HOMOSEXUALITY
IN
HISTORY

HOMOSEXUALITY
IN
HISTORY

Colin Spencer

HARCOURT BRACE & COMPANY
New York   San Diego   London

Copyright © 1995 by Colin Spencer

Library of Congress Cataloging-in-Publication Data
Spencer, Colin.
Homosexuality in history/Colin Spencer.
p.   cm.
Originally published as: Homosexuality, a history, Fourth Estate, London, 1995.
Includes bibliographical references and index.
ISBN 0-15-100223-1
1. Homosexuality—History. 2. Homosexuality, Male—History.
3. Gays—History.   I. Title.
HQ76.25.S684   1996
306.76'6'09—dc20   95-39474

Printed in the United States of America
First U.S. edition
A C E F D B

CONTENTS

ᔐᙏᙅ

FOREWORD

Throughout my life I have been shocked by homophobic responses. Unable to accept the homophobes' usual explanation that their reaction is based on divine law as interpreted by biblical exegesis, I have never been able to understand why it should exist at all. Obviously, there must be both a social and a political need which allows such violent and emotional negation to flourish, but why are some societies amiable in their attitudes to same-sex loving, while others are choleric? Why do so many societies feel the need to persecute, punish, maim and slaughter males who exhibit that sexual preference? Nothing, I decided, but a world history of the subject, could begin to explain what I wished to know.

I set out to write a comprehensive history, but once I began to read the source materials, I soon discovered that it would need the work of several lifetimes to complete it and it would fill at least a hundred volumes. I also knew that I could not merely extract one facet of sexuality without placing it in the whole social and historical context, and this would entail, in one very real sense, a history of sexuality itself. I have had, then, to be highly selective. I have used my own curiosity as a guide, working back from our present attitudes to homosexuality in an attempt to discover from what compound of arcane beliefs they stem. My search was made all the more intriguing by being constantly fuelled by academic work published in the last fifteen years (the subject, after all, has only just acquired scholarly respectability) in Britain, Europe and the USA.

For reasons of space I have had to omit much material from the Orient (though I have stressed the difference in attitudes towards sex there), the developing countries, and much modern ethnographic research in Africa, the Americas and Melanesia. Nor have I been able to do justice to lesbianism, first because very little on the subject was ever written down (in male-dominated cultures the women were left to their own devices, kept within their own quarters and for the most part men were indifferent to what happened in secret), and second because, for many centuries, men placed such emphasis upon penetrative sex that it was believed that women could not really cohabit with any degree of fulfilment. Such is the vanity of men. Third, as lesbianism was only rarely a criminal offence, there are very few court records or documents of any kind. There are already some excellent historical studies of the subject written by women (see Bibliography). Finally, I have not been able to do anything like justice to modern feminism and gay liberation – again, excellent studies already exist.

This book takes the view that our sexuality is a product of specific historical conditions, that our sense of gender is constructed rather than biologically fixed. However, I also believe that each individual has a genetic predisposition which prompts the choice of structure that is available. Society and the individual unite as an entity. So, in a sense, this volume straddles current theories, though to scrutinise the psychology of a particular historical personage is not part of its remit.

I deliberately did not wish to stray into private psychology where the discourse on homosexuality was stuck for most of this century. The 'binding mother/absent father' syndrome, or any other psychological pattern, seems to me insulting, unhelpful and in the end entirely abortive. Exceptions to generalisations can be legion, but inevitably they are dismissed by the proponents of the original theory. In my view, homosexuality should not be explained away, *it just is*. What needs to be investigated is the view which succeeding societies have had of it. I have attempted to trace the conditions which mould the manner in which sexuality is expressed, showing how it is influenced by tradition, culture, economics, land-ownership, the availability of the breeding pool of women, organised ethics, semiotics and social identification – what one might term the political/cultural structure of a society. Oddly enough, ethics, in themselves, do not seem to have influenced same-sex expression except by either allowing it to be overt or by attempting to suppress it altogether.

Homosexual activity throughout history can be divided into five different types of relationship. First, relationships with a gap in years between man and boy or woman and girl; these also embody some kind of initiation or tutorial, a rite of passage for the young in their journey to the adult world. Second, those which involve one member cross-dressing, where there is a powerful element of transvestism which may entail a complete change in social role-playing. Third, a couple equal in age and social circumstances. Fourth, an unequal partnership which crosses class barriers. Fifth, the same which crosses barriers of race. The last two are likely to share something of the tutorial or learning aspect of the first.

In a recent essay[1] the point is made that in all human societies, other than those under the influence of the Christian religion, it has been legitimate for males to have sexual relations with each other. There were two restrictions: that they also married and produced families and that the adult male was always the penetrator. This custom inevitably meant that the immature males, sometimes mere boys, played the passive role; often this became a rite-of-passage ritual. Such cultures existed worldwide and lasted for many thousands of years.

Today, we find such social structures difficult to understand, for the very subject of the sexuality of children is fused in our minds with ideas of sexual domination. But an awareness of other cultures from the past should give us a greater understanding of our own sexuality, and enable us to control and understand the present.

In the ancient world there was no need to distinguish sexual activity with the same gender from that with the opposite gender, nor was any social opprobrium attached to gender at all; instead, ignominy was reserved for passive sexual acts. There was no need for such a word as 'homosexuality' because the concept of it did not exist. (Because of this, I have tried not to use the word 'homosexuality' too often when discussing the past, but when I have fallen back on its use, it is because I believe it is helpful to the reader.) Up to and after the Renaissance, a 'sodomite' still did not mean anything other than a male, and bisexuality in social terms was thoroughly acceptable. But gradually, as the world neared 1700, a radical change took place; the idea crept in that all men who enjoyed same-sex experiences were both effeminate and criminal, and a homophobic society was born. The reasons why this occurred are fascinating and complex, for they relate to radical social changes which began in the mid-seventeenth century.

The word 'homosexuality' first appeared in English in the 1890s when it was used by Charles Gilbert Chaddock, the translator of R. von Krafft-Ebing's *Psychopathia Sexualis*; it had originally appeared in German in 1869 in an anonymous pamphlet. Havelock Ellis commented that it was a 'barbarous neologism sprung from a monstrous mingling of Greek and Latin stock'. Though J. A. Symonds used the word in a letter in 1892, it was one of many words that were being conceived and used then to describe same-gender sexuality. Why suddenly should words be sought for this erotic activity? One is inclined to be facetious and ask whether it existed before 1892. If not, its history is a short one of only just over a hundred years. Of course, that is absurd. People experience many things without fully understanding them or being able to give them a name – gravity is an obvious example. In the nineteenth century, before 1892, the term 'inversion' was used, a word that covered everything considered deviant at the time. The coining of new words and expressions is a sign of social change in action; new words mark new inquiries and, we hope, an enlargement of understanding. Sexuality itself is a marvellous barometer of such change and as the word 'heterosexuality' was coined in 1888, you might say that the words existed because Krafft-Ebing and Havelock Ellis needed them for their work in understanding human sexuality.

I believe that sexuality exists in all its depth and complexity, regardless of how society tries to control or guide it. Some would say it is the greatest force within us and perhaps this is why we show such fear of it, continuing to subjugate and tame it, often when there is no need. 'Uncontrolled sex' is linked in our minds to barbarism, to the decay of the fabric of civilisation, perhaps to our own evolution (but observations of primates show a group perfectly able to accommodate its sexuality and not in the least disturbed by its less orthodox manifestations). Perhaps this is why for so many centuries society has reserved its greatest moral censure for unorthodox sexual behaviour. What a different history we might have had if 'morals' had been exclusively concerned with how humane and tolerant a society was, instead of being obsessed with how we have an orgasm. The terms 'right' and 'wrong' and the concepts of 'good' and 'evil' have always been loaded with unspoken sexual relevance.

This sexual past is a totally different world which the modern reader at first may find alien, but it has to be true that any history of sexuality is in fact a history of society's cultural interpretation of human eroticism. A French anthropologist, Maurice Godelier, commented in *New Left Review*: 'It's not sexuality which haunts society, but society which haunts the body's sexuality.'

In order to understand the homosexual impulse throughout history we must begin by seeing where that haunting started and where it lies within our sexual evolution. The expression of homosexuality of either gender is closely entwined with the role of women in the social structure. So, throughout history, the act of non-procreative sex has been very much entangled with the social rituals of procreative sex. Sadly, I have had to conclude that our western societies have grown latterly more homophobic than before, not necessarily in legislation but in moral attitudes. It was with great relief that I discovered many societies of the past entirely free of such a taint.

1

PREHISTORY
AND
EARLY CIVILISATIONS

There are three ways in which we can learn about our sexuality in prehistory: first we can look at the evolution of man and see whether a study of primates will tell us anything; second, we can study hunter/gatherer tribes today and speculate from the ethnographic evidence; third, we can look at early myths and sagas and note how same-sex loving was viewed in those texts which have survived.

However, *one* aspect of sexuality can hardly be studied without considering the whole of human sexuality. A glance at zoology informs us graphically that the sexual impulse is dominated by the selfish gene, the driving force ensuring the survival of the species. The need to procreate, to give birth to the next generation, is so powerful that it has been used as an argument for the unnaturalness – indeed the irrelevance – of same-sex loving.

MAMMALIAN SEXUALITY

The oestrus cycle of female mammals is limited to ensure that there is time to nurture the young until they become independent.

At the same time there is a steady supply of and no limit to the amount of male eggs or the frequency of their release. The male animal has a great reservoir of eggs and a frequent desire to release them, from adolescence, through his prime and waning only slightly in old age.

Zoologists have until recently been reticent about discussing homosexual behaviour in mammals. Is it because it appears so common that it was not worth mentioning, or was it considered irrelevant or even perhaps too obscene a subject for scholarly study? Alas, for many years it was the latter, an inhibition, even a revulsion, caused, as we shall see in later chapters, by homophobic societies. So zoologists must have looked away on country walks whenever they saw cows in a field mounting each other, unaware perhaps that the farmer would be grateful for this display, because it indicated that the cow underneath had come on heat and could be taken from the herd and inseminated. Mammalian sexuality revolves round the oestrus cycle.

Male behaviour towards females differs in different species; here are three examples which cover the range. There is the brief contact, like that of the hamster which devotes a minute or two to copulation, then returns to his solitary burrow. The male ungulate (deer, zebra, antelope), on the other hand, stays with the female for a whole season, throughout the breeding time. Last, the male hyena lives with the female and helps to bring up the young.

If the female does not need the male other than for procreation then the males are dispensable. When this occurs, male bonding, that may include homosexuality of some variety, is almost certain to exist. However, the more complex the life of an animal, the more likely it is that the males have other functions for the female and her young: generally defence, hunting or some kind of food-gathering. It is in the females' interest to pick the strongest and cleverest male. In animals this explains mating rituals and also, as Darwin showed, extraordinary anatomical developments to proclaim dominance, such as the male frigate bird's ballooning chest or the antlers of a stag. Sexual selection means that only a minority of the males get to breed, while all the females get to breed at least once. The males exhaust themselves in competition and the females pick out the winners as studs.[1] The successful male can mate with as many females as he can cope with.

Clearly, most young males should have no trouble in winning the females for themselves, but the conditions under which they can rise in the hierarchy and become effective breeders are constantly made more complex by the dominant males. For example, in antelopes there is a strict hierarchy of age among the males. The six-month-old youngsters are subordinate to one-year-old males who in turn are subordinate to the nearly adult males, and all are subordinate to the properly adult males. Then they have a ranking based not on age but on strength, condition, weight and the secretion of a gland upon their foreheads. A challenging male antelope will approach the dominant male who lowers his head slightly, the challenger sniffs the forehead and nearly always retreats. If he does not, they fight.[2] (If the selection of a mate is as complicated as this in the antelope, consider how much more complex such a mating ritual must be in human society.)

So, if young males cannot copulate with a female on heat what do they do with their excess sexual energy? An early answer to this question, which had become almost unmentionable, was an off-hand remark in 1945 which noted that 'copulatory play was both varied and frequent in immature animals, homosexual, hetero-sexual, exhibitionistic and masturbatory activities occur'.[3]

More recent observation has given us new insights. Sexual be-haviour between two primates of the same gender is often a positive solution to the rivalry between young and mature males. When the dominant male has laid claim to all the females, the younger males seek and obtain protection from the superior adult by adopting a feminine posture. They also become objects of symbolic or real sexual assault.

Sexuality also flourishes between young males if they have been isolated in a group after the dominant males have appropriated all the females. A study by Frans de Waal[4] of bonobo chimpanzees describes playful wrestling and tickling which soon turned into erotic games – juvenile males with erections fellating each other – or group sex, with fondling of each other's genitals and much tongue kissing.

The chimpanzee is now thought to be more closely related to us than any other of the giant apes, but it is the bonobo in particular which has been called the most intelligent of all animals and the ape most resembling our ancestors. Bonobos stand and walk on two legs more often and with greater ease than other apes. Photographs of them upright resemble illustrations of *Australopithecus* – the early hominids. They are the only primates happy in water, wading and hunting small fish, even swimming. The females are willing to mate in the missionary position throughout their lives, not only with males but also with each other. The male bonobo's genitals are among the largest among the primates, and relative to body size they are possibly bigger than those of the human male. Nor are they bashful when displaying the organ: its bright pink colour makes it stand out against their dark fur; they present the organ by arching their backs and spreading their legs and flicking their penises up and down. The males will embrace face to face with mutual penis-rubbing or mount each other, but they do not ejaculate. This behaviour appears to be an intense form of bonding but not particularly orgasmic. The males never mount juveniles and infants without their consent, the contacts are brief and friendly and often sought by the youngsters themselves.

An interesting example of a lone and independent female was the chimpanzee named Puist observed by de Waal.[5] Puist was an adult of rather burly frame who refused to mate with any male. Though she had her genital swelling every month, and although she was always attractive to the males at this time, she refused all their advances. She would masturbate in a rather desultory fashion and when other females showed a genital swelling Puist would mount them, thrusting in a masculine manner. When the males gathered around a female on heat, Puist was among them; when a female refused one of the males, Puist joined with the female in ejecting the suitor. A primate example of female solidarity.

PREHISTORY

Like zoologists, and for the same reasons, anthropologists have been notoriously reticent about divulging much in the way of sexual information on the tribes they have studied. Anthropological records have tended to treat same-sex loving as a phenomenon, hiding references to it in a passing remark or a footnote. Thankfully, this attitude has gradually changed and recently, to offer one example, a detailed study of homosexuality in Papua New Guinea and the Melanesian islands (such as Fiji and the Solomon islands in the Pacific Ocean) has been published.[6] The tribes studied ranged from small to large: the population of the Etoro was 400 while that of the Marind was 6,000.

Until the arrival of Westerners in the nineteenth century, it is thought that the lives of these peoples continued unchanged for thousands of years, so a study of their rites and customs, some of which are still practised today, gives us an important link with the past. The evidence from linguistics and immigration patterns suggests that the tribes practising some forms of homosexual ritual in Melanesia first colonised the lands around 10,000 years ago.

Many of the tribes engaged in initiation rituals between old and young, and transvestism. There is, too, some evidence of equal adult partnerships, but never in tribes which favoured the homosexual initiation of young boys.

This study also shows that each tribe had its corresponding view of the role of women in that society. So how the tribe views women dictates the ideology and character of its homosexual structure. Or put another way, how males construct creation myths and where they place the female principle dictates the variety of accepted homosexual behaviour.

Ritualised Pederasty

Each of the tribes studied had remarkably different rites and rituals involving sexuality, yet many based their ideology on the ritualised homosexual insemination of young boys. Take the Marind and the Kiman tribes. Here every boy past infancy was taken away from his mother and the women's house to sleep with his father in the men's house. At the first signs of puberty, his maternal uncle was appointed to penetrate the boy anally, thus feeding him with the sperm which would make him strong. The boys remained in this phase for about three years.

The Marind tribe had the Sosom ritual, at which no women were present. Sosom was a castrated giant who wore a string of severed human heads around his neck. A large red phallus stood in a clearing in the bush and the boy-initiates were brought to it, their hair dressed in a hieratic fashion. The older men danced and then there would be a male orgy where for the first time any man could penetrate any boy-initiate. This was the only time in the Marind calendar when promiscuity was allowed. Marind girls also went through stages of initiation where they were assigned a maternal uncle who, with his wife, had a special tutorial relationship with the girl, but there was no sexual relationship.

The Marind viewed their women in a quite different way from other tribes. The women were placed in a subordinate role, rather like a junior gang of men; they often dressed as males, were treated with a mixture of rudeness and kindness and went on hunting trips with the men. Their myths associated the female genitals with excrement. In sham fights between men and women, the latter might be pelted with excrement. In one of the largest cults, a female effigy, Excrement-woman, stood at the apex of the ritual and was burnt at the end. In these rituals male aggression was powerfully expressed in a way which was not apparent in daily life. Women were a secret, a mystery to be admired, resented and deeply feared. Their value system ranked homosexuality higher than heterosexuality which, in their myths, was always associated with castration anxiety and death. Sosom, the giant, while fornicating with a goddess was castrated by her; his other name is Anus-man.

The Marind male did not stop his homosexual practices when he married. In the course of producing a family he might be called upon to be his nephew's pederast for three or four years. And of course he would take part in the annual Sosom ritual orgy.

Yet another ritual involved the bride having to pass her wedding night in the house of her new husband's male kin and to accommodate them sexually all night. The resulting mixture of semen and vaginal fluids was carefully collected as it was thought to contain powerful magic. Mixed with food, it was used to cure the sick; mixed with mud, it was pasted over wounds to heal them. The semen from homosexual intercourse was disdained, it had to be semen which dripped from a woman's vagina after intercourse, preferably with a variety of males. This rite was repeated when women resumed menstruating after the birth of a child. There was another cult in which the women took a more important role and were given food by the men which had semen produced by masturbation mixed into it.

These rituals were intended to increase the women's fertility. However, Marind women suffered from a greater incidence of sterility than other tribes. It is thought that excessive copulation may have caused inflammation of the cervix. The Marind and the Kiman both inseminated their youths, but they also both gave ritual emphasis to the power of heterosexually-derived substances – the semen and vaginal fluids. Also, both tribes had complex rituals that involved sex and food and a connection between maternal uncles and nephews.

The Big Nambas of the highlands of the island of Malekula are a patrilineal culture which still accords women an extremely low status. Their name refers to the large and erect penis-sheaths worn by the adult male.

Everything was owned by the chief, including the food, women and boys. All the chief's subjects had to keep their heads at a lower level than his. One old ex-chief, Kali, had twenty-seven wives and their faces had to be hidden from commoners. The chiefs had absolute power – the only meat they could eat was human flesh. Great reverence was placed upon the head, hunted in war, and upon the head of the penis. The homosexual ritual with the boy-initiates was intended to strengthen the glans penis. There is some confusion as to who the boy-initiate's partner was; one ethnologist believed it to be the boy's paternal grandfather,[7] but others understood the older male partner to be a substitute relation who not only acted as the inseminator but also as a guardian and tutor. Whoever they were, they referred to each other as wife and husband. There was, too, a metaphysical aspect to the homosexual coupling, for the participants believed they could generate a power to transform themselves both physically and spiritually.

The first ethnologist to write about Malekula in detail was Bernard Deacon (who tragically died there at the age of twenty-four). He happens also to have been the most candid in his comments on the Big Nambas' homosexuality, observing: 'every chief has a number of boy-lovers, and it is said that some men are so completely homosexual in their affections, that they seldom have intercourse with their wives, preferring to go with their boys.'[8] The final ceremony of the initiation ritual could involve circumcision. In the case of the Big Nambas, all of the foreskin was thrown into a river (a practical reason, one imagines, for the sheaths which would protect as well as enlarge the penis), and the boys then went into seclusion for thirty days while the wound healed. Deacon describes the jealousy of 'the boy's husband' who feared that some other man might have intercourse with his boy in this time. He was allowed to nurse the boy and help heal the wound, and only when it was healed could he resume his 'marital rights'. Deacon adds: 'the rationalisation which the natives put forward for their homosexual practices is that a boy-lover's male organ is caused to grow strong and large by the homosexual acts of his husband.'

Though each tribe studied had variations on the ritual there were themes common to many, one being a holy reverence for sperm. It was thought that to penetrate a young boy was to plant the seed for his own sperm; that he could not grow to be a strong, powerful man and hunter without those years when sodomy was a daily practice. One tribe, the Sambia, placed greater emphasis and reverence upon semen than any other. They lived on the edge of the Highlands of New Guinea (Papua) and numbered about 2,300 people. Relationships between the sexes were highly polarised: there was a strict division of labour (women were responsible for gardening, food preparation and childcare; men hunted, ruled and went to war); their hamlets were divided into male and female spaces; married women were regarded as lecherous and over-sexed, while young women were prudish and shy. The men feared that they would lose their strength and be contaminated by the women.[9] Prolonged postpartum taboos forbade coitus for anything up to two and a half years after the birth of a child. Further sexual intercourse in marriage was spaced out, perhaps only once every two or three weeks to avoid depletion, premature aging and death. Without doubt the male was the socially preferred and valued gender.

But males could not attain puberty without semen, for it was thought that their bodies did not produce it naturally. The Sambia believed that pre-pubertal boys had to be fed with semen, so from the age of seven they were separated from their mothers and lived in the men's house, where they had to avoid even the sight of women for the years in which they grew up. During this time the boys underwent sex initiation rituals. In the first, they were taught to perform fellatio upon the older boys or men, swallowing the valuable semen. (Association was made between the semen, mother's milk and the ritual, secret bamboo flutes, the latter playing a vital part in all their ceremonies.) By the third stage of initiation, the boys changed roles and began to fellate the new, younger initiates. When a boy showed signs of sexual maturity, there was a ceremony, after which he joined the men and became a hunter. There was among the Sambia much discussion about the different flavours and textures in semen. Boys were revered for the amount of semen they could produce as well as its quality. Both partners were forbidden to reverse the sexual roles, and the younger boy was always placed in the passive position and generally took on a female name or title. Relationships appear to have been both erotic and tender and the men usually remained close friends – though not sexual partners – all their lives. Institutionalised female homosexuality was very rare and little is known about it.

These brief accounts make it obvious that it was not only the women but also the boys who were dominated by the men; all of these rules, taboos and rituals emphasised and intensified the totalitarian power of the male. It was not so much the semen that was revered as the adult male who produced it, the object of the rituals being to enhance the mystique of the male.

It has been argued that ritual pederasty goes back to the palaeo-lithic,[10] fusing the reverence for semen with the eating of brain tissue and the brain marrow within the spinal cord, so that head-hunting and cannibalism would become an inevitable part of the same belief. Here were stored all the manly virtues of courage, fortitude, bravery and skill in hunting and warfare. Pederasty imparted the same qualities through the semen to the next generation of males.

Transvestism

In a study of different societies where transvestism was an acceptable part of the social structure, it was discovered that it occurred only in societies which had a very low sex differentiation between genders.[11]

In ten Melanesian tribes that do not practise ritualised pederasty there is strong evidence of some form of tranvestism. The Wogeo men are competitive, wishing to 'give birth', so they simulate menstruation by penis bleeding. They also have a ceremony which involves a female transvestite impersonating a pregnant sea-monster. The Orokaiva have an initiation ceremony in which a group of women dressed as men 'attack' the young boys with spears in a pseudo-homosexual manner. This pantomime confusion of gender is a dominant theme in many of the initiation rites. Among the Orokaiva it is thought normal for women to fight, and they have their own weapon, a quarterstaff, which they use on other women, their husbands and their fathers-in-law.

Throughout these tribes there are many parts for male transvestites in the performance of rituals with sacred and secret themes. It is believed that sacred knowledge could be communicated only in coitus between a same-sex couple, the transvestite representing the spirit. But there also seems to be enormous fun and riotous sexual antics in mimed play during these staged occasions, not unlike a drag act in a local pub. Two men from the Bedamini tribe would dress as witches; one wearing a large bamboo penis, the other placing a slit, unripe papaya between his thighs. They chase each other and simulate intercourse to cheers and obscenities from the crowd.[12] In the Duke of York islands and in the Iatmul tribe, homosexual intercourse is portrayed, an older man always penetrating a younger, but the Iatmul dress the male couple as women and one wears a symbolic clitoris in his anus. The dance which is so much a part of these performances always communicates homosexual eroticism as well as heterosexual. This 'is the bodily interdependence of the same-sex couple moulded over years of intimate experience with each other. It is through the close awareness of one's partner that each is able to realize his own godlike identity. Each makes the other into a god.'[13]

Hence, though there is such a partnership as a male couple, it is in no sense similar to that of a Western gay couple. The dance had religious importance, both men representing spirits, costumed and masked. The homosexual experience is a secret, so never becomes a label for a relationship, yet much overt joking and horseplay goes on in public. Men and women tend not to be intimate, but male couples hold hands in public, hug and sleep together, but even these things cannot be interpreted solely as signs of a sexual relationship, for such things are thought of as private business. However, as most of the young men are bachelors for some years, as adultery is deeply frowned upon, as masturbation is thought to weaken the body and spirit, homosexual relations are the only socially acceptable sexual outlet left.

By far the most well documented incidence of transvestism occurs in the tribes of both North and South America. The word *berdache* (sometimes *bardash*) possibly comes from the French *bardache* or the Italian *bardaccia* (meaning catamite) or the Spanish *bardajo* (kept boy) but none of these crude and inexplicit definitions remotely fits the subtle, practical and often mystical role of transvestism in the Americas. One feels the word was chosen, and retained, to hide the reality behind the practice. It reflects the European settlers' dismay, horror and confusion at the discovery that role switching in gender could be socially absorbed with equanimity. Yet women in the American Indian culture were both honoured and powerful.

The *berdaches* have been noted in at least 113 tribes in North

America, but are thought to be common to all. *Berdaches* are mostly males dressed as females, but there are also plenty of examples of women dressed as men. Dress, however, is the least of it, for they take on the lifestyle, ethos and labour of the opposite sex, which naturally includes sexual favours. *Berdaches* seem to be popular, they have no lack of partners, nor is there any opprobrium attached to a man having sex with a *berdache* for they are completely absorbed within the social structure. If a boy in infancy finds himself unsympathetic to male pursuits, such as tracking and hunting, and finds he enjoys sewing, gathering and cooking, he will simply begin to cross-dress and his new gender becomes immediately acceptable. There is no question of any physical abnormality, it is simply that he prefers to take on the role of a woman. The women themselves welcome the *berdaches*, because they can help with the jobs that the women sometimes find too strenuous. There are also cases of *berdaches* deciding to cross back and become men again, joining the hunters; one afterwards became a chief and married seven wives.[14] In some tribes the change is only partial, the *berdaches* going on hunting trips dressed as men, then changing back into women's clothes at home. Sometimes the decision to become a *berdache* is taken because the boy has had a dream, before his male puberty rite, where a female goddess orders him to become a woman. Female *berdaches* marry other women and again such couples are accepted. There is also an element of reverence associated with the role of the *berdache*; many are thought to be gifted with second sight, and can read portents and signs, and many also take on the role of shaman and play a signific ant part in seasonal festivities.

Similar cases of socially acceptable transvestism are found in ethnic groups in North Asia (the Chukchees and Aleuts), in the Far East, Indonesia and Africa. There is a fascinating account, written at the end of the nineteenth century, of the shamanistic inspiration in the Chukchees. The call by the spirits was dreaded by the youths, yet once heard they could not deny it. There were several stages in a youth's transformation, the first being that his hair was braided and arranged in the female manner. In the second stage he began to wear female dress. In the third stage:

he throws away the rifle and lance, the lasso of the reindeer herdsman, and the harpoon of the seal hunter, and takes up the needle and seal scraper. He learns the use of these quickly because the spirits are helping him all the time. Even his pronunciation changes from the male to the female mode. At the same time his body alters, if not in its outward appearance, at least in its faculties and forces. He loses masculine strength, fleetness of foot in the race, endurance in wrestling, and acquires instead the helplessness of a woman. Even his physical character changes. The transformed person loses his brute courage and fighting spirit, and becomes shy of strangers, even fond of small talk and nursing small children. Generally speaking he becomes a woman with the appearance of a man.[15]

Shamans go back to the Upper Palaeolithic. The migration of peoples carried the practice vast distances, possibly, for example, from Siberia to the Americas. The Polynesians may well have brought transvestism to Madagascar. Where the women had power, as in the Palaeo-Siberians (the Kamchadal wives had the sole right to dipose of family property), transvestism became common. Indeed, one can see the reasoning: if women are treated with respect and have power in society, why not pretend to be one? Also, where there is a low degree of gender differentiation, as in Tahiti or Java, no one much notices if men dress as women or vice-versa, any more than they take notice of the gender of anyone's sexual partner.

Another well-known example of transvestism stems from a matter of sexual need rather than mysticism. When the Thonga tribe of Mozambique were brought to Johannesburg in the nineteenth century to work the mines, the women were left behind, yet European strangers entering the camp saw a large number of young, animated females. These were *tinkhentshana*, boys who had placed carved wooden female breasts upon their chests and who would entertain and dance with the men. Each had a 'husband'. At night, after the dance, they would insist that their 'husbands' give them 10 shillings and they would then remove their 'breasts' and comply with their 'husband's' sexual demands. There had been large numbers of prostitutes frequenting the camp area, but they were chased away as the Thonga preferred the boys. It then became standard practice for the supervisor to examine a new gang of workers and to select those they felt might be happy to assume the transvestite role.[16]

GREEK MYTH

There are a great number of ancient myths which hinge upon the abduction and love of a youth, and nearly all of these are stories about initiation. These myths may be descriptions of an authentic practice or ritual, the myths having survived although the original practice has disappeared. We know that homosexual ritualised pederasty existed in the archaic Indo-European world outside Greece, in that great family of peoples which stretched from the Atlantic to the Ganges.[17] There is a pattern which they share: the youth or boy is a pupil, disciple or apprentice, while the older lover is a master, warrior, teacher and model. Quite often, the myth involves an abduction and travel outside civilisation, to a wild forest, an untamed area where the older man will reveal a knowledge of life, some inherent wisdom which is incarnate in a gift such as a chariot, a suit of armour, magic invulnerability or prophetic knowledge. Sometimes the beloved disciple dies, only to be reborn, or he performs an exploit that proves his astonishing prowess. He then becomes the adult male warrior himself, or becomes king, or he excels in a skill for which his lover was renowned as: Philoctetes is an archer, Pelops wins the chariot race, Hyacinthus ascends to heaven.

The most famous male couple in Greek myth is Zeus and Ganymede, but Apollo too was constantly stealing beautiful youths: Cyparissus, Admetus, Hymenaeus, Carnus, Hippolytus and others. Heracles loved Philoctetes, Nestor, Adonis, Jason and many more. Adonis was abducted by Dionysius. It is perhaps stating the obvious, but women do not appear in these myths of initiation. Where, one might ask, are the mothers of all these golden youths and what do they think about the abductions? As we have seen in the ethnographic examples, the mothers and the rest of the women accept the role that the young boys are about to play, for they have been taught that this is how boys become men. Only in this manner is the future of the race assured. But again, we can also see, that if pederasty is to take place within the social structure as a sacred ritual, women have no role to play and must exist, compliantly, off-stage.

MATRIARCHIES

There is evidence to suggest that over 25,000 years ago society believed in and was structured around a concept of the goddess. Sculptured figures of grossly fat females have been discovered across Europe from Spain to Russia. It is thought that these goddesses represented a profound power which animated the universe; she had three aspects, the three faces of the moon, maiden, mother and crone. Incarnations of the goddess were in the female shamans who would go into trances, perform rituals and dances. When women controlled the ideology, it meant they could also control society and their own sexuality. Palaeolithic counting-sticks, ancient moon calendars, indicate that women were in control of their menstrual rhythms.[18] Culture, religion and sexuality were intertwined. It is thought that the shaman priestesses led group sex rituals in which the whole community shared.

In this women's world, how did same-sex loving express itself? We do not know, but we can speculate, partly from later evidence of the cult. Men were there to serve the goddess. Male sexuality had to be controlled to allow the strongest, cleverest and healthiest of males and females to mate. The less perfect could expend their sexual energies where they would not hinder the future of the race. As homosexuality can never be procreative, it would seem likely that such activities would be blessed, but also tightly controlled by the women. Ritualised pederasty would be as likely to be approved of by the women as in a male-dominated society.

EARLY CIVILISATIONS

As we have seen, many of the small kinship-structured tribes were matrilineal. Often, these were also avunculate (brothers had a special relationship with their sisters' children). Some incorporated the pederastic rites of a coming-of-age ritual. But urban settlement replaced this with patriarchy. The first four Egyptian dynasties traced descent through the mother, the rest through the father. For commoners, inheritance was first through the mother, then it changed to the father. Evidence from Greek mythology suggests that an early matriarchy existed which had disappeared by the Homeric age.[19]

But why did this change occur? Domestic settlement within river valleys and at the head of estuaries, where there are both fresh water and the richest food supplies, has its drawbacks. To settle is to make oneself vulnerable; buildings and fertile land have to be fortified and protected, a settlement needs defenders to ensure that greedy neighbours will not steal, pillage and finally conquer what is rightfully yours. Because part of the life of women is giving birth and nurturing offspring, the defenders become an army of strong, young males. Once an army exists, the settlement might just as well use it, not only to defend but to wage war, to capture trade routes, precious raw materials and a labour-force of slaves to till the fields, build the temples and serve at tables. Before long, the army takes over and becomes the settlement's first priority. Thus the women lost the power they once had, becoming subject to laws which men were free from. Male sexuality was given the utmost freedom, while women's was oppressed. So materialism, possessions and property all strengthen male dominance and aggression, leading to women's subjugation.

Mesopotamia

Once a settlement is established, property, goods, furnishings and land increase the status of the individual. Such wealth and power is too attractive to be dissipated, hence the anxiety felt by property-owners over inheritance. How can the dominant male be absolutely certain that the child who will inherit his wealth and property is really his son? As we have seen, the ownership of property leads inevitably to the repression of women. In the early civilisations of Mesopotamia, the extensive fragments of legal codes still extant (dating from 2375 to 1726 BC) are extremely detailed on laws which circumscribe the lives and rights of women. Nor do any of them prohibit homosexual acts, though the subject is hardly mentioned.

Nevertheless, religious belief in the great goddess and the cult of the shaman priestess flourished in Mesopotamia. 'A prostitute, compassionate am I', reads a Sumerian clay tablet describing the goddess Ishtar.[20] Sacred prostitution was the central part of the ritual in the Temple. The priestess performed a sacred marriage to ensure the fertility of the country and the great fortune of the new king, for the king copulated with the holy priestess at the beginning of his reign. There were lesser priestesses who were also musicians, singers and dancers, certainly some of these were men who also copulated with both men and women. The goddess Ishtar had turned these men into women as a demonstration of her awesome powers.[21] Yet though Ishtar was an all-powerful presence and though prostitution was revered and was also an important economic factor in the running of the Temple, women's role in society began to be secondary to that of men.

It is clear that the purpose of marriage was procreation, not love or companionship; wives were valuable pieces of property. Society was male-orientated, the phallus being an object of enormous reverence. (Many clay phalli were found in the remains of the temples of Ishtar.) There was a law which stated that if a woman hurt a man's genitals she would have her eyes torn out. The wives were to raise children, and a childless marriage was grounds for

29

divorce. Adultery was viewed not as a sin but as a form of trespass against a man's property.

We know that homosexuality flourished. However, within archaic societies, as in the ancient world, there was simply sexuality. The only disgrace connected with sexual expression concerned the type of act and the status, not the sex, of your partner. This is a common theme within various cultures, and we shall return to it.

The Babylonians loved to divine the future and we still have one of their manuals which prophesies on the basis of sexual acts. It would seem that if a man had intercourse with the hindquarters of his equal, he would be foremost among his brothers and colleagues. If he had intercourse with a male courtier for a whole year, all worries would leave him. But if a man had intercourse with his male slave he would be troubled. Evil itself would strike him if he went with a male cult prostitute.[22] Thus, while to penetrate anally someone of high social status or one's equal could bring good fortune, it would be risking bad luck to seduce one's slave. Men who preferred the passive role (unless they were temple servants) were regarded as inferior.

Human sexuality was linked with the fertility of nature, and in each new year the priest and priestess copulated to ensure the creativeness of the earth. There are countless terracotta models of couples fornicating in all manner of positions, including males who appear to sodomise standing up. Anal penetration seems to have been extremely popular in Mesopotamia. The temple priestess permitted it to avoid pregnancy and many of the incantations for happy sexual unions mention it, yet nowhere is there mention of the love of women for women.

Egypt

Though we know much more about ancient Egypt than almost any other archaic civilisation, there is not one legal text extant. We have instead tomb pictures that revel in every possible sexual activity and position. We have stories of gods, goddesses and hermaphrodites who also endlessly copulate. The phallus was revered; the god Min was ithyphallic (having an erect penis) and always depicted holding large cos lettuces (the milky white sap in the stem was thought to be an aphrodisiac). One legend dealt with the god Seth, his sexual love for Horus and his attempted rape of him. It is a curious tale, open to many interpretations, and like much else about Egyptian sexuality fails to convince one of either a positive or a negative view of homosexual love.

The idea that women could enjoy sexual intercourse was a major irritant to the ancient world; it meant of course that because they so enjoyed it women might go in pursuit of it just as men did. Then women would no longer be at home, mothering the children and ruling over a well-run household, obedient to their husbands. If women enjoyed sex then anarchy would surely erupt. The adultery of women was condemned ruthlessly, it was a reason for divorce and could be punished by burning at the stake, while male sexual freedom was encouraged. If a couple failed to have children, then the husband was allowed to take a female slave to mother his children by proxy. (No question here of the fault perhaps being the man's.) After his death such children would be both emancipated and legitimised. Girls were married at around twelve or thirteen, while boys were married a little later, aged fifteen or sixteen. The more aristocratic men delayed marriage until they were twenty. Sexual frustration found an outlet with female slaves or prostitutes of either sex.

The men were circumcised by a priest and the ritual was performed *en masse*. We have an account written by one boy who boasts that not one of the 120 men cried out when they were cut. Herodotus thinks that they were the first nation to practise circumcision, and Strabo that the Jews borrowed the tradition from the Egyptians. It is also suspected that they circumcised girls, but like so much else there is no certain proof one way or the other.

It is interesting that the Egyptians had no taboo against brother and sister incest, in fact, any offspring was considered to be of spiritual significance. (Parent–child incest was not valued in the same way.) Their ethical code was based upon the life after death; if you could embalm the body then surely you must be able to preserve the soul too and you would be judged in the after-life for your actions in this one. To keep within the path of righteousness, so inscriptions on the pyramids of Gizeh tell us, was the goal. To do that you had to speak the truth and do the truth, for it was powerful and enduring. We know from the Egyptian Book of the Dead that it was thought wrong to steal, to covet, to tell lies, to commit adultery and to kill – at least half of the sins forbidden in the Ten Commandments as revealed to Moses. (I stress these ethnical standards because some readers might feel that if incest and homosexuality were approved of, then ancient Egypt was a nation without moral sense.)

In warfare, however, standards differed, for they ritually cut off the penises of their defeated enemies, in the ultimate act of the conqueror – depriving the dead, or wounded, enemy of their symbolic fertility. This was also an efficient method of obtaining a tally of the defeated after battle. Enemies taken prisoner became slaves, a valuable and necessary prize in Egyptian warfare when such vast building enterprises were continually underway. (The Temple of Amon at Karnak in Thebes was a quarter of a mile long; 100 men could stand on each of the capitals of the columns in the nave of its great hall.) The pharaoh Merneptah in the XIXth Dynasty listed among the booty of the defeated Libyan army, 6,359 uncircumcised penises. It is also thought that the Egyptians sodomised their enemies, as this was considered an insult of great significance. Like the Mesopotamians and later civilisations, they thought that a grown man who submitted to anal intercourse had lost his masculinity. To call a man womanly was insult enough, but for the man to allow himself to be treated like a woman meant that he was baser than a slave. From this alone, we can see that their view of women was low indeed.

To return to the strange myths of Seth and Horus: 'Seth made his penis erect and put it between Horus's buttocks . . .' Seth was a god, the brother of Osiris whom he killed, nailed into a coffin and flung into the Nile. Horus was the son of Osiris, so we appear to be back with uncle and nephew pederasty, but this myth is unhappy with such a relationship: 'for Horus put his hand between his buttocks and received Seth's semen. Then Horus went to tell his mother, Isis: "Help me, Isis, my mother. Come and see what Seth has done to me." And he opened his hand and let her see Seth's semen. With a scream she cut off his hand and threw it in the water and conjured up a new hand for him.'[23]

The act of anal penetration is foiled, though Seth believes it has been successful, but Isis is horrified to see Seth's semen and cuts off her son's hand as if the hand itself has become polluted. Seth was the only god who never married or had children. What was so obscene about the semen, one wonders? Masturbation was an acceptable practice – the gods did it: Min, the ithyphallic god, another guise of Horus, masturbated – while anal penetration of both sexes was also talked of quite casually. A coffin text of the IXth and Xth Dynasties consists of magical passages to be recited after death; one referring to Atum, a god, boasts that he has no power 'over me, for I copulate between his buttocks'.

But the myth gets stranger, for Seth goes to the nine gods – the Ennead – and tells them that he has played the male with Horus. At this news the Ennead scream aloud, belch and then spit in the face of Horus. Horus, 'he who is on high', who is identified with the living pharaoh, the state god and successor to Osiris, is here shown to be nothing but a woman, for he has taken on the position of a woman in sexual intercourse. It is clear that the Egyptians felt that men dominate women and kings dominate subjects. But when Seth claims the throne, Horus becomes his slave. But Horus strongly denies that he has been raped by Seth and to settle the matter the Ennead call forth the seed. The seed of Seth replies from the depths of the Nile where it had been cast, thus proving Seth to be a liar. But here again is another odd twist. The original myth tells us nothing about the seed of Horus when he was foiling anal penetration, but he must have ejaculated for the seed of Horus issues forth from the forehead of Seth in the shape of a golden disc which another god, Thoth, immediately seizes, placing it on his own head as an ornament. Thoth was the god of wisdom and the divine scribe, the inventor of hieroglyphs, the 'Lord of Holy Words'. Thoth's disciples boasted that they could decipher his books of magic which could command all the forces of nature and subdue the very gods themselves. They called him, three times, very very very great and the Greeks translated that as Hermes Trismegistus, the source of mystical wisdom in the Hermetic literature of the Graeco-Roman period. Does the golden disc, which could have emanated from fellation, mean that the seed of Horus, passing through the god who was a force of evil, then became an integral part of divine wisdom? There is a code locked within this story which resists attempts to unravel it.

Bisexuality in the male was accepted as natural and never drew adverse comment, but passive homosexuality made the Egyptians feel uneasy. What if a king showed such a feminine disposition? Again, a puzzle, for Amenhotep III, called the Magnificent, a great hunter of lions and husband of Queen Tiy, at the end of his reign had himself portrayed in female attire and maintained a bevy of royal male favourites. His successor and son (though some dispute this) was Akhenaten (1370–1352 BC) who was strong enough to form a new religion and in his lifetime break away from the priests of Amon, supplanting him with a new deity. Akhenaten also appeared in reliefs with his co-regent and son-in-law (or it could also be his eldest son) Smenkhare, obviously showing him affection and often both were naked – a rare convention in the depictions of royalty. Smenkhare is even given titles and endearments that had been used before of Akhenaten's queen and concubines.

It would seem that, as there was no distinct word for homosexuality or the homosexual person, no such category existed as an idea. Nor was there any concept, I must stress, of a bisexual person – there was only male sexuality. (I doubt whether there was a concept of female sexuality, only of female fertility, birth and motherhood). There was certainly no ideology based on boy-initiation and the pederastic act, though there is, as we shall see, strong proof that this form of the male rite of passage occurred at the time of the Egyptian civilisation elsewhere in the archaic world. Two customs, I believe, explain why: early marriage, and the lack of any taboo against sexual relations with slaves or prostitutes of either sex for young males before marriage. Sex was available, lying around, as it were, rather like food and drink and deemed just as necessary. If you were of the temperament not to find sex as enthralling as others did, you studied for the priesthood and prepared for a life of celibacy.

Even though Egypt was a flourishing trade centre it seemed to have been amazingly insular in its ethical and religious concepts, borrowing nothing from its neighbours, not even from the equally sophisticated civilisation of Mesopotamia. But there was another civilisation, further away, which also showed the same autocracy and insulation, and the same highly relaxed attitude to bisexuality.

China[24]

Around the Yellow River and its two tributaries, the Wei and the Fen, China in the Zhou Dynasty (1122–256 BC) was a loose confederation of states which nominally acknowledged the Zhou king, and which were linked together by kinship and dynastic marriages. The surviving accounts of this time convey both a lively and a charming impression of open homosexuality in court life. No precise words for homosexuality as a way of expressing sexual love existed; again it is obvious that it was not categorised as being different from love between men and women. In the early poems, the term '*mei ren*' is used, meaning 'beautiful person' of either sex, and the men in these poems are vigorously enthusiastic about each other's beauty. Later, the term '*chong*' is used, meaning 'favour' or 'regular patronage', denoting that type of homosexual love which crosses class barriers.

The earliest surviving collection of poems, *Classic of Odes* (*Shi jing*), were memorised and recited (like Homer's epics), so they originate far earlier than their collection in the seventh century. One poem celebrates the admiration felt by two athletic noblemen, another the intimate camaraderie felt between two virile warriors. Even though literature was restricted to a small court elite in early China, other poems make it clear that court life incorporated an open expression of affection between two men. Marriage was a class and social bond – two families came together in marriage to combine wealth and position – romantic love was an experience that occurred outside marriage, whether with men or women. There was nothing untoward about a married man having a passionate and intense homosexual attachment. Stories are legion.

It was an obvious way for handsome young men to get on in society. One of the first stories is about the favourite of Duke Ling of Wei (534–493 BC), one Mizi Xia, who hearing of his mother's illness broke a rule of court by jumping into the Duke's carriage and riding home. The punishment for anyone using the Duke's carriage was to have his feet amputated, but when Duke Ling heard of it he was deeply touched at the filial strength of his favourite. Another time Mizi Xia, strolling with the Duke in an orchard, bit into a peach and finding it highly delicious and very sweet he gave the remaining half to his lover, who again was deeply touched by his thoughtfulness. But some years later, when Mizi Xia's looks had faded and when the Duke's passion had waned, he was accused of some trivial crime against the Duke. This time the Duke pointed out that Mizi Xia had already stolen his coach and even given him half a peach to eat, so no crime would astonish him.

What is interesting about this perceptive little tale of love lost is that the favourite could just as easily have been a girl. Yet other tales, at least at their beginning, start in a way which seems to hinge upon questions of class and male honour. Rulers could not be propositioned by their courtiers, the punishment was death, yet there are stories where courtiers are so lost in ecstatic admiration for their lords that they give way to temptation and express their love. Duke Jing of Qi noticed a minor official staring at him and asked why. The courtier very boldly said, 'If I speak I will die, but if I do not speak I will also die. I am staring at the beautiful Duke.' Whereupon the Duke exclaimed: 'He lusteth after me. Kill him.' His adviser pointed out that it is not philosophically correct to resist desire; besides, to hate love is very inauspicious.* The Duke was swayed by this argument and promoted the minor official to become a retainer at the ducal bath. (One wonders what

---

* In the fifth and fourth centuries BC, rival philosophies, the so-called 'hundred schools', flourished. One of these was inspired by Confucius, but it was also the age of the great Taoist classics, *Chuang Tzu* and *Tao Te Ching*.

went on in the bathroom. Certainly, the retainer would now see more of the beautiful Duke. One hopes he did not suffer agonies of frustration.)

Many royal favourites, if they were also intelligent and efficient as well as handsome, became administrators and were placed in positions of power. History is full of such personages of either sex. The dying King Wen of Chu was concerned that his favourite Marquis Shen would suffer when he no longer had his protection, so he ordered Shen before he died to flee to the state of Zheng where he knew he would find royal protection.

In all these stories there is a candour and honesty which is refreshing. This story stems from the seventh century BC but it reads like a piece of nonsense in today's news. The ruler of Cao had heard that Chonger of Jin had double ribs and when he took refuge with the Duke, he grabbed the opportunity to peek at this anatomical curiosity. He and his wife drilled a hole in the wall of Prince Chonger's bath chamber and found the Prince in sexual play with two of his male retainers. This prompted a grandee's wife to remark that Prince Chonger's retainers seemed capable of becoming ministers of state.

By the end of the Zhou Dynasty commentators seemed worried about the fusion of sexual favours and political power. A political text in the Guanzi anthology speaks out: 'just because a man happens to be rich and eminent or pleasant featured and attractive, he will not necessarily turn out to be wise and alert when placed in office.'

However, there is one example where a beautiful lad was used for territorial gain. When Duke Xian wished to attack the enemy at Yu, but feared its ruler Gong Zhiqi, he sent him a 'beautiful lad to ruin an older head.' The plan worked and Duke Xian attacked Yu and took it.

These are all early examples of love and lust crossing class barriers, of homosexual attachments being used as a social ploy in worldly advancement, in gaining wealth and power. As court life was strictly hierarchical, this is not in the least surprising. Unfortunately there is no information from this early time of the sexual life of commoners, though as the ruling elite tend always to be copied in their style and customs, we can be fairly sure that there was no opprobrium, and maybe even some *cachet*, attached to same-sex love.

Contrary to what was about to happen, the ancient world appeared to have accepted sexuality in a relaxed manner. The legislation that existed favoured men, largely because of the importance of property and inheritance, but no single ethical belief had selected and favoured one expression of sexuality over another, nor had a concept of what is 'natural' or 'unnatural' been defined. All this was about to change, starting around 600 BC.

II

THE CONFLICT: GREEKS AND JEWS

Western culture is rooted in and moulded by the past, most of all by the Hellenic 'golden age' and the biblical ethos of Hebrew belief. These two ancient cultures were so wholly in contradiction in how they viewed women and sex, in how they treated boyhood, the concept of pleasure and the idea of the divine, that we are accordingly schizophrenic in our attitude towards sexuality and still, socially and psychologically, bear the wounds of that conflict.

THE GREEKS

Crete

In Crete, goddess worship probably lasted longer than anywhere else; Minoan wall-paintings of men wearing women's clothes indicate that a cult of male prostitution was also practised. It is interesting, then, that from this island we also have an account of the seduction of boys – a social convention of the time.

The Greek historian Ephorus (405–330 BC) wrote a fascinating account of the pederastic conventions in Crete, but all we know of his lost work comes from Strabo of Amaseia, a writer who lived two hundred years later. In his books of geography (all that has survived of his work), Strabo describes at length the erotic conventions of abduction, whereby the lover told the friends and family of the desired boy that he was planning to abduct him. The boy's family and friends put on a token show of resistance and pursued the abductor, that is, if the would-be lover was of suitable rank and honour. If not, the resistance and pursuit would be for real and family and friends would wrest the boy from him. However, if the boy had no lover and no one attempted to abduct him, then social shame befell the family.

According to Cretan custom, the most desirable boys were those who were brave and intelligent, not the most beautiful. The lover gave the boy presents and took him into the forests and mountains where they lived for about two months. In this time the lover taught the boy how to hunt, how to live in the wild and how to be an honourable man. He also made love to the boy and it is clear from the text that he penetrated the boy anally. But they were not alone all this time; some of the boy's friends and relations would accompany him and they all hunted and feasted together.

After two months the boy was sent home with presents. There were three – each of symbolic significance – an ox, a suit of armour and a goblet. Back home the boy would sacrifice the ox to Zeus, and there was a procession and a feast. It is clear that what was being celebrated was the fact that the boy had taken his first step towards manhood. Such festivals were popular occasions as the whole community was able to share in the feasting; only the smoke and the aromatic herbs were given to the god, for these were seen to waft towards heaven. The boy thus became a benefactor to the town at the same time as showing piety and gratitude to Zeus.

Wine was drunk at banquets and symposiums in civic and ritual ceremonies, hence the gift of the goblet conferred the right to become part of the banquet (women and children did not drink wine). And the gift of armour promoted the boy to the status of warrior and protector of the state. This custom was rooted, it is believed, in the prehistory of Europe.[1] It is odd that the early sagas are not imbued with such stories while the Greek myths are full of them.

Homeric Sagas

There is no overt homosexuality in Homer and very little in Hesiod, yet the warriors Achilles and Patroclus were accepted as great homoerotic examples from the fifth century BC.

There are various versions of the childhood of Achilles. His mother, Thetis, wanted to make him immortal, so at night she would hide the child in a fire. Peleus, Achilles' father, saw the child writhing in the flames and took his son and gave him to Chiron, a centaur. In the mountains the child was fed on the innards of lions, wild swine and the bone marrow of bears. However, when Achilles was nine, hearing that Troy would not be taken without him, Thetis disguised the boy as a maiden.

This account, of course, has echoes of the initiation cults. Admittedly, the centaur Chiron does not penetrate the young Achilles, nor is Achilles abducted by the centaur, but that figure in itself represents the wild man and their sojourn consuming lions' entrails is in a wild place. It is interesting, too, that in the next stage Achilles is disguised as a girl. He is finally saved from a trans-vestite life at court by Ulysses, who comes seeking for him to take him to the siege of Troy. It is possible that an earlier version of the myth conformed more closely to the initiatory ritual.

Over the years there has been much quibbling among scholars and translators of the Homeric texts. Some suggest that there has been misinterpretation and even subtle censorship of the more overtly homosexual lines. In Book XVI of the *Iliad*, Achilles asks the gods to rid the world of all humanity except Patroclus and himself. This line was omitted by the Alexandrian editor Aris-tarchus, who also omitted another line from the beginning of Book XIX where Achilles mourns his lover's death, and Thetis finds him, 'Lying in the arms of Patroclus/crying shrill'.

Aeschylus, in a play that is lost to us except for one-line frag-ments, made Achilles the older lover and teacher of Patroclus. Plutarch tells us (and Athenaeus quotes the same line) that after

Patroclus' death Achilles looked down upon his naked lover's body and talked of the 'coitus of his thighs', saying angrily: 'You had no reverence for the holiness of thighs, ungrateful after all our frequent kisses.'

When the Homeric sagas were created and memorised, part of their intention was to celebrate the physical prowess and intellect of the hero. We know that initiation rituals of boys were part of the social structure of the time, yet physical homosexuality in the sagas, for the most part, has to be inferred. It is thought that if the authors refused to speak of it directly there must have been some taboo, originating from the elite of the time who may have considered pederastic practices to be unsuitable for heroes. This view, if it existed, did not last for long, for in the sixth century BC there was a huge flowering of lyrical homosexual poetry, much of it still extant.

Lyric Poetry

Greek poetry of the sixth century is passionate and yet austere. Sappho's celebration of lesbian love (she came from the isle of Lesbos, hence the name) has a severe power, as if it was written yesterday:

> I have had not one word from her
> Frankly I wish I were dead.
> When she left, she wept
> a great deal; she said to me, 'this parting must be
> endured, Sappho. I go unwillingly.[2]

Solon has a more breezy touch:

> Blest is the man who loves and after early play
> Whereby his limbs are supple made and strong
> Retiring to his house, with wine and song
> Toys with a fair boy on his breast the livelong day.[3]

Solon was a great legislator and wrote much verse in praise of boys, so here we have the first clear indication that such love was not only approved of but had become an integral part of the whole social structure.

Anacreon, born about 570 BC on the isle of Teos, wrote: 'Come, pledge me, dear boy, your slender thighs.' His greatest love was Cleobulus: 'I am mad about Cleobulus, I gaze at Cleobulus.' It is said that the poet was asked why he wrote verses to boys and not to the gods, to which he replied: 'But the boys are my gods.'[4]

Other poets of the time, writing in a similar vein, include Alcaeus, Theognis, Ibycus and Pindar. It is clear from this work that the Greeks loved youthful beauty, and that such beauty included that of the mind, intellect and spirit. The poet is the teacher/master, the loving companion who tutors his beloved in the path of honour and virtue. The relationship is not just sexual; indeed, if it becomes a matter of lust and lust only, then the poet disparages such barbarism. Nor was the teaching always on such a high plane: the master taught his beloved the ways of the Greek world and how to behave in society. Etiquette was very important, as was the idea of moderation, for pleasure must not rule life. In all this it is clear that homosexual love was considered to be far superior to heterosexual love.

Women in Classical Greece

During that great Athenian period of Pericles and Plato, that flowering of philosophy, literature and architecture which has so profoundly inspired Western culture, women were divided into whores, courtesans, and wives and mothers. Only property-owners had the vote, while the whole economy was based upon slave-ownership (so much for the cradle of democracy). Boys were taken away from their mothers at the age of seven to be educated (rather as in the English public school system) but girls did not receive a formal education. Only courtesans were expected to converse with wit and knowledge on the world's events. Girls were taught by their mothers how to prepare wool and spin it, how to weave, sew and make clothes.

Married women were kept in the inner recesses of the house, in the women's quarters, forbidden to show themselves in public unless accompanied by an older, trusted confidential male of the household and a female slave. We read that after the fearful defeat of Chaeronea (338 BC), the women of Athens dared venture only as far as the doors of their houses, where, half senseless with grief and anxiety, they inquired after their husbands, sons, fathers and brothers – but even this was considered unworthy of them.[5] This was the battle where the Sacred Band of Thebes, made up of 150 couples of lovers who had remained undefeated for so long, were all finally slaughtered. Each died heroically beside his lover to prove that he had deserved such love. Perhaps the Athenian men felt that the women had no part in the grieving; if so, it shows how Athenian women were ousted to the margins of society and of male consciousness.

Solon passed legislation on a host of seemingly small matters. For example, when women attended funerals and festivals they were permitted to take with them no more than three pieces of clothing, and no more than an obol's worth of food and drink (about 10 pence). At night time they could go out only in a carriage with a lighted lantern. Solon was refining and strengthening the rule of primogeniture. In an earlier age of warriors and fighting heroes, women led much freer lives. The family unit was a large one which included several wives and concubines. With the rise of an affluent middle class with property to inherit, however, there was a need to regulate the family and restrict the freedom of wives and mothers. As husbands moved away from the home, spending their time at the gymnasium or in debate at symposiums, so the wife became more and more imprisoned at the domestic hearth.

Xenophon (b. 432 BC), the historian, wrote a treatise on domestic management in which he tells us that the ideal bride must live under strict supervision before marriage, seeing, hearing and saying as little as possible. She should know no more than how to make a cloak from wool. After marriage she must be chaste and sober-minded, capable of allotting to every maidservant the task best suited to her; she must keep together and make intelligent use of the money and property acquired by her husband; but her chief task was the rearing of children, governing them wisely.

Plato summed up the position of women crisply enough in his *Laws*, in a speech against Neaera: 'We have courtesans for our pleasure, concubines for daily personal service and married women to bear us children and to manage our house faithfully.'

The plight of women did not go unnoticed by the great dramatist Sophocles. In *Tereus*, of which we have only a fragment, he has a wife commenting: 'I have often observed that such is the lot of womankind – that we are a mere nothing.'

Did these wives ever take their revenge, one wonders? Perhaps in small ways, illustrated by an amusing story told by Plutarch. King Heiro was ridiculed by an opponent for the bad smell of his breath. He runs home in a rage and asks his wife why she has never drawn his attention to it. The wife replies: 'But I thought all men smelt like that.'

Xenophon has Socrates say: 'Surely you do not suppose that lust begets children?'[6] No, he goes on to say, there are streets and brothels for all that; wives are chosen carefully so that they will produce for us the best children. But what Socrates did not say was that men and boys were there to satisfy lust. In fact, Socrates took great care to warn men of the snares of sexual attraction and, as far as we know, took similar care not to become sexually infatuated himself, though he admitted that there was seldom a time when he was not in love.

Hedonism

The word comes from the Greek *hedone*, meaning the enjoyment of life, particularly the sensuous enjoyment of love. It is perhaps this heritage which explains our fascination with the Greeks; or is it because their hedonism was also, rather paradoxically, entwined with ethical values? (There were, of course, few outlets for hedonism for women in their tedious round of household duties.)

There was an astonishing cult of youth which was exclusively male, except in Sparta where naked girls and boys fought in wrestling matches. Male nakedness was universal at the gymnasia, at public national games, at contests for the prize of beauty at Lesbos, at Tenedos, in the Temple of Ceres, at Basilis in Arcadia, and in the temples of Venus at Corinth. This custom dates back to 720 BC when the Greeks allowed all contestants in the Games to appear naked. Because male genitalia tend to swing a bit in physical action, they were tied with a thin piece of cloth called a *kynodesme*; vase paintings show athletes tying the cloth. The Greeks regarded male genitalia with a kind of awe – something akin to the way Melanesian tribes revered the penis and the sperm – as mystical instruments of propagation, symbols of the life-producing force. Thus the phallus became a religious symbol, capable of breaking the spell of the evil eye. The phallus appeared on gates and entrances, or standing separately. Called Hermes, square stone pillars were surmounted by a man's bearded head and bore male genitalia, nearly always erect. The Hermes were used as border stones and house guards facing away from the house and shrines. Other phalli were carried in the hand, sometimes decorated with little claws, wings and bells, rather like worry-beads or a rosary. The phalli were also used in religious ceremonies, especially at the cult of Dionysius.

Much rarer were the amulets depicting female pudenda, mainly it is suggested because it was thought they had less power. Often they were depicted as a ripe, split fig.

The celebration of hedonism encouraged sexual expression. Nothing was banned, though laws existed to control excess. There were no purification rituals or days of abstinence after menstruation, as in other societies of the time. Masturbation was regarded as natural if men had no opportunities for copulation with others. They also used dildoes, called *olisboi* or *baubon*, which originated in the wealthy city of Miletus and were widely exported. Herondas, the poet, has a verse where two women discuss the scarcity of *olisboi* and end up by going to a shoemaker, Cerdon, who will make one for them. A bowl of Pamphaeus in the British Museum shows a naked courtesan with two *olisboi* in her hand and a flagon of oil in which to dip them. In a fragment of Aristophanes, a list of the aids to beauty that women need includes *olisboi*, among the details of cosmetics, jewellery and hair supports.[7]

Bisexuality

Athenian sexuality is far more complex and contradictory than it may first seem. For though the social norm was undoubtedly bisexuality, this concept was ringed about with many qualifications. There were also many instances of behaviour which did not conform to the norm but which were nevertheless quietly accepted.

A man was expected to marry once he reached the age of twenty-five and to produce a small family. (Various forms of birth control were practised, as well as abortion and infanticide.) Women married earlier, often as young as twelve. It was not socially approved of for a man to be exclusively a lover of boys, and the literature is full of warnings against men who hang about the gymnasia ogling beautiful youths. In a fragment of a poem, Plato speaks to a youth called Aster: 'Look at the stars. Oh, if I were the heavens I could look on you with thousands of eyes.' Alexander the Great, too, appears to have been almost exclusively homosexual. We must speculate, too, that there were plenty of men who preferred women.

A balanced bisexuality, whereby a citizen was married, was in love with a boy and was also seen to go with courtesans or had a mistress, was normal behaviour. It was said of Alcibiades, who was notorious for his beauty (he appears in Plato's *Symposium* with a tale of his inability to seduce Socrates) 'that in his adolescence he drew away the husbands from their wives, and as a young man the wives from their husbands'.[8]

The poet Meleager writes of how women ignite a fire within him but boys hold the reins of desire. Which way, he asks, must he go, to the boy or to his mother?

Theocritis, a pastoral poet, writes of a woman rejected by her lover who wonders whether the lover lies with a woman or a man.

Xenophon, mentioning the moment when prisoners of war were released, talks of the soldiers prompted by desire smuggling off a good-looking boy or woman.[9]

Social acceptance of bisexuality as the most natural of responses was as deeply ingrained in the consciousness of Greek society as the idea of exclusive heterosexuality being the only normal and natural impulse is in ours. These are, of course, examples of societies where the citizen's sexuality has been constructed rather than biologically fixed.

In both Plato and Xenophon, however, we see contrasting examples of a genetic disposition favouring one form of sexuality over another.

Ethics[10]

Plato's *Symposium* is central to an understanding of the ethics of Greek sexual behaviour. Pausanias describes two kinds of love: the first, inspired by Aphrodite, is common love which moves men of little worth to give their affections without distinction to women and boys. These men are more in love with bodies than souls. Socrates summed it up when he said: 'If anyone is found to be the lover of Alcibiades' body, he has fallen in love, not with Alcibiades, but with something belonging to Alcibiades.' The second love, inspired by Aphrodite Urania, is a heavenly love for boys shown by distinguished and noble men who chose their beloveds with care and sensitivity, committing themselves to the boys' welfare and education. Plato's work explores how the love of boys was a means of acquiring wisdom.

There were rules for this second kind of love: the boy could not give in too easily or show eagerness for fear of losing his reputation and honour; the lover had to prove his loyalty and his worth. It was essential for the boy to be certain that his lover was not interested only in his body.

To counter the notion that all this idealised pederasty was a minority interest pursued by the philosophical elite, we have the evidence of Aeschines, a legal orator who wrote speeches for tribunals to persuade the jury of the justice of his cause. The jury were ordinary country folk, not particularly educated or sophisticated, so an orator could not afford to outrage or shock them. The content of the orator's speeches is likely to reflect popular morality.

In one case Aeschines prosecuted Timarchus whom he claimed

had lost his political rights because he had prostituted himself. First, though, Aeschines had to make it clear that he in no way condemned homosexual love. He pointed out that the law forbade slaves to be the lovers of free boys, then he went on to describe the courtship of a free-born boy as giving that boy an opportunity to show his propriety and good manners – the Platonic ethos, in fact. In his speech Aeschines went on to celebrate the great homosexual lovers of the past and present, praising their moral virtues as well as their beauty: 'Men who were the most beautiful, not only among their fellow citizens, but in all Hellas, men who counted many a man of eminent chastity as his lover.' Aeschines here is stressing the modesty and moral control of other youths, as well as admitting a little later that he too was a lover of boys and wrote them erotic verses.

There was a serious issue at stake behind this case. Timarchus had accused Aeschines of betraying Athens by signing a peace treaty with Philip of Macedon in 346 BC. Aeschines argued that Timarchus had no authority in the courts for he had lost all his civic rights because of his private life. Under Athenian law the prostitute lost his rights while the customer did not. This law reflects the general feeling that passivity was not suitable for adult males, who should have grown out of that phase much earlier. Aeschines asks the court how they could dare to let Timarchus go free when he is a creature defiled with the sins of a woman, though he has the body of a man. Timarchus was a kept man, not a street prostitute, and Aeschines had to prove that to have a series of lovers keeping you is as bad as being a whore. Both male and female prostitutes were taxed on their earnings, yet women did not suffer quite the same level of social disapproval as male prostitutes. Was it because the cult of youth and its idealised love carried such philosophical weight, it was difficult to accept the more squalid side of homosexual life?

One of the most famous speeches in the *Symposium* is that made by Aristophanes which suggests that at the beginning the human race was made up of three genders. There were double males, double females and a male and female stuck together. Each had four arms and four legs and moved by cartwheeling. But they became too proud and annoyed the gods who took a blade and severed each of them in two. Aristophanes then tells us that each half has been searching for its twin ever since and defines love as the desire and pursuit of the whole. This parable now has enormous psychological power: we all know that feeling when in love that we have at last discovered our 'twin', even if it is not for life. But did it have this symbolic power then? I suspect so, for it is given prominence in the book even though it contradicted the current ideology. These couples are of the same age, the double male is not a man stuck to a boy. So the parable can reflect adult love psychologically, both heterosexual and homosexual, but it does not begin to explain pederasty or paedophilia. Historians think that paedophilia is better explained as the continuing tradition of the ritual initiation, the rites of passage, that boys had undergone to become men, which had lasted for many thousands of years across the world.

Passive Love

At what age were boys seduced? It was frowned on, though there were no laws against it, if the boys were under twelve. Certainly from twelve to fifteen boys were thought to be of an age when they should have found a male lover.

After the courtship when the boy at last acquiesced and his family approved, what form did their love-making take? The lexical implication is clear enough: the boy submitted as a woman does, he served as a subordinate.[11] This does not fit in with intercrural (between the thighs)* intercourse which by its nature has to be more equal. Besides, the graffiti discovered at Thera have specific references to anal intercourse. Also, the plays of Aristophanes are full of references to buggery, and there are many verses which praise the beauty of the buttocks, the arse and anal penetration itself.

---

* Both 'intercrural' and 'interfemoral' mean to achieve orgasm by rubbing the penis between the thighs.

The boy remained the passive partner until he was around seventeen or eighteen – this was the accepted norm – but there were many cases of youths remaining passive much longer, as indeed there are references to young boys wanting to be active with boys of the same age. The youth eventually became a man at the age of twenty-five, and from then on he took the active role, first choosing a boy, and then getting married.

In actual practice these rules were constantly being infringed. The comedies of Aristophanes revel in such contradictions, for though passivity in adult men was an occasion for scorn, this did not seem to have much effect in making it that unpopular. In *The Frogs*, Dionysius confesses to Heracles that he is in love. No, he says shamefully, not with a woman, or a boy, but with a man. And worst of all, the man is Cleisthenes who is noted for his effeminacy.

Love between two adult men occurred often, but only the 'effeminate' man incurred the social opprobrium. The slang terms used for passive homosexuals are variations on 'broad-arsed', while those for active homosexuals accentuate a brutish masculinity – rough, black or hairy-arsed.

Women in Love

Plutarch tells us that in Sparta all the best women love girls, and if it happens that two of them are in love with the same girl, then they try to co-operate and improve their beloved. Yet what opportunities, one wonders, did the Athenian housewife have for love and sexual passion? She was brought up to show duty, obedience and respect to her husband and to care for and nurture her children. One hopes somehow that many love affairs occurred in those women's quarters so hidden from the world.

There is one amusing picture from Lucian of Samosata, in the fifth of his *Dialogues of the Courtesans*.[12] Clonarium and Leaena, two courtesans, are gossiping. Clonarium has heard that Leaena is the lover of a rich lady from Lesbos, Megilla, who loves her like a man. Leaena agrees that this is true, then goes on to say how very masculine Megilla is, for she has shaved her head but wears a wig in the day to disguise it. She has not got a 'man's thing' for she has her own way of making love which is much pleasanter. Megilla tells her that though she was born a woman, her desires are all those of a man. Leaena refuses, alas, to give any more details of Megilla's love-making. How very familiar this description sounds to us today, for Megilla resembles the modern concept of a transsexual.

There is one myth which sheds some light on how the Greeks regarded women. Zeus and Hera were quarrelling over which sex obtained the most pleasure out of making love. Zeus claimed women did and Hera insisted that men must. Then Hera thought to ask Tiresias, for after all he had been both man and woman and must be the final arbiter of the quarrel. Tiresias said that there was no doubt about it, women obtained the most pleasure out of sex. This so infuriated Hera that she struck Tiresias blind. It is interesting, first, that the Greeks suspected women of having this huge and avid appetite for sex, and, second, that such an appetite had to be hidden and not publicly acknowledged. No wonder women were kept under such strict conditions, for surely they were much feared.

Could institutionalised pederasty exist without this subjection of women? It is doubtful. Once women gain more equality the expression of homosexuality changes also, to something resembling a more equal relationship. It is as if when male domination of women exists, then the male child is also dominated, taught and moulded in a particular way, and more equal sexual relationships are scorned as being imperfect.

THE HEBREWS

The second great culture which has influenced Western mores is that of the ancient Hebrews. Israel was a patriarchy and Yahweh an awesome and bloodthirsty *pater familias* of the twelve tribes. It is clear from the beginning that the Jewish opinion of women was low; it was Eve, after all, who was responsible for the Fall with the assistance of a snake, the eternal symbol of the phallus.

The Hebrew attitude to marital sex, as revealed in the Talmud, however, has echoes of a modern sex manual in its detail; this was a society, it is clear, where sex within marriage was highly valued, pragmatic and sensible. At times the directions in the Talmud show great consideration for married women, though it can be disparaging to women as a whole. The wife and mother in the home plays a vital part in the religious function of the Sabbath and the family.

The Hebrew attitude to homosexuality is complex and equivocal; it appears to be related very closely to relations with neighbouring countries and whether or not they were battling against alien cultures. Israel provides an example of a culture which was totally different from any other in Asia Minor or the Mediterranean.

The Jewish wife was owned by her husband, as elsewhere, but the women's domestic obligations were, and still are, given a religious significance. Every Sabbath the woman of the house kindles the candles with a blessing to God. The father takes a cup of wine and recites the Kiddush, sips from the cup and passes it to the wife and children. Then he recites the praise of the virtuous wife from Proverbs 31 which includes the phrase that she is in price 'far above rubies'. There is more praise in the apocryphal Ecclesiasticus 25–6: 'Happy is the husband of a good wife . . . the beauty of a good wife is like the sun when it rises in high places.' This praise of the female within marriage should be set against the thanksgiving to be recited by men from the authorised Jewish daily Prayer Book: 'Blessed art thou, O Lord our God, King of the universe, who has not made me a woman.' (How did wives and daughters feel when such sentiments were uttered? one wonders.)

The patriarchs of the Old Testament, Abraham, Isaac and Jacob, all had many wives; there was an anxiety which small tribes inevitably exhibit that the men must go forth and multiply. Polygamy continued for some thousands of years. Like the number of cattle you owned, the number of wives was a sign of affluence and power. Solomon was said to have 700 wives and 300 concubines. The Talmud sanctioned polygamy, though there were different versions of how many wives a man might have. One authority said that a man may have as many wives as he pleased, while another stated no more than four was suitable. Polygamy was outlawed in Judaism only in the eleventh century.

Men were expected to marry after the age of eighteen. Girls could marry after they had ceased to be a minor at the age of twelve. There was tremendous social pressure on men to plant a vineyard, build a house and take a wife. It was said that up to the age of twenty, 'the Holy One, blessed be he, watches for a man to marry and curses him if he fails to do so'.[13] In Deuteronomy (24.5) it is suggested that the new husband should not leave his wife to go to the army or disappear working, but should stay at home for a year and enjoy his wife. How many times he should have intercourse with his wife was also laid down, with the directive that he should take care to bring his wife to orgasm. For it was thought that women conceived more often if they experienced orgasm. Affluent men might have intercourse every night, labourers twice a week (but if they had to travel much, then once a week would do), sailors might copulate only once every six months, camel drivers once every thirty days and scholars once a week on Friday nights.

Marriage was a religious duty; a rabbinic saying was that a man who does not marry is not fully a man. Celibacy was not favoured, so priests and rabbis ought to be married and the High Priest was compelled to marry. Divorce was also very easy for the man, who could divorce his wife for any inadequacy including the quality of her cooking. It was thought that the ease of divorce by the man improved the standard of marriages. The idea that the worth of the woman was disparaged seems not to have occurred to the patriarchs. We bear the marks of such attitudes still.

The Great Taboos

Because male sexuality in marriage was so highly valued, every other sexual activity, even the most trivial, was banned. For example, a man was forbidden to hold his penis even while urinating. It is thought this ban existed for fear that the man might begin to masturbate, and one Talmudic writer even suggested that such an act should deserve the death penalty. Indeed, the Lord slew Onan for spilling his seed, so this measure had divine sanction. (Onanism is now thought to be *coitus interruptus*.) Semen lost in sleep was also a source of concern; the skin and every garment the semen had touched had to be washed and were considered unclean until the evening. After such an impure event it was thought a short period of continence was in order.

This was as nothing, however, to the defilement of menstruating women who were regarded as unclean for seven days along with everything they touched, sat or reclined on. Men who had intercourse with women at such times also became unclean for seven days, as did the bed that they copulated on. Later in Judaism this unclean period could be shortened by having a ritual bath, the *mikwa*.

Like the Greeks, the Jews also feared women if their sexuality was not regularly appeased. Talmudic writers prohibited women from keeping both slaves and a pet dog, while the punishment for bestiality was death for both the animal and the woman. There is almost nothing about lesbianism; the Hebrews felt that women could do little of significance among themselves without men and the act of penetration.

Though men could not hold their penis while urinating (aiming the jet of urine must have been a problem), their attitude to the penis was equivocal. As was the custom among the Egyptians, phalli were severed from a defeated army and brought home. David brought Saul the foreskins of 200 Philistines, obviously a precious gift as Saul then gave David his daughter in marriage (I Samuel 18.27). Circumcision was also a way in which the phallus was revered, marking the male infant with the sign of his race, though, as we have seen, the custom is an ancient one. In the Old Testament it is a sign of the covenant that the Hebrews have with Yahweh.

The Crucial Texts

The argument that the Hebrews abominated homosexuality above all else is based on several biblical passages. This is to ignore other stories which give a positive picture. Some of the references refer to the cult of male prostitution:

> There shall be no harlot among the daughters of Israel. And there shall be no sodomite of the sons of Israel. (Deuteronomy 23.18–19)

> And there were also sodomites in the land: and they did according to all the abominations of the nations which Yahweh drove out before the children of Israel. (I Kings 14.24)

> And he broke down the house of the sodomites, that were in the house of the Lord, where the women wove coverings for the Asherah. (II Kings 23:5–7)

In the early days of the formation of the Hebrew nation, people were surrounded by cultures which celebrated male temple prostitution. Hittite texts document transvestite eunuch priests; Babylonian and Assyrian texts refer to the priests who chanted, played music, wore masks and carried a spindle, a symbol of women's work. They were thought to have magical powers and all the references to them indicate that they had been castrated, and that they submitted to anal intercourse. Eusebius, as late as the fourth century AD, indicates that the priests of the moon goddess were still practising such cults on Mount Lebanon until Constantine had the shrine destroyed.[14]

As part of Asia Minor, the Hebrews were influenced by the Egyptians, Canaanites, Phoenicians and Mesopotamians. At various times in their history they incorporated other peoples' customs and beliefs, while at other times there were powerful movements to reject outside and alien cultures in order to establish their own. Time and time again this is reflected in the biblical texts: 'After the doings of the land of Egypt wherein ye dwelt, shall ye not do: and after the doings of the land of Canaan, whither I shall

bring you, shall ye not do: neither shall ye walk in their ordinances' (Leviticus 18.3).

It seems likely that, in those phases when the nation of Israel was
fighting for its independence and religious identity, many of the
verses which exhort the people to remove the sodomites are allied
with instructions to destroy the idols. These are plainly religious
instructions. The coverings which the women weave for the Ash-
erah are coverings for the phallus which would have been
decorated in different ways at different times of the year. But we
need to look closely at the translation of the word 'sodomite'.

First, in the King James translation 'sodomite' does not have its
modern connotation. Then 'sodomy' covered all sexual acts of any
kind, between people of either gender, which were not vaginal
penetration in the missionary position. Second, the Jewish scholars
who translated the Bible into Greek in the third and second centuries BC had great trouble in rendering the Hebrew word '*kadash*'
into Greek. In Hebrew the word means 'sacred' or 'hallowed'. It
was such a problem that the translators chose six different Greek
terms for the one Hebrew word, none of which would have suggested homosexuality to the theologians of the early church who
relied on the Greek translation. So these passages were not used as
condemnations of homosexuality until the mistranslation of the
words into English in the early seventeenth century.[15] There was,
of course, no precise word in the ancient world in any of the languages – Greek, Syriac, Aramaic or Hebrew – which meant
homosexual, substantial proof that the concept of a homosexual or
homosexual behaviour did not exist, though the idea of same-
gender sexual intercourse or love is very occasionally referred to.

We find it in Leviticus (18.22) where there is another passage
which appears, at face value, to be simple enough: 'Thou shalt not
lie with mankind, as with womankind: it is abomination.' But the
Hebrew word '*toevah*' translated here as 'abomination' means
something ritually unclean, on a par with lying with a menstruating woman. The same Hebrew word is used when condemning
temple prostitution, and when calling the Gentiles 'unclean'. So
the original verse, one theory goes,[16] has none of the elements of

evil which it later acquired. The Greek translation stresses the 'ritually unclean' meaning and early theologians regarded it as a directive associated with idolatry and temple prostitution, or as being on the same level as the many detailed dietary prohibitions which were applicable to Orthodox Jews, but had nothing to do with Christianity.

However, a critic of the theory argues that '*toevah*' implies great repugnance, that pollutions involving elements of the taboos are equally offensive, for everything prohibited by Yahweh in Leviticus is totally wrong. Leviticus, scholars now think, was compiled and written immediately after the Babylonian exile (500 BC), though some of it may well have been gathered together during that period (roughly 680–520 BC), for it shows the influence of the Zoroastrian religion in its emphasis on purity and cleansing doctrines. Zoroastrians prohibited male homosexuality, again in an attempt to establish a pure religious form which owed nothing to cult temple prostitution.

At this time in Jewish history Judaea was devastated: the ruling classes had been deported, its cities were in ruins, there were no kings, no leaders. But there were priests, and the Holiness Code (Chapters 17 to 26) in all its detail gives a structure for religious authority based upon sacrifices, purity and pollution. It says that if the people obey these rules, then Yahweh will return to lead his people again. All the disasters, the defeat and the exile are explained away through the guilt and sin of the people.

Sodom and Gomorrah

The most notorious story in the Bible – which gave its name in the Latin languages to a word which over the years meant a variety of sexual acts disapproved of by the church – has become the basic weapon in the homophobic armoury. 'Sodomy' had a different meaning in the Middle Ages, referring to anal penetration of either sex or to positions where the woman was on top of the man, or to copulation with an animal. Up to and throughout the Renaissance, the crime of the two cities of Sodom and Gomorrah was considered to be 'sexual licence', which as part of orgiastic partying would have included buggery and bestiality. More recently, the crime which the men of these two cities committed (the women appear to have vanished) has become firmly established in people's minds as homosexuality. It is, frankly, a very silly story but one which still causes controversy.

Sodom and Gomorrah were two of five cities on the plain of Jordan; archaeological evidence indicates that the area was fertile in the Middle Bronze Age (2000–1500 BC), for fresh water then flowed into what we now know as the Dead Sea. The cities were devastated by an earthquake around 1900 BC, which ignited the oil and petroleum deposits in the area, causing a conflagration which must have been extraordinarily dramatic and terrifying; an unforgettable vision to be passed on from generation to generation.

The Book of Genesis is a compilation which scholars have dated as being written at three different times. Some of it was written as early as 900 BC, about one thousand years after the earthquake which destroyed the cities. Other parts were written in the seventh and fifth centuries BC. Genesis begins with a history of the world which includes the Creation and flood myths; these borrow much from Mesopotamian sources. Then it goes on to tell the story of Abraham and his sons, the patriarchs of Jewish history, which is the point at which the Sodom and Gomorrah story is told. As there is about a thousand, or even fifteen hundred, years between the events and the writing of them, it is clear that Genesis is history based on myth and folk tales which, like Homer's epic poetry, would have had a long oral tradition behind them. History, we must always remember, reflects the opinions and emotions of the time in which it is written; it is a highly subjective craft as each era sheds a different light upon the past.

As this story is central to homophobia, it is important to place it in context. Genesis tells of the sons of Noah after the Flood. One descendant of Noah's son Shem was Terah, who lived at Ur of the Chaldees. He had three sons, Abram, Nahor and Haran, but Haran died leaving a son, Lot. Terah and family, intending to migrate to Canaan, leave Ur and travel up the Euphrates. But they stop and settle in northern Mesopotamia. Then the Lord speaks to

Abram, telling him to complete his journey, for 'I will make of thee a great nation'. Abram, taking his wife, nephew and servants, sets off and arrives in central Palestine. Here the Lord tells him that the land is given to him and his descendants. There is an almost paranoid need in ninth-century historians to prove their territorial rights, for the patriarchs were always on the move. Even after this gift from God Abram does not stay and work the land, but moves south and, in the midst of a famine, crosses over to Egypt. This was customary among the various nomad tribes of Egypt's neighbours and the host country appears to have made them welcome. However, this welcome was no doubt helped by the fact that the Pharaoh fancied Abram's wife, Sarai, and as he was told by Abram that she was his sister, they all lived very comfortably for some time. As Abram was wealthy when he left Egypt, one can only draw the conclusion that he sold his wife's favours to the Pharaoh, but the historians draw a veil over this.

The family return to Palestine, but now they have greater herds and larger households and Lot breaks away from Abram to find pasture of his own. He goes to the plain of Jordan and to the city of Sodom. At this point we are told that the men of Sodom were 'wicked and sinners before the Lord'. There is no particular sin specified. Could it be that they were pagan? Yet paganism or idol worship remains unsaid because the compilers of the oral tradition knew full well that at this stage, before the revelation of the Lord to Moses via a burning bush, no distinct religion had yet been revealed to the patriarchs. Abram built two altars in Palestine to the Lord for sacrificing, and continued to have the occasional conversation, but that was all. It is not feasible that the men of Sodom would have been cast out at this time merely because they were pagans.

Some time after Lot has settled among these 'wicked men', the cities are in revolt against their rulers in Elam, which is far away beyond the Tigris. The king of Elam puts down the revolt, defeats the five cities and takes away as prisoners Lot and his family. Abram musters 318 warriors from his own household and recaptures Lot from the rearguard of the victorious army. So we have in these stories a picture of Abram as a roaming cattle-rancher who is also in close conversation with God (always about land; at one point the Lord promises Abram land from Egypt to the Euphrates), who pimps for his wife and who at a moment's notice can turn into a warrior chief.

Because Sarai is barren Abram is allowed to fornicate with the maid (a Mesopotamian custom, as we have seen) but then the Lord makes Sarai pregnant in her ninetieth year and Abram in his one-hundredth year is circumcised. This is the covenant with God and they are renamed Abraham and Sarah.

God informs Abraham that he is going to destroy Sodom and Gomorrah. Again no crime has been specified, but we have seen that cult temple prostitution had been common in Mesopotamia since at least 2000 BC, and as these are vassal cities it might seem reasonable to suppose that they had adopted such rites. It would accompany the pagan idol-worship mentioned above. However, God specifies only two of the five cities, the other three do not seem to have been destroyed, though they are unlikely to have been very different in their customs of belief and worship.

There then occurs an amazing passage in which Abraham haggles with God over how many righteous people in Sodom and Gomorrah can be saved. Abraham shows himself to be far more compassionate than God, who is pictured delighting in punishment. Two angels arrive at the gate of Sodom. (Angels in the Old Testament are described as the sons of God and as messengers from God.) Lot is waiting at the gate and recognises the angels. He takes them back to his house and makes them a feast. But the men of Sodom surround the house and ask Lot to bring out the men so that they may 'know them'. The Hebrew verb for 'to know' is very rarely used in a sexual sense; in only ten out of 943 times in the Bible does it refer to carnal knowledge. Yet the men's request seems to be more alarming than mere curiosity, for Lot offers his daughters to them and describes them as not 'knowing' men (Genesis 19.8). The men reject Lot's daughters and insist that the angels be brought out. As one might expect, the angels can perfectly well defend themselves and they strike the men blind. The angels then warn Lot that they will destroy the city in the morning and he must save his family.

Lot flees the city the next morning with his wife and two daughters. The cities are destroyed by fire and brimstone but Lot's wife pauses to look back and is turned into a pillar of salt.

Chapter 19 ends with the two daughters of Lot getting their ancient father drunk then sleeping with him so that they might conceive, which they do. Incest here between father and daughters does not incur the wrath of the Lord. But what was the crime of these cities?

The earthquake and holocaust observed from afar must have been a terrifying sight. Cities alive with people and animals, thriving markets, temples and palaces were suddenly destroyed without warning, the buildings falling and fires igniting with flames of a hundred feet or more. In order to make sense of such an event, the best explanation seemed to be that it was divine punishment for a human offence. The crime seems all the more significant for not being precisely named, allowing later writers, interpreters and translators to be specific and to use the story for their own purposes. By the time Genesis was written down, man's infamy had been linked with disasters such as floods and earthquakes. It is a link which was to grow stronger down the ages.

The early Christian fathers did not see the story of Sodom and Gomorrah as having anything to do with homosexuality. Origen, who wrote at length about the powerful battle between the flesh and the spirit, analysed the story of Sodom and Gomorrah and interpreted it in terms of hospitality. In Origen's view, Lot escaped the fires of destruction because he had opened his home to strangers. Origen was more concerned over the incestuous act of the daughters. As the whole human race, according to Genesis, is based upon incest (Cain's wife has to be his sister), one might argue that Lot's incest was merely in an honourable tradition. St Ambrose also saw the story in the same terms, saying that Lot placed hospitality above the modesty of his daughters.[17] Even as late as the fourteenth century Piers Plowman thinks that over-plenty and sloth were the reasons for the destruction of the cities.

The use of the story of the destruction of the Cities of the Plain as textual dogma against homosexuality does not survive a close scrutiny of the lexical data. It is a prime example of a myth whose interpretation reflects the changing prejudices of succeeding societies.

Lovers

The most ecstatic prose of the Old Testament is contained in the Song of Solomon and in the description of the love shared by David and Jonathan. The Song is a hymn to sensual sexuality, and transcends gender. Later priestly editors may have deleted the sex from Saul's love for David and his for Jonathan, but they could not erase it all. We are told that Saul loves David greatly (I Samuel 16.21), but when he learns that David and Jonathan have become close friends he flies into a jealous rage and curses his son. 'Thou son of the perverse rebellious woman, do not I know that thou hast chosen the son of Jesse to thine own confusion, and unto the confusion of thy mother's nakedness?' (I Samuel 20.30). We read that 'The soul of Jonathan was knit with the soul of David, and Jonathan loved him as his own soul' (I Samuel 18.1). When both Saul and Jonathan are killed in battle, David laments and recalls that Jonathan's love had been 'wonderful, passing the love of women' (II Samuel 1.26). This is obviously a heroic love in the Greek mould, reminding one of nothing so much as Achilles and Patroculus or the Mesopotamian epic, *Gilgamesh*, with Gilgamesh's love for Enkidu.

Yet there is another possibly homosexual couple in the Old Testament – Ruth and Naomi. Ruth begs Naomi: 'Intreat me not to leave thee, or to return from following after thee: for whither thou goest, I will go; and where thou lodgest, I will lodge: thy people shall be my people, and thy God my God' (Ruth 1.16). This appears to be an all-embracing devotion; if it contained a physical side, it is unlikely that anyone would have been aware of it.

The evidence so far shows that when the Hebrews denounced homosexuality it is the idolatry that accompanies it which is loathed. But other evidence suggests that in their minds there is little doubt that homosexual acts are unclean. One might ask why the love that David bore Jonathan does not fall into this category.

The Holiness Code

Hebrew thought and religious jurisdiction work on a system of opposites; order is considered as clean, while disorder is unclean. The two must not be mixed. 'You shall not plough with an ox and an ass together' (Deuteronomy 22.10); 'You shall not sew your field with two kinds of seed' (Leviticus 19.19); 'You shall not wear a garment of divers sorts, as of wool and linen together' (Deuteronomy 22.11). In the same way, mixed marriages are forbidden (Deuteronomy 7.3), nor must a man of mixed blood or a bastard attend the assembly of the Lord (Deuteronomy 23.23). 'A woman shall not wear that which pertaineth unto a man, neither shall a man put on a woman's garment' (Deuteronomy 22.5).

Jewish dietary laws are highly selective and attempt to impose order upon the animal kingdom. Herbivorous animals are clean, while carnivorous animals are unclean. Animals must be unblemished, so must a priest and so must a man. Dwarfs, hunchbacks, people with defective sight, injured feet or hands, the blind and the lame, those with scabs and itching diseases are all listed as men who may not attend the assembly of the Lord (Deuteronomy 23.1). But the worst injury of all is those with male members cut off or crushed testicles. Eunuchs and castrated animals are unclean.

Based on Genesis and the story of Adam and Eve, the solid kernel of life is man and woman and their family. Male seed wasted was an unclean act which had to be ritually purified. Because Jews were constantly exhorted to go out and multiply, to procreate and fill the earth, semen must be deposited only in the female uterus. This perhaps explains why the Jews seem to be indifferent to women copulating together, for they were obviously irrelevant to the future of the race. But two men together in sexual congress fly in the face of the imposed 'natural' order.

In the Mishnah (AD 200), the first text which fixes Hebraic teaching in a written form, homosexuality is punished by stoning, but only the active partner is killed. Later in the Talmud both partners are condemned to death. Earlier, in the second century BC, *The Testaments of the Twelve Patriarchs* contains many exhortations against committing the sin of Sodom. This is the first time the link between Sodom and homosexuality is made; it is not unreasonable to suppose that Israel under Greek domination felt alienated and deeply affronted by Greek customs and rituals which so obviously celebrated homosexual love. Texts were written in an urgent attempt to defend Israel against such influence.

This fear imbues the Holiness Code, and Rabbinic and Jewish literature. Western culture has inherited this fear to such a degree that it is still vigorously alive today, fuelling homophobia and injustice. Certainly much of Leviticus and Deuteronomy, as well as suitable Pauline quotations from the New Testament, have become the bedrock of fundamentalist denunciation today. Fundamentalists seem unaware of the accretion from clumsy and inadequate translations which is inclined to dog all ancient texts, so that the original meaning is all too easily misinterpreted.

III

꩜

ROME, THE EAST
AND
EARLY CHRISTIANITY

THE ROMAN EMPIRE

Rome, from the earliest times, followed the tradition of ancient
civilisations (except, as we have seen, that of the Hebrews) in
celebrating male bisexuality. This was not solely a matter of classical Greek traditions influencing the Romans, though there is little
doubt that they did, for there were also radical and striking differences between them. The origins of Rome, some scholars believe
(while others question this), like those of the Greeks, lie in a far
more ancient culture, that of the Indo-Europeans.

At first it was accepted without question that boys and beautiful
young men were sexually desirable. This gradually changed, however, for in the later Roman Empire the concept of sexual
asceticism took over. Some scholars argue that this change
occurred quite independently of the spread of Christianity.

The Years BC

The famous myth of Romulus and Remus, the twin founders of
Rome suckled by a she-wolf, can be interpreted as a homosexual

initiation story. Mars, the god of war who fathered Romulus and Remus, was the male principle which dominated Roman thought and culture and was associated with Indo-European expansion. (A box discovered at the site of the ancient Latin city of Palestrina-Praeneste shows a naked Mars surrounded by several youths, which could be an initiation scene.)[1] If we recall cave drawings of shamans in animal skins – worn to absorb the ferocity of the carnivore – and the significance of swallowing semen and its equation with breast milk, as well as the ritual ceremonies which boys and youths underwent to become men, then she-wolf suckling begins to take on another and greater dimension.

Greeks and Phoenicians had settled in Sicily by the eighth century BC and the Etruscans took their Astarte worship from the latter. It is very possible that they also took the cult of ritualised pederasty from the early Greeks. The first mention of Etruscan sexual tastes comes from Theopompus (fourth century BC) who wrote: 'They certainly have commerce with women, but they always enjoy themselves much better with boys and young men. The latter are in this country quite beautiful to behold, for they live lives of ease and their bodies are hairless.'

For the Roman, virility was the greatest prize, an essential requirement for the adult male, allied with power and dominance and the whole concept of the conqueror. This is yet another phallocentric society where the male is defined as the bold aggressor. The Roman *pater familias* was an absolute master. It is interesting to note that, unlike the Greeks, the Romans were prudish over nudity, preferring their statues to be clothed. The Roman male is never allowed to seem vulnerable, for he is a man of war. In sculpture, the armoured torso is made to resemble the naked body with muscles, nipples and navel.

The Roman boy was raised to rule the world, first with the force of his arms, second with the superiority of his laws, and third with the authority of his language. From his childhood he had to impose his will upon lesser people, the slaves of the household and those beneath him in class. There is no doubt that he observed and was taught that this dominance extended also to sexual desire.

Male Roman sexuality was based upon the law of the rape.[2] All great, colonising empires include subjugation of victims as part of their sexual structure. The Greek pederost idea of courting a boy, flattering him and persuading him of the honour and integrity of the lover's intentions was utterly repugnant to the Roman spirit, for such behaviour showed a submissiveness alien to the nature of virility. However, the love of boys was popular enough, though from what we know of the Lex Scatinia (passed around 226 BC and designed to regulate Roman sexual behaviour), a sexual relationship with a free-born boy was punished by a fine. Cicero condemns such love, stating that, to his mind, the practice had its origins in the Greek gymnasia 'where that kind of loving was free and permitted'.[3]

Instead, it was slave boys that the Romans were allowed to love. Cicero himself continued to love his Tiro, even after freeing him from slavery. The elder Seneca records a case in which a freedman is criticised for allowing his patron sexual favours, but the lawyer responds that 'sexual service is an offence for the free-born, a necessity for slaves and a duty for the freedman'.[4] Juvenal tells us that young Armenian lads were always seduced when they came to Rome. There are plenty of references which indicate that slaves were bought especially for their sexual prowess and charms. In the plays of Plautus there is a host of sexual innuendoes about slaves, including a much repeated way of teasing a slave to remind him of what his master expects of him – to get down on all fours.[5]

It is far from clear that it was only slaves the Romans lusted after. Polybius, a Greek historian who visited Rome in the second century BC, comments that most young men had lovers. Sextus Propertius, a poet of the first century BC, prayed that his enemies would fall in love with women and his friends with boys. Though there was a natural horror about using free-born boys as lovers and inflicting the position of sexual passivity upon them, it undoubtedly crept into behaviour quite early on.

The Roman calendar contained a feast day not only for women prostitutes (26 April), but also one for male prostitutes (25 April). Later, Augustus taxed their earnings but also gave them a legal holiday. There seems little doubt about which prostitutes earned the most money, for the men were more like high-class courtesans. Cato (recorded by Athenaeus) was extremely angry about how much they cost, complaining that he had to pay 300 drachmas for a jar of Black Sea caviare, but the services of a pretty boy cost the value of a whole farm property.

Roman Women

Unlike Greek women, Roman women were not sequestered in their own living quarters buried within the house. Far from it; women were educated and took part in cultural life. They also took personal charge of their sons and were expected to indoctrinate them with society's patriarchal values. Women had to be proud of being Roman, but although they had status outside motherhood and the home, they could not be part of the legislative and judicial assemblies. No wonder they excelled in exercising 'power behind the throne', that secret labyrinth of hidden diplomacy.

On the whole, Roman women were not made to feel inferior or thrust to the margins of society, though certain customs seem to contradict this. For example, they were admitted to banquets only up to a certain point, to the second part of the feast (*secundae mensae*) when the wine was served. This was because wine might enflame women's passions.

Like Caesar's wife, women had to be above suspicion. If they led a chaste life free of all scandal, they were heaped with honours, eunlogies and praise, but adultery was severely punished. The betrayed husband was allowed to hand over the man to his slaves to be sodomised, or to have his nose and ears cut off, or to be castrated or tortured by anal rape with a mullet (its barbs would inflict great pain) or a radish root. Finally the man might be killed. One man caught in bed with a married woman claimed he was carrying on an affair with a male slave of that household. Though to have sex with a slave owned by another was to incur some punishment (usually a fine), it was obviously preferable to the penalties inflicted on an adulterer. These punishments were, of course, in force to protect primogeniture, to ensure that the son and heir was spawned by the husband and owner of the property. Married women were nothing like as oppressed as in classical Greece, possibly because heterosexual love was more highly valued. Many of the Roman poets have left us love poems addressed to both men and women.

What did the women think of their bisexual husbands, sons and lovers? Alas, no comments by women have come down to us, but we do have comments by men and the picture they give is of jealous women carping and nagging. Juvenal, Martial and Petronius all depict women thus in an unflattering light. 'Having caught me, wife, in a boy, in a harsh cross voice you rebuke me and tell me that you too have a backside,' wrote Martial.[6] But after all, bisexuality was the status quo; women for the most part must have accepted it quite simply as an integral part of male sexuality. Yet seeing your husband besotted by some lad must sometimes have prompted caustic comments like those Fortunata makes to Trimalchio in the *Satyricon*. (Fortunata, though, was a prostitute before her marriage.) Generally, it must have been thought that because the social position of women was not imperilled by their husbands' love of boys or young men, these were not dangerous rivals and could be accommodated with at least a show of indifference.

Men, however, were not willing to accommodate women's homosexuality. In the *Satyricon* we have a picture of Fortunata with Scintilla: giggling and smooching, vulgar and pretentious, they are presented to us as the kind of women who may very well sink into depravity. Lesbianism affronted the Roman male because it took away his right to give pleasure. It was seen as an attempt by the woman to usurp the man. If a woman could do this in the bedroom, might not she go on to dominate in the courts and on the battlefield? Martial, in particular, seems terrified of this, presenting the sexual life of Philaenis as gross and virile. She penetrates boys and possesses twelve virgins in a day; like a man she prefers cunnilingus to fellatio: 'When she is lustful . . . she guzzles girls' middles.' Such women, as depicted by Roman writers, devote themselves to athletic activities, drink copious amounts and vomit at dinner.

Male Sexuality in the Roman Empire

Though the Lex Scatinia had banned the seduction and love of free-born boys, it did not seem to halt its practice. Men, the poets tell us, were sighing for the love of boys, imploring their favours and suffering over their betrayals.

> May I have a boy with a cheek smooth with youth. Honeyed Juventius, while you were playing I stole from you a sweeter kiss than sweet ambrosia.

Ignoring the law, men openly attempted to seduce boys, pestering them in the streets, so a new law was promulgated (*De adtemptata pudicitia*) which was intended to punish the cruising lecher. It covered not only free-born boys, but married women, widows and virgins as well. The Romans, however, went on courting boys as they had done before.

By the second century BC a change in sexual mores was apparent. The idea of the dominant Roman male, the conquering hero, was being softened by the influence of Greece. Boy-love was in fashion. If a Roman wanted secure affection, respect and faithfulness, then he chose a wife. But if he wanted sexual passion, anguish and romantic ardour, he chose a youth. This now became a fashionable as well as a socially acceptable practice and was celebrated in literature. What the original Roman conquerors feared most seemed now to be happening: if free-born boys became the passive adored loves of older men, might they not still have a longing for passive love when adult?

Though devastating scorn was poured upon the adult man who was passive in sexual relations, there were plenty of examples which flouted public opinion. The philosopher Seneca, though married, preferred athletes to boys. But it was not the sexual practice that was detested so much as the lack of virility shown by the adult. For the Romans, pleasure was virile, but to accept it was servile.[7] Whether one went with boys or girls was of no relevance, but what one did sexually was highly significant. Of all sexual acts, fellatio and cunnilingus were abhorred.

A man could use his slave to perform fellatio on him, that was common enough, but for a man to fellate his slave was to turn the world upside down. This act, which gathered so much social opprobrium, would surely, you might think, vanish altogether. Yet their literature is so full of such incidents – the poets condemn it, speaking of a slave-owner's breath that stinks of spunk – that the act seems to have been commonplace.

Juvenal, by the end of the first century AD, considered that Rome had sunk to such depravity the men no longer paid to have someone beneath them, they now paid for someone to go on top. Men showered themselves with perfume, hung trinkets about their necks, knotted scarves about their heads, extended their eyebrows with soot, painted their eyes, gathered their long hair in golden nets and, armed with mirrors, rubbed bread pellets into their faces to make their skin smoother. The final mockery was for these men to marry each other, even bringing a dowry for the so-called husband.[8] This practice must have been much encouraged by its imperial adherents: Nero married his castrated slave, Sporus, and kissed him frequently in public. According to Suetonius, he later changed his gender identity and married his freedman Doryphorus, imitating the cries and lamentations of a maiden being deflowered.

Juvenal also cautioned husbands against such effeminate men because their women consulted them. Such men were treacherous; where gender boundaries remained undelineated, information percolated through which could undermine virility. But, as always, upon this vexed question Roman society was equivocal, and never more so than in its attitude to Julius Caesar.

Caesar, who had a well-known affair with Nicomedes, the King of Bithynia, was called 'the queen' in public assembly by Octavius, for he had been seen as a cup-bearer at a banquet given by Nicomedes with other *exoleti* (passive homosexuals). Caesar was mocked in public. It is said that he wore his toga in such a way that it swished languidly upon the ground. But he also had a reputation for seducing women, among them at least two queens: Cleopatra, undoubtedly the most famous, and Eunoe, wife of King Bogudes of Mauritania. He also seduced the wives of Pompey, Crassus and Servius Sulpicius. Not for nothing was Caesar named *omnium virorum mulier, omnium mulierum virum* (wife to all men and husband to all women).

Caesar, then, was not only the leader of a Roman conquering force, but his potency was inevitably linked with his prowess in the battlefield. A man who had such a reputation could be allowed to slip occasionally, it was felt, into the passive role and still be a man. Caesar's character fulfilled Roman expectations. He was physically strong, he had great military skill, forbearance and tenacity and he was highly sexual. If the soldiers loved and approved of Caesar, it was because he was a winner in bed as well as a winner in war. Ovid wrote, 'every lover is a soldier'[9] – a popular concept in the ancient world which goes back to Sappho and Homer.

Stories of the Roman emperors and their illicit and often bizarre sexual peccadilloes are legion. The historian Suetonius made such tales notorious, from Tiberius at Capri and his small boys nibbling at him as he swam, to the transvestism and murderous cruelty of Caligula and Nero, who both delighted in incest as well as forms of copulation with boys and men. There was Galba who liked mature, vigorous men; Otho, who wore a wig and massaged his face with bread pellets to prevent his beard from growing; and Commodus of whom it was said, 'every part of his body, even his mouth, was defiled by intercourse with both male and female', and who kept a little boy naked but adorned with jewellery at his side. Tatian wrote that the Romans collected boys like others collect herds of grazing horses.[10]

There was also the romantic ardour of Hadrian for his former slave Antinous. After his death, Hadrian honoured him by building him a city, Antinoöpolis, and by placing statues and busts of him in every major city of the empire. Many still exist and stare out at us with a magnificent brooding melancholy. So great was Hadrian's despair at Antinous's early death that a cult, like that of the Egyptian Osiris, formed around the dead boy.

The Roman male still saw himself as the aggressive dominator, believing that when he forced others to submit he was dispensing pleasure. *Hic habitat felicitas* (here dwells happiness) reads the inscription beneath an erect phallus. So certain were the Romans of this that childhood hardly existed for boys in the frantic rush to become adult aggressors. Boys became entitled to take a wife at fourteen and to exercise their rights without the involvement of a tutor. No wonder Romans felt that male passivity was a retrograde step, erasing male dignity in forfeiting power and allowing utter subjugation.

In AD 342 the Emperors Constantius and Constans introduced the death penalty – burning alive – for passive homosexual behaviour, despite the fact that Constans, according to Aurelius Victor, was a homosexual himself, being renowned for his scandalous behaviour with handsome barbarian hostages. However, there are no records of any victims. In AD 390 Theodosius reaffirmed the imperial hatred of what is described as 'the infamy of condemning their manly body, transformed into a feminine one, to bear practices reserved for the other sex'. Here, it is male prostitutes who must be publicly burned; again, it is unknown whether there were any victims. In AD 438 the law was again amended, this time to include active homosexuals, but homosexual prostitution was still tolerated and taxed by the Christian emperors in all the cities of the empire. Obviously it was a valuable source of state income.

It was Justinian in AD 533 who punished all homosexual acts with burning and castration, and it is he who brought in the injunction of divine law. Christianity united with paganism, and homosexuality was outlawed and brutally punished. This code was prepared by a commission headed by Tribonian – a pagan. The law did not have the desired effect and stricter laws were passed in AD 559. Justinian's court historian, Procopius, claimed that the motives behind this law (which was unpopular and did little to halt homosexual behaviour) were political and not religious, arrests on charges of homosexual behaviour being a convenient method of removing unwanted people.

THE RISE OF STOICISM

All societies change, but the larger and more complex a society is, the greater the rate of change. When Rome's power was growing in those centuries before Christ, it was led by various ruling factions, the great families, all of whom were in competition with each other. Each *pater familias* had total power over family, household and estates, so controlling people was a relatively simple matter. Once imperial power had been centralised, the noblemen changed from being princes in their own right to being servants of a prince, while their prestige and success now depended on their good relations with their peers. What men did at home and how they behaved now became common knowledge, and once-powerful men could be scorned or satirised – in rare cases even punished – for their behaviour. Men who were used to giving orders to others became incapable of giving orders to themselves. But in a society rules are essential; civilisation can be measured by the manner in which we share the disadvantages and the advantages of life in a group. Rules give structure and form to a society, and conformity with them adds status and lustre to a man's position. Hence the new rules adopted tended to be those which emphasised conservatism and respectability.

These new rules were reinforced by the lower classes, the plebeians, who copied and aped the classes above them. The more respectable the lower classes were, the greater their chances of rising within the system. To be respectable was to repress natural desires and emotions, to moderate behaviour, to appreciate the new stoical thinking which conferred a certain philosophical dignity on a man.

Plebeian self-repression and sexual moralising led to a change in emphasis from the bisexual male to the heterosexual male, marriage and family. The Stoics taught men to channel their sexuality into marriage, if not to repress it entirely, and to dominate their impulses and control their passions by reflection. Seneca and Musonius Rufus praised chastity as the ideal, yet Seneca was known for his affairs with men. There seems to have been that gulf between ideals and practice which is a constant theme throughout history. Philosophers who formed the neo-Platonist school – Plotinus, Porphyry and Iamblichus – all urged their pupils towards vegetarianism and celibacy, both seen as methods of refining the spirit. All this paved the way for the adoption of Christian values, but it also meant the rigorous exclusion of homosexual ideas and behaviour. How successful it could be is another story.

There is another powerful motive behind repressive legislation: that of pleasing and placating the gods. Citizens of the Roman Empire were born into the world with a life expectancy of twenty-five years; only four out of a hundred men and fewer women lived beyond the age of fifty. It was a population 'grazed thin by death'.[11] There was continual pressure to produce children. For the population of the Roman Empire to remain steady, each woman would need to produce an average of five children. Natural catastrophes played their part in decimating the population. Earthquakes, droughts, fires, floods and visitations of locusts as well as continual warfare on the borders of the empire led to enormous loss of life. It may well be pertinent that in AD 542, between Justinian's two anti-homosexual laws, there had been an outbreak of bubonic plague. In Constantinople, 'at the height of the scourge mortality exceeded 500 a day', of which Procopius, pertinent as ever, observed 'that its marked characteristic was that it carefully spared the wicked'.[12]

For a few hundred years the Christians had been the scapegoat. Tertullian had pointed out that the Christians were the cause of every public disaster; whether the Tiber overflowed or the Nile failed to do so, if famine occurred or pestilence, it was the Christians who were to blame. Justinian pointed out that the decisions made by the four great Ecumenical Councils were as valid as imperial law. These forbade swearing and blasphemy, they made adultery a capital offence and ordered clerics not to gamble or to go to the theatre or races, as well as proscribing male homosexuality (lesbians were not referred to). Considering the sexual life of Justinian and his wife Theodora,* such injunctions were

---

* According to Procopius, Theodora once remarked she wished she had more than three orifices so as to increase her pleasures.

deeply hypocritical. However, the belief that natural disasters were caused by gross immorality in society had ancient roots, still not completely eradicated. We can speculate that this new legislation merely drove prohibited practices underground, and the majority of people did not take it that seriously, knowing that it was the rich and powerful members of the church and court who would suffer.

Before we examine the rise of Christianity, let us take a brief look at how other societies at that time considered homosexuality.

THE EAST

India

It is impossible to disentangle individual expressions of sexuality from Indian sexual awareness which is highly intense, detailed, complex and both sacred and pragmatic. There is no doubt that homosexual behaviour and love existed in the sub-continent from the earliest times. The great pantheon of Indian Hindu gods and goddesses includes hermaphrodite deities, transvestite deities and others which change their sex. Possibly this derives from the idea that the Supreme Being was thought to possess both male and female principles, while Tantrism taught that every man has in him a female element and every woman a masculine element.

Excavations in the Indus valley have shown us the beginnings of Indian culture, around 3000 BC. (The earliest part of the Vedic literature began to be written down 1,500 years later.) Among the findings were many representations of the phallus and the yoga position of an ithyphallic figure. This fertility god is thought to be a proto-Shiva. Later, in the epic poem the *Mahabharata*, Shiva is both a god of sex and asceticism, of virility and destruction; and his lingam or phallus shows he is sexually intensified by asceticism.[13]

Sex was not only considered to exist for procreation; it could also be engaged in for pleasure, for power and even for magic.

There were many sex manuals, and much of their advice dwells on the giving of pleasure. Much more than Greek culture, Indian culture celebrated pleasure and particularly sexual pleasure, but it was always allied with mysticism. Copulation was one method of getting in touch with deeper layers of consciousness and understanding in a more profound way the enigmas of god. Pleasure, though, tended to be defined from a male point of view. All sexual positions were described in detail and all orifices were used in intercourse. As the anus was considered one of the most important centres of psychic energy, its significance was emphasised in Tantric texts. To animate the rectal area was to energise the artistic, poetic and mystical faculties.

Sometimes the penis itself was worshipped, the phallus of the guru kissed and adored. Phalluses were worn about the neck. All manner of dildoes (made of candlewax, baked clay, bone or wood) were used by both men and women to give themselves pleasure; there was no shame whatsoever in masturbation, for the god Krishna was believed to practise manual orgasm. Mothers stimulated the penises of their infants and gave a 'deep massage' to their daughters as a form of affectionate consolation. A fixed stone phallus in a secluded part of the temple served for the ritual defloration of temple girls and virgins.[14] Hinduism also taught that there was a third sex, whose main function was to provide alternative techniques of sexual gratification. There was a strong belief in the mystical power of semen.

Up to 1948, when India achieved independence, some of the Hindu temples still had women and boy prostitutes. There are also groups of male transvestite or transsexual devotees of the Mother Goddess (Parvati, Bachuchara Mata) who sing, dance and beg for alms in the cities of northern India. They also engage in homosexual prostitution.[15]

Homosexuality has never been an issue in Indian culture, though some Hindu texts frown upon it and others consider such acts must be ritually cleansed. These are texts which are steps towards greater asceticism and such Indian thought dwells on ways of reserving the semen so as to intensify male vigour and intimacy with the god. For this reason, the spilling of seed in an homosexual act would not have been approved of.

China in the Han Dynasty[16]

There seems to have been a great flowering of homosexual behaviour which stems from the emperors and their courts throughout the Han dynasty (206 BC to AD 220). Official histories of the period include lengthy biographies of all the emperor's favourites. There was much competition at court to become a favourite, for wealth, power and position inevitably followed. A modern historian lists ten openly bisexual emperors and their favourites throughout the time of the dynasty.

One of the last emperors of this dynasty, Emperor Ai, died without sons and a designated heir. He attempted to give the succession to his lover, Dong Xian, but that was too much for his political enemies and Dong Xian was forced to commit suicide. The court was exceedingly fashion-conscious, striving to catch the eye of the Emperor: 'the courtiers competed to ornament themselves as seductive beauties . . . in contrast Dong Xian wore a simple garment of misty plain silk. It draped upon him like cicada wings.'

It was Ai and his favourite who gave a phrase to the language to denote homosexual passion. The story goes that Ai was sleeping in the daytime with Dong Xian next to him stretched out across his sleeve. When he awoke Ai did not want to wake Dong, so he cut off the sleeve of his garment in order to rise from the bed. All of Ai's courtiers then imitated the cut sleeve as a tribute to the love that their emperor had for Dong. From then on homosexuality was referred to as the passions of the 'cut sleeve'.

Favourites were allowed free access to the concubines' quarters. Sometimes a favourite would seduce one of the emperor's concubines and would be punished accordingly. Though bisexuality was accepted as perfectly normal behaviour, there was no stigma attached to being either completely heterosexual or homosexual. The historian comments dryly on Emperor Ai: 'by nature he did not care for women'. Martial emperors, considered to be quintessentially masculine by historians, such as Emperor Wu who spent his long reign subjugating the surrounding non-Chinese peoples, also had their great favourites. Wu's favourite was Han Yan. He too was famed for riding and archery and was skilled in warfare. So homosexual life at court was not only a matter of intrigue, clothes and cosmetics (in time these would come to be associated with effeminate behaviour and passive homosexuality), for Chinese perceptions of homosexuality at this time were 'primarily aesthetic, literary and anecdotal, not moral, social, religious or scientific'.[17]

Early Japan

Empress Jingu (AD 170–269?), an almost legendary figure who was said to have established Japanese hegemony over Korea, visited the palace of Shinuno, when in the province of Ki. At that time it was always dark, and when the Empress asked why, she was told it was because two priests of two Shinto temples had been buried together. Again, the Empress asked why. She was told that Shino and Ama had been good friends and when Shino died of an illness, Ama was distraught and wished to be buried in the same grave. So he killed himself and they were buried together. The Empress ordered that the tomb be opened and each body was reburied in a different place. From that moment, the sun shone and night and day were divided again.[18]

This is thought to be the first description of homosexuality in all the Japanese chronicles. At first reading it would seem that the love of the two friends was considered so heinous that it stopped the sun rising, or at least plunged the area into perpetual gloom. However, considering the sunny outcome when separate burials take place, it looks as if the taboo was against the idea of two priests who had officiated in separate temples being buried in one coffin. As a few hundred years later there are Rabelaisian stories of homosexual exploits, often illustrated, and as the Empress Jingu lived roughly at the same time as the end of the Han dynasty in China when homosexuality was commonplace, the story cannot really bear the homophobic interpretation which later Japanese historians gave it.

HOMOSEXUALITY IN HISTORY

There is in Japan a long cultural tradition of homosexual love, especially pederasty, and, as we have seen elsewhere, such expression tends to have its roots in rite-of-passage rituals found in prehistory. 'The Japanese do not share Western views about the sinfulness of sexual relations. To them they have always seemed a natural phenomenon like eating, which is to be enjoyed in the proper place. Promiscuity is in itself no more of a problem than homosexuality.'[19]

Half of the civilised world, then, had no repressive measures at this time against homosexual behaviour; on the contrary, some societies positively celebrated it.

EARLY CHRISTIANITY

Two thousand years ago, a tiny strip of the Mediterranean coast at the edge of Asia Minor stood alone in its abhorrence of homosexuality. This was due to the inheritance of the culture of Israel. Yet this statement is not strictly correct. We have already seen that a swing towards a more conservative morality in ancient Rome occurred at about the same time. Nor was early Christianity completely clear where it stood on these matters.

The early Christians had to fight hard for survival among a plethora of different religious sects, all of them embracing with fervour the teachings of a divine master or masters, many of them also disciples of Jesus. Any new group is helped to find and define its own identity by being challenged by its competitors, and many of the Gnostic★ sects celebrated homosexuality as a means of becoming nearer to God in ways very similar to those of Tantric Hinduism – a form of heightened sensuality which was prolonged into metaphysical illumination. The popularity of such sects could well have been a stimulus, driving the early church further

---

★ From 'gnosis', the knowledge of the divine truth revealed to an individual through vision or contemplation, without it being first communicated to the priests or a church.

towards asceticism. Again, many of the Gnostic sects also believed in gender equality and had women priests as well as male. Rich widows found such sects sympathetic and were liable to leave their fortunes to them, so several Gnostic sects were very rich indeed. The Greek historian Procopius talks of 'unheard of riches' which the Senate or the Roman state could not compete with. He was speaking of Arianism★ which Justinian attempted to destroy, one suspects so that he could rob the church of all its wealth. Seeing how easy it was for women to gain more power and influence in these sects might well have encouraged the early church to strengthen the Pauline misogyny with which it was riddled.

In Paul's letters to struggling Christian groups dotted around the Mediterranean, time and time again he makes it clear that women are to be repressed:

Wives, submit yourselves unto your husbands, as unto the Lord. (Ephesians 5.22)

. . . suffer not a woman to teach, nor to usurp authority over the man, but to be in silence. (I Timothy 2.12)

And Adam was not deceived, but the woman being deceived was in the transgression. (I Timothy 2.14)

Women, Paul makes clear, are a danger to the spiritual authority of man, to the untrammelled journey of the spirit towards God.

Paul is equally clear in his directions about sex. His manner seems to be that if you must have sexual relations, though God would rather you didn't, then those relations must be kept strictly within marriage. The first epistle to Timothy (1.9–10) details God's moral laws and those in need of them, including 'them that defile themselves with mankind'. In the first chapter of Romans, in a

---

★ The movement begun by Arius (250–336), a Christian priest of Alexandria, whose teaching affirmed the created, finite nature of Christ. He integrated Neoplatonism with a literal and rationalist approach to New Testament texts. Arianism is considered to be an early form of Unitarianism.

piece of invective against pagan believers, Paul speaks of a God who washed his hands of all the pagans and gave them up to 'vile affections: for even their women did change the natural use into that which is against nature: And likewise also the men, leaving the natural use of the woman, burned in their lust one toward another; men with men working that which is unseemly'. The Christian church down the ages has based its attitude towards and teaching about homosexuality on these texts, regarding it as a great sin.

As we have seen, when subjection and repression of women occurs it is often combined with ritual pederasty. Laws against homosexuality in Christian societies did not stop its practice: it drove the expression of it underground. Though the subjection of women was not twinned with pederasty in Christian society, it was accompanied by severe brutality in the upbringing of children, especially boys, and the likelihood of secret pederastic exploitation. As the subjection of women hinges upon the use of masculine power, that same power was certainly used in the rearing of infants.

As the early Christian leaders – Clement of Alexandria, John Chrysostom, Eusebius of Caesarea, Gregory of Nyssa, Ambrose and Jerome – constantly praised virginity, approving of sexual relations only in marriage. Most of them cited the Leviticus prohibitions against homosexuality. It should be remembered that Paul taught that the Second Coming was imminent. The early church believed that such an event could occur at any moment, that the heavens would rend and the heavenly host appear to divide humanity into the just and the wicked. No wonder that sexual desire, in its haphazard spontaneity casting its net wide over all manner of lust objects, was looked upon with such terrible fear and revulsion. Besides, semen was viewed with holy reverence; like blood, it ran through a man's veins: 'To make love was to bring one's blood to the boil, as the fiery vital spirit swept through the veins, turning the blood into the whitened foam of semen.'[20] Tertullian, making the idea very clear, writes: 'in that last breaking wave of delight, do we not feel something of our very soul go out from us?'

There is here a subtle change in society's view of masculinity. Was not the most masculine man, the most virile man, the man who kept most of his vital spirit, the man who lost little seed? Quintillian wrote that to preserve the masculine voice, 'strong, rich, flexible and firm', a man should abstain from sex. No wonder the later Roman Empire embraced Christianity (albeit slowly), for it fitted into the ideas then held of austere and responsible government in home and society. Early Christianity was deeply influenced by these philosophical concepts, and in its earnest and urgent desire to be cleansed and ready for the Second Coming its strictures on sexual expression became more and more fierce. The Book of Revelation (14.4) describes a procession of the redeemed as consisting of male virgins not defiled by women.

Up to AD 313 (when Emperor Constantine was converted), no overall doctrine on sexual matters prevailed. Instead, each bishop exercised authority in his own diocese, differing on how significant sexual expression was. One must speculate that some bishops were lax while others were not. In AD 521 Justinian put to death two bishops, Isaiah of Rhodes and Alexander of Diospolis, for their seduction of younger men. Procopius writes in *The Secret History*:

> The prosecution of these offenders was conducted in the most irregular fashion, since the penalty was imposed even where there was no accuser, and the word of a single man or boy, even if he happened to be a slave forced to give evidence most unwillingly against his owner was accepted as final proof. Men convicted in this way were castrated and exposed to public ribaldry.

Gibbon tells us the horrific details of the execution of the two bishops:

> A painful death was inflicted by the amputation of the sinful instrument or the insertion of sharp reeds into the pores and tubes of most exquisite sensibility; and Justinian defended the

propriety of the execution, since the criminals would have lost their hands, had they been convicted of sacrilege. In this state of disgrace and agony, the two Bishops ... were dragged through the streets of Constantinople, while their brethren were admonished by the voice of a crier, to observe this awful lesson and not to pollute the sanctity of their character. Perhaps these prelates were innocent. A sentence of death and infamy was often founded on the slight and suspicious evidence of a child or a servant ... and pederasty became the crime of those to whom no crime could be imputed.[21]

Perhaps the paranoid and often hysterical voice of John Chrysostom set the tone for such barbarism. Earlier (he died in 407) he had inveighed against homosexuality within the church. Those people

who have heard the Scriptures brought down from heaven, those do not consort with prostitutes as fearlessly as they do with young men. The fathers of the young men take this in silence: they do not try and sequester their sons, nor do they seek any remedy for this evil. None is ashamed ... there is some danger that womankind will become unnecessary in the future with young men instead fulfilling all the needs women used to.[22]

The legal age at which a boy became a man was fourteen, but here at the end of the fourth century in Asia Minor and Roman Syria, boys received their sexual initiation, which would be homosexual, at the age of ten, sometimes even earlier.[23] This was the age at which John Chrysostom recommended the boys be placed in the care of monks who would educate them up to the age of twenty. But were the boys much safer there? Even when the boys were taken out to the desert fathers and left in a cave with a pious recluse, the accounts we have of seduction by sex-starved monks are legion.[24] Someone so permanently anxious as Chrysostom must have found homosexual licentiousness all around him. A pagan writer who lived at the same time, Libanious, described the stroking and fondling that went on beneath the blankets at the winter feasts and how this would inevitably lead to fellatio. Chrysostom also complained that churchgoers attended services only to stare at attractive women and boys. He cautioned parents not to let their son's hair grow long. Long hair, he said, made a boy look effeminate, softening the ruggedness of his sex. Long-haired boys, Chrysostom believed, were particularly attractive to pederasts. Clip the locks all around, he advised, and attain severe simplicity. Chrysostom was disliked by many because of these passionate views, but the telling point in this extract is his comment about the indifference of the fathers. This tells us clearly that homosexuality was still socially acceptable.

Another Christian writer, Lactantius, points out that pederastic practices were regarded as honourable. Epictetus, a stoic philosopher whose teaching was much admired by the early Christians, spoke of heterosexual and homosexual attraction in equal terms.[25] Libanius in his *Moral Discourses* tells us that pederasty was rife in Antioch; in his discourse on passion it is only homosexual love that he speaks of. Of a man's enslavement to love he writes: 'There is no request, however impossible, that the boy he loves can make which the man wounded by love does not regard as an absolute necessity to fulfil.'

It is perhaps difficult for us to discover exactly what was the truth, but it would hardly be surprising if bisexual expression, which had continued perfectly acceptably for some thousands of years, did not wither away overnight because a small elite, a few religious ascetics and philosophers, had for some obscure reason started to preach against sex altogether. It would have been another matter, of course, once Justinian's brutal punishments began to take effect; such horrors must have sounded a cautionary note to even the most reckless.

We should not forget either that these first few hundred years after Christ were a maelstrom of philosophical and mystical ideas, where nothing remained stable for long. Many pagan writers accused the Christians of sexual indulgence. One work defended the Christians against the charges of ceremonial fellatio and temple prostitution.[26] That these charges were made suggests that some of the Christian sects were similar in their ceremonies and beliefs to Gnostic groups. Many were named after minor characters in the Old Testament such as Seth, or after their charismatic leaders – Montanus, Marcion, Arian, Elchasaios. Each had a different version of the divine truth, interpreting the past in their own way. Some, like Marcion, eschewed the Old Testament. Others, like Elchasaios, rejected the Epistles of Paul. All in varying degrees celebrated or recoiled from sex.

It was Manichaeism (founded by Mani, born AD 216) that most disturbed the church. If we are to believe St Augustine, who was a Manichee himself for ten years, we do have some idea of the sexual ritual performed by the Elect (that is, the elite; the rest of the Manichees were called Hearers). All emanations from the Elect were holy, even their burps, but the most revered essence was semen. Coitus interruptus in some form, with either gender, was enacted. Flour was sprinkled upon the semen and the mixture was cooked and eaten. Augustine tells us: 'their Elect was forced to consume a sort of eucharist sprinkled with human seeds in order that the divine substance may be freed.[27]

The Manichees viewed men and women as equal, but they believed that propagation was bad because all matter was evil, while only the invisible spirit was good. Hence, all copulation should be sterile, so as not to create more matter. This view obviously favoured homosexual relations. From then on, the heretical movement for the most part became sympathetic to homosexuality, though for obvious reasons, it was not a widely publicised facet of their belief. But it fuelled the hatred and disgust of Christians like Augustine of Hippo and would continue to do so for centuries to come.

I would suggest, then, that homosexuality and heresy became entwined very early on, so that the church saw heretics not just as blasphemers, but also as demonic in their sexual corruption, sinning in the most flagrant and profound manner. As for churchmen discovered to be homosexual, it was not only that they flouted

Leviticus; such men were behaving heretically. No wonder the monasteries took steps from the very beginning to halt such behaviour.

The founder of monasticism, St Basil of Nyssa, wrote in AD 375 that monks guilty of unseemly behaviour with others would be disciplined in the same way as adulterers. If men were discovered to have engaged in sexual relations with boys they would not be admitted to communion, even at death. The same penalty was decreed for female prostitutes and women discovered in adultery. St Basil's admonitions went into the most precise details. Young monks must not approach closely to one another; when addressing each other, they must cast their eyes down; they must never touch each other. Adolescent boys must never sleep beside each other; if there was more than one boy to a bed, then an old monk had to sleep between them. Monks must always be alert to sexual temptation, the key to good life being absolute celibacy.[28]

It was St John Cassian (AD 360–435), the monk, ascetic theologian and founder of the abbey of St Victor in Marseille, who had the greatest influence on the further development of monasticism. In his *Institutes of the Monastic Life*, written between 420 and 429, he describes the six stages that advance towards chastity. What he is describing is not the beatific state, but the negative signs which will destroy it. The very first sign of progress is when the monk awakes and is not smitten by carnal impulse. The second stage is when voluptuous thoughts do not disturb his mind. The third stage is when a glimpse of the world outside does not arouse lustful feelings. The fourth stage is when throughout the day the monk feels no stirrings or movement of the flesh. (Cassian is too discreet to mention an erection.) The fifth stage occurs when he is not touched by the remotest thought of sexual pleasure while reading about human procreation. The last stage is when, in sleep, there are no visions of voluptuous temptation. In this final stage there must be no 'involuntary pollutions' during sleep. Overeating and impure thoughts in the day, Cassian taught, could lead to this: 'It is a sign of the corruption that festers within and not just a product of the night. Buried in the depth of the soul, the corruption has come to the surface during sleep, revealing the hidden fever of passions with which we have become infected by glutting ourselves all day long on unhealthy emotions.'[29] It is no surprise to learn that St John Chrysostom had a huge influence upon his thought and theology. Cassian, like St Basil before him, advises his monks never to remain alone with one another, even for a short time, or withdraw with each other or take each other's hands. Monks that infringe these rules have committed a grave offence and remain under suspicion. How powerful is Cassian's fear of sex and how devastatingly influential such a paranoid fear was to be in years to come, fuelling the Inquisition and the sadistic bleakness of monastic life.

Yet in great contrast to this, a few years earlier the poet Ausonius (AD 310–95) had a passionate relationship with St Paulinus, the bishop of Nola, and they wrote to each other some exquisitely tender love poetry which set a model for the literature of medieval Europe. Both considered their love to be eternal, that they would in the next life still be locked in an embrace. Whether their love had physical expression we do not know, but the ardour of it is undeniable. This was publicly known and found acceptable. Set against the revolting punishments of Justinian and the purgatorial asceticism of Cassian, the question of how early Christianity considered homosexual relations becomes to a certain degree enigmatic.

New light has recently been shed on the enigma by the discovery of male-to-male Christian marriage ceremonies which involved the burning of candles, the joining of the right hands, the binding of those hands by the priest's stole, the Lord's Prayer, communion and a kiss. Such ceremonies existed in their thousands throughout the centuries and Montaigne probably witnessed one of the last in the sixteenth century (see p. 141). How acceptable they were to the majority of Christians is not known; certainly a small minority of homophobes inveighed against all expression of same-sex love throughout the Christian centuries with what sounds like ever-increasing hysteria.[30]

Even St Augustine confessed to homosexual love in his youth, describing the desolation he felt when a friend died: 'I felt that my soul and his were one soul in two bodies, and therefore life was a horror to me, since I did not want to live as a half.' Augustine knew his Plato and one feels in this sentence he is consciously reflecting the allegory of Aristophanes in *Symposium*. But Augustine adds: 'I contaminated the spring of friendship with the dirt of lust and darkened its brightness with the blackness of desire.'[31] This renunciation, with its terrible negation of instinctual life and love, would have a horrifying impact upon the world and most of all on young men who aspired to become nearer to God. For centuries to come they saw in male human affection the forked tale of the Prince of Darkness and renounced it in fear and trembling.

IV

THE CELTS, FEUDALISM AND ISLAM

While the Roman Empire flourished and declined, other peoples who were to influence the culture of Europe grew in power. Sadly, we know very little about some of them, though they are a significant part of our genetic breeding pool, and many of their so-called 'pagan' beliefs have left powerful images in our consciousness.

THE CELTS

These fascinating peoples have been unfairly pushed to the margins of history, by scholars dazzled by the classical world, but they deserve our attention. They were agronomists of enormous skill and knowledge, exporting grain and food to the southern Mediterranean; they were craftsmen in metal; jewellers of extraordinary skill; and brilliant technicians in the manufacture of chariots and armoury. At the peak of their military power their territory extended from Britain to Turkey, for they gave their name to Galatia. By 250 BC they had migrated to the Iberian peninsula and northern Italy.

The Celts occupied those lands which the new Christian religion would colonise as the Roman Empire dwindled and concentrated its power in Byzantium. The Celts' beliefs, their social structures and sexual mores would, in that first millennium AD, be seemingly swept aside, but in reality they were merely overlaid by Christianity. Unfortunately, the Celts left no written evidence of their lives, for the Druids forbade the writing down of their knowledge. We have to rely instead on Greek and Roman writers.

It is thought that the gods in the Celtic pantheon were at first spirits associated with forests, rivers and lakes, and had no visual anthropomorphic form. There is an endearing story that when Brennus the Celtic leader was defeated at Delphi in 279 BC, on learning that the Greek gods all had human form he broke out in scornful laughter.[1] Later, the Celtic gods borrowed some of their imagery from Rome, while other striking creatures, such as a beaked and winged horse, were very obviously exclusive to them.

The Greeks and Romans thought the Celts were remarkable for their height, strength, muscularity and fair colouring, but they were judging the warrior class they met in battle. This aristocratic warrior society practised extensive male sexual coupling; Aristotle (in *Politics*) observed that the Celts esteemed love between men. Diodorus Siculus gave us a fuller picture:

> The men are much keener on their own sex; they lie around on animal skins and enjoy themselves, with a lover on each side. The extraordinary thing is they haven't the smallest regard for their personal dignity or self-respect; they offer themselves to other men without the least compunction. Furthermore, this isn't looked down upon, or regarded as in any way disgraceful: on the contrary, if one of them is rejected by another to whom he has offered himself, he takes offence.[2]

It is the passivity of grown men that Diodorus finds so extraordinary, the fact that they are warriors who allow themselves to play the part of women in the sexual act. This was difficult for a citizen of the Roman Empire to understand.

Polybius (200–118 BC), the Greek historian who wrote a massive history of the rise of Rome, describes a battle between the Celts and the Romans in 225 BC. The Celts had marched on Rome but were hemmed in by two Roman armies. The Gaesatae were a professional band of Celtic warriors who fought naked for metaphysical reasons, believing that their bodies would thus become more fully infiltrated by the life forces of nature. Polybius wrote:

> They took up their positions in front of the whole army naked and wearing nothing but their arms ... the movements of the naked warriors in the front ranks made a terrifying spectacle. They were all men of splendid physique and in the prime of life, and those in the leading companies were richly adorned with gold necklaces and bracelets. The mere sight of them was enough to arouse fear among the Romans.[3]

Considering the Romans' distaste for nudity in opposition to the Greeks' love of it, one speculates as to whether their distaste was founded on such experiences, so that nudity for them equalled barbarism. Psychologically, fear and eroticism are closely entwined, a compound of adoration, love, awe and desire. It is hardly surprising, then, that the ancient world has so many examples of warrior heroes closely bound by male love-ties.

The Celts began to settle in Britain from the eighth century BC and had finally colonised it by 250 BC. There are indications in the folk stories and lyrics of Ireland that the affection between warriors was a powerful and binding emotion.[4] We must not forget, too, that the very first tales of King Arthur and his Knights sprang from Celtic mythology, though most of the stories we are familiar with now are later medieval embellishments. Yet, perhaps, in that close camaraderie of Arthur's Knights, bound by fervent idealism, we see something of the warrior friendship that existed in Celtic society.

Celtic society was divided up into priests, the Druids who came from the elect, the aristocracy, who were also the warrior class, and beneath them the farmers and rural labourers. It was a male-dominated society: a woman was subject to men, to her father before marriage, to her husband after marriage and to her sons or her father or her nephew when marriage ended. In Welsh law a woman's protector received a payment in token of that protection on her marriage.[5] Irish law classified women among the 'senseless', that is, the slaves, foreigners and imbeciles, who could not make contracts nor engage in sale and purchase. Marriage was arranged between families, constituting an alliance between them and a means of controlling property. Virginity was considered essential in a woman up to marriage, then she was expected to be faithful.

Much of what we know about the Celts came from the transition period between pagan and Christian and is therefore blurred. It is clear that some of the changes were dramatic, from warlike to peace-loving, for example, or from a highly-charged sexuality to a passionate celibacy. Their attitude to women did not seem to change much, though, for they managed to extract from Christian mythology the same ambiguity they had been saddled with before. A poem written by St Columbanus on women goes:

> That the proud tongue of an evil woman has.
> Woman (Eve) destroyed life's gathered crown;
> But woman (Mary) gave long-lasting joys of life.

BARBARIAN TASTE

As the Roman Empire declined so their sense of their own superiority grew and the difference between what they felt to be their civilised behaviour was seen in contrast to that of the barbarians. More and more the criterion used for judging what was civilised or not was a sexual code. The Taifali were a people who had settled between the Carpathians and the Black Sea, during a time when the Gothic peoples had moved into the Ukraine (AD 150–230). When the Huns invaded in 375, the Taifali were forced back towards the Danube and Roman territory. It was then that Ammianus Marcellinus, a Roman soldier and an historian, came across them. He wrote: 'We have learned that these Taifali were a shameful folk, so sunken in a life of shame and obscenity that in their country the boys are coupled with the men in a union of un-mentionable lust, to consume the flower of their youth in the polluted intercourse of those paramours.'[6] His tone of prudery strikes one as a bit bizarre, considering that Roman poetry only two centuries before had celebrated the love of boys with almost hysterical fervour. However, times had changed. Ammianus lived from AD 330 to 395, a time when pederasty, though in existence in parts of the empire (such as Antioch), no longer had overall approval. This passage, however, has been accepted by scholars as an example of the still living tradition of the rite-of-passage ceremony. Once the Taifali boys had killed single-handedly either a boar or a bear, they became men and were no longer the paramour of an older man. It is very reminiscent of the initiation rituals of the early Greeks described on p. 40.

Procopius notes that the Heruli, whose young men served their elders until they had proved their courage in battle, also had a similar practice. Like other societies, including classical Greece, they were expected to change sexual roles overnight. Whether they did or not is another matter.

GERMANIC TRIBES[7]

By the end of the fifth century, Germanic tribes★ had taken over the Latin West. These were rural peoples, brilliant horsemen, hostile to cities, who conquered the territory of the Roman Empire west of its capital, Constantinople. Their sexual mores denigrated women and passive men and exalted the love of comrades and the bravery of warriors.

Effeminate adult men of the Naharvali (later to join the Vandals)

★ The Franks, Visigoths, Vandals, Anglo-Saxons and many others.

may well have become priests. Tacitus tells of transvestite priests who held ceremonies in forests to two brother-deities that he interprets as being Castor and Pollux. Cult transvestism was certainly common in Scandinavia, for a Danish historian wrote in the twelfth century with some disgust of the womanly priests at Uppsala. In the Old Norse Eddas and Icelandic sagas, the words denoting receptive male homosexuality were among the most powerful terms of abuse. As we have seen before, prisoners of war were used in this manner, and to use a man as a woman was considered the deepest, most potent insult.

Before the tribes' conversion to Christianity, there was no ceremony of marriage. Instead, there was marriage by abduction and ravishment without the consent of the woman or her family. If there were men who disliked this manner of acquiring a wife, there was also marriage by consent. The first year of marriage was regarded as a trial period and could be terminated if the wife did not become pregnant. Unfaithful women were punished by having their heads shaved, being driven from their homes and publicly beaten. For men, however, these unions were not sexually exclusive; married men could maintain several concubines, generally servants or slave girls, but the children of these unions had no claim on their father's estates.

German laws of inheritance did not make the sexual life of a young man simple. At the death of a father, land went to the eldest son who could then marry. Younger sons underwent initiation rites at adolescence and joined a religious society dedicated to Wotan. They spent their time fighting, hunting and stealing, and remained bachelors for life. Only when they inherited land could they marry. As we have seen, women were expected to abide by strict rules of chastity and were punished severely for violating them; if a husband discovered his wife committing adultery he had the right to kill both parties without any legal penalty.

Heterosexual opportunities for these rampaging bands of young men must have been haphazard and fraught with danger. It is no surprise, then, to find that the adolescent boys joining the fringes of such a society would have been used sexually until they too had proved themselves in feats of robbing, killing or drinking. Similar bands of wild young men existed in Norse and Irish Celtic society. In them, power is associated solely with the masculine. Semen being the essence of the male, special strength is acquired by those who ingest the semen of the powerful. It is fascinating to see how this idea had exerted power over the male psyche, ever since pre-history. Many folk tales attest to it: the mandrake, which had magical powers, grew from the semen which was ejaculated by hanged men; while the Norse gods, the Aesir, who included Odin and Thor, gained arcane knowledge through swallowing semen.

Though the Germanic tribes ridiculed, scorned and lambasted passive homosexuality, they were in an equivocal position, for all the males, after all, started off as being passive. Procopius (in *The Vandalic War*) tells the story of how the Vandals captured Rome. It seems that the Vandals selected with great care 300 of their most beautiful boys, who also had to be strong and of high birth. These they sent to the Roman patricians to serve as house slaves vulnerable to the sexual favours of their masters. Then at a predetermined day and hour, each boy was to rise up and murder his master, flinging open the gates of Rome to their countrymen. The Germanic tribes' horror of male effeminacy, which they identified with passive sexuality, in this case was obviously approved of when it gained them great military advantage.

EARLY FEUDAL SOCIETY[8]

As Rome declined, so did the urban centres of its civilisation in the West. Rome itself was sacked twice and by AD 500 was a crumbling ruin. But as the great city centres were erased, the peasant economy and a network of agricultural trade and markets found a new life. Yet these, as scholars (in particular, Boswell) have pointed out, were hardly conducive to a sophisticated sodomitical milieu. It is difficult to uncover what these rural societies thought of sodomy or male loving. Not much, one would hazard a guess, for life went on as it always had. Although Christianity was spreading northwards and infiltrating new lands, pagan gods were still worshipped. Throughout the hundreds of years of transition there was a mixture of new and old beliefs, many of which still remain as folk tales and superstitions in our own society.

Medieval beliefs about sexual morality rested upon a mixture of ideas and attitudes found in late antiquity. The rationale that supported these ideas did not come into existence until the generation of St Augustine and St Jerome, about the time that Christianity became the state religion of Rome. They then, as we have seen, slowly became part of law. Christian sexual morality did not begin to become doctrine until the fourth and fifth centuries, and it started very slowly to be transformed into law from the middle of the sixth century.

However, for many hundreds of years, what the new religion said on sex was not always clear or consistent, nor was the way in which rulers, kings and clerics behaved. Clovis, King of the Salian Franks (481–511), on the day of his baptism felt he had to confess to male sexual relations; Gregory of Tours (538–94), on the other hand, recounts with no surprise an incident in which the Count of Javols insulted a bishop by asking him in front of King Sigibert: 'Where are your husbands, with whom you live in shame and disgrace?' It would seem that this anecdote reflects the continuing tradition of the classical world, that sodomy carried no shame or dishonour while being the passive partner did. Latin poetry of the sixth, seventh and eighth centuries did not describe same-sex loving in terms of sinfulness.

In the first millennium of Christianity, patristic doctrines of sexual morality were propounded. These doctrines have become the foundations of sexual law and theory in our own time. One of the great peculiarities of this early church thinking is that morality is identified with sexual conduct. The medieval sexual tradition created powerful taboos which have coloured and influenced Western culture. Why Christianity should so intensely concentrate upon sex to the exclusion of other moral areas (common humanity and justice, distribution of food, employment, property and wealth, for example), deserves a study in itself. Neither Judaism nor Islam ever identified sex as something intrinsically evil, though both had strict moral sanctions on sexual conduct. Nor is this view based upon any statements of Christ, who said little about sex except to disapprove of adultery and promiscuity. Perhaps such views reflected those of the churchmen of the time, who were appalled at the sexual licence around them and felt the need for ethical standards to control it.

These ideas were gradually accepted as part of the developing canon law of the church, and from this a complex and sophisticated legal system grew. The ideas behind this structure were based on notions derived from antiquity, the first being the Hebraic idea that sex was for reproduction only. The church, though, rejected any pleasure or sensuality that might be attached to marital sex; rather, it took the idea that sex was closely related to the divine and the sacred. This was almost a pagan idea which had infiltrated Gnostic beliefs, attracting followers in the climate of sexual asceticism of those years. Another idea that became attached to this was the notion of what is 'natural'. This, as we know, changed in all societies and is actually whatever reflects the beliefs of the majority at the time. Medieval moralists used the term with abandon, and the concept still has enormous power.

Unfortunately, both this idea and the notion of the sacredness of sex had an equally strong dark side; sex could also be a defilement of the spirit, it could be 'unnatural' and therefore evil, and an individual had to be purified and cleansed.

Alcuin (732–804), the Anglo-Saxon poet, teacher and cleric who spent his first fifty years in Yorkshire and then accepted an invitation from Charlemagne to lead the Palatine school at Aachen, wrote poetry of considerable homoerotic value, emphasising the sacred and idealistic aspects of his love. At the court of Charlemagne, that same erotic element presided over Alcuin's circle which included some of the most brilliant scholars of the day. Most of his pupils had pet names, derived from classical allusions, many from Virgil's *Eclogues* which is itself full of homoerotic elements. When Alcuin was not writing poetry to his students, he was writing letters to his friends and these too are afire with passion. This, for example, to a bishop: 'how would I sink into your embraces . . . how would I cover, with tightly pressed lips, not only your eyes, ears and mouth but also your every finger and your toes, not once but many times.'

There are countless examples of passionate attachments among the clergy at this time and in the next few hundred years. The church does not seem to have been much bothered. In the eighth century the Venerable Bede referred to anal intercourse with a wife as a sodomitical crime. Hincmar of Reims (806–82), an archbishop and theologian who greatly influenced Christian thinking, applied the term 'sodomy' to all non-procreative sexual acts. He also defined as 'against nature' any sexual release of semen with a nun, a relative, the wife of a relative, a married woman, an animal, or by oneself whether through manipulation or any other means. Hincmar lists homosexual acts with sloth and gluttony, far removed from the nefarious sin which Chrysostom and other interpreters of St Paul had made them out to be. The church viewed adultery, fornication and bestiality as being far more serious.

St Boniface also redefines 'sodom' and its sins when he remarks that it is rumoured that the people of England have rejected legal marriages in favour of adultery and that 'from such unions will be engendered a degenerate and ignoble people burning with lust'. Later, Boniface was to describe exactly what he meant by the term 'sodomitical lust': 'despising lawful marriage and preferring incest, promiscuity, adultery, and impious union with religious and cloistered women.

ISLAM

Arabic society, which was male-centred, polygamous and considered women to be inferior, remained the same in its essentials after its conversion by the Prophet Muhammad. We have seen before that in such societies it is almost inevitable that young boys are enjoyed and exploited sexually. Once Islam was accepted with fervour, behaviour was hedged about with moral absolutes; though nothing much changed, what was written and said about sex did change.

Muhammad was born in Mecca about AD 570 and died there in 632. In the Koran Allah is said to have created man from dust and earth but also from drops of semen and congealed blood. In opposition to the Hebrew Yahweh, Allah is a sexual being and Islam valued sex highly. In fact, again in opposition to the asceticism of the early Christians, Muhammad was opposed to celibacy and preached that marriage was incumbent on all men and was the highest good ordained by God. For those men who could not be monogamous, then polygamy was acceptable, but regardless of how many wives a man had, they should all be treated with kindness. (How kindness is defined is another matter.)

In some small way Muhammad reformed some of the older Arabic customs that affected women. Women retained their right to their dowry. Anal intercourse and oral–genital contact was not permitted without the wife's consent. Girls were married at twelve or thirteen. Though the punishment for a woman accused of adultery was death (being walled up alive in a room), it was necessary to produce four witnesses to prove the accusation. Women were seen as highly erotic creatures, always about to give trouble to men. Nudity in both men and women was thought obscene, but no part of a woman should ever be seen except by her husband, so women were heavily veiled in public. When male visitors entered the home all the women had to retire and stay behind a curtain.

After the death of Muhammad, as the Arab Empire grew, Islamic scholars created a detailed system of behaviour called the *Hadith* (meaning the 'tradition'). Eventually there were around 600,000 of these sayings which, not surprisingly, were often in conflict. They hold the same place in Islam as does the Talmud in the Jewish community. But they are not as helpful in understanding the place that homosexuality had in Islamic society as one might suppose. It would seem that the law often took one view while society happily continued in another. This disparity could occur in the writings of individuals; for example, al Ghazali, the mystic theologian who died in 1111, wrote poems to the boys he loved but also expressed strong disapproval of homosexuality. Ibn Khaldun, the historian and sociologist, wrote strongly homoerotic poetry but thought that those who committed homosexual acts should be stoned.[9]

The *Hadith* regarded all heterosexual intercourse outside marriage as a sin (as well as homosexuality, which was put on a par with adultery or fornication), but as it allowed both polygamy and concubinage a man might have plenty of variety in his marital life. Yet were there enough women to go around? The Arabic language has a huge vocabulary of homosexual terminology, including dozens of words to describe male prostitutes. As complete segregation of the sexes was a hard and fast rule, the social life of men was spent with other men. Homosexuality must have seemed to be the only possible sexual expression.

Mirror for Princes, written by Kai Ka'us ibn Iskander in 1082 for his eldest son, is a guide which says: 'as between women and youths, do not confine your inclinations to either sex . . . find enjoyment from both kinds.' He added the suggestion that his son might in the summer 'incline towards youth and during the winter towards women'.[10] It is an urbane and civilised piece of writing and nothing else perhaps so quietly and powerfully communicates to us how ordinary and acceptable the bisexual male was thought to be. Many authors made no pretence of being anything but bisexual: Beha Ed-Din Zoheir, a poet of thirteenth-century Cairo, disdained by his mistress, 'went to find a young and obliging boy. Beautiful as the moon and the stars'.[11]

Arabic medicine was much admired and influenced many European thinkers and physicians, but Christian medicine would not have much liked the observation made by a Jewish convert to Islam, Samau'al ibn Yahya (died 1180), who wrote that eminent men had turned to youths because their physicians had warned them that intercourse with women would cause gout, haemorrhoids and premature aging. Islamic literature made it clear that sexual relations between a mature richer man and a subordinate youth were commonplace and never concealed.

William of Adam, a Dominican friar, was horrified at Muslim carnality and concluded: 'In the Muslim sect any sexual act at all is not only not forbidden, but allowed and praised.' He complained that Christian boys were sold into slavery in Egypt and turned into prostitutes. Jews living in Egypt and Spain also turned towards pederasty. William wrote: 'These Saracens, forgetting human dignity, go so far that men live with each other in the same way that men and women live together in our own land.' Again, mature men who took the passive role were scorned and it was felt necessary to explain it away – too high a consumption of hashish perhaps? Or some genetic reason that might be explained by a follower of Aristotle.★

Boys dressed as women and with their faces made up were part of the harem of rich men in Afghanistan at least down to the nineteenth century. Sir Richard Burton noted: 'the Afghans are commercial travellers on a large scale and each caravan is accompanied by a number of boys and lads almost in women's attire, with kohl'd eyes and rouged cheeks, long tresses and hennaed fingers and toes, riding luxuriously . . . they are called travelling wives and the husbands trudge patiently by their sides.'[12]

How Islam saw the role of women is again summed up in Iskander's *Mirror for Princes* when he writes about daughters: 'Do not teach her to read and write, that is a great calamity. Once she is grown up, do your utmost to give her in marriage; it were best for a girl not to come into existence, but being born she had better be married or buried.'

The existence of harems made relationships between women almost as commonplace as male homosexuality. Lesbianism features in Islamic erotica, but it is almost a taboo subject. The view that lesbians are also witches is reflected in the *Arabian Nights* collection of stories. Men do not like to think that they may be completely redundant in that basic pleasure, so indications of lesbian love in the harems might have been ignored. Certainly, for

★ In the pseudo-Aristotelian *Problemata Physica* the physiological explanation for the passive male is that the semen is deflected towards the rectum.

many centuries the West had considered the harem to be a centre of sensual lesbian indulgence. As a sixteenth-century writer, Pierre de Bourdeille, put it when describing a painting belonging to the Comte de Chasteau-Villain: 'a number of fair ladies naked and at the bath, which did touch, and feel, and handle, and stroke, one the other, and intertwine and fondle with each other, and so enticingly and prettily and featly did show all their hidden beauties.'[13] Such scenes were, of course, nonsense. In reality liaisons had to be highly discreet, for harems were full of political intrigue, the women plotting against each other for their own son's future as a possible heir to the sultanate.

Ahmad ibn Yusuf al Tayfashi (died 1253) gathered together in *Nuzhat-al-Albab* (*Delight of the Hearts*) an obscene collection of observations, poems and stories on the subject of debauchery, and was particularly interested in stories about homosexuals and pederasts.[14] In Chapter 6 he delineates the characteristics of homosexuals and male prostitutes, speaking also of their attractive lodgings furnished with books and wine, decorated with doves and singing birds. He goes on to declare that homosexuals can be recognised by the way they stare directly at one, a direct gaze which is often followed by a wink. The typical homosexual has thin hairy legs, he says, and when he walks his hands and legs sway. Many of the stories concern mature men chasing beardless boys. He also notes mature men who seek others like them, and these he reckons have short lives as they risk being mugged or murdered. Some stories celebrate homosexual seductions, including many about Abu Nuwas, a poet who praised both boys and wine, but though he is teased he is never vilified. Other stories present the paedophile as a villain, and yet others tell of bisexuals who love 'to eat both figs and pomegranates', who can be described as men of ill-repute. A theme that runs throughout the collection is that of a beautiful boy who has to be kept in seclusion away from the advances of lascivious men.

The stories in this collection can be used to 'prove' that homosexuality was widely approved of, or that it was a matter of indifference, or an abomination. Possibly all three attitudes operated at the same time in different degrees.

LATER FEUDALISM[15]

In twelfth-century Spain, Muslim writers considered the Christian clergy to be particularly addicted to homosexual relations, while the rest of Christian Europe fulminated against the sodomitical vice of the Saracens. In another great irony, there were several Jewish poets and rabbis of that time who wrote homoerotic verse. Boswell lists six Jewish poets and singles out Judah Halevi as one of the most prominent who constantly wrote poetry and epigrams to beautiful boys and even transformed a heterosexual Arabic poetic jest into a homosexual one. It is fascinating to speculate how such Jews coped with their cultural tradition, filled as it was with so much biblical and Talmudic text inveighing against homosexual relations. Alas, we must remain unenlightened, for there is no example of a Jew meditating upon the subject.

From the ninth century there was an urban revival in Europe, and this slowly renewed a vigorous homosexual underground culture. Many cities were communes which afforded opportunities for self-government which engendered an atmosphere of liberty and tolerance. Contributing to this atmosphere was a rediscovery of the ancient world where writers such as Ovid, Plutarch and Seneca were read and enjoyed.

However, the Christian church had, as always, its bevy of bigots eager to declaim in the Chrysostom tradition. There was Benedict Levita who in the ninth century forged a document calling for sodomites to be burnt. St Peter Damian composed *The Book of Gomorrah* which accused priests of having carnal relations with their spiritual advisers; Damian suggested that many clerics avoided doing penance for homosexual acts by confessing to other homosexual clergy. He thought that homosexuality as a vice 'surpasses all others in uncleanness . . . it opens the doors of hell and closes the gates of heaven'. Pope Leo IX was not much impressed by this polemic, telling Damian that 'you have written what seemed best to you'.

Between the end of the sixth century and the beginning of the eleventh, a new branch of Christian moral literature came into being – the Penitentials. These were handbooks of punishments for offences to be used as a guide for confessors in dealing with sinners who wished to be reconciled with God. A glance at these Christian penances shows us more clearly how the church viewed homosexuals. Four to eight per cent of the rules concern homosexual offences, a few even mention lesbian practices. Penances are graded according to the age, rank and the method of arousal. As a benchmark, a single offence of heterosexual adultery by a married man could have been atoned for by eighty days of bread and water followed by fourteen years of fasting. While homosexual inter-femoral intercourse rated forty days and mutual masturbation thirty days. But there is much inconsistency in the penances, which differ from country to country and change with time. For example, the penances above applied only to married men; it would seem that single men might do what they liked without punishment, except in seventh-century Ireland where homosexual acts among boys are discussed in the Penitential of Cummean. And in another Irish Penitential, Finnian, boys who experimented with anal sex had to undertake two years of penance while grown men had three years, and those for whom it had become a habit were assigned seven years.[16] Oral sex, either homosexual or heterosexual, merited greater severity. 'Let him who puts semen in the mouth do penance for seven years,' declared Theodore of Canterbury. But Archbishop Theodore's Penitential is notably severe. Finnian and others did not think fellatio a greater crime than anal sex. Theodore thought that if a wife committed adultery the husband had a right to divorce her and marry another; he also considered that masturbation warranted thirty days of fasting. The Penitentials occasionally mentioned female autoeroticism and lesbianism. They were highly censorious if a mechanical aid, such as a dildo, was used; rather more censorious than when males used a mechanical device for masturbation. Lesbian relations are not treated with much severity. Far more frequent mention is made of acts of bestiality.

The recommended penances vary so much according to the country, the time and the author, that it is difficult to extract an overall picture of the effect such literature had. What does not change is the matter-of-fact acceptance of homosexuality as a common occurrence throughout Christian Europe.

How influential was the church in early feudal society? The question hinges upon the relevance of the act of confession itself. Most people confessed once – upon their death-bed. Throughout the sixth and seventh centuries the church had great difficulty in persuading people to confess and do penance, and it was not until 1215 that the fourth Lateran Council required confession to occur at least once a year. Up to then the evidence suggests that the burgeoning morality of the feudal church affected the clerics but few others; it would take a combination of other factors to produce the anti-homosexual legislation of the twelfth century, discussed later. In the meantime there was no lack of homophobic critics.

Peter Damian's successor in bigotry was Ivo of Chartres who told the papal legate that Ralph, Archbishop of Tours, had requested the King of France to install the archbishop's lover, one John, as Bishop of Orléans. As John had also had sexual relations with the king and Ralph's brother, who was the previous Bishop of Orléans, John had become notorious and had been nicknamed Flora, after a famous courtesan. But Ivo seems to have objected to John's youth more than his promiscuity, claiming that this would make him a mere puppet of the Archbishop of Tours. Though Ralph was unpopular with the pope, Urban II, though Ralph's lifestyle was well known – popular songs were composed about him – the consecration of John went ahead, and he ruled effectively as Bishop of Orléans for forty years.

Burchard, Bishop of Worms (died 1025), carried on in the Hincmar tradition and classified homosexual acts as a variety of fornication. But in 1102 the Council of London laid down that in future 'sodomy' must be confessed as a sin. St Anselm, the Archbishop of Canterbury, refused to publish this edict and in a letter to the Archdeacon William wrote: 'This sin has hitherto been so public that hardly anyone is embarrassed by it, and many have therefore fallen into it because they were unaware of its seriousness.' As St Anselm had been a pupil of Lanfranc and as both men had written highly emotional letters to each other and to other men, perhaps they were prejudiced in their rejection of the edict. Anselm frequently addressed letters to his 'beloved lover'. It is extraordinary to think that the sentiments expressed in the following letter had no physical expression, for Anselm was devoted to the monastic ideal of celibacy. Anselm wrote: 'Wherever you go my love follows you, and wherever I remain my desire embraces you . . . How then could I forget you? He who is imprinted on my heart like a seal on wax.' It is interesting, though, that in the edict 'sodomy' appears to have been used in its more limited modern sense to mean only homosexual anal penetration. There seems to have been a change of meaning, for by 1230 when Jacques de Vitry (who declared that it was Muhammad himself who had introduced sodomy to the Arab world) described Paris as being filled with sodomites, it is doubtful that he meant married men who committed anal penetration with their wives. No doubt it is pertinent that the edict above was never published; perhaps Anselm and others in the church knew that the majority of churchmen would be thus indicted. The king of the time, Henry I, was well known to be in sympathy, and his heir, William Atheling, who was later drowned, had a court which historians were inclined to name as 'sodomites' or 'intemperate and foppish youths'.

Nevertheless, the pope at the time, Leo IX, was strenuous in his efforts to enforce clerical celibacy and was the first pontiff to take action against married clergy. The first Lateran Council of 1123 declared marriage for clergy to be invalid. The hundred years after 1050 marked a phase of high papal morality and spiritual reform within the church, yet nothing was done about the high incidence of homosexual romance within the church itself; it was, for the most part, ignored. For the people, however, the homosexual liaisons of those clerics who loved gods more than goddesses, as Walther of Chatillon put it, were a popular subject for satires, poems and songs. One was about a reforming bishop keen to enforce the law on clerical marriages because he had no need of one: 'The man who occupies the bishopric is Ganymedier than Ganymede.'

So-called effeminacy in men was lampooned and vilified as it always had been (and still is, for that matter), but were the objections to effeminacy or merely to *outré* fashions which suggested wealth, elitism and leisure? Orderic on the court of William Rufus of England is splenetic: 'the effeminate predominated everywhere and revelled without restraint, while filthy catamites, fit only to perish in the flames, abandon themselves to the foulest practices of Sodom.'[17] Yet he is the only writer to connect effeminacy with homosexuality; others merely declaim against men dressing and acting like women and growing their hair long.★ In 1108 the Council of Westminster condemned long hair in men and clerics were known to become barbers at court. Other commentators on William's court do not single out the sins of sodom, but talk of sexual excess of all types, the king being given 'insatiably to obscene fornication and frequent adultery', while his courtiers, who had been called 'effeminate catamites', were charged with violating the wives and daughters of the Anglo-Saxon nobility. Hardly the picture of a homosexual king and court.

Another medieval king, Richard the Lionheart, was renowned for his love of men including, when he was Duke of Aquitaine, an affair with Philip, King of France: 'they ate every day at the same table and from the same dish, and at night their beds did not separate them. And the king of France loved him as his own soul; and they loved each other so much that the king of England was absolutely astonished at the passionate love between them and marvelled at it.' There was nothing remotely effeminate about Richard, of course, a crusader and warrior devoted to hand-to-hand combat. Another of his lovers was a young knight, a crusader, one Raife de Clermon, whom he freed from Saracen captivity. Richard was undoubtedly pious and constantly in the company of prelates, there was no shame attached to his predilections and nothing hidden. Though he did repent on several

---

★ The word 'effeminacy' changes its meaning throughout history. In the Renaissance it meant men who were lovers of women and spent time with them. The evidence here points to a court obsessed with fashion, pleasure and trivialities.

occasions 'that sin' (*peccatum illud*), public confessions being a tradition of the church, there is no sign that it was regarded as a more serious sin than many others.

Bernard of Morlaix wrote that homosexuals were 'as numerous as grains of barley, as many as the shells of the sea, or the sands of the universe'. The cities, the countryside, even holy places were awash with unashamed and unabashed homosexual behaviour.

The problem of masculine women and effeminate men much exercised the medical writers. Albertus Magnus, the teacher of Aquinas, being an Aristotelian, propounded the view that hermaphrodites also possess the secondary organs of the opposite sex, so that in intercourse they can easily become both active and passive. This explains the church's nervousness over any sexual position in marriage other than the missionary one. If a woman is on top, surely she must have lesbian tendencies. Or if the woman is on her hands and knees and is penetrated from behind, surely this is too close to bestiality. Besides, such a position could be taken to be an act of sodomy.

Other writers obviously felt uneasy with this blurring of gender and stressed the negative qualities of hermaphrodites, the lustfulness of masculine women and the maliciousness of feminine men. Their bodies were misleading so they could be charged with fraud, they were deceitful and liars.[18] No wonder Tiresias suffered among the sorcerers and soothsayers in the circle of Dante's Hell devoted to the punishment of fraud.

Peter of Abano wrote a commentary upon the pseudo-Aristotelian work *Problems* and explained:

> some exercise the wicked act of sodomy by rubbing the penis with the hand; others by rubbing between the thighs of boys, which is what most do these days; and others by making friction around the anus and by putting the penis in it the same way as it is placed in a woman's sexual part.

At least here we have a definition of sodomy – it means any sexual act committed by two males. This extract comes from a chapter which is an heroic attempt to explain why some men derive sexual pleasure from anal stimulation. Abano declares that the pores and passages which generally convey the semen to the penis are blocked in the case of eunuchs and effeminate men. These vessels terminate at the base of the penis or around the anus and the seed can be dispersed by rubbing in those areas. Albertus Magnus gives a remedy for sodomy, which is to apply ash of hyena fur mixed with pitch to the man's anus. Other medical writers thought that homosexuality was inborn, while William of Saliceto identified the cause of lesbianism as either uterine prolapse or abnormal enlargement of the clitoris.[19]

The eleventh and early twelfth centuries were periods of liberality and tolerance compared with what was to come. The growth of feudalism came at a time when society managed to accommodate a great many different beliefs; Catholics co-existed with Arians, Muslims with Jews, Manicheans and pagans. Civil law had not begun to regulate sexual morality in any overbearing manner, and the church exercised only a limited influence over its flock. All this was to change.

THE MIDDLE AGES

Throughout the twelfth century a different tone creeps in when issues of sexual deviance are discussed. It is a dark, judgemental and arrogant tone which brooks no dissension. It is the tone of the Inquisition which came into being a hundred years later. (Pope Gregory IX instituted the papal Inquisition in 1231 for the apprehension and trial of heretics.) Raymond of Penafort attempted to define the term 'unnatural' in sexual practices and pronounced that it was any form of sexual activity save that between man and woman using the appropriate organs: 'All other sexual practices should be rejected, and if not punished, severely castigated as sin.' Justinian's declaration that sexual licence caused disasters, such as famine, pestilence and earthquakes, was exhumed and became a stock item in the rhetoric of medieval vituperation. The third Lateran Council of 1179 thought it necessary to adopt a canon prohibiting 'that incontinence which is against nature.'[20] It also decreed that clerics guilty of such unnatural vice must forfeit clerical status or be confined indefinitely in a monastery. Laymen must be excommunicated and entirely excluded from society. There was a gradual feeling in the church that sodomy was the greatest crime, far worse even than incest between mother and son.

Sodomy was slowly becoming a symbol of much else where fast economic growth occurred, especially in the northern cities of Italy, northern France, Flanders and the Rhine valley. These cities were anxious to be independent of the Holy Roman Empire. They were ruled by lesser nobles and wealthy merchants, the latter having little interest in religion or in persecuting heretics, for much of their wealth came from charging interest on money loans and the church considered usury to be a grave sin. Yet being upwardly mobile, they aped the customs and more, of the true aristocracy.

In opposition, another new class began to form, the shopkeepers and artisans who desired more influence in government, who saw usury as yet another tool of their oppressors and who resented a merchant class aping the old elite. But they were also in opposition to the hereditary aristocracy and the church, who by then were notorious for their ostentation, wealth and over-consumption of food, wine and sex of every description. Sodomy came to be seen as a quintessential part of this unrestricted greed and a reason for the plight of the underprivileged. Where the new middle classes gained political power in Lombardy and Tuscany, they enacted legislation against both usury and sodomy.[21]

As heretics were also believed to be sodomites and as usurers were sometimes called heretics, sodomy and usury were linked in the popular mind. Dante placed them both in the same circle of Hell. That the heretics actually favoured homosexuality is probably true; certainly the Bogomils, the Manicheans and the Cathars held very similar beliefs. All were Dualists, believing that flesh belonged to the devil and that procreation entrapped a soul in evil matter. Thus, acts of sexual release that were not procreative might be favoured over those that were. The orthodox church thought that unnatural sexual orgies occurred in the heretics' rituals and ceremonies and they publicised this gross sinfulness to the general populace so that heretics might be heartily loathed.

At the same time there was a rise in anti-semitism. In 1173 when Thomas of Monmouth published his account of the ritual murder of a Christian child by the Jews, the child, William of Norwich, was soon canonised and Monmouth's account became a source for mass hysterical hatred of Jews, leading to their persecution all over Europe. The third Lateran Council of 1179 issued a series of statutes to curb Jewish authority in economic and social life and to limit their interaction with Christians. By the following century Jews appeared in popular literature as 'thieves, kidnappers, usurers, assassins, murderers and traitors.'[22] It would not be long before sodomites joined them.

Thus the second half of the thirteenth century saw a growth in legislation against homosexuality. Popular belief saw it as a common crime among the clergy and as flourishing in towns and cities. Hence, the most severe penalties occurred in city statutes and ordinances; some writers have seen these as a reflection of anti-clericalism. In Castile a royal edict forbade monks to leave their orders, then continued to speak reluctantly of a terrible sin 'that one man desires to sin against nature with another . . . if any commit this sin, once it is proven, both be castrated before the whole populace . . . then hung by the legs until they are dead.' The legal school of Orléans also required castration for the first offence, dismemberment for the second and burning for the third. This punishment seems so hysterical and impractical that one is led to speculate that it was intended more as a deterrent than as a responsible act of law. The Bologna statutes of 1288, on the other hand, are simple and pragmatic; they replace the earlier fines for homosexual offences with death by burning. Siena prescribed hanging by the 'virile member'.[23] Between 1250 and 1300 most of Europe passed legislation against homosexual activity which incurred the death penalty.[24]

There is very little evidence that these laws were ever put into effect, but one suspects that if they were there were other reasons behind their use. As in Justinian's court, political trouble-makers could be neatly disposed of with false accusations, especially when their wealth could then be legally purloined into near empty royal coffers.

The Trial of the Templars[25]

A case in point is that of the Templars, a military–religious Order founded in the Holy Land in 1119, and their fanatical persecution by Philip IV of France, nicknamed *le Bel*. Philip himself is an interesting study. Called fair for his height and blond good looks which were delicate and almost feminine, he resembled his daughter Isabella, who married the first Prince of Wales soon to become Edward II, one of the supposedly most notoriously homosexual of the English kings. Philip's father, Philip III, was also well known for his liking of young men.

Philip IV grew up with a loathing of homosexuality which was almost paranoid. The bishop of Pamiers had said of him: 'such was our King of France, who was more handsome than any man in the world, and who knew nothing at all except to stare at men.' An equivocal remark, given Philip's homophobia, but Philip had another obsession, a longing to go down in history as a king of great piety like his grandfather, Louis IX, who was eventually canonised during his grandson's reign. Yet Philip spent most of his time hunting and left the running of his kingdom to a circle of close advisers. An anonymous writer from the early years of Philip's reign attacked the king because he had surrounded himself with 'villani' – thieves and plunderers, brutal, corrupt and malignant men. That Philip, with his aspirations towards holiness, should then follow their advice and turn upon one of the most revered and pious groups of Christians, the Knights Templar, and accuse them of blasphemy and heresy, including idol worship and sodomy, might sound odd except that Philip was hungry for land and money and the Templars were one of the richest religious Orders with their treasury in the heart of Paris. They also had extensive property in the Crusader states of Palestine and Syria, they enjoyed ecclesiastical and jurisdictional privileges from popes and monarchs, and they functioned as bankers helped by the international nature of their organisation.

The Knights Templar were astonishingly powerful in the medieval world, yet in the early hours of Friday, 13 October 1307 Philip ordered the 2,000 Templars of France to be arrested, charging them with a detailed list of crimes and taking over their property and wealth. Philip had a compulsion for pitting himself against great men: in 1301 he had charged Pope Boniface VIII with simony, sodomy, parricide, nepotism and heresy. Certainly Boniface may well have been guilty; he was reputed to have said: 'Why, there is no more to going to bed with women or boys than in rubbing one hand against the other.' There had been a great quarrel between Boniface and Philip and Philip attempted to kidnap the pope. The bizarre situation tore Christendom in half, but then Boniface, not surprisingly, died a month later from a heart attack. A new pope had to be found who could stand up to the growing power of the monarchy, especially that of France. Philip IV was obviously a king who was not afraid of taking on the power of the church.

The new pope, Benedict, endeavoured to calm the political climate, but he died a year later. Then the cardinals chose a Gascon, Bertrand de Got, who became Clement V. Clement had been chosen because he did not belong to either of the warring factions and he appeared innocuous enough not to cause more trouble. So in 1307 Clement V, though seeing the arrest of the Templars as an affront to his dignity and the jurisdiction of the church, was not prepared to do battle with the French king.

That same year Philip's twelve-year-old daughter married Edward and he was crowned king. The reports of the coronation dinner where Edward spent more time caressing his favourite Gascon, Piers Gaveston, than paying attention to his child bride must have disturbed his homophobic father-in-law. Indeed, Philip made it clear there and then that he would co-operate with England only if Edward also agreed to arrest all the Templars within his lands. The pope, endeavouring to put himself in charge of the situation (and no doubt tempted by the Templar riches) issued a bull ordering all the monarchs of Christendom to arrest the Templars and sequester their lands in the name of the papacy.

There is no doubt that the Templars had been in decline for some time. In 1207 Innocent III had condemned them for their pride and their abuse of their privileged position. With an uncanny echo of Philip's charges, Innocent had said that they 'yield to the doctrine of demons, they mark the sign of the cross on the chest of any vagabond'. And he went on to say that adulterers, usurers and criminals were all buried in their cemeteries. They were accused of hindering the crusade of St Louis in 1248 for their own profit. In 1291 the Templars lost the last fortress in Palestine at Acre and the survivors fled to Cyprus. The last Grand Master was Jacques de Molay, already middle-aged when he became Master at the end of 1293.

Historians still cannot agree on whether the Templars were guilty or not, though there is a general consensus that they were innocent. One of the most constant and gravest charges, which must have sent shivers of horror through the medieval populace, was that the Templars worshipped a severed head. Those Templars who confessed all described the head differently; some said it was covered in silver, others that it had a long beard, others that it was two-faced and so on. But no head was ever presented as evidence, and certainly Philip would have done so if he could. Nor was there any evidence of heresy, blasphemy or homosexuality, other than the confessions which were constantly revoked. The charges sound absurd: new recruits to the Order had to spit upon the crucifix, had to kiss the penis, anus or base of the spine of the older knights in an initiation ceremony, where they were also encouraged to have sexual relations with their brother knights. These are routine allegations which all the heretic groups were charged with. They worshipped a cat which entered the chapel backwards, they urinated on the cross or spat out the Host in a latrine. All of the charges had their roots in folk lore and superstition, and were part of the stock apparatus of propaganda which had been used for centuries by the church to discredit its religious and political opponents.

The great problem for Philip was that no one confessed unless tortured and he had to rely upon the Inquisition to obtain incriminating evidence, but it was tame and muddled. Besides, from the evidence of the dispositions it is clear that the Templars were no longer a military establishment. They were more likely to be shepherds, stewards, agricultural workers, carpenters, ploughmen or winesellers. Some of them were over fifty and had not entered the Order until they were in their forties. They were simple men, uneducated and not at all versed in political machinations who scarcely understood why they were being threatened, much less the nature of the charges. What they did understand, though, were the threats of torture, and the fact that the government was intent upon having positive answers to their questions. Out of the 138 dispositions which have survived from those first hearings in Paris, only four Templars denied everything and insisted on their innocence. When threatened with torture, one of these changed his mind. Philip tortured the Grand Master, Jacques de Molay, and all the leaders. Under torture the Templars confessed sacrilege and heresy, but very few would sign confessions of sodomy. Jacques de Molay, before he died by burning, cursed the French king and all his heirs (and it is true that the royal line died out).

Edward II

It is to Edward II's credit that though he exiled the Templars, he never tortured or imprisoned them, or allowed the Inquisition into England. Most of the Templars fled to Scotland where it seems likely that the warriors among them took Robert the Bruce's side and fought at Bannockburn a few years later in 1314. The King of France had found that the charge of sodomy was one of the most effective accusations for character assassination. It would remain so.

Historians have also destroyed Edward's character and reign with charges of feebleness, indolence and homosexuality. They have always spoken of his intemperate love for his first favourite Piers Gaveston, a Gascon nobleman and knight. Both Piers and Edward were bisexual and both married. Edward had four children borne by his wife Isabella and one bastard son. Piers, like

Richard I, was a highly skilled horseman and warrior, and the barons loathed him because he always defeated them at jousting. They also resented the influence that the Gascon nobleman had at court, but they never singled out a sexual relationship for their abuse. Edward, too, was disliked for what were thought of as his 'unkingly' occupations. There was something of the Renaissance prince about him – he loved music and dancing, he wrote poetry and there is some evidence that he helped to design the gittern, the forerunner of the violin.* He was skilled in swimming, rowing and water sports, he adored exotic animals (he kept a pet lion), fine clothes and jewellery.

England was more used to the ways of his father, Edward I, whose chief concern had been war but who had left his country bankrupt and in debt. Edward II, it is true, was far more suited to run a country estate than a kingdom. That the barons rose up against him and Piers was due less to their homosexuality, than to their complete lack of tact and diplomacy. They treated the barons with scorn, never sharing land and wealth with them and Piers was loaded with gifts of titles and land, clothes and jewellery. One title, that of Duke of Cornwall, was traditionally given only to a member of the royal family and this understandably infuriated the barons who murdered him in 1312. He was buried in three gold embroidered cloaks at Edward's chapel at Kings Langley.

Edward, too, was murdered, but on the orders of Isabella and her lover Mortimer. The story is that he was put to death by the insertion of a red-hot poker into his anus; this was so that they could exhibit his body which would show no traces of violence, although this was never done. (Pigs used to be slaughtered in this manner in the belief that it tenderised the flesh.) The story of the red-hot poker comes from Geoffrey le Baker, a chronicler well known for fictionalising events. His chronicles were written thirty years after the murder, by which time Edward had become almost a saint in the eyes of the public who flocked to Gloucester to see his burial place and believed he had miraculous powers. Isabella was

---

* There is a fine gittern dating from Edward's reign at the British Museum.

still alive, exiled from the court by the king, her son, for her part in the deposition of his father. There is, then, some reason to believe that the red-hot poker story was devised by Isabella to destroy her late husband's now saintly reputation. Gloucester Cathedral was rebuilt in the splendour we see today because the pilgrims still flocked to Edward's tomb. Indeed, some people would like the tomb to be opened and the remains, if any, inspected, for there is also some evidence that Edward escaped from Berkeley Castle and ended his days in northern Italy.[26]

It is clear from both the treatment of the Templars and the deposition of Edward II that where homosexual charges are made, the truth is almost impossible to determine. From the evidence of Edward's life, it seems to me probable that homosexuality was not an issue. Sodomy had only been made a capital crime linked with sorcery, apostasy and heresy by his father in 1290. What became a scandal was the inept running of a bankrupt kingdom by a monarch and his advisers who were concerned only with lining their own pockets. Disasters were hastened by the onset of the Little Ice Age (caused by the advance of polar and alpine glaciers, and lasting until around 1700) which destroyed harvests and crops and led to years of famine. In the last ten years of his reign, faced with mounting debts, Edward violated the constitution and overrode all notions of respect for ownership of land. This behaviour was far more serious than his bisexuality which was regarded at the time as inappropriate and highly charged emotional infatuation. It did, however, provide ammunition for Edward's enemies and contributed to his downfall. It is this which has left an unjust smear upon his life and reign.

Roaming Heretics

Despite the move towards totalitarianism in both church and state, the second half of the thirteenth century saw the rise of great popular movements, such as the Brethren of the Free Spirit, in which bands of vagabond monks called Beguines and Beghards (women and men), claiming to be a mendicant Order, roamed across Europe. They lived off alms, calling out 'God's bread'. They dressed as friars in robes which were often coloured, or split from the waist down, with hoods covered in patches. Around 1290 they increased in number. On the whole they were literate and articulate, and they preached with great popular success. The clergy were often dismayed by the Brethren's subtlety, the eloquence of their teaching and the skill with which they handled abstruse theological concepts.[27] But the church was also horrified at their message, for they translated the Bible into the vernacular, told stories from it and interpreted it to the people. They preached that God was contained within the spirit in all people. Gnosticism had returned to haunt the church.

Gnosticism taught that redemption came with spiritual knowledge, and that everyone could find God in both meditative silence and in the delights and pleasures of this life. What is more, these wandering preachers taught that all passions of the flesh were not only harmless but could also be beneficial, in that God was found in pleasure, so no sexual act could be a sin. In the eyes of the church, this could lead only to anarchy. Indeed, churchmen thought they saw it all around them. Such statements as that of Johann Hartmann – 'The truly free man is king and lord of all creatures. All things belong to him and he has a right to use whatever pleases him' – struck terror into the soul of the orthodox church. Such people were obviously heretics and deserved to be burnt. The anger against them was all the more intense because sodomy was considered a particularly common vice among the clergy. In fact, the church was slowly losing its control over such acts which were treated as 'reserved sins' requiring recourse to a bishop. The parish priests were left to deal with fornication, masturbation by boys under fourteen and by girls under twenty-five, together with irregular heterosexual intercourse which meant either coitus in unusual positions or anal and oral sex.[28]

Both canon and secular law grew in volume between the years 1243 and 1348 (the year of the Black Death). The legislation on homosexuality in this period now involved the secular authorities, and it became defined as a major capital crime attracting far more attention than it ever had from the municipal law-makers. I would suggest this is not because there was suddenly a great deal more of it, but because it had become associated with other heinous offences and was a symbol of dissidence and anarchy.

Yet homosexual practices do not appear to have diminished because of the increased penalties against them. Why should Pierre de La Palude have to explain at length why the church could not marry homosexuals?[29] Surely it was because he knew that same-sex marriage ceremonies occurred in churches and had done so ever since the early church, and that however much the church fulminated against same-sex practices, others gave them the blessing of God.[30]

V

❧

MEDIEVAL EUROPE
AND
NEW WORLDS

THE BIRTH OF THE HOMOPHOBIC STATE

By the middle of the fourteenth century, society's view of sexual identity was quite different from what it had been in the ancient world. This radical change was brought about by the combined autocracy of church and state which refused to countenance bisexuality. A man's sexuality was now touched by the divinity of God, it became sacred (women were so marginalised that they had not yet been considered). In practical terms, any sexual expression outside marriage, or positions and acts within marriage which were not vaginal penetration in the missionary position, were contaminated by the devil. Gradually, all 'deviant' acts became grave and flagrant sins against the divinity of God. The only sexual expression that escaped condemnation was female prostitution and the bordello, which the church for the most part ignored.

This change to a heterosexual 'ideal' could not expunge the expression of bisexuality from all levels of society, including the church. Instead, it created a form of schizoid thinking in both the individual and the state. Now the expression of bisexual feeling had to be thought of as something else, unless it became blatantly and publicly obvious and the state was forced to take action. It is from this time, when the concept of bisexuality was discarded from the consciousness of society, that a polarity began to establish itself between the Other (what is repressed) and the Self (which is publicly acknowledged); between that which will later be called homosexual, which must be hidden, and the status quo, the heterosexual, which needs to be publicly enhanced. Human sexual nature, in the way it was considered socially, was divided into two parts, homosexual and heterosexual, as if they were mutually exclusive. From this time onwards an underground society which thought of itself as catering for the tastes of homosexuals began to flourish in the cities and towns of Europe. Some historians have claimed that this split took place much later, when the idea of homosexuality as a separate sexual identity was first invented – namely, the end of the nineteenth century when the word itself was coined: 'The sensuality of those who did not like the opposite sex was hardly noticed in the past.'[1] This may well have been true up to the twelfth century but not afterwards, as the examples in this chapter testify. The term used in literature to describe emotional and sexual love between men was 'masculine love'.[2] Examples can be found in Bacon, Heywood and Michelangelo's grandnephew (see below).*

Why was bisexuality not erased from society when the church and the state used such virulent propaganda and rigorous laws against it? Moreover, the offence was a capital one. The answer is a social one compounded of economics, property and masculine anxiety over the validity of heirs. Virginity was a condition of marriage, valued because a man had to be certain his wife was faithful and his sons were his own. A man did not marry until he could set up his own home, a process which took some years, so he was unlikely to marry before he was about thirty. Wives tended

---

* The term 'masculine love' was used as late as the second decade of this century by E.M. Forster in his posthumously published novel *Maurice*, to describe the love between Maurice and Alec.

to be much younger: girls from the aristocracy and the daughters of rich merchants were married off from the age of ten or even earlier, though the average age was around thirteen, at puberty.

So what opportunities for sexual expression did a man have until he got married? He could persuade a girl to sleep with him by promising her marriage when they could afford it. But girls throughout the ages know how fragile such promises are. Then there were prostitutes, but they cost money and there was always the risk of disease. Better by far, it must have seemed, to strike up a friendship with an apprentice and hope the whole sexual arrangement could be both casual and discreet. In the houses of noblemen the servants slept together in crowded conditions, often two or three in a bed. If the other servants heard any noises, the creaking of a bedstead or groans of pleasure, they on the whole kept quiet for they too were far from innocent. (Later, in Renaissance England, we shall see cases which illustrate this.)

Though the upper-class adolescent male was expected to behave in an aggressive manner, he actually had to be passive until he was accepted into full manhood in his late twenties or early thirties when he got married. Males in their early teens began as passive partners to older men who in turn served them as active models and teachers for adult status. Court records in Florence and Venice indicate that these youths in their turn developed into active sodomites when adult. Men who did not make the change from passive to active were seen as being subversive to the structure of society, for they were undermining the correct path to adult status.[3] How reminiscent all this is of classical Athens. It is illustrated in Benvenuto Cellini's *Vita* where the young Cellini dresses his male neighbour in drag and presents him at a dinner as a beautiful prostitute. Later, Cellini rejected, often violently, any hint of homoeroticism. However, double standards were a necessary ploy, for in the larger world of Christendom itself, sodomy was becoming a serious offence.

Beginning in fourteenth-century Europe, homosexuality, already associated with heresy and usury, was linked to something more sinister – sorcery and demonism. It is then hardly surprising that human nature dealt with this by pretending that the act of homosexual coition was something quite else. As a hungry man taking a few crumbs does not think of it as stealing but as feeding himself, so must the fumbling around in the dark, the furtive mutual masturbation with an apprentice, have seemed something necessary and even modest. Surely, what they were doing could not possibly be that sin which state and church considered so loathsome that the very details of the trials were often burnt with the offenders, for it was believed that the naming and detailing of the acts might pollute the hearer and encourage yet more sin.

The Emperor Justinian's link between sin and natural disasters continued to have a huge influence on the popular imagination, particularly at a time when the plague struck Europe and swept aside boundaries of territory and class. Preachers across Christendom were not slow to link the gross sins of the flesh with the visitation of disaster and disease, which no prayers could stop.

The Black Death of 1348–50 killed an estimated one-third of the population living between India and Iceland. It led to economic chaos, a dearth of agriculture, social unrest, profiteering, frenetic gaiety, wild expenditure, and social and religious hysteria.[4] Afterwards, it raised great concern over how the population might regain its pre-plague level. Law-makers in the generation after 1348 began to see sodomy as a grave threat to the repopulation of society.[5] This is reflected in the severe and gruesome punishments visited upon those convicted of deviant sexual practices.

The legal theorists, unhappy with the biblical account identifying that it was the men of Sodom who invited the angels to come outside so as to 'know' them, decided that sodomy must have begun with the women of Sodom and Gomorrah, who had not been content with copulation with men but had dreamt up new and obscure pleasures, which the men of these Cities of the Plain had eagerly followed.

Both men and women convicted of sodomy could be burnt alive. However, the age of the offender was taken into account, presumably bearing in mind that adolescent youths served a sexual purpose for the older male before he was married. Perugian boys between the ages of twelve and fifteen who consented to sodomy could be gaoled for three months, while boys above fifteen were fined as well as being gaoled. Convictions seem to be rare, too; that, coupled with the lighter sentences, shows an understanding of the plight of the defenceless apprentice who must have found it difficult, if not impossible, to fight off an older man. The fines become larger with the age of the man, but if they had not been paid within ten days the offender was stripped, tied by the genitals, paraded naked through the streets, beaten, then expelled from the town. A man over thirty-three was to be burnt and all his property forfeited to the city. The accused were denied the right of counsel in presenting their defence. Burning seems to have been reserved for the most vicious. cases like homosexual rape; other offenders were most likely to be whipped, fined and exiled.[6]

Because of the popular belief that sodomy was rife among the clergy, a special magistrate was appointed in Florence in 1432, with the extraordinary title of Official of the Curfew and the Convents, to deal specifically with sodomy.[7] The curfew covered student activity which was also thought to be particularly licentious. According to St Bernardino of Siena, Florence and other Tuscan cities had a notorious reputation for homosexual licence, so much so that Genoa would not hire Tuscan schoolmasters. In 1375 Benvenuto da Imola found the University of Bologna infested by sodomites whom he publicly denounced. Warned by a sympathetic priest, however, they all fled.[8]

Witchcraft now began to be associated with taboo forms of sexuality. Masturbation and even nocturnal emissions caused great concern, for it was believed in some quarters that devils collected the semen and used it to create new bodies for themselves. One Caesarius of Hesiterback, who wrote in the thirteenth century, began this fiction and after the fourteenth century the anxiety over witches began to grow, swelling to an astonishing and ugly degree in the ensuing centuries.

Pope Innocent VIII (1484–95) issued a bull, *Summis desiderantes affectibus*, specifically to encourage and justify witch-hunting. The bull claimed that demons, called incubi (male) and succubi (female), assumed human form to have violent sexual intercourse with unsuspecting people, thus causing still-births, impotence and sterility. Any human being could also be a demon, especially one who was enticing and seductive, who tempted you into sexual congress. These demons had once been angels, but they had fallen due to their intemperate lust. Theologians did not explain how angels, as part of the heavenly host in paradise, could feel physical lust, for surely they were members of a different species. Therefore intercourse with them amounted to buggery or bestiality. One ecclesiastical authority added: 'to which sin is added also malice against religion, sodomy, adultery and incest.' Witch-hunters always had accounts of monsters, part human and part animal that were born after such unions. Later it was believed that convicted homosexuals must also be children of such a union.

Naturally, it was thought that demons would be far more likely to try intercourse with women than with men, because women were far more licentious than men. St Thomas Aquinas argued that devils in the form of succubi seduced males and thereby received their semen; then changing shape they became incubi and poured this semen into the females. All this complicated demonology shed a new and terrifying light upon masturbation, for it was also believed that witches could make the penis disappear. Once that had happened, only the witch herself could make the penis reappear. No one knows how many witches were burnt, beheaded, hanged or whipped to death in the centuries from 1450 to 1793, the year in which the last 'witch' was burnt in Poland. Millions of women were accused in this time. An inquisitor at Como in Italy is quoted as saying that he burned 1,000 witches in one year (possibly 1523).[9]

Homosexuality as an integral part of satanism was given added resonance by the notorious demonist Gilles de Rais (1404–40). Orphaned at eleven, brought up by his maternal grandfather, married when he was sixteen to a rich heiress, Gilles de Rais quickly became one of the wealthiest men in France. He fought for Charles VII against the English and protected Joan of Arc, twice saving her life, and as a reward was made Marshal of France. He returned to his castle in Brittany after Joan had been executed, and he set up a court rivalling the king's in grandeur and riches. He decorated his château, maintained a large train of servants, heralds and priests, was a munificent patron of music, literature and pageants. But this effort nearly bankrupted him and when his family restrained him from mortgaging the rest of his lands by securing a decree from the king, he turned to magic and alchemy in a search for gold. He scoured the countryside for young boys to sacrifice, using satanism in the hope of gaining knowledge, power and riches by invoking the devil. Sexual assault on the boys was obviously part of the ritual, before the unfortunate innocents were killed. His activities went unchecked for over ten years, in which time he had abducted, tortured and murdered more than 140 children. He was tried at Nantes, condemned for heresy and sentenced to death for murder. He is thought to have served as a model for Bluebeard (also set in Brittany) which first made its appearance in a collection of stories by Charles Perrault in 1697, though the gender of the victims has been changed in this version of the story. Though de Rais's story of ugly serial-murder fuelled Christian prejudice against pederasty, it is rather the saga of a bankrupt satanist than of a Platonic boy-lover.

SLAV SEXUALITY[10]

The Orthodox Slavs comprised three national groups: the Serbs, Bulgarians and Russians. They adopted Christianity later than Western Europe, beginning to be converted in the ninth, tenth and eleventh centuries. They were the heirs to the empire of Byzantium, and their church was based in Constantinople. They were largely a conglomerate of pastoral and rural communities and because of their geographical intimacy with Greece, it would seem likely that they would also have been heirs to the sexual idealism of the classical era.

But Slav culture seems to have bypassed the ancient world, and its ideas on sexuality were taken from the early church fathers.

Homosexuality quickly became one of the major crimes against God, particularly because pagan religions had been so tolerant towards a whole range of sexual practices.

The three requirements for licit sex were procreation, vaginal penetration and a variation of the missionary position, the 'horse' position, in which the man sits astride the supine woman, as in a saddle. The reversal of this position, with the woman astride the man, horrified Slav sensibility. All other sexuality constituted a 'sacrifice of semen to the Devil without purpose'.

There were many gradations of sin, penance and punishment in the Byzantine canon law which help us understand more clearly how their society regarded sexual transgressions. A clear distinction was drawn between male homosexuals who engaged in anal intercourse and those who engaged in mutual masturbation. Homosexual intercourse involving anal penetration was treated as seriously as heterosexual adultery or bestiality. The offence carried a penance of fifteen years, though more lenient sentences of up to seven years were more generally given. When giving penances priests had to take into account the age of the offender, how often he transgressed, in what way, and whether he was married. Priests were understanding if the culprit was under thirty and completely exonerated boys under twelve of knowing the seriousness of what they were doing. If a child under five was sexually abused then the abuser took on all of the sin; if the child was over five but not legally an adult, then it was the parents' responsibility for not teaching the child how to avoid sin. Two or three minor homosexual exploits in the young were viewed as being relatively insignificant, though warnings of what it might or could lead to were inevitably given.

Bachelors were given greater indulgence than married men whether their sin be fornication or homosexuality. In an interesting reversal of the view held in the ancient world, some canon law looked on the passive partner with less seriousness than the active. Orthodox churchmen considered the initiator of the sin to be worthy of the greater condemnation. This shows, of course, a naive view of sexual relationships; perhaps desire was seen as more akin to rape than to love. Where the homosexual partners alternated between being active and passive, the case was seen as most shocking.

Intercrural homosexual intercourse was seen as a minor offence, slightly more serious than masturbation. The usual penance given was a fast of eighty days with fifty prostrations a day – double the penance for masturbation. The details of intercourse were scrutinised and noted with meticulous care: for example, if the hands were used in mutual masturbation as well as rubbing against the thighs, that counted as a much more serious offence. Highly serious too was the idea of a man making himself look like a woman by shaving off his beard. Kissing another man with lust carried a penance of forty days. None of these rules, penances and punishments seems to have had much effect, however.

Elizabeth I's ambassador to Russia, George Turbervile, thought that the homosexuality he encountered in Russian society was a product of 'a savage soil, where laws do bear no sway', and where 'lust is law'.[11] While Samuel Collins, an Englishman who visited Russia in the seventeenth century, commented that 'Russians were naturally inclined to Sodomy and Buggery'. However, such words then had nuances unfamiliar to us. 'Buggery' could mean both bestiality and homosexuality. 'Sodomy', too, could also mean bestiality. 'Sodomitical villanies with men and beasts', was how one writer put it in 1688.[12] But it could also be a heterosexual sin. The use of such words then would have indicated debauchery, which would probably have included some form of homosexual behaviour. But it is likely that there would have been young bawds as well as young boys and possibly a goat to broaden the range of erotic delights.

On the whole, lesbianism was not treated very seriously. It was deemed to be a kind of masturbation, and the penance was a year of exclusion from communion. But if one woman engaged in homosexual relations by sitting astride another, then she had to be flogged because to use the position recommended for marital heterosexual intercourse was both obscene and blasphemous. Lesbianism, traditionally, was linked with paganism. It was believed that lesbians prayed in the midst of their love-making to female spirits and led pagan rites themselves. But the association of illicit sexuality with either the devil or some heretical or pagan beliefs was never far below the surface of the medieval Christian world.

RENAISSANCE PLATONISM

In fifteenth-century Italy, humanism took flight upon the rediscovery of classical Greece and the philosophers of Athens. Humanists had to take on board (with some relief and eagerness, one imagines) the Greeks' positive attitudes towards and justifications for homosexuality. They were certainly not slow in doing so, for here, in one glorious package, was a reason for idealising homosexuality and removing from it the taint of sin and depravity forced on it by the church.

Marsilio Ficino (1433–99), an Italian philosopher, theologian and linguist who translated and interpreted Plato, could write his observations upon love and sex without, it would seem, attracting any shred of opprobrium: 'The reproductive drive of the soul, being without cognition, makes no distinction between the sexes', and is 'naturally aroused for copulation whenever we judge any body to be beautiful'. For this reason, 'it often happens that those who associate with males, in order to satisfy the demands of the genital part, copulate with them.' There can be no doubt, he observes, that some men 'naturally love males'.[13]

Ficino was riding the crest of the wave, for a mania for the culture of ancient Greece and Rome was spreading across Italy. The statues of that era which had been dug up had previously been crushed into dust for limestone, but now they were cleaned, polished and put on display, then sold to the highest bidder; even a limbless torso was revered, copied and sold for an astonishing amount. The classical world became the new fashion: merchants descended into debt in order to build their villas in the classical style; cardinals had their heads carved in marble in the style of Roman emperors; naked youths, gilded all over, formed living statues at the coronation of Pope Alexander VI. It became the fashion to scatter one's letters with classical allusions and to transform Christian figures into classical ones: nuns became vestal virgins, saints became gods, Christ was changed into Apollo and God into Jupiter. Classical literature was read with enthusiasm, the more salacious the better. Juvenal, Ovid, Martial were all hugely enjoyed for their picture of a licentious and completely bisexual ancient Rome. Lorenzo Valla (1407–57), philosopher, humanist and literary critic, wrote a work in praise of pleasure, *De Voluptare*, which was a defence of the work of Epicurus, but Valla's readership took it as a guidebook to the sensual pleasures available to man.

This widespread embracing of pagan culture alarmed the church, yet it too was susceptible and the popes behaved more like decadent, spendthrift Caesars than Vicars of Christ. As Luther was to write to Pope Leo X: 'The Roman court, which neither you nor any man can deny is more corrupt than either Babylon or Sodom – according to the best of my information – is sunk in the most deplorable and notorious impiety.'[14] So the church let the humanist tide run over it, becoming more extravagant and worldlier than ever, unable to unite its own teachings on sodomy with the practices of some of its priests. The situation at times became ludicrous.

Florence, concerned about its declining birth-rate, which it blamed on sodomy, was forced to recruit female whores from other cities. Like Venice, it outlawed female to male transvestism to stop prostitutes from dressing like boys to attract clients. The authorities faced a serious dilemma, and for the most part they turned a blind eye, aware that bisexuality was common to all. Fra Bernardino spoke in his sermons of the unhappiness suffered by the wives of sodomites, but he considered all non-procreative sex as unnatural, lumping all acts together as sin. Occasionally the authorities had a purge, but there were only fifty prosecutions for sodomy in Florence between 1348 and 1461, while the death sentence was carried out in only around 20 per cent of the cases. In

Genoa there was roughly one execution per year, and in four-teenth-century Venice, sodomy was rarely prosecuted.[15]

In Venice, a 1467 regulation ruled that as the vice of sodomy was of much concern, both women and boys found 'broken in the hinder parts' when visiting surgeons or barbers to be treated should be reported to the council.[16] On Christmas Day 1497 the Doge went to hear a sermon at the Church of San Marco and was told by Timeoto da Lucca that if he closed the churches against plague, he should rather eliminate the causes of the plague by banning blasphemy, usury, the policy of aiding the rich at the expense of the poor, the selling of justice and the societies of sodomy. The convents of nuns, he added, were nothing but whorehouses and public bordellos. Prostitutes must not hawk their wares in masculine garb or masculine manner. The Doge ignored the sermon, but men caught openly in homosexual acts either fled the city or were banned from it, though nobles were often executed. The passive partner always earned a more lenient sentence in Venice, so nobles sometimes pleaded their passivity in the act and were let off with a whipping. As Venice was dependent upon its fleet, the merchant-banker nobility in particular were concerned with the idea of God's wrath enveloping sinners in a Sodom and Gomorrah-style conflagration. In 1420, the authorities claimed that there was so much homosexuality on Venetian ships 'it is surprising that divine justice has not sunk them'. To help the Council of Ten (who ruled Venice) to catch homosexual sailors, they promised a 500 lire reward to those who turned them in.

Not only was the law flouted, in humanist Florence the oppressive concept of the demonic was also to some extent rejected and ridiculed. How else could one explain the painter Giovanni Bazzi (1477–1549) signing his tax returns 'Il Sodoma'? There is a delightful picture of him in Vasari's *Lives of the Artists*:

his manner of life was licentious and dishonourable, and as he was always keeping boys and beardless youths around him of whom he was inordinately fond, thus earning him the name of Sodoma; but instead of feeling shame, he gloried in it, writing stanzas and verses on it, and singing them to the accompaniment of the lute.

How else can one account for what so many writers and painters said in public? Flamino Nobili wrote that Plato and other Greek philosophers had judged a youth's beauty more fitting than a woman's to excite amorous desires. Ariosto (1474–1533), author of *Orlando Furioso*, wrote quite blithely that all humanists engaged in homosexual activity. In Canto 25 of this work, Bradamante, a young Amazon, is shorn of her hair and thereafter is mistaken for her twin brother. Asleep in the forest she is passionately kissed by a Spanish princess. Bradamante confesses she is a girl but the princess is not in the least deterred and takes her back to the palace, showering her with clothes and jewels. At night,

> One sleeps, one moans and weeps in piteous plight
> Because her wild desire more fiercely glows.[17]

Bradamante returns and tells her twin brother of the adventure. At once he dresses in women's clothes and goes to the princess, pretending to be Bradamante. He is welcomed with loving arms and in bed at night, when his true gender is discovered, he declares it is magic. They live together for several weeks as two loving women without anyone else knowing the truth. Though the lesbian nature of the princess seems to switch quite comfortably, this still must be the first tale to deal sympathetically with lesbian emotion since Sappho.

Benvenuto Cellini's autobiography tells of a beautiful and talented youth, Luigi Pulci, who made a career out of seducing Roman bishops, from one of whom he sadly contracted syphilis. Angelo Poliziano (1454–94) wrote Greek epistles begging kisses and caresses from young men and he is supposed to have died because he rose from his sick-bed in order to serenade a youth.[18]

One man clearly saw the great divide between the fashionable pursuit of humanism, with its reverence for classical culture, and the tradition and ethics of the Christian church. Girolamo Savonarola (1452–98) could not ignore what he called the blind wickedness of the peoples of Italy. He found humanistic paganism unbearable, for it corrupted manners, art, poetry and religion itself. In 1482 he took up the post of lecturer at the Convent of San Marco where he began to preach against the viciousness of the clergy and the tyrannical abuses of the government. In a sermon of 1494 he charged that Florence had become infamous for sodomy. He had great rhetorical power and could move his audience to tears or petrify them in horror over the agonies of the damned. Great fires were built to burn those books which celebrated the classical past, but much else went into them as well. The 'burning of the vanities' destroyed ornaments, false hair-pieces, lewd pictures, and gaming cards and tables. His power alarmed both the pope and the Medici who eventually contrived an ecclesiastical trial. Savonarola was hung and burnt at the stake. Afterwards, a Florentine member of the council was supposed to have remarked: 'And now we can practise sodomy again.'[19]

It is clear that we are discussing bisexuality, though writers constantly fall into the trap of talking about 'homosexual' Renaissance artists. Although Benvenuto Cellini was charged with sodomy three times, he also had affairs with women and eventually married. When his rival, Bandinelli, publicly called him a 'dirty sodomite', Cellini, lying but nevertheless with great bravado, answered: 'I wish to God I did know how to indulge in such a noble practice; after all, we read that Jove enjoyed it with Ganymede in paradise.'[20] Caravaggio openly painted his boy models for a patron, Cardinal Francesco del Monte, who himself had homosexual interests. Caravaggio was notorious in his passion for boys but also had relationships with women. Pieta Aretino seduced a married woman but also chased boys.

The subjects of many paintings were the classical archetypes of masculine love: Apollo, Narcissus, Cupid and Bacchus. Ganymede alone appeared in several hundred paintings and sculptures. Two painters who seemed to have only platonic relationships with women while also having close and emotional attachments to their assistants, were Leonardo da Vinci and Michelangelo. In 1476 Leonardo, along with four other Florentines, was anonymously accused of sodomy with the seventeen-year-old boy Jacopo Saltarelli. There was to be a trial and Leonardo spent two months in gaol, writing appeals for help to his family, friends and patrons. Eventually pressure was put upon the authorities and the charges were dropped. Leonardo was twenty-four.

According to Vasari, Leonardo was well-liked, he was charming, generous, beautiful and strong, and immensely kind to animals – he would buy caged birds to free them. Later in life he was charged with the same offence, but few details are known. He went on to have a series of assistants, all of whom seemed to find special favour, the most renowned being one Salai who would steal money from clients' purses, sell bits of equipment from the studio and generally behave in a thoroughly irresponsible manner, only to be forgiven and possibly indulged even more by his master. (Leonardo left Salai a bequest in his will and a dowry for his sister.) The painter turned away from the male nude in his work (his St John the Baptist is an androgynous dreamer, a youth who has learnt the ultimate secrets too early) and went on to paint those Diotima-like women, mysterious, ethereal and highly enigmatic.

The women in Michelangelo's paintings look as if they have worked out at the gym, pumping iron. There is no sensuous love of the dimpled soft flesh of women, for they are all heroic amazons. Michelangelo's statue of David is considered to be a classic example of homoerotic art (though to my mind the David of Donatello is far more seductive, a sleek classical ephebe). Michelangelo himself wrote:

You must know that I am, of all men who were ever born, the most inclined to love persons. Whenever I behold someone who possesses any talent or liveliness of mind, or displays any excellence in action or grace of body, I am impelled to fall in love with him. I give myself up to him so entirely that I no longer possess myself, but am wholly his.[21]

Vasari tells us that Michelangelo at fifty-seven loved Tommaso Cavalieri more than anyone else, and the two stayed close until Michelangelo's death at the age of eighty-nine. His drawing of Ganymede is but one in a series in which he expressed his passion, the 'prisoner of an armed cavalier'. The sonnets he wrote to Tommaso are particularly moving:

> Your will includes and is the lord of mine;
> life to my thoughts within your heart is given;
> my words begin to breathe upon your breath . . .
> Why should I seek to ease intense desire
> with still more tears and windy words of grief,
> when heaven, or late or soon, sends no relief
> to souls whom love hath robed around with fire?[22]

Michelangelo's grandnephew, known as Michelangelo the Younger, prepared the poems for their posthumous publication in 1623. He altered the gender in all the love poems to imply that they were written to women. In a note scribbled in the margin, not discovered until 1863, he indicated that the poems must not appear in their original form because of the 'amor . . . virile' ('masculine love') expressed in them. By then this term had become entrenched in Renaissance culture as a way of describing men who had a homosexual orientation.

The popular picture of the Renaissance genius is of a man (the immensely talented women painters have been almost ignored) who had no financial worries, being secure in the care of a benevolent patron, and whose personal life was a romantic homosexual idyll filled with a succession of handsome youths. These young men with their Italianate faces, sensuous and dark, still stare out at us from the paintings. Havelock Ellis in his book *Sexual Inversion* (published in 1897) is partly to blame for this picture, for he lists a glittering hall of fame which includes artists, writers, monarchs and aristocrats.[23] But, of course, it was not like that at all. Leonardo was tormented by his passions; when he commented on his depiction of Christ as an androgynous youth, he alluded bitterly to his sodomy accusation. 'When I painted Our Lord as a boy, you put me in gaol; if I were now to paint him as a grown man, you would do worse to me.'[24] Later, he wrote: 'The act of coitus and the members that serve it are so hideous . . .'[25] He must have lived through those two months in gaol knowing that he could be fined, or stripped naked and whipped, or even at the last resort burnt. Michelangelo was similarly tortured; his poetry and paintings are magnificent because they communicate such intensity of pain. Both artists show us the longing and aspiration for the divine coupled with a loathing for flesh. They are heirs, there is no doubt, of the medieval tradition, with its deep hatred and fear of sex, and to the powerful and compelling idea that the body's desires obscure and halt the souls' journey towards the divine. Though influenced by its visual heroism, they are not heirs to the culture of the classical world.

In 1580, on a trip to Rome, Montaigne noted that at the Church of St John marriages were being held for male couples. Remembering the twelfth-century denunciation of this ceremony, we can infer from Montaigne's observation that homosexual marriages blessed by Christian sacraments had a long, but obscure, history.[26] Montaigne also tells us that in Rome if these male married couples were then found to be living together in a carnal union, they were arrested and burnt at the stake. It is possible then that the male marriage was permitted at that time as a purely Platonic union. Nevertheless, these were exciting times to live in, for other worlds were impinging upon Europe, worlds with customs and traditions alien to Christendom, worlds which Christian missionaries wrote of with horror, for the sin of Sodom appeared to be everywhere. These 'other' peoples, though, were barbarians.

NEW WORLDS

The Incas began to build their empire only a century before the Spaniards arrived. The Mochica and Chimu civilisations which preceded them left no written documents, but remnants of broken pottery show enough representations of various sexual positions in coitus, some of which are homosexual, to suggest that there was no taboo attached to same-sex relations. Bartolome de las Casas, writing in 1542, tells us that Mayan parents supplied their adolescent sons with boys to use for sexual pleasure before marriage, but that if someone else committed sodomy on one of these boys it was tantamount to rape.[27] Young Mayan men lived in men's houses until they married at around the age of twenty. In a few Mayan regions, phallic cults existed. They appear also to have had that same custom, last seen in the ancient world, of sodomising their prisoners to indicate that the men were effeminate in defeat.

Sodomy, the Spanish also discovered, was almost universal among the Aztecs, involving children as young as six. Boys would dress as girls to make a living out of prostitution. An Aztec god, Xochipili, was the patron of male prostitution and homosexuality, while priests performed sodomy as a religious ritual. The Yauyos, who were part of the Inca Empire, had public houses filled with men with painted faces dressed in women's clothes. In other parts of the empire, boys were dedicated to the temple to be raised as girls, and chiefs had ritual sex with these boys on certain festival days. Also *berdaches* (see p. 23) were common in all the kinship-based Indian groups of Central and South America. The picture we receive is of many small groups with their own traditions and rituals, having a wide acceptance of homosexual practices, rather similar to the archaic civilisations of the Near East.

However, both Inca and Aztec laws decreed death by burning for homosexual offences; the latter went further, extending the death penalty to include female homosexuality and transvestism. Though these laws were in theory applicable throughout the empires, there seems to have been little enforcement of them. In Aztec society women were thought of as inferior – fathers advised their sons not to become entangled with them at too early an age – and effeminacy was spurned and ridiculed. The Spaniards were shocked and horrified at the homosexuality they found. Once in power they began to burn the sodomites. When Balboa came to Panama, he killed forty transvestites by feeding them to his dogs. This story is told by Peter Martyr who claimed that the people blamed the transvestites for the natural disasters they had been afflicted with – the storms, floods, famine and diseases – hence the slaughter. But there is some doubt as to whether this was actually what the people said or an interpretation offered by the Europeans who had often made the same connection at home.

It was not only in the West and the Americas that new discoveries were being made. As Christian missionaries journeyed east the same horrific customs were revealed. In the spring of 1541, Francis Xavier left Lisbon to become the first Jesuit missionary to go east and visit China. A few months later, three shipwrecked Portuguese found themselves upon a Japanese island. When they returned to Macao in China and then to Goa, they spread stories of the Nippon archipelago. Francis Xavier was eager to visit and arrived in Kagoshima where he stayed for ten months. He then moved to Kyoto to request an audience with the supreme sovereign of the empire. His party visited a large Zen monastery and discovered 'abominable vice against nature so popular that they practise it without any feeling of shame. They have many young boys with whom they commit wicked deeds.'[28] The Japanese were very surprised and laughed at him. Xavier left without any word.

The Jesuits found that the sin of Sodom was also widespread among the Samurai; indeed, everywhere they went they found it. In an attempt to get the Christian message through to their hosts, they described the sin as 'something so abominable that it is more unclean than the pig and more low than the dog'. Sometimes the Japanese lords were very angry and told them to leave, at other times they seem to have been merely amused. At last the Jesuits found a young lord, Otomo Yoshikata (1530–87), who expressed a wish to be converted. Nevertheless, he was hesitant about being baptised, for he had fallen into 'those sins which he must abandon'. It seems that the habit of loving young pages was very popular among the nobles. Otomo was finally baptised in 1576, though it would seem that he was still unable to relinquish his passions.

In 1551 Francis Xavier left Japan and died on the island of Macao late the following year. It is said that he favoured the Japanese above all the Asiatic peoples he had met and considered that in time they would all convert. As to their great sins, no successor of Xavier was able to do much about them. In despair, one Valegnani wrote to the Jesuit General complaining, 'the gravest of their sins is the most depraved of carnal desires, so that we may not name it. The young men and their partners, not thinking it serious, do not hide it. They even honour each other for it and speak openly about it.' Valegnani took four young Japanese back to Europe with him but when he returned in 1590 the persecution of the church had begun. In forty years Jesuits had converted 3 per cent of the population but now all European missionaries were ordered to leave the islands. Some stayed on and in 1637 all were seized and massacred.

Japan settled down to a new order, sealed off from the rest of the world. The great cities were prosperous, Buddhism was widely accepted, and the custom of homosexuality became popular, under the name of *shudo*, not only in the classes of samurai and monks but also among the bourgeoisie.

No doubt this was given some impetus by the lifestyle of the Shoguns. We have an account of the third Shogun, Lemitsu (1604–51), from François Callon, the head of a Dutch company at Nagasaki. Writing home he commented: 'the low opinion in which he [the Shogun] holds women and the shameful inclination he has towards boys have always kept him from marriage.' Nor did court life change much with the fifth Shogun, Tsunayoshi, who kept around 150 male concubines in his palace. The Korean ambassador commented:

> There are many male favourites who surpass young girls in beauty and attractiveness; they much exceed them, in their toilet especially, painting themselves with false eyebrows, making themselves up, dressing in coloured robes decorated with designs, dancing with fans; these beautiful young men are like flowers. King, noble, or rich merchant, there is no one who does not keep these beautiful young men.

Shudo, like the concept of the love of boys in classical Greece, was a philosophy. It had been developed by Buddhist monks and the Samurai in the medieval years, and it laid emphasis on morality and spirituality. Ijiri Chusuke, author of *The Essence of the Jakudo* (1482), uses the word for the first time when he writes of *shudo* in the abbeys of Kyoto and Kamakura. He portrays a world of warriors and nobles where lovers swear eternal love whether their partners are noble or common, rich or poor. Men must be full of good-will and loyalty, nor caring if they lose rank or property because of their love, continuing to be moved by the spirit of *shudo* and its way. The poet Sogi (1421–1502) also writes of the *wakashu*, the young boy or youth who was loved. He must have a pure and simple heart, be both tender and noble, must never fail to respond to passion from an older man, even if he is not pleasing. He must study hard, write poetry and never forget that he too will grow old. For, to have been loved provides happy memories for one's old age.

A book written in 1643 offered guidance to the *wakashu* from a Buddhist point of view, stating that *shudo* must conform with the idea of humanity. So many beautiful young men, the book for the friends of the soul says, are without soul and do not respond to admiration. But even when you cannot take the one who loves you into your heart, you should try and work some sense of duty into your conduct.

The etiquette of *shudo* was explained in countless texts. 'You must have only one lover in your life, otherwise there would be no difference between you and prostitutes or worse,' writes Yamamoto Jocho (1649–1719). Then he turns to the Samurai lover and addresses him: 'Homosexual pleasure must never be pursued at the same time as pleasure with women.' Jocho himself was bisexual and married, as were all the Samurai. The pattern is the same as in the ancient world: the future Samurai is loved by adult men up to the age of his majority, then he loves adolescents, and a few years later he marries and begets children. He still has his *wakashu* if he so desires, whatever the books of etiquette say. A character in Saikaku's *Five Women in Love* says: 'Between the pleasure one has in a man and that which one obtains with women there is no difference.' In the literature there is no mention of fellatio, intercrural coitus or even mutual masturbation, only of anal penetration and again, as in classical Greece, this form of copulation was hymned in praise.

The world of the Samurai was all about appearances. Jocho goes into great detail about how the Samurai should look: always carry rouge and powder with you, he advises; sometimes you find that you look pale, if so pause and apply rouge. In the Sengoku era Samurai would perfume their hair with incense and put on make-up before going into battle. They believed that even in death their faces should never look disagreeable. In warfare they were always accompanied by their adolescent lovers, teaching them the skills of battle and the code of honour.

It is interesting to note that in the Manchu front in the war between China and Japan (1880–83), a German living in Tokyo found the old Samurai spirit flourishing. Friends marched arm in arm and officers told of scenes 'where a soldier in love with another had fought at the risk of his own life, rushing willingly to the deadly spot'.

The Yuan and Ming Dynasties of China[29]

We have already seen that bisexuality flourished in Japan's great neighbour to the west. The Jesuits made their 'horrific' discoveries there too. Matteo Ricci, visiting Peking in 1583 and again in 1609-10, found that male prostitution was lawful and openly practised. In a puzzled and troubled tone, he wrote: 'there are public streets full of boys got up like prostitutes. And there are people who buy these boys and teach them to play music, sing and dance. And then, gallantly dressed and made up with rouge like women these miserable men are initiated into this terrible vice.'[30]

The Tang and Song Dynasties (220 to 581 BC) had continued in the same bisexual tradition as before (there are numerous stories of the favourites of Emperors), but this high point of Chinese culture was suddenly disrupted by the Mongols who swept across China and established the Yuan dynasty which lasted eighty-eight years. Opinion is divided over how popular homosexuality was among the Mongols. One Western visitor accused them of being 'addicted to Sodomy or Buggerie', yet there was also a law which had been passed before the conquest of China called the Great Yassa which invoked the death penalty for those guilty of both adultery and homosexuality. The fragments we have of the Yuan legal code in China do not mention the subject.

The dynasties that came after the Mongols were aware of the romantic homosexual tradition, of intrigue and romance, of sexual competition and social climbing, for it all still continued. The stories of the past, such as the shared peach and the cut sleeve, had become classics and had entered the language. With the advent of printing, reading became a popular pastime. But it is in humour, stories and anecdotes that we can catch a glimpse of how ordinary people live and think. Many of the stories reveal a common acceptance of bisexuality. 'A man got into bed on his wedding night and immediately seized his wife's buttocks and wished to do it that way,' begins one story. Another recounts how the husband's male lover moved freely within the family circle, even into the couple's bedroom. One day the wife's mother arrives and asks what relative the man is. 'He's my husband's husband,' the wife replies. Another joke tells of a virgin lad who was penetrated for the first time and found it very painful. Afterwards, 'He ran about wildly a few hundred steps, showing his arse to a passerby and asking. "Excuse me, sir, but look and tell me, please, is the prick still in there?"'

Ming sources reveal glimpses of homosexual love from a range of classes and regions. Though homosexuality was known as the 'southern custom' in the provinces of Fujian and Guangdong, it seems to have been popular in the north as well. In Fujian there was a form of male marriage, a ceremony in which the older man referred to the younger as an 'adoptive younger brother'. A carp, rooster and duck were sacrificed, and the men smeared each other's mouths with the blood and swore eternal loyalty. The ceremony concluded with a feast. The younger man moved into the older man's household and was treated as a son-in-law by the family.

It is clear from Chinese fiction that servants in the richer households were accustomed to perform sexual favours for their masters. In *The Golden Lotus*, the insatiable Ximen Quing, after countless bouts of copulation with wife and concubines, turns to his young male servant Shutong who obliges in return for various privileges. Shutong is later discovered by one of the master's concubines with a female servant, and runs away. One could hardly have a better example of rampant bisexuality, or of the prevalence of master–servant relationships, a subject barely touched upon so far. We see both elements in another erotic novel, *Prayer Mat of Flesh* by Li Yu, where a scholar is intent on having an operation to make his penis larger by grafting the penis from a dog on to his own. He has decided to return to his boy servant for a farewell visit after ignoring him in favour of women. The boy asks why he should return now and the scholar explains how large his penis will become and then says: 'The tiny gate of your rear chamber will then be quite impracticable. Now do you see why I have spoken of a farewell visit?' The boy agrees that his master's penis may be on the small side but it was in good shape, so why be in a hurry to operate? And the master explains that 'while men esteem dwarfs, women prefer giants'. The boy then asks if he might, after the operation, be allowed to come along and watch his master seduce women, because he could then seduce the maids. The master agrees and the boy in gratitude redoubles his efforts to make the last night pleasurable.

The frankness of Chinese literature allows us these insights into what the West has decreed is forbidden territory. Sexual happiness among couples is partly based on the accommodation, size and elasticity of organs and orifices. A thin, curved but long penis might well be a more satisfactory organ for sodomy than a short thick penis, for the former would massage the prostate gland without causing pain when entering the anus. The Chinese stories explore and invite such speculations and do it with gusto and humour.

VI

RENAISSANCE ENGLAND

Because church and state had banned 'deviant' sexuality, terrified of its pagan, heretical nature, people reacted in different ways when expressing their sexual identities. Some were racked by shame and guilt and wanted to hide their preferences; these on the whole seem to have been those men who desired other men and who thought they deserved society's condemnation because they were passive. Other men, who gloried in their natures, tended to be boy- or youth-lovers, for this was still considered acceptable.

As towns grew and urban centres became crowded, there was a proliferation of great houses with large staffs. Where servants from different households met, gossip and scandal revolving around sex and money were meat and drink. Also, the court at this time set the fashion and tone for the self-seeking and affluent, while life beyond the court tended to be a pale reflection of it.

MASTERS AND SERVANTS

In the large households of the gentry, where hundreds of servants

were accommodated, there was ample opportunity for sexual relationships between master and servant. Such exploitation was so
common, so much a part of the working conditions of the time,
that the authorities for the most part turned a blind eye. It was
only when a flagrant injustice was done that they were forced to
act, as in the case of Richard Finch, a London merchant, who was
called before the Middlesex Justices in 1609 charged with abusing
Nicholas Wheeler with whipcords when he was quite naked.[1]

Because the Justices of the Peace were keen to exclude illegitimate children from dependence on the poor rate, there was
pressure upon unmarried servants to find alternative sexual outlets.
Opportunities for homosexual relationships were, as we have
already noted, aided by cramming male servants together into
small rooms, sometimes even the same bed. Meredith Davy, a
labourer from Minehead, was charged in 1630 with having sexual
relations with his master's apprentice, John Vicary, with whom he
shared a bed. There was a witness in the room, another servant
who was woken when the boy cried out. Davy seems to have been
bewildered by the prosecution, 'denying that he ever used any
unclean action with the said boy'.[2] King James I was openly lecherous with his male favourites, so it is hardly surprising that there
was some confusion, and prosecutions seem to have been almost
arbitrary. It was a world where the gentry – in almost all cases –
got away with committing the crimes for which ordinary people
were punished.

Perhaps the most renowned master–servant relationships were
those in the household of Sir Francis Bacon. These were not so discreet either, for Lady Bacon wrote with asperity to her elder son,
Anthony, about her younger son, Francis: 'I pity your brother yet
as long as he pities not himself but keepeth that bloody Percy –
yea, as a coach companion and bed companion: a proud, profane
costly fellow, whose being about him I verily believe the Lord
God doth dislike.'[3] The master–servant relationship must have
been the only socially acceptable way in which two adult men
might continue to live together. Whether or not Percy genuinely
loved his lord and master we have no way of knowing. John

Aubrey later mentioned that Francis Bacon was a pederast, though a contemporary, Sir Simonds D'Ewes, writes of it also in his autobiography. D'Ewes was an antiquarian, Puritan, writer and moralist. In his diary entry for 3 May 1621 – the date of Bacon's censure by Parliament – D'Ewes vents his feelings:

> Would he not relinquish the practice of his most horrible and secret sinne of sodomie, keeping still one Godrick, a verie effeminate faced youth, to bee his catamite and bedfellow, although he had discharged the most of his other household servants: which was the moore to bee admired, because men generallie after his fall begann to discourse of that his unnaturall crime, which hee had practiced manie years, deserting the bedd of his ladie, which hee accounted, as the Italians and the Turkes doe, a poore and meane pleasure in respect of the other.[4]

Lady Bacon longed for grandchildren but was destined to be disappointed, for her elder son, as she must have known when she wrote to him about Francis, was also homosexual. In 1579 Anthony Bacon succeeded to his father's estates, but the following year he left for the Continent and did not return for twelve years. He settled in Montauban, was friendly with Henry of Navarre, Montaigne, Philip Sidney and Madame du Plessis-Mornay. But he upset the latter who took her revenge by accusing him of sodomy. As a priest, Benoist Grealou from Cahors, had been burnt alive for the same crime in 1563, this was a crisis. Some of the pages gave evidence: they said that the English gentleman spent hours, day and night, in his room with his pages. Isaac Burgades, they said, would mount a younger page, David Boysson, and they couldn't see anything wrong with it.[5] One of the lackeys, Barthelemy Sore, claimed that the master buggered all the boys and then bribed them with sweetmeats to keep quiet.[6] Henry of Navarre intervened, an appeal was made and the sentence quashed. Anthony returned to London and shared lodgings with Francis.

Percy was not the first servant to have a sexual arrangement with Francis Bacon, who seems to have had a particular fondness for young Welsh serving-men. His household in 1618 contained a total of seventy-five attendants, twenty-five of whom were gentlemen waiters. Bacon was so generous with money and other gifts that his servants flaunted their possessions and his behaviour began to be talked about. It is possibly this fact above all others which shocked society, for if servants started to ape their masters and were given an income to go with the lifestyle, the world would be turned upside down.

The satirists made much of the subject and the Earl of Rochester a little later says:

> There's a sweet, soft page of mine
> Does the trick worth forty wenches.

Somehow, if the sexual partner was a boy then the whole business could be laughed at; it was more or less like going with a girl, for boys were used as passive objects.

Bacon, however, in his work, referred to something else, something which disturbed society, for he wrote of the love shared by two men of similar age. (As we have seen, a passive older man was regarded as a freak.) In the essay 'Of Friendship', he uses the vocabulary of friendship to disguise his allusions to homosexuality: 'Nuptial love maketh mankind, friendly love perfecteth it', and, 'if a man have not a friend he may quit the stage'. It is said that this essay was written for Tobie Matthew who had appeared in a play at Gray's Inn in 1595 and who became Bacon's most intimate friend. In 'Of Marriage and the Single Life', he praises unmarried and childless men as being the best friends, masters and servants, and as being the creators of the best works with the greatest public merit. Finally, in 'Of Beauty', only male beauty is discussed.

Bacon married at the later age of forty-five and the marriage was childless. In his last posthumously published work, *New Atlantis*, he uses the phrase 'masculine love' and it is clear from the context that he is speaking of a male homosexual orientation. It is also clear that for the Renaissance audience the term 'masculine love' was not ambiguous, it simply denoted the male–male content of the love. Bacon idealised such love, separating it from 'libertinage' which referred to men who frequented courtesans, brothels and other dissolute places. What is more, he mentions masculine love in the same sentence as friendship of the most faithful and inviolate kind, implying that they can easily be mistaken for each other.[7]

EFFEMINACY AND APPAREL[8]

Bacon also linked a man's behaviour to the clothes he wore, and pointed out that a man, 'if he labour too much to express (good forms) he shall lose their grace, which is to be natural and unaffected'. How did, one wonders, men inclined towards homosexuality recognise each other? In what way did Francis Bacon chose his servants? As men at court went in for sumptuous dress, jewellery and make-up, in what sense was the term 'effeminate' used at that time?

'Masculinity' was recognised and defined by sumptuous display, living up to the sartorial expectations of the crown which, in Elizabeth I's reign, were immense. Such displays did not decline in the least in her successor's reign, for James I was homosexual and enjoyed masculine beauty. Critics of the court accused it of vice, luxury and effeminacy, criticism which fuelled the rise of Puritanism. The Puritans' credo owed much of its strength to rural ideology which stated that to follow the latest fashion was as effeminate as excessive display. Defenders of the court ethos argued for a morality of masculine display which made it essential for high expenditure to be the prerogative of nobility. They justified this as magnificence not extravagance, as manliness not effeminacy.

It was believed that dress and manners were not mere externals but were manifestations of internal worth and graceful supplements to nobility. A sign of inward goodness was outward beauty, just as appearance denoted status, silk and satin were noble, flannel and fustian humble. The higher the status, the richer the fabric, but effeminacy *was* found in over-extravagance, in lack of balance and taste:

a man must not embellish himself like a woman, for his adornments will then contradict his person, as I see some men do, who put curls in their hair and beards with a curling iron and who apply so much make-up to their faces, necks and hands that it would be unsuitable for any young wench, even for a harlot who is more anxious to hawk her wares and sell them for a price.

So wrote Giovanni della Casa in *Galateo* (1558). Elsewhere, the same author links immoderate dress with homosexuality: 'Your garments should not be extremely fancy or ornate, so that no one can say that you are wearing Ganymede's hose.' Effeminacy involved using the symbols of bravery and heroism in the wrong manner, over-stating, embellishing in excess. Men should apply make-up, but not too much. Casa points out that James I advised his son, Prince Henry, to be 'moderate in your raiment', for there should be courtesy in dress as well as in manners.

Sumptuary laws were a guide, reaching their zenith under Elizabeth I. No one under the degree of earl was permitted to wear cloth of gold, silver, or tinselled satin; no one under the degree of husbandman was allowed to wear hose made of cloth costing more than two shillings per yard. It was a royal prerogative to regulate the display of social distinctions.

In this context it is interesting to see how Christopher Marlowe used clothes to communicate homosexual passion in his writing. Marlowe (1564–93) was killed in a brawl in a tavern at Deptford just before reaching thirty, and it is astonishing that he left such a large corpus of verse and plays, though sadly many are unfinished. Perhaps his most famous line – 'Come live with me, and be my love' – was said by a shepherd to a lad. The poem is shaped by Virgil's second Eclogue, which was about Corydon persuading Alexis, the boy he loves, to come and live with him by promising him gifts. The shepherd promises the boy clothes – a cap, smock, woollen gown – which gradually become more exotic: lined slippers with gold buckles, a belt decorated with coral and amber. No doubt these adornments would have been frowned upon by both Casa and Bacon as excessive, but Marlowe was a master of exuberant decoration. He contradicted every tenet of good taste that we have explored above.

In *Dido, Queen of Carthage* Jupiter promises Ganymede peacock feathers and jewels, but Ganymede wants more in return for his sexual favours. Venus calls Ganymede 'that female wanton boy'. In Marlowe's work we constantly find a crossing of genders. In *Hero and Leander*, Neptune mistakes the naked Leander for Ganymede and almost drowns him while caressing him. The god gives him 'gaudy toys to please his eye', bracelets and more jewels, but Leander tells Neptune, 'You are deceived, I am no woman, I'. He must have been used to this error, though:

> Some swore he was a maid in man's attire,
> For in his looks were all that men desire.

Marlowe rhapsodises about Leander's naked beauty: his uncut hair rivals the Golden Fleece; the moon goddess yearns to be in his arms; his body is as straight as Circe's wand, a bewitching instrument of seduction; Jove could lap nectar from Leander's hand; his shoulder is as white as ivory; the immortal fingers of some unknown god have left their imprint upon his spine which is 'the heavenly path' to the paradise of his behind; his eyes, cheeks and lips are lovelier than those of Narcissus and even the celibate Hippolytus could not have resisted falling in love with him. What is more, he is no Narcissus, for this wondrous beauty is entirely unaware of his own magnificence.

Though Marlowe in his translation of one of Ovid's Elegies writes 'Love is a naked boy' (X.15), most of the boys in his works are adorned in fancy dress and jewels. Sometimes they are in drag, and they are certainly androgynous. In *Edward II* Gaveston plans some Italian masques to entertain the king and describes:

> Sometime a lovely boy in Dian's shape,
> With hair that gilds the water as it glides,
> Crownets of pearl about his naked arms,
> And in his sportful hands an olive tree,
> To hide those parts which men delight to see,
> Shall bathe him in a spring.

PEDERAST OR SODOMITE?

As we have noted, up to around the thirteenth century the idea of bisexuality was alive and well. Then church and state began to destroy it. Men became aware that their bisexual nature was being erased, or redefined as either sodomy or pederasty, leaving them with no name for what they felt. The textual evidence of both Marlowe and Bacon suggests that Marlowe was content to use classical imagery, while Bacon used the term 'masculine love'. There is other evidence that boy-love was acceptable because it reflected ancient Greece and an era of philosophy and idealism, while sodomy became even more despised. That the two became confused was inevitable.

Richard Barnfield (1574–1627) published *The Affectionate Shepherd* in 1594, a pastoral that owed much to Marlowe's 'Passionate Shepherd'. Nevertheless, Barnfield was rather more explicit than Marlowe; there is no question here of what gender the beloved is.

> But I began to rue the unhappy sight
> Of that faire Boy that had my hart intangled;
> Cursing the Time, the Place, the sense, the sin;
> I came, I saw, I viewd, I slipped in.

The homoerotic voice is powerful and undisguised, especially with the punning Caesarian allusion.[9] Yet it is not without the Renaissance legal rhetoric on the subject of sodomy, in that sin is not mentioned once but thrice.

If it be sinne to love a lovely Lad;
Oh then sinne I, for whom my soule is sad.

Some scholars have argued that this is nothing but a literary exercise; indeed, Barnfield himself printed a disclaimer saying that such a love between a shepherd and a boy was a fault which he could not excuse. Barnfield's commonplace book reveals a robustly pornographic and heterosexual being (which, of course, does not preclude bisexuality). However, the sexual inclinations of the writer are almost irrelevant, for the fact remains that a pederast or boy-lover was presented as a romantic figure which readers would recognise and some would relate to. This suggests that such figures were a recognised part of society.

Certainly the boy prostitute in Thomas Middleton's satire, *Ingling Pyander* (1599) ('ingle' was slang for tart) was familiar:

> . . . sometimes he jets it like a Gentleman
> Otherwhiles much like a wanton Courtesan
> But truth to tell a man or woman whether,
> I cannot say shes excellent in ether.
> But if Report may certifie a truth,
> She's nether or ether, but a Cheating youth.

The 'lovely smiling Parragon . . . of Bewtie' was in 'Nymphes attire', unlike in Florence or Venice where the female tarts dressed as boys to entice their customers. The author loved this creature whom he calls Pyander: 'Never was boy so pleasing to the hart,/As was Pyander for a womans part.'[10] No doubt this too, was a literary exercise, this time in the mode of Juvenal, but one doubts that the subject would have been chosen had there not been a public eager to read it.

In Nicholas Udall's play *Ralph Roister Doister* (1541) the plot revolves around Ralph's love of Dame Custance which is constantly being upset by the mischief of Matthew Merrygreek. Yet on two occasions this last character bemoans the fact that he is not a woman and cannot marry Ralph himself. As Udall in that same

year had been charged with sodomy, which ended his head-
mastership of Eton, it would be interesting to know whether the
sequence in the play got extra audience participation – cheers or
boos – but we have no playgoer's account. Udall was set free after
a year and even became headmaster of Westminster, so it is
thought strings in high places were pulled with success, for the
charge could have incurred the death penalty and would have done
so for the first time.

Time and time again we have society condemning the passive
partner in sodomy, but as contemporary homosexuals well know,
men seldom chose to be either exclusively active or exclusively
passive. They may have a highly charged sexual relationship without penetrative sex. In Bacon's emphasis on the love and devotion
of friends, one detects relationships which are far richer than those
restricted to physical release. Bacon is one of the first historical
figures that we know of who seems to desire an equal relationship
with an adult man (not feasible for him as his partners were his servants) which contains great emotional content. He must have been
appalled at the violent crudities and the obscene jokes that always
attended a crime of sodomy, though, one suspects, he would have
been mollified and reassured by the king's sentimental attachments
to his young men.

Though a law was passed in 1290 decreeing the death penalty for
anyone convicted of sorcery, apostasy, heresy or sodomy, it was
not until 1533 that a statute under Henry VIII made buggery committed with mankind or beast a felony punishable by hanging.
There seems to have been a sub-text to this statute at that time.
The king was in the midst of fighting the church and wished to
weaken it, especially by taking its property. Sodomy was rife
among the clergy and especially in the monasteries. By making it a
felony under secular law he took it out of the realm of the ecclesiastical courts, so a conviction meant that the felon lost property
to the crown. When Mary ascended the throne in 1553, it was repealed, giving jurisdiction back to the ecclesiastical courts. But in
1563 the Act was revived by Elizabeth who wanted it known that
she was in the Protestant tradition and her father's heir.

There were, however, very few prosecutions. The Essex Quarter Sessions for 1556–1680 do not show a single case of sodomy, while the Essex Assize records for 1560–1680 show only one.[11] It is perhaps astonishing that there are not more, for homophobic feelings must have been encouraged by much of the popular literature. A didactic poem on the Creation and early history of the world occupied an honoured place in many households next to a copy of the Bible. It was written by a French Huguenot, a trusted counsellor of Henry of Navarre, Guillaume de Salluste du Bartas (1544–90), and its language and emotion is crude, yet because of its Protestant message it had a huge success in its English translation by Josua Sylvester. This is du Bartas on the end of Sodom and Gomorrah:

> For while (O horror) in the stinking mire
> Of his foul lust he lies a lightning flash
> Him and his love at once to dust doth dash:
> The abhored bed is burnt, and they as well
> Coupled in plague as sin are sent to Hell.[12]

It is difficult to imagine a society in which this vigorous hyperbole was an integral part of the culture alongside the romantic lushness of Marlowe's plays. But then it is possible that the readers of du Bartas would have considered that all those who frequented the playhouses were in moral sin anyway. Certainly the theatres were known as places where you could find boys for pleasure. And the plays themselves, where boys played women's roles, must have been a source of titillation, *double entendre* and comedy, much of which we miss now when the parts are played by women. How, one wonders, could a boy play the splendour and passion of Cleopatra? Perhaps in that question we are missing the reality of bisexuality which was still largely acceptable in the Renaissance. Certainly, no one expresses it better than Shakespeare in his sequence of Sonnets.

SHAKESPEARE AND THE SONNETS[13]

Published in 1609, the first 126 sonnets are love poems to a beautiful youth, while the rest are devoted to a dark mistress. But a close reading reveals a far more detailed story, and the sequence can be broken up into phases.

Sonnets 1 to 19 praise the rare and ravishing beauty of a youth and urge him to procreate so as to save that beauty for posterity, though at Sonnet 15 the poet changes to the thought that his beauty will become immortal through the verse. Sonnet 18 ends:

> So long as men can breathe or eyes can see,
> So long lives this, and this gives life to thee.

Shakespeare never once employs the first person, but from Sonnets 10 to 14 there can be detected a state of emergent love which at last is declared in Sonnet 20:

> the Master Mistress of my passion,
> A woman's gentle hart but not acquainted.

Few lines could express so succinctly the idea of bisexuality. 'Acquainted' carries with it a pun on the noun 'quaint', slang for the pudenda, so a paraphrase might be, 'a woman emotionally but not physically, a man capable of entrancing both men and women'.[14] Freud, speaking of classical Greece and writing of the love of boys, observed: 'The sexual object is a kind of reflection of the subject's own bisexual nature.'

But there is a problem in Sonnet 20. Shakespeare has a mistress but he is 'prick'd out' for women; the speaker's passion has been evoked but there seems no acceptable mode of expression. At the end he offers non-sensual love, but this is temporary, for either the passion will subside or the friends will engage in physical love. If we leap to Sonnet 52 it is clear that there now exists a sexual relationship between Shakespeare and the youth; the former is 'as the rich, whose blessed key/can bring him to his sweet up-locked treasure', but he will not survey his treasure 'every hour' for fear of 'blunting the fine point of seldom pleasure'. If we refer to a dictionary of slang we find that 'sweet' refers to sexual intimacy and 'treasure' to genitalia, while 'point' can refer to the glans or the whole penis. A reading of the whole sonnet sequence with reference to Eric Partridge's study *Shakespeare's Bawdy* is illuminating.

Where sexual passion exists, so inevitably does jealousy; the sonnets are riddled with it. In Sonnets 33 to 35, the lover reacts bitterly to his friend's sexual intimacy with someone else. Sonnets 40 to 42 speak of a possible intimacy with a woman, the same woman to whom the poet is attached. Sonnets 48, 49, 57, 58, 61 and 69 deal with the poet's anxieties about loss of love. Sonnets 76 to 86 speak of a triangle, which includes Shakespeare's competitor, another male and a poet. In Sonnets 87 to 96 the lover is haunted by the thought of losing the beloved. In Sonnets 109 to 112 and 117 to 120, it is now Shakespeare who is guilty and seeks forgiveness from his friend. Sonnets 133 to 144 speak of the mistress and the triangle that involves her, the poet and the friend.

Shakespearian scholars have argued for years about whether or not the sonnets contain a saga of homosexual love. Their uneasiness over this subject was summed up by W.H. Auden in 1964: 'it won't do just yet to admit that the top Bard was in the homintern.' It seems incredible that there should be such fudging of what is surely so obvious. Some scholars, and Auden was one of them in his introduction to the Signet edition of the sonnets, refer to a 'mystery rather than an aberration' and a mystical vision of Eros. G. Wilson Knight considers it a matter of 'homosexual idealism' by which he means a 'strong sexual impulse' wholly divorced from 'physical vice'. Scholars have tied themselves in knots attempting to avoid the conclusion that Shakespeare had a loving, physical relationship with an unknown young man of excessive beauty (there is no textual evidence to point to him being of noble birth).

The sonnets contain an over-abundance of possible meanings, they are full of puns, there is a constant intermingling of hetero-

and homoerotic longings. Unfettered by strictures of gender, the imagery flows on, lush and delicate, witty and contradictory. Surely this reflects the paradox of bisexuality, a paradox that Western society has never willingly accepted. Auden was possibly right to say what he did, but wrong in that he lacked the courage to reveal Shakespeare's bisexuality himself.

TWO KINGS

Henry III of France and James I of England were both contemporaries of Shakespeare. The two monarchs were also bisexual, though history likes to remember them as notorious perverts.

Henry (1551–89), Duc d'Anjou until 1574, was one of three sons of Henry II and Catherine de Medici. He was his mother's favourite and a brilliant soldier. In command of the royal armies, at the age of eighteen he defeated the two Huguenot leaders at Montcontour in 1569. Five years later, on his way to his coronation, he stopped in Venice expressly to enjoy a night with Veronica Franco, the most famous courtesan of her day. He is largely remembered for his extravagance. He loved ceremonies, balls, fêtes and surrounded himself with a host of 'Mignons', handsome young men dressed in the height of fashion. Henry had a mistress and was said to be in love with the Princess de Conde, but his formidable mother arranged a political marriage for him which failed to produce an heir. Syphilis brought into the Valois line by his grandfather Francis I was thought to be the reason why the three grandsons failed to procreate, though one of Henry's younger brothers also had romantic relationships with boys.

The Mignons have been represented as a group of effeminate swaggering dilettantes – their fashions and manners were much copied by young men in England – but Henry was keen to arrange grand marriages for them all and most of them had wives and mistresses as well as male friendships that may or may not have also been sexual. The Mignons obviously took delight in shocking their contemporaries. A diarist of the age, Pierre de L'Estoile, wrote in 1576: 'These pretty mignons wore their hair pomaded, artificially curled and recurled, flowing back over their little velvet bonnets, like those of whores in a bordello, and the ruffs of their starched linen shirts were a half foot long.'[15]

There is no doubt that the king was strongly emotionally attached to some of them. (St Megrin was killed in a duel and buried in Henry's own church, nicknamed the 'temple de Mignons'.) In 1589 a fanatical Jacobin friar gained admission to the king and fatally stabbed him. He was succeeded by the Protestant Henry of Navarre who renounced his religion to become Henry IV.

The end of James I of England was not violent, though his beginnings were. His father, Darnley, had been murdered by a gang of drunken Scottish louts. His mother, Mary, Queen of Scots, had been exiled and he was crowned king when he was one year old. Starved of affection as an infant, he craved love all his life and became entirely malleable in the hands of anyone who offered it. At the age of thirteen he fell in love with his cousin, Esme Stuart, Lord of Aubigny, who was a thirty-three-year-old French courtier. But three years later he too was exiled for suspicion of playing the Catholic cause.

In 1590 James married Anne of Denmark, a Protestant princess, and dutifully produced heirs which strengthened his right to the English throne to which he succeeded in 1603. Anne had a separate household at Somerset House and James had a series of favourites, handsome young men who quickly became 'gentlemen of the Bedchamber'. All were ennobled by James and all made their fortunes. Several were married off to heiresses, but some fell in love with women and married of their own volition, causing great unhappiness to the king. The most famous of James's favourites was George Villiers, who became Duke of Buckingham. James nicknamed him Steenie because of his resemblance to St Stephen in a stained-glass window in the royal chapel, while George referred to the king as Dad. We have the love letters which they wrote to each other over a ten-year period. The king signed himself not only

'Dad', but also 'husband' while he addressed Buckingham as 'my sweet child and wife'. Nor was their love affair discreet, far from it. A contemporary, Francis Osborne, wrote: 'In wanton looks and wanton gestures they exceeded any part of womankind. The kissing them after so lascivious a mode in public and upon the theatre, as it were, of the world, prompted many to imagine some things done in the tyring house that exceed my expression no less than they do my experience.'[16]

This relationship provoked a debate in the Privy Council when John Oglander testified in 1617 that: 'The King is wondrous passionate, a lover of his favourites beyond the love of men to women.' James defended himself, readily confessing that he loved 'those dear to me more than other men', and ending his statement by saying: 'Jesus Christ did the same, and therefore I cannot be blamed. Christ had his son John, and I have my George.' Yet the whole court witnessed daily the lascivious nature of their relationship, and every morning a troop of handsome young louts from the street were scrubbed, primped and curled, then led around the throne to amuse the king. Parliament felt uneasy and showed it, so James felt obliged to dissolve Parliament altogether in 1621 and thereafter lost control of his kingdom.

There was plainly one rule for the court and one for the rest of the land. Prosecutions for sodomy did not stop when James was king. In 1607, a barber, John Slater, was charged with sodomising the son of a neighbour. In 1613, Alban Cooke of Hoxton was charged with buggery with a man under twenty years of age. And it would seem that there was a male brothel in Hoxton, owned by Queen Elizabeth's cousin, Lord Hunsdon: satirist and playwright John Marston wrote:

> At Hoxton now his monstrous love he feasts
> for there he keeps a bawdy house of beasts.

Even more extraordinary was the statement that James himself made in *Basilicon Doron*, his defence of absolute monarchy: 'So is there some horrible crimes that yee are bound in conscience neuer to forgiue: such as Witch-craft, willful murther, Incest (especially within the degrees of Consanguinitie), Sodomie, poisoning and false coine.' Obviously James did not connect the crime of sodomy with the love-making he and Steenie got up to. Or else he was blatantly lying. This is a huge problem in our understanding of the past and my only explanation, explored earlier, is that he genuinely accepted two opposing concepts. This makes James's attitude not singular at all, but similar to that of most, if not all, Renaissance males.

WHO WAS THE SODOMITE?[17]

Where did the king see this horrible crime of 'Sodomie'? Indeed, where did society see the sodomites, and were king and society in agreement in their detection of them? The satires of Ben Jonson, Edward Guilpin, Richard Brathwaite, John Donne and Thomas Middleton all contain similar pictures of the sodomite, who is a young man-about-town with his mistress on one arm and his catamite on the other. He is indolent, extravagant and debauched. The vice for the satirists belonged to the gentry. It came, so Edward Coke said, from 'pride, excess of diet, idleness, and contempt of the poor'. George Turbervile thought that it came from drunkenness, 'such filthy sin/ensues a drunken head', while the Puritan writer John Rainolds thought it was a sin to which 'men's natural corruption and viciousness is prone'. William Bradford, the governor of the Plymouth colony, wondering why sodomy and buggery had broken out, reasoned that it was 'our corrupt natures, which are hardly bridled, subdued and mortified'. All of these writers were not describing an abnormal predisposition, they were describing basic, undisciplined human nature, the world of fleshly delights without the transmutation of God's word. This was the climate of opinion which gave birth to puritanism.

The puritanical hatred of the theatre is explained by claims that the theatre was a haunt of sodomites. Edward Guilpin wrote that a sodomite is someone who is 'at every play and every night sups with his ingles'. Philip Stubbes, a pamphleteer, wrote that after the play is over 'every mate sorts to his mate, everyone brings another homeward of their way very friendly, and in their secret conclaves covertly play the Sodomites or worse'. The Puritans would not have countenanced the transvestism of the boy-players, which also inevitably stimulated an erotic reaction in the audience. There is every reason to believe that the boy-players were adored, loved and lusted after as favoured catamites. In Ben Jonson's play *Poetaster*, the elder Ovid, on learning that his son is to become an actor, replies: 'What? Shall I have my son a stager now, an ingle for players?' The theatre was bound up in the Puritan critic's mind with a hatred of the court and its influence.

The sodomite, then, seems to have been a young debauchee. What is more, we have a graphic example of one in the Earl of Castlehaven, one Mervyn Touchet, twelfth Lord Audley, who was tried in 1631 on a count of rape and two counts of sodomy. The trial is important because it set a legal precedent which lasted well into the twentieth century. But the case also illustrates very clearly that it is not so much the type of sexual act which outrages society as the affront to taboos about class.

At the age of twenty-four the Earl, who already had an estate at Fonthill, inherited a fortune from his father. He then married an heiress and begot a son, James. When his first wife died he married another heiress, Lady Anne Stanley, widow of Lord Chandos. They arranged a marriage between Lord Audley's son, James, and Lady Anne's daughter as a way of keeping the wealth in the family. The day after their wedding Castlehaven called upon each of his manservants to enter the room and to expose his member to Lady Anne: 'he forced me to look upon them and to commend those that had the longest.'[18] Three manservants were thereafter brought into the marital bed – Henry Skipworth, Giles Broadway and Amptil – and sexual relations occurred between Castlehaven and the servants and between the servants and Lady Anne, who was forced by her husband to endure the servants' assault which nevertheless sometimes failed. These servants were all given large salaries by Castlehaven.

What is singular about the case is that Castlehaven insisted that his wife indulge in what he was enjoying. His behaviour would have gone unremarked if he had limited his sexuality to his male servants, and the trial would not have occurred at all if he had not involved his wife and then her daughter. The trial became notorious as an example of sodomite behaviour, yet Castlehaven was acting within a heterosexual context. He obviously liked to demean and humiliate his wife, and was a voyeur in the heterosexual act. The details remind us more of the literature of the Marquis de Sade (who flourished 150 years later) than the life of a closet homosexual.

Castlehaven insisted that his step-daughter, the twelve-year-old Elizabeth Brydges, lay with Henry Skipworth (by far his favourite youth) in the presence of himself and other servants. Twice Castlehaven had to apply oil to Skipworth's member in order to make penetration possible. But it was the wish behind this act of rape which so shocked and horrified Castlehaven's peers, for the Earl wanted his step-daughter to be the mother of Skipworth's progeny and for them to inherit the estates and titles. He was, in fact, disinheriting his son's issue and his own.

Not surprisingly, in 1630, when his son James had come into his majority, he brought these facts and their orgies to the attention of the courts. Six weeks later Castlehaven was arrested and confined in the Tower of London. To intensify the alienation from his peers, Castlehaven was also suspected of Roman Catholic allegiances and this further inflamed the prejudice against him. Some historians see his trial as a virulent reaction to the court of James I and an indirect attack upon his son, Charles I, who was considered to be sympathetic to Rome. It must also be stressed that an early prosecution of a nobleman, Walter Lord Hungerford, in 1540 on charges of sodomy with a servant, also had a treasonable context; Hungerford had ordered his chaplains to prophesy the date of the king's death and whether he would defeat his enemies.

At the Castlehaven trial, his servants testified to what had happened and went into details of where orgasms took place. One said that the Earl had emitted between his thighs rather than penetrating him. Therefore, technically, this was not sodomitical rape.

Castlehaven protested that the servant was incriminating himself, was a participant, so could not be a legal witness against him. But the Lord Chief Justice disagreed, claiming that he could be a legal witness until he was convicted of a felony, otherwise such truth of this nature could never be discovered. This became a legal precedent which led to the convictions of numerous sodomites and later homosexuals over the next few centuries.

Castlehaven's wife and step-daughter also testified against him and he was found guilty of rape. He had held his wife down while one of the servants penetrated her. Lord Coventry of Aylesborough told the Earl that 'having honour and fortune to leave behind you, you would have the impious and spurious offspring of a harlot to inherit'. It was this that really stuck in the peer's gullet. It is interesting to note that not only was Skipworth called a harlot but his offspring were accused of impiety. Thus, in Lord Coventry's eyes, the lower orders could taint religion as well as dishonouring class.

The Attorney-General, Sir Robert Heath, described Castlehaven's crimes as 'pestiferous and pestilential', which, if not punished 'will draw from heaven heavy judgements upon this kingdom'. He went on to accuse Castlehaven of prevaricating with his religion, being a Protestant in the morning and a Papist in the afternoon.

Castlehaven was also found guilty of sodomy. Only fifteen of the twenty-six jurors thought him guilty, but a majority verdict was enough to convict. Castlehaven was beheaded, then his servants were also charged with rape and sodomy based on those testimonies they had given against Castlehaven. They were hung at Tyburn.

Many of Castlehaven's servants had been plucked out of the lower classes, only too ready, one imagines, to exchange penury for life as a servant to the earl. Vagabonds were to prove a growing problem within society. William Harrison in 1577 thought that there were over 10,000 roaming the countryside, but this is considered to be a conservative estimate. The Lord Mayor of London in 1594 suggested that there were at least 12,000 beggars in London alone. By 1602 it was thought the number had grown to 30,000.

Known as 'masterless men', vagabonds were a sign of great social change. Roaming the country in search of work, often evicted from their land, they were rejects of a society in which the population was rising and which was in economic transformation. The authorities feared them, for they belonged to no parish, church, or social stratum, and were a mob that could not be relied on unless paid:

> under the surface stability of rural England, then, the vast placid open fields which catch the eye, was the seething mobility of forest squatters, itinerant craftsmen and building labourers, unemployed men and women seeking work, strolling players, minstrels and jugglers, pedlars and quack doctors, gypsies, vagabonds and tramps.[19]

It has been suggested that this underworld, which was mostly male, which was ever-changing, absorbing wandering children and orphans, fuelled both the army and navy, provided settlers for Ireland and the New World, and in its sexual practices was largely sodomitical. This has to be speculation, though contemporaries Thomas Dekker (in *The Bellman of London*, 1608) and Thomas Harman (in *The Fraternity of Vagabonds*, 1575) both mention it.

VII

PURITANISM
AND THE RISE
OF THE WORK ETHIC

In the second half of the seventeenth century there began a vast shift in the sensibilities of Western society which started in England. In an astonishingly short time this fuelled a virulent homophobia, encouraged by the authorities. These social attitudes have moulded twentieth-century concepts of sex and gender so it is important to understand the various forces at work at that time.

THE ZEALOUS REFORMERS

The idea that all sexual expression outside Christian marriage must be repressed was reinforced by Protestantism. The most influential reformers – Luther, Calvin and Zwingli – attacked Roman Catholicism on three fronts: its ecclesiastical structure – the relationship of the pope with the bishops and the church councils; its theology; and its morality. And it was sexual morality which, naturally enough, most concerned the reformers. They disagreed on celibacy for priests, who were hardly renowned for it anyway, because they believed it encouraged homosexuality. They wanted to present sex within marriage in a more positive light, keen for people to see it as a blessing bestowed by the Creator and not as a flaw in human nature engendered by sin.[1]

Their ideas about Christian marriage, once put into effect, would in a very short time begin to strengthen the ideological and social power marriage held within society. This, in turn, disparaged all forms of homosexuality. The reformers detested the idea of clandestine marriage by consent alone, they wanted a marriage to be legally binding only if it had parental consent; all other marriages became invalid without this. They also rejected the idea that marital sex must be only for procreation. Martin Luther (1483–1546) spurned St Jerome's condemnation of the married man who burned with lust for his wife.

John Calvin (1509–64) thought as the early church fathers did that celibacy was superior to marriage, but any deviation outside marriage was treated as a sin. Marital sex was virtuous in his eyes as long as the couple observed modesty and propriety, though he thought some acts inside the marital bed, such as *coitus interruptus*, were monstrous because they extinguished the hope of new life.

On the whole, the reformers agreed broadly that sex within marriage was a good thing, for it symbolised and embodied conjugal affection. This was an astonishingly new idea which, as it percolated down into communities attempting to live a devout life, was to relieve a great burden of anxiety and dread. Such a new idea played its part in binding communities together, though it was slow to take hold in society at large. We see its repercussions on same-sex male loving only in the eighteenth century.

The reformers, however, were far more ferocious in their attitude to extra-marital sex than their opponents, the Catholics, had ever been. Fornication, Luther declared, was evil, bad for the soul, body, family, fortune and honour. Huldreich Zwingli (1484–1531) in Zurich also recommended stiff penalties for all sexual licence. Calvin believed that the sight of a harlot would provoke people into reforming their own lives. Many of their followers were even more zealous, and considered adultery and prostitution as stemming from serious mental and spirital flaws. One reformer – Bucer (1491–1551) – argued that the civil authorities should punish adultery by death. In the sixteenth century in Strasbourg, men were drowned for bigamy, beheaded or burnt for incest and sent to the stake for sodomy. It was firmly believed that if the civil authorities did not punish the sinners, then God would do it instead. There was a cautionary tale told by Samuel Saxey of the couple who kept an adulterous rendezvous at St Bride's church when a fire broke out and burned them to death.[2] The same author found much spiritual exaltation in the fact that a prostitute was hung for adultery. In this climate it was unlikely that the reformers would have any understanding of or compassion for deviant sexual behaviour; Catholic condemnation was merely reinforced by new ethical zeal. From the evidence of prosecutions, two new aspects of deviance begin to appear, transvestism and lesbianism. These we will look at later. But it is important to examine Calvinism more closely, for it was to have a huge influence in the colonies of the New World and remained for centuries a living ethic at the heart of society. In fact, it is alive and flourishing now, and still fuels modern homophobia.

Calvin believed that God's plan for mankind's salvation lay within biblical text, but because the Bible was a mystery to the illiterate and full of obscurity and enigmas for everyone else, he began a scheme whereby ministers appointed by the Congregation would interpret biblical text according to Calvinist dicta. He transformed the city of Geneva into a theocracy; taverns were abolished, card-playing, dancing and the theatre prohibited, the Sabbath kept inviolate. He effectively got rid of all his opponents, who were exiled or fled, for Calvin was thorough in rooting out sin and bringing the unbelievers to trial, using the death penalty without compunction. In the four years between 1542 and 1546, forty-eight persons were executed, thirty-four of them for witchcraft.[3] Between 1555 and 1678 there were sixty-two prosecutions for sodomy and thirty executions.[4] After such a blood-bath, few opponents remained, but Geneva prospered nevertheless because it took in refugees fleeing Catholic persecution in the Low Countries, France and Spain.

Calvinism simplified morality and gave its believers great hope. Calvin believed that the Fall of Man had made people so deeply corrupt that their only hope was the grace of God, but God saved only the elect, the new Israelites. The elect themselves would come to realise their favoured state and act accordingly, choosing to do the right things. The spiritual part of man, his soul, would learn to control the flesh, the body, which was always inclined to do wrong. A new emphasis was placed upon masturbation by all the reformers; they claimed it was akin to sodomy and ought to merit more severe penalties than fornication or adultery. Even spontaneous orgasm was wrong and should be fended off. People should lie very still if they felt an orgasm about to come and pray to God to save them from any pleasure.

Calvin maintained that the damned would do wrong anyway because they could not help it, having already been rejected by God for his salvation. But the new Israelites could always be recognised by their demeanour, modest clothes, their standards and upright life, their observance of the Sabbath, their Bible-reading and their participation in the sacrament. How Geneva must have been transformed in those years when Calvin ruled like a monarch. Among the Protestant communities, Calvinists felt themselves to be the spiritual aristocracy, and they exported their ideas to Scotland and New England where they flourished more or less intact.

The result was a work ethic of industry and self-improvement, of pride in the home and family, of a simple morality where problems were solved by prayer, self-sacrifice and abstinence, where this life was seen as a passing phase to be lived through in fear that the gift of paradise might be taken away by a bad deed or thought. Those not of the faith were considered to be damned unless they could be converted and saved; violent suspicion flared to life at the impact of strangers or alien customs; judgements were quickly made and enforced; compassion for others outside the fold was not given but stifled because it was not required. It is a world we in Western society all recognise, for it is closely connected with our cultural roots and has carved out many of our institutional, moral and legal structures. It is a world which has repressed homosexual expression and punished it cruelly in the last five hundred years.

For by the end of the seventeeth century, Protestant Puritans 'had resurrected some of the most draconian provisions of medieval sex law and enshrined them in statutes and casuistic manuals where they lingered until the second half of the twentieth century.'[5]

THE PURITANS

For a short time the Calvinist principle held total power in England. During the Interregnum (1649–60) the Puritans imposed a restrictive morality upon the land. Theatres, alehouses, brothels and gambling houses were all banned along with the traditional village sports of cock-fighting and bear-baiting. Adultery and sodomy were made capital offences, and fornication carried a penalty of three months' imprisonment. Though Cromwell, unhappy over what he felt was increasing immorality, wanted more prosecutions, there seem to have been few attempts to put such punitive measures into practice. A few years before the Interregnum, in 1643, the Reverend John Wilson, vicar of Arlington, had confessed to buggery with many of his parishioners and, what is more, 'openly affirmed that Buggery is no sinne'. Wilson was not prosecuted but only deprived of his benefice.[6] In 1640, John Atherton, Bishop of Waterford and Lismore, was hung in Dublin together with his lover, John Child.

In Puritan England there was a spirit of revolt among people angry at the dearth of entertainments, and it is possible that many scandals were discreetly ignored. Certainly the prosecutions bear out such an idea, for they concentrated on blasphemy, Sabbath-breaking and fornication, the last because of the threat to the parish of the cost of illegitimate children. But Puritan rule was short-lived, unlike in the colonies where it took root. Cases like those of Bishop Atherton and the Earl of Castlehaven were made much of in the next century, when pamphlets about them were written and sold to encourage the rising tide of homophobia.

In New England the Puritans were a miscellaneous group of Quakers, Presbyterians, Congregationalists and Calvinists. They were in broad agreement that God had given man the Bible to direct his thinking, for it contained all wisdom and the necessary guidance for life. Hence, sodomy was regarded as a particularly heinous crime, bestiality was thought of as a horrific sin (the animal being burnt alive in front of the sinner before they were hanged)★ and both oral–genital sex and masturbation were also thought to be dangerously sinful.

The very first English settlement at Jamestown proclaimed the death penalty for sodomy, adultery and rape in 1607. Sir Thomas Dale, Governor of Virginia from 1611 and 1616, made it clear that chastity was a 'virtue much commended in a souldier'.

In Virginia in 1624, Richard Cornish, a shipmaster, was executed for forcing a young man to have sexual relations, but this is another controversial case, for his brother strongly denied it had ever happened. Afterwards, the two men were pilloried, had their ears cut off and were indentured for protesting that Cornish was innocent. This whole case may have been engineered by the authorities who had an interest in getting rid of Cornish.

In 1637, John Alexander and Thomas Roberts were found 'guilty of lude behaviour and unclean carriage one with another, by often spending their seed one upon another'.[7] Alexander was sentenced to be whipped, burnt in the shoulder with a hot iron and banished from the colony. Roberts, his indentured servant, was whipped but not burnt or banished. The sentence was lenient because no penetration was proved.

William Plaine, a married man, was executed in New Haven in 1646, for sodomising two men in England and corrupting 'a great part of the youth of Guildford by masturbations . . . above a hundred times', but what seems to have outraged the authorities most was that Plaine questioned the existence of God.[8] He was called 'a monster in human shape, exceeding all human rules'. The language fuses sex with religion; Plaine insinuated 'seeds of atheism' into the youths he seduced. In the same year a black slave, Jan

---

★ Thomas Granger, aged sixteen, was executed in 1642, having been found guilty of buggery with a mare, a cow, two goats, five sheep, two calves and a turkey. The animals were burnt in a great pit.

Creoli, in the New Netherland colony, was 'condemned of God ... as an abomination'. He was choked to death then burnt to ashes. The kindling used is referred to as 'faggots', the first time the word was combined with the crime of sodomy. Tragically, the ten-year-old boy, Manuel Congo, 'on whom the above abominable crime was committed', was flogged and also burnt.[9]

In 1655 the New Haven colony published a body of laws which include a mention of the crime of lesbianism. This is the first time it appears upon a statute book. It quotes Romans 1.26 as a precedent, interpreting it thus: 'called in Scripture the going after strange flesh, or other flesh than God alloweth, by carnall knowledge of another vessel than God in nature have appointed.' When 'Sodomitical filthiness' is mentioned, it is followed by the parenthesis '(tending to the destruction of the race of mankind)'. It is important to realise that when people take the Bible literally, the destruction of Sodom becomes a real fear; not to believe that the colony could be destroyed by fire and earthquake if sodomy was not punished would show an heretical lack of faith.

There were few aristocrats among the settlers, for any who made the journey did not stay for long, so there was no *laissez-faire* spirit, no libertine philosophy that might soften the effects of punitive legislation. Most of the immigrants were hard-working, middle-class people who felt they could look down upon the indentured servants, felons and slaves who made up the rest of the community. In their effort to be a class apart, they set a great importance upon appearances – their clothes, manners and domestic life. Sex was something outside all this, something to be feared, tamed and fiercely subjugated if at all possible, rather like the great expanse of alien territory on the edge of which they now clung.

Yet in these new territories there were very few executions and not many prosecutions for homosexual offences. It was as if the community preferred not to observe, or, if they did, not to bring the miscreant to trial. When two men were accused of sodomy in 1635, the governor of New Hampshire refused to try them. In 1677 a citizen of Windsor, Connecticut, had to post a bond for future good behaviour after repeated attempts at sodomy with a variety of men over thirty years. In a new and expanding society spread with tiny hamlets and small towns, everyone knew everyone else and what they were doing, so there was little privacy and a strong sense of community, of striving to succeed together. One can imagine that friends and neighbours might turn a blind eye to sexual indiscretions for as long as was possible.

THE COURT AND THE NOBLE LIBERTINE

Castlehaven's trial and execution might have dampened the spirit of aristocratic debauchery, if that was really what had been punished. The Restoration and the court of Charles II, however, celebrated its return with a vengeance. The very fact that Puritanism had been defeated in England, while its spirit was still growing abroad, seemed to encourage libertinism and to induce the sodomitical rake to become more outrageous still. The twenty-four-year-old Sir Charles Sedley stood naked on the balcony of an inn in full daylight, 'acting all the postures of lust and buggery that could be imagined'. He also abused the scriptures and boasted that he had such powder to see 'as should make all the cunts in town run after him'. Pepys notes that story in his diary and adds that two of his acquaintances declared that 'buggery is now almost grown as common among our gallants as in Italy, and that the very pages of the town begin to complain of their masters for it'. The Restoration brought to flower for the very last time the bisexual man who romped with enormous gusto, quick to respond to the charms of women and youths. Gone was any bewilderment or guilt about sexual identity which had begun to creep into the soul of Elizabethan man.

John Donne (1572–1631) wrote of those who

> in rank itchy lust, desire and love
> The nakedness and bareness to enjoy
> Of thy plump, muddy whore, or prostitute boy.

Not since the heyday of the Roman Empire had it been quite as
acceptable for men to satisfy their sexual feelings with either
gender, without being labelled as having particular inclination
towards one or the other. No one inquired very deeply into relationships between women, for in a phallocentric society it was
considered that nothing serious could occur without penetration.
Charles II himself was promiscuous and though there was never a
hint that he was anything but exclusively heterosexual, his court
was rife with bisexual intrigue and assignations.

John Wilmot, the Earl of Rochester (1647–80), wrote several
verses celebrating the love of boys, including:

> Nor shall our love fits, Chloris, be forgot,
> When each the well-looked link boy strove t'enjoy
> And the best kiss was the deciding lot
> Whether the boy fucked you, or I the boy.

Rochester's drama, *Sodom or the Quintessence of Debauchery*, was
performed at the court of Charles II. In it the King of Sodom pro-
claims: 'that bugg'ry may be us'd/Through all the land, so cunt be
not abus'd.' When Rochester sent a friend his valet, a young
Frenchman called Saville, he wrote: 'The greatest and gravestof
this court of both sexes have tasted his beauties.'[10]

We are still very much in the world of the young man-about-
town with a mistress and a catamite on either arm. The libertine is
bisexual and makes no value judgement on his sexual partner, he
appears indifferent to the idea of a preference for either. Another
example is that of the lawyer John Hoyle, the lover of the play-
wright Aphra Behn, who had been called an 'atheist, a sodomite
professed, a corrupter of youth and a blasphemer of Christ'. Hoyle
had been arrested for buggering a poulterer, William Bristow. He
was also a friend of Sir Charles Sedley who described his republican conversation in a tavern. He died in a drunken brawl that he
had begun when 'railing against the government'.[11] This period
was, in fact, though they could not have suspected it, bisexuals'
last chance to show their nature to society plainly and honestly.

For the attitude to same-gender sexuality had changed dramatically by the beginning of the following century.

Even as the seventeenth century closed, the aristocratic libertine found he had to be cautious, taking care not to flaunt his proclivities, for the court of William and Mary had become chastened. Though scandal, rumour and innuendo about William and his catamites were rife, the king himself was discreet and also kept a mistress, Elizabeth Villiers.

William of Orange (1650–1702) was the son of William II, prince of Orange, and of Mary, the daughter of Charles I, so was fourth in the English succession. He had been born eight days after his father's death. As a youth he was thought to have great vivacity and charm, though later he was known for his reserve. He was popular in the Netherlands, especially when he took up arms, trained an army and fought the combined might of France and England. In 1677 he married his cousin Mary, daughter of James II, then Duke of York, which further strengthened his claim to the English throne. Ten years later his father-in-law had so outraged and alienated the English Parliament by his Romish sympathies and policies that William was asked to intervene. In 1689 James II abdicated in favour of William and Mary.

The new king brought to the English court a Dutchman, Hans William Bentinck, whom he later made Earl of Portland. Bentinck was known as the king's 'first favourite', and for years there had been rumours that William had an interest in young men and would advance their careers in return for sexual services. The king himself is recorded as saying: 'It seems to me a most extraordinary thing that one may not feel regard and affection for a young man without it being criminal.'[12] At the royal palaces both Bentinck and his replacement, Justus van Keppel, had specially-designed adjoining bedrooms with the monarch. This was supposedly to facilitate important political conferences at night. Within the king's circle quarrels would break out with Bentinck (who was then around forty) about which young men should be advanced as potential favourites for the interest of the king and what payments they should deserve. His major quarrel was with James Stanhope.

Once in England, William showered Bentinck with titles, property and a small private fortune. (Bentinck's wife – the sister of Elizabeth Villiers – died in 1688 and he did not remarry until 1700.) In the lavish dispensation of wealth, property and titles to his favourites, William's court resembled that of James I. It was said that if you wanted to marry an heiress and rise at court, then you began as a gentleman to the king's bedchamber. Though it was well known that the king favoured these handsome young men, it was accepted that he was always the active partner and thus was equally interested in women. (This could well be propaganda, for the king had no children from either wife or mistress, and no favourite would have been foolish enough to have told the truth if the king had demanded penetration.) As long as this was so, sodomy was still acceptable, just as it was acceptable that young men were passive. But Bentinck at forty was considered far too old to be a catamite.

Dryden wrote a play, *Don Sebastian*, about a Portuguese king who likes men more than women, but it is clear that the author's disapproval was reserved for the older men who played the passive role. Nevertheless, there was plenty of satire about the monarchy:

> to find old Popery
> turned out and replaced by Almighty Sodomy
> But here content with own homely joys,
> We had no relish of the fair fac'd boys.
> Till you came in and with your Reformation,
> Turn'd all things Arsy Versy in the nation.

Queen Mary, too, felt strong passions for her own sex. Frances Apsley was seven years older than the queen, and Mary wrote letters to her signed 'your loving obedient wife' and referred to her as 'loved blest husband'. Apsley must have been a striking personality for Mary's sister, Anne, also worshipped her. When Anne became queen, the women who were her close and affectionate allies were seen as political problems because their influence was so great.

Because there was a movement towards driving homosexuality underground, drama, intrigue and subterfuge were rife at court. Elizabeth Villiers, Bentinck, and various other noblemen were mixed up in a curious tale involving the remarkably beautiful Edward Wilson who was killed in a duel by John Law (later to become a financier of huge influence) in 1694.

Wilson, the son of a nearly impoverished Norfolk family, was the talk of London in the year before his death because of his extravagant lifestyle – he got through £4,000 in one year. John Evelyn pondered in his diary how the younger son of a man of only middling wealth could exist in such fabulous style, 'in so extraordinary Equipage', without any visible industry or income. Beau Wilson's sudden affluence and his grand lifestyle provoked much rumour.★ It was thought that he must have been kept by a rich and eminent lover – but who? Thirty years later, in 1723, a slim volume entitled *Love-Letters Between a certain Late Nobleman and the Famous Mr Wilson* was published. This caused renewed speculation as to who the lover might have been.

Some of Wilson's story emerged after his death (or murder as it was believed). As Captain Wilson he had been sent to Flanders under the command of his uncle who was colonel of a regiment, but he was sent home, the colonel stating that Wilson was far more suited to be a courtier than a soldier. After only six months in England he was observed to be living in great splendour. Also in Flanders fighting for King William was James Stanhope – the courtier who had quarrelled with Bentinck over a position as gentleman of the king's bedchamber. Stanhope was well known for his bravery, he and Wilson were both about twenty, and it is possible that they might have met there.

Stanhope returned to London at the height of Beau Wilson's fame, but he was so deeply in debt that he had to ask his father for funds. (By 1703 it was well known that Stanhope was a sodomite:

★ The term 'Beau' was used to describe men who dressed extravagantly with some of the bravura of the old-time rake. According to Trumbach, part of their style was sodomy with boys.

'Stanhope, that Offspring of unlawful lust . . . who thinks no Pleasure like Italian Joy,/And to a Venus Arms prefers a Pathick Boy'.)
One of Stanhope's fellow officers, Lord Huntingdon, became a
close friend and ally. Their correspondence, amounting to dozens
of passionate letters (still in the archives at Chevening), dwells on
the memories they had of young men they had both slept with.
Huntingdon writes: 'What would I not give to tell you this my
wicked Stanhope over a glass of champagne in Paris with two or
three pretty smiling unthinking fellows that know nothing and do
everything.'[13] However, because of his poverty, Stanhope is an unlikely candidate for Wilson's mysterious benefactor.

It has been suggested that Wilson's lover was the king himself,
for the munificence exhibited implies unlimited wealth. In this version of the story, Villiers and Bentinck become allies in their
jealousy of Wilson and plot to murder him. There is one piece of
evidence to support the theory that they purchased John Law to
kill Wilson: when Law was arrested, the king insisted that he be
tried for murder, but Law escaped from prison and fled abroad
helped by money from outsiders.

Yet another suggestion is that it was the king's catamite, Bentinck himself, who was Wilson's lover. Certainly he was rich
enough to keep Wilson in such an opulent style. It was known that
he was unfaithful to the king, and he was also unpopular with
Elizabeth Villiers who encouraged the king to replace him. However, a publication of 1708, *The Unknown Lady's Paquet of Letters*
written by a Mrs Manley, claims that it was Villiers herself who
kept Wilson: 'To placate him, she lavished on him, coaches, sad-
dles, hunting, race horses, equipage, dress and table, spoiling him
to such a degree that he became the admiration not only of the
town but of the whole world'. Villiers was always veiled and in
disguise when the couple met, but when Wilson became too
curious and ripped off her veil, Villiers arranged for Law to
murder him and then supplied Law with the money to flee to
France.

The love letters published in 1723 tell a different story. Most
scholars believe they are fiction which uses Wilson's real name to

revive the story in order to inflict political damage on John Law and either Stanhope or the Earl of Sunderland. Others disagree. The letters are florid as was the style of the time, but I cannot say I felt the impact of real people in the grip of real emotions or real sexuality. Instead, the sub-text is one of sex for sale and an urgency to buy.

Charles Spencer, the third Earl of Sunderland, who died in mysterious circumstances in 1722, was identified as the unknown nobleman after the letters had been published.★ Sunderland was also in Flanders in 1688, with his tutor at Utrecht, and it is possible that he may first have met Wilson there. The letters show that Sunderland – if it was him – was thoroughly besotted with Wilson's physical charms, bathing him and revelling in his nakedness: 'I may wrestle with it, and pit it, and pat it, and—it; and then for cooler sport, devour it with greedy kisses.'[14] Sunderland liked Wilson to dress up in women's clothes, but Wilson made Sunderland pay for all the pleasures. When visiting the theatre he discovered Sunderland with a mistress and flew into a rage. Sunderland wrote back: 'thou alone art every, and all the Delight my greedy Soul covets.' In turn, Sunderland became jealous of Wilson when he saw him being kissed by another man. We could infer that the earl introduced him to a circle of noble sodomites and Wilson became a high-class prostitute. There is evidence that Sunderland organised a high-class sodomites' circle.

In the meantime, according to this version of the story, society was anxious to discover the source of the young man's wealth, so the earl put about a story that Wilson was being kept by Villiers, the king's mistress. On hearing of this she hired John Law to find out the truth. He discovered that every night Wilson took a sedan chair to a private house in Hyde Park Corner and did not appear again until the early hours of the morning. But the house was a

---

★ Thomas Seccombe's life of Wilson in the *Dictionary of National Biography* states that in 1695 the love letters first appeared and that the nobleman was Sunderland. On a copy of the letter, in the British Museum Library, according to Norton, the nobleman is also identified as Sunderland.

lodging house and because the spies were refused a room they believed it to be a front. They then discovered that the house had a back entrance, and forty-five minutes after Wilson entered the front door a well-dressed woman would leave by the back door and take a chair to the earl's house in Piccadilly. After three or four hours she would return to the lodging house by the back door, and Mr Wilson would leave half an hour later by the front.

John Law revealed Wilson's disguise. He then may have black-mailed both Wilson and Sunderland, or inveigled himself on to the latter's pay-roll. Some time later, Law killed Wilson after forcing a quarrel with him and then quickly running him through. The inference is that Wilson had asked for too much money from the earl who had paid Law to murder him. When Law escaped from prison he was helped by Sunderland.

Law went on to work for the Bank of Amsterdam and became an innovative driving force in the rise of capitalism. He established the pre-eminence of paper money over metallic, which resulted in an expansion of French industry by the system of credit.

The Earl of Sunderland came of age in 1694 and married a great heiress, Lady Arabella Cavendish. She died in 1698 and he married another heiress, Lady Anne Churchill. In 1717 he married a third heiress, Judith Tichborne. In 1721 a satire *The Conspirators: Or, The Case of Catiline* was published, with a barely disguised dedication to Sunderland. Catiline (thought to be the earl) 'married several times, but chiefly as people suspected for the convenience of strengthening himself by Alliances with Great Men, rather than out of any affection for the Ladies . . . some of his Ganymedes were pampered and supported at a high Rate at his Expence.'

Sunderland by then was First Lord of the Treasury, while Stanhope was Prime Minister (having ousted both Townshed and Walpole in 1717). Both men were forced to resign because of their responsibility for the collapse of the South Sea Bubble, one of the first great failures of capitalism. Soon after the Bubble burst Sunderland, aged forty-seven, was found dead. It was thought that he had poisoned himself, but the government was anxious to disprove this and after an autopsy had been performed it was pronounced that the earl had died from natural causes. Not only had the South Sea Bubble collapsed and the earl was implicated in the fraud, but the Wilson love letters had just been published – might they have been the last straw? That was the gossip of the taverns and coffee-houses.

It is interesting that, at the turn of the century, people in high office, such as Stanhope and Sunderland, were well known as sodomites, had scurrilous and bawdy verses written and sung about them, and yet were able to ignore the slander and continue in office. Seemingly it did them no harm, for even as the mob howled abuse and threw refuse at sodomites in the stocks, the noblemen remained aloof. We must not underestimate the influence of the court, for these noblemen merely reflected the king's own behaviour.

Some years later, however, the Scottish antiquary, the Reverend Robert Wodrow, recorded in his diary for 20 September 1727 that 'the abomination of Sodomy is too publick' and that the 'Earle of Sunderland was the first who set up houses for that vile sin, and when this was like to break out, poisoned himself, to prevent the discovery'.

What had happened in the fifty years that separated Rochester from Sunderland? There had been a sea-change in how society saw the sodomite and how sodomites saw themselves. We cannot imagine Rochester or any of those Restoration personalities committing suicide because of their sexuality; quite the reverse, as we saw with Sir Charles Sedley upon the balcony. This great shift within society heralds the beginning of modern social behaviour.

There is another case which marks the radical changes that occurred in social attitudes towards sex at this time, the trial for sodomy in 1698 of Captain Rigby, who attempted to seduce a boy in a park. Rigby was a beau who had been entrapped by a Thomas Bray, a member of one of the societies for the Reformation of Manners. These were new crusading groups encouraged by Queen Mary that sought out and prosecuted sodomites, prostitutes and Sabbath-breakers, organisations that sprang from the roots of Puritanism and, with royal favour, flourished.

Rigby had been tried for sodomy at a court martial early in the year and had been acquitted. Bray considered him guilty and plotted with the constabulary to entrap him. The bait was a nineteen-year-old servant, William Minton, who had previously met Rigby in the park on Guy Fawkes' night to watch the fireworks. On that occasion Rigby had taken Minton's hand, squeezed it and 'put his Privy Member Erected into Minton's hand; kist him, and put his Tongue into Minton's Mouth'.[15] They arranged to meet in a private back room at the George Tavern in Pall Mall. In the next room were a clerk of the court, a constable and two assistants who were to burst in when they heard the codeword 'Westminster'.

The conversation between Rigby and Minton as recorded in the trial is of particular interest. After Rigby had told him that 'he had raised his lust to the highest degree', he sat on Minton's lap, began kissing him and asked 'if he should fuck him'. Minton replied that only women were fit for that sport and asked how he could do it with a man. Rigby answered that the women were all diseased with the pox and went on to say he would show him, for it was done in their forefathers' time, and the French king and the Tsar of Muscovy did it. Then Rigby pulled down Minton's breeches and 'put his finger to Minton's Fundament and applied his Body close to Minton's', whereupon Minton ran towards the door calling out his codeword. The four officers rushed in and seized Rigby. He was convicted and sentenced to stand in the pillories near the George Tavern for two hours each day, fined £1,000 and imprisoned for a year.

Rigby's explanation that the whores all had the pox was true. John Dunton, a bookseller and publisher, in 1710 thought prostitutes had 'burnt so many beaus that now he-wores are coming into use'. Dunton explained that this was a new society, calling themselves sodomites, 'men worse than goats, who dressed themselves in petticoats'.[16] At Rigby's trial it was the fact that he 'spake most blasphemous words' which most outraged the authorities, for Rigby had suggested monarchs did unspeakable things. Rigby was the last of the libertine rakes. His attitude to sex with lads was casual; he preferred them for they were less likely to have the pox. Besides, he implied, everybody did it, even the very highest of the land.

Rigby's case also marks the point when effeminacy began to be allied with sodomy. One of his critics blamed his actions on the 'effeminate madness' of the fop, though he assumed that fops were also interested in women. But Rigby was a beau, set apart from society, an over-dressed man with extravagant and bizarre tastes. Beaus were not soberly and decently dressed like those men who believed in the moral ethic of work and duty.

Up until this point 'effeminate' had been used of men who were so interested in women that they spent too much time with them, fascinated by their beauty. Fops, rakes and beaus, all extravagantly dressed men, were called effeminate, meaning promiscuously heterosexual.

THE MOLLY HOUSES

As early as 1709 it is clear that society was aware of a new type of sodomite, the 'molly' men who met in secret in discreet clubs and taverns (soon to be called 'molly houses'), at least half of whom began to cross-dress. The word 'molly' stems from a moll, slang for a female prostitute. It is apparent from the records that the mollies, the tranvestite men, were often also married, so it would seem that bisexuality had changed its expression too.

In 1726 a London molly house owned by one Margaret (Mother) Clap was raided by an agent for the Societies for the Reformation of Manners. The agent, Samuel Stevens, visited the house several times over a period of months and took notes of each visit:

> I found between 40 and 50 men making love to one another, as they called it. Sometimes they would sit in one another's laps, kissing in a lewd manner and using their hands in-decently. Then they would get up, dance and make curtsies, and mimic the voices of women . . . Then they would hug,

and play and toy, and go out by couples into another room
on the same floor to be married, as they called it.[17]

Some molly houses were in private rooms in taverns, where there
was music, songs, drink and dance. It was obviously not difficult
to gain admittance, for the Societies' agents apparently had no
trouble. None of them ever reported being subjected to homoerotic advances, so these places seem to have been fairly innocent
havens of entertainment, places where men could change into
female finery and adopt what they felt were female manners.

Much thought seems to have gone into the costumes:

> Some were completely rigged in gowns, petticoats, head-
> cloths, fine laced shoes, furbelowed scarves, and masks; some
> had riding hoods; some were dressed like milk maids, others
> like shepherdesses with green hats, waistcoats, and petticoats;
> and others had their faces patched and painted and wore very
> expensive hoop petticoats, which had been very lately in-
> troduced.[18]

There was a long-standing tradition of cross-dressing among
street-walkers. Over a century earlier, Thomas Middleton in
Micro-Cynicon, published in 1599, had said: 'The streets are full of
juggling parasites/With the true shape of virgin's counterfeits.'
Female prostitutes dressed as boys in fifteenth-century Florence
and youths were to dress as girls in nineteenth-century Vienna.
But the men who went to the molly houses were, on the whole,
not prostitutes. It was fertile ground, though, for young men on
the make, one of whom was Ned Courtney. By the age of
eighteen, Courtney had been in prison several times and was obviously a petty criminal and a cheerful tart. He worked at the
Cardigan's Head at Charing Cross and at the same time acted as a
'molly-cull' around Covent Garden. Nor, outside the molly
house, were the men obviously homosexual in the sense that they
carried their 'female-guying' back home or to their work. Both
costume and manners were adopted for the time they spent as a

molly. Sometimes when they were raided all signs of effeminacy vanished, for they fought back and defended themselves.

The first published reference to this new phenomenon appears in Ned Ward's *The London Spy* (c. 1700), which has a chapter headed 'Of Mollies Clubs', so it is likely that they grew up in the previous decade.

> There was a particular Gang of Sodomiticall Wretches in Town who call themselves Mollies and are so far degenerated from all Masculine Deportment . . . that they rather fancy themselves as Women, imitating all the little Vanities . . . of the Female Sex . . . not omitting the indecencies of Lewd Women . . . to commit those odious Bestialities that ought for ever to be without a name![19]

The class of the men arrested after raids is particularly interesting, for there is no trace here of the aristocratic rake. (This is not to say that the noble libertines did not cross-dress, but it is more likely that they did so in the privacy of their own homes with a few like-minded intimates.) The molly houses were for the working and middle classes. At the trials the first two to be prosecuted were Gabriel Lawrence, a milkman, and William Griffin, an upholsterer. Later there was Mr Grant, a woollen draper, and Mr Jermain, described as 'late clerk of St Dunstans in the East'.

The genital activity involved much manual groping, as we have heard, but the outcome among the 'married couples' would often be anal penetration. Interestingly enough, there seem to be hardly any accounts of oral–genital contact among all the cases recorded from this time.* I surmise that this is basically a matter of hygiene. Oral sex seems to have been rediscovered (remembering that it was highly favoured in the ancient world) in the nineteenth

---

* Trumbach mentions one incident in 1704 where it is recorded that John Norton took hold of the privates of John Coyney 'putting them into his mouth and sucking them'.

century and to have been imported from America – no doubt it accompanied the rise in the popularity of the bathroom.

The sexual act occurred in another room, but was often attended by others who had been at the 'wedding'. It is surprising how casual these events seem, as if in one sense they were socially acceptable. Yet the outcry at the trials and the violence of the demonstrations at the executions show us a society hysterical with rage and revulsion. It seems to be another paradox.

Margaret Clap's house was described as 'the public character of a place of rendezvous for sodomites', and 'notorious for being a molly house'.[20] The neighbours of the molly houses knew what was going on, for they were fairly easy to find and visitors were not grilled on their habits and preferences. So they were not hidden places of sin or secret clubs, which they could well have been. In a very real sense, then, society tolerated them, yet they were persecuted throughout the eighteenth century. In 1726 both Lawrence and Griffin were hanged at Tyburn. The next month there were further trials and hangings and because there was such a public outcry against the mollies the authorities set out to trap them in known homosexual cruising places – St James's Park, Moorfields and Lincoln's Inn.

Mollies convicted of sodomy were sent to the pillory, fined and imprisoned for anything from six months to three years. Young Edward Courtney, who had turned King's Evidence at the trial of Mother Clap's establishment, identified a number of men who were then arrested and tried. The *London Journal* for June 1727 reported:

York Horner and Robert Whale stood yesterday in the Pillory at Charing Cross for keeping a House of Entertainment of Sodomites . . . and for attempting to commit sodomy . . . they were so loaded with Dung and Dirt that they appeared like Bears . . . in short, if the Populace had been suffered to exert their desired Resentments . . . they must have received their Exit upon the spot.[21]

The pillorying of a group of mollies would so excite the mob assembled around the Old Bailey that by noon all the business of the sessions was halted and the shops from Ludgate Hill to the Haymarket would be closed. In the pillory the condemned had to endure the rage and fury of the people armed with sticks, bricks, stinking fish-heads, offal, dead cats and rotting vegetables. From 1720 to 1740 mollies stood in the pillory nearly every week.[22] It is a wonder that not more people were killed suffering this ordeal. In April 1763 an unidentified man who stood in the pillory at Bow for sodomy was killed by the mob. Others were saved at the last moment by constables and taken back to prison. What is disturbing, of course, is that the authorities tolerated such uncontrolled inhumanity for well over one hundred years. It has left its mark upon society, for such hatred lies at the core of homophobia.

Richard Smalbroke (1672–1749), the Lord Bishop of St David's, in his New Year sermon in January 1728, congratulated the Societies for the Reformation of Manners on their success: 'that those abominable wretches, that are guilty of unnatural vice have been frequently detected and brought to condign justice, is very much owing to the laudable diligence of the Societies.' Indeed, the Societies were not slow to congratulate themselves, claiming that now the streets were purged of night-walking prostitutes and 'most detestable sodomites'. One wonders whether the bishop ever observed the barbarism of the mob and the hatred the members of the Societies had unleashed.

Puritanism blurred any discussion of sexuality by dragging in concepts of absolute good and evil so crude in their definition that they became weapons of social revenge in the hands of the ignorant. The reforming zeal of Puritanism gave people an agressive ethic by which they could express their anger. They were taught that it was correct to feel righteous anger at the sinful and to punish them cruelly, for that can be one path to salvation.

For the first time in history, society had designated a group of men as 'contemptible' because of their sexuality. Before this time sodomy had certainly been thought of as a sin, but it was something which all mankind might suffer from in the fall from grace.

Now, only certain individuals were characterised by the sin. This change from the general to the particular was a radical one and it had its uses. Homosexuality could now be confined. It was so socially beyond the pale that no one would readily admit to being a sodomite. Men who had feelings towards their own sex not only kept quiet about it and attempted to repress it, but they also saw that if they wanted to express their feelings a profound change in costume and manners was expected of them.

The mollies became easy targets; socially they were recognisable by their choice of costume and milieu. It is as if they had taken the role of victim upon themselves and offered themselves up to be punished. Why this willing sacrifice to society's punitive judgements? Puritan ideology insisted that the male psyche was severed and parts of it were dismissed and damned. The mollies followed the authoritative credo; in their adoption of female mannerisms and costumes they cut themselves off from the socially approved part of their gender, the acceptable face of masculinity.

Although the dangers of frequenting a molly house were considerable, the institution survived well into the nineteenth century, though it lost the transvestite image.

GENDER AND CAPITALISM

It seems astonishing that this huge change in public perception occurred within fifty years, but a multiplicity of factors came together at the end of the seventeenth century to bring it about. The largely agricultural society, in which both men and women were labourers, gave way to a mercantile society in which feudalism finally died to be replaced by the petit-bourgeoisie. This brave new world, where the market ruled, 'depended on the spread of a new personality type, one able to control animal urges and to delay the satisfaction of present wants for future gains, one governed by internal constraints'.[23] Middle-class people now redefined gender roles and the role of the family itself. They placed a high premium upon self-discipline, hard work and frugality, for class distinctions were now comparatively fluid and by these means a person could rise in the world to positions of power, wealth and authority.

Men went out into the world to trade and make their fortunes, while the women stayed at home and became the living symbol of the husband's wealth and position. The end of the seventeenth century saw the first stirrings in the birth of capitalism which turned the male into a competitive animal. The need to drive the market economy for personal profits becomes, as we know, an overriding obsession and is effective in inhibiting any emotional intimacy with other males much less sexual closeness.

There was an astonishing increase in the population of England from 4.9 million in 1680 to 11.5 million in 1820. Between 1791 and 1831 (the core years of the Industrial Revolution) it grew 72 per cent from 7.7 million to 13.28 million, the fastest rate of increase anywhere in Western Europe. Life expectancy at birth increased by six years from about thirty-two in the 1670s to thirty-nine in the 1810s. Fertility rose two and a half times faster than mortality. The burgeoning population crowded into urban centres which grew into a seething morass of human hunger and desire.

The emphasis on sexuality within marriage was something that Calvinism had stressed positively. But the age of marriage was still late, around twenty-eight for men and twenty-six for women between the years 1600 and 1850. The celibacy rate declined from 25 per cent in 1641 to 10 per cent in 1690. The beginnings of the Industrial Revolution meant a little more money for the lower classes, which meant savings could be put aside and a commitment to marriage made. The relationship between money and sex was explained by Thomas Malthus (1766–1834), a theory which shocked the Tory poet Robert Southey. That the economic and the sexual spheres were 'intimately connected' was not used to explain away the new hostility to the sodomites and mollies, yet, 'compared to earlier periods there was certainly open hostility to non-reproductive sexuality – to masturbation and homosexuality'.[24]

The end of the seventeenth century also marks the beginnings of a new social obsession which would become a driving force in the commerce of the industrial age about to dawn – that of social emulation. With the new petit-bourgeoisie eager to rise, we have a social structure in which everybody watches everybody else, eager to discover new styles and modes, the details of public display. By the eighteenth century almost everyone had a money income and was prepared to spend it. A huge increase in small rural factories producing non-essential goods occurred at this time – toys, pins, lace, glasses, cards, puppets and toothpicks. The class that bought these items was neither the poor nor the rich, it was the middle-income market, the artisans and tradesmen, the engineers and clerks. The textile industries began to flourish, turning out cottons, woollens, linens and silks. Crockery in new designs poured out of the Staffordshire potteries. Birmingham factories produced buckles, buttons and brooches. But most significantly, publishers were booming, women's journals, stories and novels were being read and they all had one theme – romantic love.

It now became fashionable to marry for love. Before, marriages had been planned by the parents and the suitability of partners was worked out strategically, for land, property and class. And though these issues still had great power to persuade and still occupied the concerns of parents, the younger generations were obsessed with 'falling in love'. Respectable society found this concept appealing, though it would have been horrified at the idea that romantic love might exist between people of the same sex. (When this happened, as we shall see, the people involved quickly became pariahs.)

> Beginning in the late seventeenth century and continuing well into the nineteenth – precisely how and why remains unclear – couples could marry with only a shadow of the claim on social and economic resources that had been required earlier. Sexual intercourse was thus literally freer because there was a freer market in matrimony, to which it was still inextricably linked.[25]

The family as consumers became enormously important. All the new goods and clothes were bought, worn and used to beguile and attract sexually, the end result being marriage and a family. David Hume (1711–76) in his essay 'On Commerce', wrote 'govern men by other passions and animate them with the spirit of avarice'. And later, 'people work harder to consume more'. Clothes and objects were used to raise the status of the family, and consumerism became the machine which activated the whole of society. Bernard de Mandeville (1670–1733), in his *The Fable of the Bees*, argued that if pride and luxury were banished, goodly numbers of artisans would starve within half a year.

Bachelors were warned to take care not to deck themselves out in too opulent a manner: 'rolling in foreign silks and linens' is likened to 'blind sodomites groping after their filthy pleasures'.[26] So the major obsession of society - consumerism – not only rejected the sodomite but also obscured him. He could find no place in it, few goods were made and none mass produced with him in mind.*

Consumerism rested on male competitiveness and social emulation, and was often driven by the idea of romantic love, all of which attacked, subdued and sublimated any same-sex emotional stirrings that might appear. Sodomites were reviled as 'monstrous sinners and beastly wretches, creatures so like dogs that even the most inhumane treatment of them could be tolerated'.[27] For the sodomite struck at the new driving force within society which brought comfort and security to the masses and helped them to rise above thousands of years of abject poverty. The sodomite could not procreate in his sexual act and his sterility also affected his role in the new consumer society.

---

* Interestingly enough, it is only very recently that consumerism has acknowledged the power of the 'pink pound', and has even begun to use 'gays' in advertising.

VIII

THE ELITE
AND
TRANSVESTISM

Homophobia became so rampant in England in the eighteenth century that even the rich and powerful, accustomed to having their vices regarded as harmless eccentricities, felt vulnerable and had to be more cautious. Some fled to the Continent. Few of them seemed to have learnt the art of discretion, though, for street balladeers had a field-day.

THE ENGLISH UPPER CLASSES

The Hervey family all tended to be fragile and pretty. Lady Mary Wortley Montagu said that the world was composed of three sexes: 'men, women and Herveys.'[1] Lord Hervey (1696–1743) was obviously bisexual; he married, had six children, had a mistress and also a passionate love affair with Stephen Fox who was eight years younger and with whom he shared a house. Fox appeared physically stronger but was the passive partner. His love letters to Hervey of 1731 show jealousy and pique at Hervey's friendship with the Prince of Wales, and a little later he is accusing Hervey of succumbing to Lady Tinkerville. However, the lampoons circulated about Hervey and Fox almost led to social ostracism. (Fox eventually married.)

William Pulteney, a political rival, wrote of Hervey as being 'a delicate hermaphrodite' and that 'you know that he is a lady himself; or at least such a nice composition of the two sexes, that it is difficult to distinguish which is most predominant'. Hervey fought Pulteney in a duel, but his delicate looks were always against him, however many children or mistresses he had. Alexander Pope in 1735 described him as the boy whom Nero castrated so that he might marry him.

A balladeer also had enormous public fun at the expense of Robert Thistlethwayte, Warden of Wadham College, Oxford, and Doctor of Divinity.

> There once was a warden of Wadham
> Who approved of the folkways of Sodom,
> For a man might, he said,
> Have a very poor head
> But be a fine fellow, at bottom.[2]

The Warden attempted to seduce a student, Master William French, a commoner at the College. They spent an afternoon together, but at supper that evening French appeared to be in a much disordered state, murmuring invectives against the Warden. French told his friends that 'the Warden did not love Women'. The friends surmised that 'a Sodomitical Attempt' had been made and advised him to prosecute. But French was anxious that if he did so he would be expelled and not receive his Bachelor's degree. The students took advice from another Fellow, the Reverend Mr Stone, and after another conference it was decided to discuss the matter with a Reverend Mr Watkins. A London solicitor was then spoken to, while Mr French composed and signed a declaration of what had happened in the Warden's rooms. Though this has been lost, one Fellow who saw it said that the details were 'too gross and obscene to be repeated', it was 'the most notorious Sodomitical Attempt conceivable'.

The Warden begged French to drop the matter. But French went home and returned with his father, who was much incensed, insisting that justice be done. Old Mr French was spoken to by the Warden and friends in an attempt to bribe him, but he remained firm. The justices of the peace decided that the case should go to the court at the next assizes. Thistlethwayte was ordered to post £200 bail. He did so, then left Oxford never to return.

The case went ahead. The college butler and the Warden's barber both told the court they had had to resist advances made upon them, but the Warden had fled to Boulogne where he died five years later.

The diarist Dudley Rider had written in 1715 that it was 'dangerous sending a young man that is beautiful to Oxford . . . sodomy is very usual and the master of one college has ruined several young handsome men that way'. There was nothing new about the Warden's activity; what had changed was the fact that a student could complain and gather support around him to go to court on the matter. This was unlikely to have happened fifty years earlier.

Quite the most controversial figure at this time managed to break all the rules, but in doing so was ostracised by English society. Nicknamed 'the Fool of Fonthill', William Beckford (1759–1844) was the richest man in England. He was also a novelist, architect, bibliophile, scholar and aesthete; his father, twice Lord Mayor of London, had also been a sugar-planter and slave-owner in Jamaica who had bought himself into Parliament as a supporter of Lord Chatham. He died when William was nine and, because he was the only legitimate son, William became heir to a vast fortune.

At the age of nineteen Beckford met and fell in love with William Courtney, aged ten, a pupil at Westminster school and regarded as one of the most beautiful youths in England. Two years later Beckford married a Scottish heiress with whom he had two children. He remained close to Courtney.

In 1784, when Courtney was seventeen, the Beckfords stayed at the Courtney estate, Powderham Castle in Devon. Courtney's aunt (who was in love with Beckford) was married to an ambitious lawyer and Presbyterian elder called Loughborough. It was he who started a rumour that Beckford and Courtney were in the same room together behind locked doors and that he heard a cry of pleasure. Loughborough tried to get his nephew to give evidence against Beckford, but both Courtney and Beckford's wife refused.

Nevertheless, it was enough to ruin Beckford's chance of a career in politics or of admittance into society. The newspapers started to circulate rumours about the country squire and his 'kitty' (Courtney's nickname). George III refused Beckford his peerage and personally wished for him to be hanged. Beckford and Courtney were forced to separate. A year later Beckford left the country to travel in Portugal where he stayed for the next ten years. After his daughters grew up he was not even permitted to visit them in their London houses. The experience made Beckford hate English hypocrisy and he continued to spend much of his time abroad. He became a great liberal thinker with compassion for the poor, he set himself up against public executions and the vile state of the prisons, and he hated fox-hunting.

Courtney's reputation too was stained irrevocably, but the experience did nothing to make him discreet. By 1810 few of the gentlemen of Torquay would visit him socially, and by the following year an Essex magistrate had enough evidence to convict him of 'unnatural crimes'. A warrant was issued for his arrest. He fled to France where he lived for the next twenty-four years.

Beckford, it would seem, was able to dismiss his persecution because he was so wealthy and because he had no other choice. Later he brought back from Portugal Gregorio Franchi, then a seventeen-year-old choirboy, who remained at Fonthill for forty years. When Beckford was away he wrote to Franchi in Italian every day.

Immense wealth also enabled Beckford to live in an ivory tower, for the tower at Fonthill Abbey was nearly 300 feet high. With the help of the leading architect of his day, James Wyatt, he turned the abbey into a pagan Gothic cathedral and filled it with beautiful youths. The estate was surrounded by an eight-mile-long, twelve-foot-high wall topped by iron spikes to keep out hunters, but also one suspects the curious, the bigots and the law itself.

There seems little doubt that after Beckford's marriage he never again felt attracted to women; in fact, Franchi seems to have been both general factotum and pimp extraordinary, acquiring youths from across Europe to serve at Fonthill. These youths were all given names: 'there is pale Ambrose, infamous Poupee, horrid Ghoul, insipid Mme Bion, cadaverous Nicobuse, the portentous dwarf, frigid Silence, Miss Long, Miss Butterfly, Countess Pox' and so on.[3] Popular rumour claimed that there were wild orgies at Fonthill and it would seem that, for once, rumour might be correct. Certainly, something not unlike the Castlehaven regime (Beckford's library contained an account of the trial),★ where servant and master were involved in eroticism together, seems likely. But Beckford was an aesthete and one suspects that the orgies would also have been costume dramas where the participants were dressed in silks and jewels.

Because of his wealth Beckford could live in the way he chose, rejecting social indoctrination. Though he lived like an eastern potentate, the ruler of a harem in a house crammed with priceless objets d'art, he paid for it by being totally ostracised. Throughout his life he kept a scrapbook of accounts of the arrest and persecution of sodomites, and often wrote to Franchi about these cases. In 1816 one John Attwood Eglerton, a waiter with a wife and children, was accused of sodomy by a stableboy. Within ten minutes the jury found him guilty and he was sentenced to death. Beckford wrote to Franchi: 'I should like to know what kind of deity they fancy they are placating with these shocking human sacrifices.'[4]

THE FRENCH ARISTOCRACY

The French aristocracy maintained a tradition of *laissez-faire* about

---

★ Ironically enough, the estate at Fonthill was once owned by the Earl of Castlehaven.

the whole subject of sodomy. In the seventeenth century sodomy was permitted in the upper classes, while anyone else caught in the act, up to the middle of the eighteenth century, was burnt alive in the Place de Grève in Paris.

Terms used for the activity included 'philosophical sin', a phrase used by Montesquieu in 1728 in reference to the Greeks, while others spoke of 'nonconformity'. When theologians studied the case of some young Christians who had been kidnapped by Berbers and then sodomised, they were pleased to note that the Muslim ravishers had converted the Christian lads to Islam first. Sexuality was still linked to notions of religious orthodoxy, so that sodomy was still equated with heresy.

Father Joseph François Lafitau compared the sexual customs of American Indians with those of the ancient Greeks, with particular reference to the 'peculiar friendships' that were common to both. He concluded that they occurred because both peoples lacked the authority of divine law.

Voltaire takes up the same idea in his *Dictionnaire Philosophique*: of sodomy he says, 'it does not pertain to human nature to make a law which contradicts and outrages nature, a law which if literally observed would annihilate mankind'.[5] Yet there was one contemporary French writer who suffered doubts. Diderot said to his friend Sophie Volland: 'Once in the public baths among a number of young men, I noticed one of astonishing beauty, and I could not help drawing near him.' He had to acknowledge that such desires would transform Western society and religion, yet his imagination seemed at times to dwell on homoeroticism. He envisaged a Marriage at Cana where: 'Christ half-soused, somewhat non-conformist, would have surveyed the bosom of one of the brides-maids and St John's buttocks, uncertain whether to remain faithful to the apostle with the chin shaded by light down.'

For the rich and powerful, as in Beckford's case, the problems raised by 'non-conformity' were rarely life-threatening. Queen Christina of Sweden could dress in male clothing while still on the throne but she abdicated in order not to marry. Her behaviour was accepted as being merely eccentric. She settled in Paris where her life was scrutinised and recorded by contemporaries, but because she was a woman of high rank she was never criticised. As queen she had fallen in love with a noblewoman, Ebba Sparre, and after her abdication she continued to write to her: 'If you remember the power you have over me, you will also remember that I have been in possession of your love for twelve years; I belong to you so utterly, that it will never be possible for you to lose me; and only when I die shall I cease loving you.'

Many incidents of lesbian activities among the aristocracy were recorded, including those of Mme de Maintenon and Henriette d'Angleterre, and it would seem that it was common behaviour in Louis XIV's reign (1643–1715).[6]

The tone of the court at Versailles was influenced by the king's only brother, Philippe de France, duc d'Orléans (1646–1701), popularly known as 'Monsieur', who, though he married twice and had three children, was known to be inordinately fond of beautiful young men. His favourite was Philippe, Chevalier de Lorraine, but there was a stream of young men, all described as attractive, who left after seeing 'Monsieur' with munificent presents and a lot richer than when they arrived.

It would seem that this tradition continued, for there is a note by Mathieu Marais, man-at-law to Prince Charles de Lorraine, Grand Ecuyer de France, that on 31 July 1722 he observed the young duc de Boufflers and the marquis d'Alincourt attempting to sodomise the marquis de Rambure. Boufflers could not manage it, whereupon d'Alincourt, his own brother-in-law, took over with the willing Rambure who made 'no attempt to defend himself'.[7]

The Chevalier d'Eon

Later the same century, another chevalier caused scandal and notoriety. Louis XV (1715-74) felt obliged to send one of his spies, M. Drouet, on a secret mission to England to discover whether or not another of his spies, the chevalier d'Eon, was a woman. Bets had been laid on d'Eon's gender – the sum of £10,000 was mentioned in an advertisement in the *Westminster Gazette* in 1776.

Drouet returned to France and confidently told the king that the rumours were true: d'Eon was a biological woman posing as a man. The British court reached the same conclusion the following year. Burke's Annual Register considered her to be the most extraordinary woman of her age, a diplomat, spy, military hero and author.

They were all wrong. D'Eon was anatomically male but managed successfully to pass as a woman from 1777 (when he was forty-nine) to his death in 1810.[8] He was born in 1728 in Tonnerre, a Burgundian town, son of a provincial noble family. He studied law and had published a treatise on financial matters when he became a spy for Louis XV and was sent to Russia. He fought in the Seven Years' War (1756–63) and was awarded the Cross of St Louis for his valour. He was sent to England as part of the peace treaty and hoped to become ambassador. Disappointed in this, Louis XV kept him on in London to spy on the English.

When Louis XVI ascended the throne in 1774, he ended his grandfather's system of spies and d'Eon was recalled. He was given a pension and declared to be female. After a great argument with the king, the church and even his mother, who all decreed that he must wear women's clothes, he very unwillingly agreed. From then on he referred to himself as La Chevalière d'Eon and complained that it took him four hours and ten minutes to complete his first toilette. The French Revolution put an end to the pension and d'Eon returned to London where he lived quietly, working on his memoirs which were never published. When he died his female roommate prepared him for burial and discovered his true sex.

D'Eon is a great mystery. There is not the slightest clue to any sexual entanglements, homosexual or heterosexual, throughout his long life. Nor would it seem that he was either a transsexual or a transvestite, for he says clearly enough in his memoirs that he hated women's clothes. What does seem apparent is that he thought gender itself was irrelevant, and he crossed the gender boundary with a fair amount of ease and elegance in an age which was redefining these boundaries more strictly. His life illustrates a reality where biological sex need not predetermine gender identity, which he saw as something more fluid and malleable. Because of this he was a lone and curious figure. When he was alive he was notorious but popular, because society viewed him as a woman who had once masqueraded as a man, and female-to-male transvestites reaffirmed patriarchal authority. Once society knew that he had been a man masquerading as a woman, people were shocked and horrified.

THE RISE IN TRANSVESTISM[9]

There had been isolated reports of cases of female transvestism in the sixteenth century. In 1566 Henry Estienne reported a case in Fontaines where a woman had been disguised and worked as a stableboy for seven years, then learnt the trade of vineyard master and married. The two lived together happily for two years, after which time, Estienne says, the dildo that she used 'to counterfeit the office of a husband' was discovered. The woman was arrested and burnt alive.

Montaigne reports another case where a group of girls from Chaumone en Bassigny decided to dress as men and went separately into the world. One of them married a woman in Montirandet but was recognised by a traveller from Chaumone. She was arrested, a dildo, described as one of the 'illicit inventions she used to supplement the shortcomings of her sex', was discovered and the poor woman was hanged.

However, from the middle of the seventeenth century there is a rise in the reported cases of female transvestism. For the 'mollies', adopting women's clothes and manners might be an evening's charade, but there was no question of them taking up the role in society and living as females. But for many women in the seventeenth and eighteenth centuries, cross-dressing was a matter of survival. Men who in death were discovered to be women made news and were the stuff of ballads; the seventeenth and eighteenth centuries are full of such cases from the pirates Anne Bonney and Mary Read to the French Genevieve Premoy who, as Chevalier

Balthazar, was decorated and admitted to the order of St Louis by Louis XIV.

Most of the women who have been studied were between sixteen and twenty-five when they decided to change their gender role, that is, from puberty to the age when they were expected to marry. Women of the lower classes (from where the majority of these cases stemmed) had about ten years to earn their living and, ideally, to accumulate a dowry. To obtain a steady job at a slightly higher wage was easier as a man than a girl. Changing from woman to man, or more likely from girl to boy, was not too difficult, though a poor person usually had only one set of clothes. Sometimes they stole men's clothes, at other times they had a woman accomplice. Sometimes the idea came unexpectedly from others: Maria van der Gijsse was begging at farms when some peasants gave her men's clothes and told her to become a soldier. Another woman, a shrimp seller, was unable to live in the closed season and was helped by being given men's clothes by a chimney sweep.

Secrecy was essential. The girl had to journey to somewhere away from her home and friends. One can only conjecture that living conditions were so bleak for many girls that desperate action of this kind was necessary. Barbara Adriaens said she 'sold her women's clothing in Utrecht and bought men's clothing in place of it' and that she first 'cut off her plaits and then went to a barber in a village outside Utrecht'.

The majority of the women became soldiers or sailors, so they were fed, clothed and had security of work for a term of service. It meant the end of penury and near starvation. They were also safe from assault, unless their colleagues suspected they were false.

In the documents and trials, some women claimed that their behaviour was predestined by God: that when they were born, a son was expected; that though in appearance they looked like women, in fact their nature was masculine. Others claimed patriotic or romantic motives which must, if they were believed, have swayed the court in their favour. A few named poverty.

Fear of disclosure must have been an ever-abiding one, and

many of the accounts detail the paranoia. Maria van Antwerpen wrote her autobiography in which she recounted an incident where the army company she was serving in marched past a house where she had been a serving-maid. She was recognised by one of the daughters of the house. Maria returned to her own home and wrote: 'I could not hide the melancholy that this unexpected event lodged in my soul, so that upon my homecoming my wife could not avoid becoming aware of it, as my dejected countenance and defeated posture gave sufficient knowledge of it.'

Exposure of the truth sometimes drove a woman to suicide. In 1765 a woman in Amsterdam killed herself after being taken in custody. Catharin Rosenbrock, who served for twelve years as a sailor and soldier in Holland, returned home to Hamburg at the age of forty-two and was promptly accused by her mother of 'negation of her feminine sex' and imprisoned for bad behaviour. Catharin too then tried to kill herself.

It is astonishing that these women could live undetected for so many years, considering how close living and sleeping quarters were. Many refused to undress or bathe in the heat of the tropics; others refused strong drink, knowing that their caution might vanish; others feared becoming sick or wounded. As many of them signed on as boys rather than men there must also have been the risk of being unable to repel the advances of a drunken sailor. Some, in fact, found companions who were let in on the secret and protected them. Others enjoyed some form of patronage because of their good looks.

Catherina Linken, tried in 1721, told how she passed as a man even in her married life, for she made use of a leather-covered horn through which she urinated and which she kept 'fastened to her naked body'. To this she had also attached a bag of pigs' bladders and two stuffed leather testicles. (One wonders if she bothered to wash and sterilise this astonishing contraption.) An English soldier, Christian Davies, used a silver tube as a urinating device which it was said she obtained from another woman soldier. Geertruid van den Heuvel 'covered her shameful parts with a leather thong with a copper clasp', so that she would have a bulge beneath her trousers.

There are many cases where the cross-dressing was used in the pursuit of a sexual relationship with another woman. Sometimes the real gender was known by the partner, but more often than not the wife was astonished when the true gender of her husband was revealed. A dislike of nudity began to permeate society in the eighteenth century, along with horror at unorthodox sexual positions, so perhaps it is not so unbelievable that sexual contact in some of these marriages took place in the dark and in only semi-nudity.

The reaction of the authorities followed a pattern. If the women involved did not wear male clothing and did not use instruments to imitate heterosexual copulation, they were treated far more leniently. In Plymouth in 1649 two women, Goodwife Norman and Mary Hammond, were brought before the court for lewd behaviour 'each with the other upon a bed'. Mary Hammond, thought to be the innocent partner, received no punishment while Goodwife Norman was made to make public acknowledgement of her unchaste behaviour. But when women successfully impersonated men, claimed a variety of masculine privileges, usurped male prerogatives and appeared also to have made their partner happy, society was enraged.

The astonishing saga of Mary Hamilton, who used the names Charles George or William Hamilton, saw her tried for fraud in 1746 for marrying a woman and posing as a man. Mary confessed that at the age of fourteen she was seduced by a neighbour Anne Johnson who then converted her to Methodism. Mrs Johnson told Mary that she often indulged in carnal relations with her Methodist sisters at Bristol. Mary and Anne began to live happily together in Bristol. But then Anne fell in love with a Mr Rogers and married him. This provoked Mary into terrible fury and jealous rages. Out of it came her decision to begin dressing as a man. To get away from the people she knew she went to live in Ireland where, dressed as a man, she became a Methodist teacher. She was then about eighteen and she took lodgings in Dublin and immediately began to pay court to her landlady, a forty-year-old widow, all to no avail for the landlady married a young cadet. Not put out by this Mary next wooed the widow of a rich cheese-monger, aged sixty-eight, and they were married. Mary deceived his wife for a time, 'by means which decency forbids me even to mention'. But then the old lady discovered the truth and Mary was forced to flee, stuffing as much money as she could into her breeches, and took sail to Dartmouth, posing as a doctor.

There she eloped with her very first patient and they married. But after a fortnight, when a storm was raging in the middle of the night, the young wife saw her 'husband's' nakedness and said piteously, 'You have not what you ought to have', so Mary fled once more. As Charles Hamilton in Wells, Somerset, she fell in love with the beautiful eighteen-year-old Mary Price and wrote love letters to her. They were married and spent the next two months happily together, but in Glastonbury Charles Hamilton was recognised as Mary Hamilton by someone who knew about the previous marriage in Totnes. This rumour reached the mother of Mary Price who then interrogated her daughter. In her need to convince her mother that her husband was really a man Mary Price divulged too much, making her mother cry out: 'O child, there is no such thing in human nature.' Such news quickly went the rounds in Wells and by the time Dr Hamilton had returned home she was abused and laughed at in the streets, dirt and refuse being thrown at her. Mary's mother had told all to the magistrate and a warrant was granted for the doctor's arrest. A dildo was discovered in the doctor's trunk. This is supposition, for the dildo is not named but an object is described as 'something too vile, wicked and scandalous of nature'. Mary Price also confessed that throughout her marriage when lying with the doctor she was entered several times.

No statute seemed to cover this outrage and the problem was to define exactly the crime that Mary Hamilton had committed. A clause in the vagrancy act was used: 'for having by false and deceitful practices endeavoured to impose on others'. It was claimed at the trial that she married fourteen women. In Bridewell, Mary made a great impact in periwig, ruffles and breeches, appearing most bold and impudent. She was convicted of fraud and sentenced to be publicly whipped throughout the winter of 1746 in four market towns, Taunton, Glastonbury, Wells and Shepton Mallet and then sent to prison for six months. But according to Henry Fielding even this did not break her spirit, for 'the very evening she had suffered the first whipping, she offered the gaoler money to procure her a young girl to satisfy her most monstrous and unnatural desires'.

Sometimes transvestism seems to have been undertaken for a specific purpose, but once its advantages were appreciated, the disguise was retained. Disguise in itself has an attraction which has deep psychological roots; losing one's known identity and moving through society as somebody else is a compelling notion. It was an idea which permeated many a novel or supposed autobiography. Masquerades, carnivals and festivals were celebrated with all manner of cross-dressing and often, if the disguise worked particularly well, it offered the chance of an alternative life. Women travelling alone had better protection if they wore men's clothes: Maria ter Meetelen travelled to Spain wearing a male disguise and was so happy that she signed on with a regiment of Frisian dragoons. Women who joined the services could be treated generously and with some sympathy when unmasked, for most had proved themselves as fighters and workers and had earned respect from their comrades. But they were also an embarrassment to the authorities, for one woman among a crowd of men could cause endless troubles. Maritgen Jans, serving as a soldier in a West Indies fort in Africa, fell ill and had to be nursed. It was then that her true gender was discovered and she was removed to a private room. The governor decided that she must be married for her own protection and sent back to Holland. Clothes were found for her, the governor and council gave her a gold chain and she had no lack of suitors who came to her bedside to woo her. Maritgen chose a thirty-five-year-old jurist, a far better match than she could have made back home, and the wedding took place only three weeks after the discovery of her sex.

There are many more cases of women who, with hindsight, one can see were astonishingly brave, expressing their desires and convictions and courting great danger. Lillian Faderman writes:

Transvestites were, in a sense, among the first feminists . . .
Only in convincing male guise could they claim for themselves the privileges open to men of their class. Transvestism
must have been a temptation or, at the very least, a favourite
fantasy for many an adventurous young woman who understood that as a female she could expect little latitude or
freedom in her life.

The Stage

There was one world where cross-dressing was not only acceptable but also popular. The Puritans had loathed the stage and
particularly the habit of boys playing women's roles, for they said,
with some truth it would seem, that these boy actors were nothing
but catamites. English theatres were closed during the Interregnum and reopened with the Restoration. At long last women
became actors, sometimes even playing male roles too. Actresses
became hugely popular, especially throughout the eighteenth
century, and in both England and France got away with exuberant
cross-dressing and bisexual lifestyles without interference from the
authorities.

The most famous actress in seventeenth-century France was
Mlle de Maupin, a singer in the Paris Opera. She played men's
roles to great acclaim, but while on tour she ran off and seduced a
girl in Marseilles. The girl discovered Maupin's true gender and
informed the authorities. Maupin was imprisoned and sentenced to
be executed, but her stage popularity was so great that public
opinion was in her favour and the sentence was overturned. She
continued to dress in men's clothes and the law turned a blind eye
to any further adventures she had in them.

One of the most famous English actresses, Peg Woffington,
played the role of Harry Wildair in *The Constant Couple* (by George
Farquhar, 1700) and was a great popular success with both men
and women. James Quinnin wrote in *A Memoir* (1766): 'it was a
nice point to decide between the gentlemen and the ladies whether
she was the finest woman or the prettiest fellow.'[10] Woffington's
ambiguity was both a mystery and an attraction.

It was a popular assumption that an actress cross-dressed to arouse and gratify men. Sarah Siddons was accused of learning the role of Hamlet and of taking fencing lessons so as to seduce her future husband, Mr Galendo. But there was also a perfectly sound economic reason for the practice: actresses who dressed as men filled the theatre. David Garrick admits of Woffington: 'she always conferred a Favour upon the Managers whenever she changed her Sex, and filled their Houses.' But Garrick felt uneasy about it. He went on to write: 'To masquerade as a man, and to do it well, is to enter a no-woman's-land beyond femininity, to exceed the limits of delicacy.'

By the early nineteenth century these feelings had crystallised into something more sinister. James Broaden refers to 'vile and beastly transformations', for by then cross-dressing was associated with 'Sapphic inclinations'. This idea of deviant female sexuality began to emerge only at the end of the eighteenth century. So we might speculate about why the female transvestite, for a time, was such a popular figure.

The actress posing as a man, pretty, charming, with lithe limbs and a perfectly flat crotch, seems an unlikely figure to appeal to male desire. Is she/he the personification of past youth, with smooth hairless cheeks? Does she/he represent same-sex eroticism, the now unattainable but, as she is in reality female, actually attainable? Is she a mirror in which the male glimpses his own castration? Male cross-dressing on stage was accepted only if it was a bad parody of femininity, so that the figure was turned into a grotesque. (We continue this tradition in the pantomime dame.)

SEX AND GENDER

The division of people into two separate biological sexes, man and woman, and genders, male and female, is a structure that is so familiar to us that it hardly warrants repeating, but it is a formulation that began to predominate only in the eighteenth century.[11] It was tied into the emerging equality between the two genders in their new roles of the male entrepreneur and the passive female status symbol. But there was also a third, illicit, gender, that of the adult passive transvestite male or molly who, it was supposed – erroneously I would argue – desired only men. The passive male, as we have seen, did not fit into the burgeoning capitalist society; in fact, such people were blasphemous to it. One way of rationalising such a blasphemy was not to talk of two genders but of three biological sexes: man, woman and hermaphrodite. Hermaphrodites were acceptable if they chose a gender, stuck with it and had sex only with the opposite gender; if they had sexual relations with both sexes, they were considered to be sodomites. (As we have seen, women, too, could commit sodomy, for the term covered any expression of unorthodox sexuality.) This classification existed because people were considered to be capable of desiring both genders, and the minority who acted upon this impulse acted within the rules of patriarchal domination. Many adult men had sex with adolescent boys and, like Rochester, saw little difference in that act from penetrating a woman.

It is a particularly phallocentric paradigm, for it is significant that sodomy contravened the gender system and broke the patriarchal code only when an adult male allowed himself to be penetrated or when a woman penetrated another woman. The only explanation for such behaviour was thought to be physiological, so they were considered to be hermaphrodites. Transvestite women who were discovered to be married to another woman were almost certainly medically examined. Hermaphrodites had been considered a source of eroticism in antiquity, but in the seventeenth and eighteenth centuries much was written about detailed physical examinations. For example, in 1675, Anne Jacobs told the magistrate of Harderwijk 'that she was more a man than a woman'. After a medical examination, she was ordered to dress as a man.[12] Cornelis Wijngraef told the court at The Hague in 1732 that at birth he was ascribed the female sex and christened Lijsbeth. She married at fourteen but the husband discovered that sexual intercourse was impossible. Her parents then shut her up in a lunatic asylum. After six months she was medically examined and pronounced to be a man; she was discharged and told to wear men's clothing. But a later examination by three qualified doctors concluded that she 'is constituted as any other female . . . no parts or members have been found contrary to this'.

Two changes occurred in theories of sexuality in the early part of the eighteenth century: the first was from a belief in two genders and three sexes to one of three genders and two sexes; the second change was that the idea that men and youths could have sex together without compromising their masculinity (in fact, in some societies gaining plus points) vanished entirely and was replaced by the adult male molly, characterised as a kind of male whore. 'Hermaphrodite' came to refer to an effeminate man who desired sex with other men; it no longer had any reference to a biological condition.

However, women who desired other women were, as we have seen, assumed to be biologically betwixt the two genders and therefore hermaphrodite. Hermaphrodites were then thought to be women with enlarged clitorises. When they apprehended such people, the courts assigned them a gender which they had to stick with if they were to stay out of trouble, for the authorities would not consider a third biological gender. The mollies or passive sodomites behaved the way they did because of the corruption of their minds, and not because of any physical abnormalities. By the end of the eighteenth century women who loved women had also joined this category. Such women were called sapphists or tommies, and what they did was called 'flatfucks' – another example of phallocentric slang. These women were also thought of as having corrupt minds but not necessarily the bodies of hermaphrodites. The sodomy statute had never included women because it was thought that sex by definition was penetrative and therefore a penis was essential. In the novels of the time, if women were described in carnal relations it was always made clear that they preferred men.

Dr Johnson's friend Mrs Thrale kept a diary for thirty years and was obviously fascinated by both sodomites and sapphists, for her diary is full of references to them. She also thought what two women did together were 'impossibilities'. Like the rest of society, she approved of the Ladies of Llangollen and visited them. Eleanor Butler, aged twenty-nine, had first eloped with Sarah Ponsonby, aged thirteen, in 1778. Their outraged families found them and took them back, but they left again and settled in Wales. They cropped their hair and almost always wore riding habits. Mrs Thrale never considered them to be sapphists, and as far as we can tell there seems to have been little erotic content to their relationship. They were highly orthodox in their opinions, hating anything radical or common. In 1790 a newspaper column described them in terms which, though sympathetic, inferred sapphic leanings. They wrote at once to Edmund Burke to ask advice about legal action, and Burke, who had some experience of suing for libel and failing, advised them not to. It would seem that the ladies were acceptable because they did not project any sexual subtext within the relationship, while women who were active sapphists were stigmatised for it.

Mrs Thrale also mentions a Mrs Damer, the daughter of General Seymour Conway, a great friend of Horace Walpole. Mrs Damer was married at eighteen, but nine years later her husband shot himself. From then on it became clear that Mrs Damer preferred women. Mrs Thrale wrote that 'it was a joke in London now to say such a one visits Mrs Damer'. At the end of the century, in her fifties, Mrs Damer had adopted some articles of men's clothing – hat, shoes and jacket – and began to court a Mary Berry (aged thirty-five). It was remarked how tender their leave-taking was, 'as if it had been parting before death'. The *Sapphic Epistle* (a satirical poem) referred to Mrs Damer as a 'tommy', the first recorded use of the term.

There were other notorious sapphists, such as Lady Caroline Harrington and her friend Elizabeth Ashe, nicknamed 'the Pollard', and there were even specialist houses, such as Mother Courage's in Suffolk Street and Francis Bradshaw's elegant house in Bow Street, where ladies of quality could go to relax. Both Lady 'Polly' Harrington and Elizabeth Ashe were bisexual and promiscuous. The latter, an actress and courtesan, was described as 'a small pretty creature . . . between a Woman and a Fairy'.[13] She was twice married before having an affair with Polly Harrington, and later left to become the mistress of Count Haszlang, the Bavarian Envoy to London. She died happily, aged eighty-four, after enjoying a 'large collection of amours'.*

By the end of the century there were only two kinds of bodies – male and female – but four genders: men, women, sodomites and sapphists. The first two were acceptable and licit, the last two were unacceptable and still considered sinful, but only one of these was illicit and still being persecuted. We might ask ourselves, why was the condemnation of the sodomite so necessary to society?

SODOMY REVILED

We can view this question from a different angle. Why was prostitution allowed to grow greatly in numbers throughout the eighteenth century? Why did numerous religious reformers do little to take girls off the streets? The physician William Buchan was reluctant to restrict prostitution for fear it would encourage sodomy. Astonishingly, St Thomas Aquinas had expressed the same view. The eighteenth century religious philanthropist, Saunders Welch, agreed with Aquinas, adding the thought that sodomy was 'a horrid vice, too rife already, though the bare thought of it strikes the mind with horror'.[14] Though the modern gender role for men proclaimed that they desired women exclusively and that all masculine behaviour flowed from such a desire, the authorities thought it best to cater for such virility by turning a blind eye to whores and bawdy houses. Prostitution was essential to the upkeep of the gender system which we have seen emerging above.

Marriage as an institution was beginning to feel the first stirrings of equality, helped by the popular concept of romantic love and by the realisation that a wife and mother had an integral and significant part to play in capitalist society as the ideal consumer.

---

* An observation by Horace Walpole who also gave her the nickname 'Pollard' Ashe.

Bachelors were not consumers in the same manner at all, but considering the age at which marriage occurred – around thirty – they did have obvious sexual needs. If they did not use courtesans or prostitutes, the fear was that they might go with a passive 'he-whore' and, who knows, develop a taste for it and become sodomites themselves. Whores, then, were a necessary safety-valve within society.

At the same time, prostitution was hated by a reformist and puritan society which held strong ideals about the sanctity of marriage. It was well known that married men also used bawdy houses and the new ideals about marriage were not impregnable to the demands of male lust. It was now thought that male and female could be intimate enough in marriage to become close friends, and for both to care for their children in a gentle and loving manner. The family became a great repository of sentiment: women and children were painted as innocent creatures, and in contrast the sodomite became more depraved and reviled. As women were valued more and more as mothers and wives, the sodomite became anathema to so-called decent society.

Thus prostitutes allowed men to establish quite clearly and in the most brazen manner that they were free from the taint of sodomy. The whore also offered freedom from the constraints of marital intimacy which itself contained intimations of 'effeminacy' as it drew the male back into the women's world. And effeminacy, of course, was only one step away from being a sodomite. Men felt they had to take care to limit the demands that the feminine domestic world made on them. So the prostitute existed as a balance for the male psyche and also as a bulwark between domesticity and the threat of real depravity.

What we see clearly in the eighteenth century is the beginning of an oppositional system of sex and gender, where the definition of masculinity is increasingly dependent upon the feminine other.[15] We also see the beginning of an anxiety about masculinity and a recurrent and almost obsessive discourse against the 'masculinisation' of women.

IX

SEX
AND THE
ENLIGHTENMENT

The translation of the Bible into the vernacular had instilled within people both respect and fear of the exegesis contained within the Old Testament. It was unquestioningly accepted that this was the voice of God himself, and that these pages contained the history of the human race and the explanation of divine purpose. Genesis destroyed any optimistic interpretation of the nature of humankind or any hope that human beings could create a civilised and satisfactory society upon earth. It was clear from the doctrine of the Fall that human nature was basically evil, and could be redeemed only by God and that the only paradise available was in the next world and not in this. The chosen people, the Jews, under the direct guidance of God, had been, it was believed, the teachers of antiquity. Plato, for example, had been the pupil of Jeremiah in Egypt.

Bossuet, a French bishop, dedicating a work on political theory to the son of Louis XIV, wrote in 1677: 'Whatever was wisest in Sparta, in Athens, in Rome; to go back to the very beginning, in Egypt and the best governed of all states, is as nothing compared to the wisdom that is contained in the law of God.'[1] And the law of God, as interpreted by him and others, thought masturbation was

219

heinous but sodomitical practices were so vile they could hardly be mentioned in a civilised language. That Bossuet wrote his dedication at a court which contained the whims and fancies of 'Monsieur' and his circle could only have strengthened the bishop's resolve.

One of the many influences that slowly dented this almost impregnable defence against knowledge was the fascinating anthropological information of distant lives. Hakluyt and his fellow chroniclers commanded a wide public, but at first the recorded customs and rituals of 'natives' only further intensified the feeling that they were barbarian savages and that the Christian world contained God's elected people. Then, as reports filtered back from the wilds of Siberia, the deserts of the Middle East, the torrid zones of Africa, the vast plains of the Americas, a fascination grew for the exotic and bizarre and an interest developed in the sexual anthropology of these distant peoples. Both Swift and Diderot thought the sexual prohibitions of the Europeans were merely arbitrary, imposed on society by a scheming priesthood.

SEX IN THE OPEN

Eighteenth-century sexual pleasure was considered by some to have been an erotic 'golden age' – albeit only for men. New expressions of scientific and philosophical thought recognised the fundamental sexuality of all living creatures. In Erasmus Darwin's evolutionary theories sexuality becomes the agent of progress, order and happiness.[2] Animal attraction was 'the purest source of human felicity; the cordial drop in the otherwise vapid cup of life'.[3] (Darwin openly brought up two illegitimate daughters.) Locke, Addison and Chesterfield all agreed that the pursuit of pleasure led to happiness and that this behaviour was dictated by nature to man. 'Pleasure is now, and ought to be, your business,' Chesterfield told his son.[4]

The Enlightenment threw off the chains of biblical text and was determined to see man's character as a *tabula rasa*. The driving force behind human behaviour was the avoidance of pain while pursuing pleasure. The true nature of *homo sapiens* was the innocence of Eden, so all desires, far from being sinful, were seen as part of the divine good. David Hume argued that erotic attraction was the 'first and original principle of human society'. New currents of philosophical hedonism, led by Lamettrie, d'Holbach and Diderot, advanced the view that sex was a basic mode of human enjoyment.[5]

All this unashamed and candid enjoyment of the flesh was discussed openly; at the same time it was also highly visible, for décolletage displayed near-naked breasts in a manner few other ages have countenanced. In London there were over 10,000 prostitutes who plied their trade upon the streets or who advertised in *The Whoremonger's Guide*. In St James's Park women carried baskets of dolls for sale, but instead of legs the dolls had a cloth-covered cylinder of about six inches long and one inch wide. Lesage, a French traveller, reported that a young woman brought her doll back complaining it was too big and ordered a smaller one. But the saleswoman insisted on being paid in advance, arguing that if the lady changed her mind again she would not be able to sell a used doll.[6] A poem was published in 1722 called 'Monsieur Thing's Origin' which describes the adventures of a dildo.

> She boldly worked him up into an Oil
> So did she make the Creature slave and toil;
> She wrought him till he was out of breath,
> And harrast Seignior almost until Death.

Another poem published in 1748 suggested that men of wealth could order life-sized dolls for their own private amusement.

The sex act was performed in public, in the parks, and even, as Boswell tells us, beneath the new Westminster Bridge. This must have encouraged voyeurism, though the parties did not undress. Contemporary pornographic prints depict the woman wearing few clothes and the man merely unbuttoned. Pornographic novels and stories began to enjoy a great vogue. Brothels and clubs catered for whipping orgies, naked dancing and shows of copulation.

Once society 'discovered' other worlds, the polygamous societies of the South Seas held great appeal for the British male. Boswell told Belle de Zuylen that within marriage he would expect to be free to pursue his sexual appetites wherever they took him. But when she said she would like the same freedom, he termed her a 'frantic libertine'. The idea of a society without sexual ownership or guilt seemed highly beguiling and the term 'free love' had popular appeal. But all this liberalism towards sex did not extend itself to same-sex loving which was now thought to be a nasty foreign vice which had been imported to England. A doctor and poet, John Armstrong, wrote *A Poetical Essay* which included the lines:

> Be Male and Female still.
> Banish this foreign Vice; it grows not here,
> It dies, neglected; and in Clime so chaste
> Cannot but by forc'd Cultivation thrive.[7]

Only one eminent thinker of the Enlightenment swam against this tide of condemnation to espouse a liberal and compassionate view of sexual relationships between the same gender.

Jeremy Bentham (1748–1832)

A Utilitarian philosopher of rational hedonism, Bentham twice wrote in defence of sexual pleasure, in 1774 and 1814. Part of his task was to examine the place of 'Greek love' in history.[8] He could find no reason for punishing its expression and went on to rebut one argument after another for its criminalisation. Bentham attempted to reconsider the penalties for sexual offences and recognised the difficulties of dealing with sex offences when many people thought sex was inherently evil anyway. He defined sex as 'any act having for its object the immediate gratification of the sexual appetite'. He proceeded to divide these into two categories: those acts that conform to public opinion and the others which do not. In the latter category he placed sexual acts between people of the same gender, people of different genders but under-age, un-married people and married people that practised adultery. Using the principle of utility, the criterion he applied was 'happiness', and whether or not the sexual act added to its sum.

Bentham observed that in the ancient world the adult lovers of boys were almost certainly bisexual, and he thought that an ex-clusive taste for the same gender was probably rare. He suspected that the persecution of sodomites tended to encourage an exclusive taste for it and that the present laws against sodomy contributed to the growth of an underground sub-culture. He thought such prac-tices had no appreciable effect upon population growth, but if they had, and that was the reason for burning pederasts alive, then monks should be roasted in front of a slow fire. He also tackled the charge of its 'unnaturalness' and thought that if sodomy was con-demned for the mere circumstance that it was not necessary for procreation, then a taste for music, for example, must also be un-natural. Bentham summed up: 'when the act be pure good, punishment for whatsoever purpose, from whatsoever source in whatsoever name and whatsoever degree applied in consideration of it, will not only be evil, but so much pure evil.' He claimed that sex was a legitimate pleasure in its own right and thought those moralists foolish who argued that 'a man is to convert the highest enjoyment that kind nature has bestowed upon him into a mechan-ical operation to make children'.

The tragedy of this compassionate diatribe is that it remained unpublished, not only within his lifetime, for reasons not too hard to guess, but also, alas, today. The whole text remains un-published. Bentham reflected: 'To other subjects it is expected that you sit down cool: but on this subject if you let it be seen that you have not sat down in a rage you have betrayed yourself at once.'[9] No doubt he was remembering a judge who, after 'consigning two wretches to the gallows' for sodomy, had an expression which Bentham described thus: 'Delight and exultation glistened in his countenance; his looks called for applause and congratulations at the hands of the surrounding audience.'[10]

Bentham is remembered for his famous axiom: 'The object of all legislation must be the greatest happiness of the great number.' But in many ways his work was too far ahead of his time – though friends and contemporaries, such as John Stuart Mill, were full of admiration for him and after his death rewrote several of his books from a mass of rough notes that Bentham left. They ignored the 'Essay on Pederasty'. We must be thankful that at least they did not destroy it.

THE SOLITARY VICE

What caused the even greater hardening of what was already an implacable hatred of same-sex sexuality? Why was it so much more offensive to people in the eighteenth century than it had been in the fifteenth, sixteenth or seventeenth centuries? Some of the factors which contributed to this change were explored in the previous chapter: the rise of both capitalism and Calvinism played their parts in changing perceptions of male and female roles. Now a new factor entered: the idea that male vigour was connected with the amassing of wealth, the storing-up of gold and land which was symbolised by the procreative force of semen itself.

Anti-masturbation literature began to enjoy a vogue in the eighteenth century. It was thought that the male had only a certain amount of semen stored within him and if he ejaculated too often he would become empty and lethargic. Ejaculation began to be referred to as 'spending', as if a loss of money was incurred. Indeed, the concept of the male as an avaricious entrepreneur, out to collect and store wealth, encouraged the view of this fusion between money and semen.

It is incredible how much male hysteria was unleashed by the subject. James Graham (1745–94), a sex therapist, a term much in vogue then, who created a Temple of Hymen at the Adelphi in the Strand which housed a celestial bed in a chamber called the holy of holies, wrote a tirade of invective against masturbation. He warned that it would lead to 'debility of body and mind – infecundity, – epilepsy, – loss of memory, – sight, and hearing, – distortions of the eyes, mouth and face, – feeble, harsh and squeaking voice, – pale, sallow and blueish black complexion.'[11] Graham continued in this vein for another 200 words. What made masturbation so threatening, leading the sinner straight to perdition, was that it was thought to be the first step on the road to sodomy. Earlier, mollies and masturbators had been lumped together as 'unnaturalists'. As carnality between mollies must perforce include some mutual masturbation, the waste of semen became a double crime. Graham was repeating, though enlarging upon, the orthodox medical view.

In 1708 a Dutch physician, Hermann Boerhaave, had warned of solitary sexual excess: 'the semen discharged too lavishly occasions a weariness, weakness, indisposition of motion, convulsions, leanness, dryness, heat and pains in the membranes of the brain.' The subject of masturbation seems to have touched upon an unconscious terror of the time.

The most well-known writing upon the subject was an anonymous pamphlet (by a clergyman turned quack) entitled *Onania*, published in England in 1723. This was devoted entirely to the pernicious disasters attendant on the solitary vice. By 1750, 138,000 copies had been sold. Other writers merely reflected its opinions. In 1760 it was translated into English and had great success. *Onania*'s power upon the public was due, no doubt, to the authority that biblical text still exerted, coupled with the mores of the new mercantile world.

A UNIVERSITY CLUB

How did young, intelligent and educated men react to all this hysteria? Were they careful to avoid all same-sex encounters? Did they limit themselves to courtesans and whores? The diaries of Pepys, Boswell and others describe heterosexual promiscuity, but if encounters with male whores had occurred they would have been unlikely to have written them down in diary form for fear of persecution.★

However, we do have letters written in the mid-eighteenth century by students at the universities of Utrecht and Leyden which give an insight into a close and undoubtedly homosocial society. The students formed a group based on 'tears and kisses, hugs and caresses' where the relationships were extraordinarily emotional and intense.[12] What makes this group of particular interest is that it comprised men who were to become distinguished names in the fields of medicine, philosophy and politics.

The Scottish philosopher and itinerant tutor Andrew Baxter (1683–1750) wrote to a young medical student at Leyden in June 1745: 'Never man was thought so much upon by another.' Such strength of passion puzzled the philosopher; the notion that a man can esteem another man in this erotic way and to such a profound degree, he mused, is the basis of a riddle. The student was John Wilkes (1727–97), then aged twenty. Baxter was over sixty.

Wilkes was later to gain a reputation as a radical libertine, for despite his squint and his round face he could charm a bird off a tree. Soon after their meeting, Baxter wrote to him: 'if ye be against this whim, which a passionate love for you has brought me to bed, I shall drop it.' Baxter was confined to bed in Utrecht, thirty miles and a day's travel by canal from Leyden. Wilkes did not object to the whim, in fact it is likely that he was flattered and pleased – Baxter, after all, was a distinguished writer and thinker – for they remained close friends until Baxter's death. When he was dying, Baxter wrote on 10 April 1749: 'My first desire . . . my dearest Mr Wilkes, is to serve virtue and religion; my second and ardent wish to testify my respect to Mr Wilkes.'

There is little doubt that this passion was wholly platonic, but we cannot come to that conclusion about another of Wilkes's student friends, Baron d'Holbach, who was to become the leading

---

★ Unlike von Platen and Casement in the following centuries.

German philosopher of the Enlightenment. In August 1746 d'Holbach wrote a long letter to Wilkes who had returned to England to stay in Aylesbury with the heiress, Mary Meade, whom his family intended him to marry. D'Holbach was torn with jealousy and said so. He recalled a long walk that they had enjoyed at Leyden, wishing desperately that he also could be in Buckinghamshire. He recalled the 'Joy, the fear of a second parting, what charming tears, what sincere kisses'. D'Holbach was wealthy and Wilkes had been to stay with him at his estate. They were to remain friends throughout their lives.

Wilkes's reputation as a libertine grew after the failure of his marriage and his involvement in the satanic activities at Sir Francis Dashwood's ruined gothic abbey of the Monks of Medmenham. These orgies were always considered to have been strictly heterosexual, but in the light f these letters that now seems unlikely.

Also among this group of students were Mark Akenside (1721-70), the pre-Romantic poet and author of *The Pleasures of Imagination*, and his lover and patron, Jeremiah Dyson (1722-76). Dyson remained true to Akenside throughout their lives, giving him an allowance of £300 per year and buying him a house in Bloomsbury in which they lived together, while Dyson's wife and family lived in another house. Akenside, who had a club-foot, continued his dual career in medicine and literature and eventually became one of the physicians to the royal family. His sexual bias was well-known, for in Tobias Smollett's *Peregrine Pickle* (1751) Akenside figures as a physician in love with the Greeks who invites Peregrine and his companions to 'An Entertainment in the Manner of the Ancients' where epicurean delights presided, especially 'sodomiticall debauchery'.★

The group at Leyden, including Wilkes, were much taken by another student, John Freeman, a Creole from Jamaica who was 'a Man of Fortune', and they waxed eloquent in praise of his beauty. Other members of the group, who referred to themselves as a

---

★ *Peregrine Pickle*, Chapter 49. The scene was omitted after the first edition.

club, were William Dowdeswell, Charles Townshend, Anthony Askew and James Johnstone.★

There can be little doubt that a discreet bisexuality continued among gentlemen, overlooked by the law because it was practised by people of eminence. But how did Akenside and Dyson react to scenes of mob hysteria and hanging at Tyburn? It is a short walk from Bloomsbury to Covent Garden and Akenside must have known that the great piazza was filled with catamites prowling for trade. Was he ever a customer? Did he feel pity or horror for the poor? In 1768 (two years before Akenside died, aged thirty-eight), the magistrate Saunders Welch reported to Sir John Fielding (half-brother of novelist Henry Fielding) that a quarter of the inhabitants of Covent Garden were 'living in filthy, obscene squalor' and were 'illiterate Paupers helpless against their fate' who had to resort to crime in order to exist. These were crimes committed by 'sodomites' who in gangs turned violent and robbed people when their overtures were rebuffed.

In 1766 the following verse was printed in *The Fruit Shop*:

> Go where you will, at every Time and Place
> Sodom confronts and stares us in the face;
> They ply in Publick at our very Doors
> And take the Bread from much more honest Whores . . .
> For Pleasure we must have a Ganymede
> A fine fresh Hylas, a delicious Boy
> To serve our Purposes of beastly Joy.[13]

This rather equivocal verse strongly implies that young male whores were freely and openly available. Hence, as Bentham had pointed out, sodomy trials did nothing to reduce the prevalence of street trade. It is possible that the trials frightened off bourgeois customers for a time, but it is extremely unlikely that men of

---

★ Dowdeswell became commander-in-chief of India and collected prints by old English engravers; Askew was a famous classical scholar and bibliophile; Johnstone was a physician and author; and Townshend, a Chancellor of the Exchequer, famed for his eloquence.

leisure and substance were much deterred from any desired pursuit, for they could always, like Beckford, disappear abroad.

THE CULT OF THE CLASSICAL

If Smollett had satirised Akenside as a lover of Hellenic art, it was due to the influence that Johann Joachim Winckelmann (1717–68) had had upon the aesthetic of the eighteenth century. Though it was never acknowledged, the focus of Winckelmann's 'rediscovery' of Greek art was its homoeroticism. It is obvious from Smollett that any lover of 'Greek art' was suspected of proclivities not countenanced by the rest of society.

Winckelmann was the only child of a Brandenburg cobbler. A local schoolmaster encouraged Winckelmann's scholarly talents and in 1737 Winckelmann enrolled to study Theology at the University of Halle. He then tutored for two years before studying medicine and science at the University of Jena, followed by another five years of tutoring. Throughout this time he was doing a prodigious amount of reading from the classics. In 1748, when he was thirty-one, he was appointed by Count von Bunau to catalogue his library. In 1755 he wrote a work which was to make him renowned in the academic world. *Reflections on the Imitation of Greek Works in Painting and Sculpture* was only fifty pages long but it was translated into French and English. On the strength of it and because he had converted to Catholicism, he landed the plum job of Papal Antiquary, residing at the Vatican. This left him with time to travel in Italy and to study classical remains. His *magnum opus*, *History of Classical Art* was published in 1764 to much acclaim.

Winckelmann's story now takes a most sinister and mysterious turn. He was invited to Berlin, but made a detour on his journey to attend an audience with the Empress Maria Theresa in Vienna. After this he went to Trieste, waiting for a ship to Venice. He took a room in the city's most expensive hotel and registered under the name of Signor Giovanni. He became friendly with a thirty-one-year-old unemployed Tuscan cook called Francesco Arcangeli. The man was pock-marked and unattractive, married, and had been in gaol for theft. For a week the two men were seen around Trieste deep in conversation. They dined alone in Arcangeli's room. After a week, Arcangeli strangled and stabbed Winckelmann, then tried to escape but was stopped in the courtyard and arrested. Winckelmann died that same afternoon.

In interrogations, there were six in all, Arcangeli altered his testimony several times: he had intended to rob Winckelmann (but though he was shown the medals from Maria Theresa, he left them behind together with money); he thought Winckelmann was a Jew, or a Lutheran, who had accused him of being a spy. His motives remained a mystery.

Winckelmann's vision of classical Greece is of a country populated by golden youths, naked and beautifully proportioned, on the verge of manhood. His descriptions of sculptures such as the Belvedere Torso or the Apollo Belvedere is fulsome, almost grossly sensual, the virility and power of the masculine both idealised and idolised. The intensity of the emotion that Winckelmann felt for them is what moved his readers who suddenly began to see the sexuality of the statues through the patina of Platonic love and ideals with which Winckelmann had covered them. His credo emerges in the opening pages of his first book: 'Good taste . . . had its origins under the skies of Greece . . . the only way for us to become great . . . is to imitate the ancients.'[14] In 'Essay on the Beautiful in Art' (1763) he shows his bias towards the male: 'I have observed that those who are only aware of beauty in the female sex and are hardly or not at all affected by beauty in our sex, have little innate feeling for beauty in art in a general and vital sense.' Later in the same essay he suggests that the capacity to appreciate beauty 'is more to be found in youths of pleasing appearance than in others'.

Winckelmann influenced artists and thinkers, stimulating the movement towards neoclassicism, turning eighteenth-century eyes away from Rome in the direction of Greece. His influence was most powerful in his native Germany where Greek classicism is plainly apparent in the poetry and literature of the next hundred years. It is of interest that the culture of Western European society absorbed so hungrily an aesthetic composed of homoeroticism, while at the same time its customs and laws punished brutally any manifestation of it in daily life. This dichotomy within caused tension and discord and no doubt, as Bentham coolly recorded, accounted for the apoplectic countenance of many a judge who sentenced a sodomite and then bought a reproduction Hermes for his garden.

What of Winckelmann's personal life which ended in such a tawdry murder? From his own youth there seems plenty of evidence of his interest in young men, though whether this was of a sexual nature is unknown. Certainly, the emotional content of his correspondence with several pupils, students and friends exhibits much tender affection and also economic consideration. 'My sole consolation in my solitude is that there must be something in me that binds me so fast to you. This must be the sole thing in me that is great. I will love you as long as I live,' he wrote to his pupil, Lamprecht. And there were others whom he confessed to loving: Friedrich Reinhold von Berg, Baron Riedesel, Baron Strosch and Prince Anhalt-Dessau. But there is no evidence that there was a sexual component in any of these close passionate relationships.

Casanova walked in on Winckelmann early one morning and surprised him with his trousers undone, lying upon a handsome boy. Winckelmann's explanation was a masterful piece of deceit and sophistry. He said that he had always admired the ancients, who were all buggers, and that he felt he should resemble his heroes more, so he had attempted an experiment with the boy. But it was no good, he said, for he found women preferable.

In a letter to an old friend in Germany Winckelmann confessed with pleasure: 'I have no worries other than my work, and have even found someone with whom I can speak of love; a good-looking, blond young Roman of sixteen, half a head taller than I am; but I only see him once a week, when he dines with me on Sunday evening.'

There is a theory[15] that Winckelmann chose Arcangeli, a particularly unattractive man, to consort with specifically to be punished.

This urge to be punished is a result of the schizophrenia within society. Unable to declare love for a beautiful youth publicly, Winckelmann, like so many others after him, felt it was his fault and that he should be blamed for his transgressions. But if the crime was kept secret then only he, Winckelmann, would know how unworthy and bad he really was. In that case he must punish himself. From this time on the need to journey on a path to self-destruction is found in the lives of homosexual men, especially when they are renowned and praised, for they cannot cope with the thought that if society really knew the truth, they would be hounded and vilified. Was the celebrity status of Winckelmann a factor in his murder? Did the cobbler's son become yet another victim of homophobic society? Or had his social ambition lured him into agreeing to be Maria Theresa's secret agent and he bungled the whole affair? Whatever the truth, Arcangeli was tried, convicted and sentenced for Winckelmann's murder and was broken upon the wheel in front of the hotel where they had stayed.

LAND OF THE FREE

At this time the American War of Independence was being fought and, as the New World too was imbued with the ideals of the Enlightenment, it is pertinent to inquire whether men labelled 'sodomite' fared any better there.

In the autumn of 1776, Thomas Jefferson and other leading citizens reviewed Virginian law, intending to reform it by stripping away all aspects of British monarchical rule and making it reflect Republican principles. Jefferson, a leading liberal, suggested with others that 'Rape, Sodomy, Bestiality . . . be punished by Castration'. Up to then these crimes had incurred the death penalty, so no doubt Jefferson and his colleagues felt they had taken a humane step. In the published Bill, polygamy was added to the list. If a woman was guilty of any of the crimes, she was to be punished 'by cutting thro' the cartilage of her nose a hole of one half inch diameter at the least'. The note to the Bill defined sodomy: 'Buggery is twofold. 1 with mankind. 2 with beasts. Buggery is the Genus, of which Sodomy and Bestiality are the species.'[16]

Two years later George Washington court-martialled Lieutenant Frederick Gotthold Enslin for attempting to commit sodomy with a soldier, one John Monhort. Enslin was to be dismissed from the service 'with Infamy'. It was ordered that he be drummed out of camp by all the drummers and fifers in the army, never to return.

Yet we have letters dated a year later, 1779, from Alexander Hamilton to John Laurens, both serving officers in Washington's army, part of his 'family' as he liked to call them, letters which abound in protestations of undying love. Hamilton's biographer writes: 'they were not merely soldiers doing a job; they were classical scholars whose thoughts and actions were coloured by the grandeur of antiquity. They lived – and often died – by the code of the heroes of Plutarch.'[17] How far the shadow of Winckelmann had reached.

Hamilton wrote:

I wish, my dear Laurens it might be in my power, by action rather than words, to convince you that I love you . . . you should not have taken advantage of my sensibility to step into my affections without my consent. But as you have done it and as we are generally indulgent to those we love, I shall not scruple to pardon the fraud you have committed, on condition that for my sake, if not for your own, you will always continue to merit the partiality, which you have so artfully instilled into me.

Laurens was married, and Hamilton often forwarded letters from his wife. At the attack on Charleston, Laurens was taken prisoner by the British. Hamilton became engaged to a Miss Schuyler. He wrote again: 'In spite of Schuyler's black eyes, I have still a part for the public and a part for you . . . as if after matrimony I was to be less devoted than I am now.'

There was an exchange of prisoners and Laurens was set free to fight the British again. In another letter, dated August 1782, Hamilton describes being delegated to Congress, and ends by saying: 'we have fought side by side to make America free, let us hand in hand struggle to make her happy.' A few days later Laurens was shot in a minor skirmish. It is not known whether he ever received Hamilton's last letter.

It is unclear whether or not this relationship contained any carnal element. Of his marriage Hamilton says: 'I intend to restore the empire of Hymen.' Why 'restore'? Hamilton was twenty-two and Laurens was twenty-five when they first met as Washington's aides. In the same letter Hamilton talks of his fiancée as loving Laurens 'à l'americaine not à la française'. The inference here is 'not in a tactile manner', for both the British and the Americans had stopped the custom between men of greeting by kissing, such exhibitions of affection were thought to be a nasty foreign habit. The authors of Satan's Harvest Home (1749) thought male kissing was an example of Italian effeminacy which led to sodomy, so such behaviour among the British was thought to be an affront.*

The correspondence, redolent with intense emotion, surely implies some physical caresses between the two young men. Yet, as they compared themselves to Damon and Pythias, well known for their passionate friendship,† heroism and Platonic love, it equally seems reasonable to suppose that there was no carnality within their relationship. However, there is also the matter of their admiration for and hero-worship of Baron Frederick von Steuben (1730–94), a major-general in the American revolutionary army. In one of those great ironies of history, if Steuben had not been implicated in a scandal back home in Germany which involved taking

---

* A German travel book of 1819 warned visitors: 'The kiss of friendship between men is strictly avoided as inclining towards the sin regarded in England as more abominable than any other.'[18]
† Damon was a Pythagorean philosopher from Syracuse, renowned for his friendship with Pythias (whose name is in fact Phintias). The latter, condemned to death, left Syracuse to arrange his affairs, leaving Damon to stand surety for him, and returned in time to redeem his friend. The tyrant, impressed, pardoned Pythias.

familiarities with young boys, the War of Independence might well have been won by the British.

Steuben went to America at the invitation of Benjamin Franklin, who had told Washington that Steuben was fired with zeal for 'our cause'. Steuben had been born into a military family and had led a soldier's life from the age of sixteen. Once in America, Congress appointed him to train the Continental forces; this became a model drill company copied throughout the ranks. In 1778 Steuben was appointed Inspector General of the army, with the rank of major-general. Once in charge he collected round him a circle of admiring young officers which included both Laurens and Hamilton. Two of them, William North and Ben Walker, he legally adopted as his sons and heirs.

If there was a core of physical expression in this inner circle of Washington's aides then they were either deluding themselves in the Winckelmann mode, believing their pure and ideal love purged the evil which society declared such sexual acts had, or they were as brave in love as they must have been on the battlefield. It was a time when scandal and homophobia were never far from the surface. They lived in a vast land where unknown territories were constantly being explored. Reports about the peoples discovered there were brought back, often by Jesuits. Father Font wrote a diary on his second journey to California in the expedition of Juan Bautista Anza (1775–6), recording men dressed as women. He wondered whether they were hermaphrodites but then learnt that they were sodomites 'dedicated to these nefarious practices'. A few years earlier Jean Bernard Bossu had written *Travels in the Interior of North America 1752–1762* in which he stated that the Choctaws were 'addicted to sodomy'.

Women who may have been bisexual were treated with rather more sympathy by the American army. In September 1782 Deborah Sampson, aged twenty-two, was excommunicated from the First Baptist Church of Middleborough, Massachusetts. The church accused her 'of dressing in men's clothes and behaving very loose and unchristian'. By that time she had already enlisted as Robert Shurtleff in the Revolutionary Army and as a member of the fourth Massachusetts Regiment she fought in several battles. Over a year later she caught a fever and was placed in a hospital in Philadelphia where her true gender was discovered. General Henry Knox gave her an honourable discharge. In 1785 she married a farmer, Benjamin Gannett, and they had three children. Throughout her life she received a pension for her war services. When she died in 1827 the US Congress passed an Act 'for the relief of the heirs of Deborah Gannett, a soldier of the Revolution, deceased'.[19]

A biography of Deborah was published in 1797 which, though written in the customary florid manner, goes into some detail about three romantic attachments to girls she had while masquerading as Robert Shurtleff. The anonymous author declares of these relationships: 'Surely it must have been that of sentiment, taste, purity; as animal love, on her part, was out of the question.' The tone is far too knowing throughout. One feels that the author had made the same observations as Moreau de St Mery, a French lawyer and politician who lived in America from 1793 to 1798. He was shocked at the disregard that parents in Philadelphia had for the manner in which their daughters formed relationships: 'I am going to say something that is almost unbelievable. These women, without real love and without passions, give themselves up at an early age to the enjoyment of themselves; and they are not at all strangers to being willing to seek unnatural pleasures with persons of their own sex.'

One is forced to conclude that the Enlightenment did nothing to liberalise either the law or the attitudes to same-sex loving on either side of the Atlantic. On the contrary, there is ample proof that prejudice against the expression of such love grew and hardened throughout this time.

THE PAGAN PHALLUS

Both the classical and the Christian worlds were phallocentric, but while the former openly celebrated the phallus, the latter suppressed all phallic imagery or else caricatured it, hoping to render such imagery harmless. Because the Enlightenment broke the stranglehold that Christian theology had upon the past, pagan worlds began to be scrutinised again and the censorship that the church had imposed was ignored.

In the majority of relationships between males, the phallus inevitably plays a significant part: it might be revered, is an object of awe, even takes on magical, quasi-mystical properties. Homosexuals tend therefore to be sympathetic to rituals and religions based upon the celebration of the human phallus. In the homophobic society born just before 1700, same-sex loving took on a new aspect, that of a revolutionary weapon; the act of sodomy had become subversive. It is in this light that the story of a small circle of eighteenth-century gentlemen pursuing archaeological research has a particular resonance.

As we have seen, Winckelmann opened up the ancient world to travellers and rich antiquarians. One of the most renowned was Sir William Hamilton,[20] the English envoy in Naples, a position which allowed him ample time to pursue his scientific studies. He was especially interested in volcanic eruptions and lava streams, he collected classical antiquities and explored the archaeological remains which that area was so rich in. It was Hamilton who discovered an ancient priapic cult in Isernia outside Naples – an account was published later by the Society of Dilettanti. Hamilton was helped and encouraged in his account of Isernia and in his rapid collection of 200 antique vases inside a year by one Pierre François Hugues. This man was a bizarre reprobate who managed to charm a wide circle of intelligent gentlemen. (Voltaire thought highly of his brain, though less of his character.) He went under the title of Baron d'Hancarville, a one-time intimate of Winckelmann, and was described as a 'drifter, forever being expelled from one place and seeking another, always in debt, often in prison'. Winckelmann wrote to his nephew that when he showed the gems to the baron he must keep his eyes on the man's hands.

Hugues was born in Nancy in 1719, the son of a bankrupt cloth merchant. As a child he began to study languages and science and quickly attained a mastery of ancient and modern languages. He once wrote of his early years: 'those gloomy days, when, by the sport of capricious fortunes, the low intrigues of Courtiers, and the ambitions of Princes, I saw, like Damocles, the fatal sword continually hanging over my head.' He was constantly being arrested and thrown into prison. With the Duke of Wurtemberg he attempted to buy the island of Corsica, but then he was arrested for stealing the Duke's silver. He travelled in the Iberian peninsula, and published a philosophical pamphlet proving that morality was a matter of political calculation. (Frederick the Great said that d'Hancarville was indeed an expert on the morality of stealing.)

Even in his eighties he could mesmerise an audience. At the Salon of Isabella Teotochi Albrizzi, one of the most famous society hostesses in Venice at the turn of the century, he could talk of Parnassus, Raphael and the temple of Segesta and keep his absorbed circle wrapt. Isabella wrote: 'his penetrating voracious eyes, his flaring nostrils, his lips which barely touch each other are the outward signs of his longing to see everything, having known everything, he wins you over with his learning and his prolific and imaginative way of speaking.'

Throughout his life he had a flair for making the past come alive, and also for drawing the most fascinating and original deductions from archaeological evidence. Whether his deductions were correct or not is another matter altogether. The fact is that d'Hancarville believed they were, and had the authority to convince the learned circle that he moved among. But the Baron also had to make a living and when he did not manage to acquire a patron he had to survive by other means. He became a salesman, a fixer for antiquarians, a pulp publisher of the erotic and pornographic in antiquity. He sold two books to Hamilton and then contrived to make a huge profit by publishing cheap copies of them.* All the illustrations of supposed antique obscenity were modern forgeries, yet Hamilton continued to retain and subsidise the baron for some years, until he was expelled from Naples on 'pain of death if he ever returned'. He then turned up in London in

---

* *Monuments de la vie privée des douze Cesars* and *Monuments du Culte Secret des Dames Romaines*. Both books are so rare today they are almost unknown.

1777 and Hamilton introduced him to Charles Townley, a rich bachelor, Italiophile and antiquarian. In Townley's Westminster house the Baron began to catalogue the finest collection of antiquities to be seen in England. Zoffany painted the scene, *Charles Townley and his Friends*, in 1781, with Baron d'Hancarville seated in the midst of the sculptures.

In 1786, *Discourse on the Worship of Priapus and its Connexion with the Mystic Theology of the Ancients* by Richard Payne Knight (1751–1824) was published. Though the book is without structure – there are no chapters – it reads like a learned dissertation and has many footnotes culled from the writings of the Baron d'Hancarville. Knight duly acknowledged that many of the ideas derived from the Baron, but he gave a 'witty, Voltairian icy form to the more ponderous learning of his mentor'. Knight's intention was also to amplify Sir William Hamilton's as yet unpublished account of the Isernia priapic cult.

Richard Payne Knight was born into luxury, but was a sickly child. His family were West Country Tory landowners who devalued book-learning because it interfered with piety and obedience. His father forbade him to study 'those pagan ancient Greeks'. Nevertheless, Knight was tutored at home and managed to acquire an education. He then wandered through Italy, eventually inheriting his grandfather's fortune. Like Beckford, whose background and early adult experiences are similar, he rebuilt the family castle, Downton, the main part being a tower to which he could retreat.

After Knight had completed Downton, he took the young painter Robert Cozens with him on another Italian tour. They travelled together as far as Naples and then separated. Cozens stayed on in Italy where he also travelled with Beckford, who became another of his patrons. Cozens was not the first or the last young man to be sponsored and cultivated by Knight, who obviously had a weakness for dashing young men, while he had few if any female friends and remained unmarried. Charles Townley, too, would remain a bachelor for the whole of his life.

In 1782 we find Townley writing to Knight complaining of

Baron d'Hancarville as a profligate bohemian, 'filling his belly frequently at my house with an occasional loan of 5 guineas', even if he compensated with 'more rational and more satisfactory disquisitions on ancient art than all I had found in the absurd books of Antiquaries'. Haskell, the Baron's biographer, talks of his intoxicating effect on those who came to know him; the Baron could win admiration even when it became all too clear that he was not the gentleman he claimed to be. It was undoubtedly this effect he had upon Knight. Like Winckelmann and Hamilton before him, like Isabella and her salon in the future, Knight became enchanted, spellbound by those learned disquisitions.

Knight became a frequent visitor to Townley's drawing room, convinced that the Baron was a genius. The Baron's book, Knight thought as he wrote to Townley, 'promises to be such an Acquisition to all lovers of Ancient Arts and History that he must at all events be enabled to complete it'. The Baron had been espousing his theory of ancient fertility rites ever since he had met Sir William Hamilton in 1764, and it was part of his wicked charm, for such topics were censored in the polite drawing rooms of Europe. If Townley and Knight were going to subsidise a book on the subject, by an author they knew to be a maverick, they must have been well aware that it would be seen as a radical and subversive act.

In 1785 the book was published in England, but in French, and Knight was given a three-volumed copy: *Recherches sur l'Origine, l'Esprit et Les Progres des arts de la Grece*. For the first time a book on art and religion absorbed the first discoveries of the religions and literature of India and the Far East. D'Hancarville was fascinated by the light that Indian sculptures threw upon Greek art and mythology, and he linked Moses, Bacchus and Osiris. The book also included a view of ancient and modern theology, a discussion of the treasures of Mount Ararat and a dissertation on hermaphrodites.

All this time Knight was working on his own book. The Society of Dilettanti sponsored it but then planned to limit its circulation – only eighty copies of *Priapus* were published. In the book Knight wished to provide a comparison between the religious rituals of pagans and Christians, hoping to demonstrate that both had the same meaning but differed in how they conveyed it. In so doing he demonstrated that the cult of fertility lay at the heart of all religions. It caused a furore, for various reasons.

First, it was an attack upon Christianity. Almost every page contains a note of scepticism about the church from its inception, criticising 'the zealous propagators of the Christian faith' who 'condemn the rites and doctrines of others and the furious zeal and bigotry with which they maintain their own'. Christian morality is the main target of the work, while enlightened paganism and its toleration of homosocial desire is praised. Second, the book dealt with phallus worship, a subject censored in polite society. Its certain companion, same-sex loving, was never mentioned in the reactions to the work but lay within the sub-text, awkward and tacit, fuelling the vilification of Knight who soon tried to buy back all the copies. A few Whigs defended him. Hamilton's nephew, Charles Greville, professed to be liberated by its discoveries; another, Roger Wilbraham, was very sympathetic but he was described by Joseph Farrington, a contemporary diarist, as 'a debauchee much given to loose conversation on such subjects as priapus'.

In the first few years after the book's publication the Dilettanti Society controlled the distribution of the copies, then, in the aftermath of the French Revolution, as aristocrats went to the guillotine, there was a rumour that the English authorities viewed *Priapus* as subversive to the national church and government. No review copies were ever sent out. Then in 1790 came an attack from T.J. Matthias in the First Dialogue of his *Pursuits of Literature* which called it a criminal obscenity, lewd and debauched, the illustrations being disgusting, 'containing all the ordure and filth, all the antique pictures and all the representations of generative organs in their most odious and degrading protrusion'. Matthias prophesied Sodom and Gomorrah if *Priapus* was to find its way into schools and colleges.

Another who was revolted by the book was Horace Walpole,

now a septuagenarian bachelor living his solitary last years in the gothic fantasy of Strawberry Hill, going to bed cushioned in peacock feathers and pink satin. The exaltation of pagan religion and Knight's claim for sexual enlightenment disgusted and offended Walpole who thought him insolent and conceited. Knight was blackballed in the London clubs. In the eyes of London society he had committed a worse crime than any Frenchman espousing liberty, fraternity and equality. It was profoundly shocking that Knight should think that phallic rites were a sacred and symbolic language when they were nothing but the lascivious designs of antiquity.

Walpole's strong antagonism to *Priapus* as both ironic and hypocritical when seen in the light of his youthful ardour for Lord Lincoln's over-large penis. Walpole had hymned Lincoln's tool, which he used on both men and women, in love letters and verses which praised his 'majestic vigour'. He had gossiped with friends about Lincoln's phallic might and even examined in minute detail the actual size of Lincoln's genitalia. The obsession that Walpole had had in his twenties now seemed to fuel his hatred for Knight's book, as if he could not endure to share a source of such obsessive delight with pagan and religious rites as described in a work of scholarship.

D'Hancarville, horrified at an abusive review of his own book, had moved to Paris where he sympathised with the Revolution, writing an amusing letter to Townley describing the documents found within the Bastille. But the Terror was too much for him and he fled to Rome and from there, a few years later, to Venice. He was now admired and revered, his conversation always dazzling. In digging into the springs of religion and creativity he had unearthed a simple explanation for all the varieties of artistic experience: all art was inspired by religion, but religion was based on sexuality. D'Hancarville died in Venice in 1805, refusing to the end to divulge, even to his confessor, how old he was.

Knight was saddled with the authorship of *Priapus* for the rest of his life. He was considered an erotic devotee of the 'Temple of Sensuality', and was caricatured as a satyr. By the 1820s his radical anti-clericalism expressed in the book had become legendary. Nevertheless, he had changed the view of the phallus from something grotesque and comic to a threatening symbol of fertility and unorthodox love. This is exactly what the Victorians loathed and did not want to learn. Knight's view of Greek myths and a religion which lay in phallic worship was anathema to later scholars. An eight-volume history of Greece by Connop Thirlwall (published in 1835) did not even mention the figure of Priapus. Greek history had to be fit for ladies and must not disturb students.

Recent scholars see Richard Payne Knight's work in a wholly different light, as being original and innovative, far before its time, almost modern in its perception in bringing sex openly into the daylight of history and mythology. As to his subject, a recent classicist has said: 'The story of phallic rule at the root of Western civilisation has been suppressed, as a result of the near monopoly that men have held in the field of Classics, by neglect of such rich pictorial evidence, by prudery and censorship, and by a misguided desire to protect an idealised image of Athens.'[21]

Whether d'Hancarville was physically loved by either Townley or Knight is unknown, but unlikely. When the Baron stayed with Townley at his house in Westminster he was around sixty. A drawing of him at Padua shows an appealing, rather boyish profile with lips parted in mischief. As a younger man he may well have had his conquests in the bedroom as well as the drawing room. He was certainly not much put out (in fact, one suspects, rather relieved) when in 1761 his pregnant mistress ran off with a monk. The sexual natures of both Knight and Townley are also unknown. Their love of Italy suggests a sexual as much as an aesthetic fascination, their cultivation of young men, their lack of female friends and the original work of Knight's *Priapus* are the only clues to them having been secret sexual renegades.

THE ROMANTIC AGONY

The homophobic society had not only produced an oppressed rebellious minority, but also the sentimentalisation of unrequited love. It is from within the despair of the black gulf of frustrated expression that the concept of 'the love that dare not speak its name' stems. As we have seen, Rochester and friends tended to shout its name from tavern balconies while Shakespeare could write over 120 sonnets celebrating the ecstasies and anguish of such love, but now, suddenly, not only had the prison walls emerged to shut out, suppress and distort the truth of the recent past, but also, in its deep anxiety, society continued to persecute and punish any sign of its rebirth.

August von Platen (1796–1835)[22] agonised over his sexuality to the extent of contemplating suicide throughout his short life. Fortunately he kept a diary (it was not published until the end of the nineteenth century) which details his travels and romantic longings. He first fell in love in his teens with a handsome young nobleman he saw at a court ball: 'I will love him to a passionate enthusiasm, I will call out his name in a fiery ecstasy when I am alone.' He continued to fall in love with handsome young aristocrats, but never dared to express his interest. His self-imposed silence led to romantic pining, to an over-sentimentalised daydreaming about the heroic virtues of the loved one. One such figure, Prince Oettingen-Wallerstein, a member of the Bavarian royal family, died in battle, forcing Platen into mourning for a lost love he had never fulfilled. Such fantasy romances tend to undermine a person's sense of reality, yet another result of the social censorship of the time.

Then Platen met another student, Justus Leibig (1803–73), who was to become famous as a chemist for his research into proteins and for the invention of artificially fertilising soil.* They had an affair. And there were others: Eduard Schmidtlein inspired 300 pages of diary entries, and Captain Friedrich von Brandenstein, 'the darling of my heart for almost a year'. In the diary it is clear that in many of these romantic attachments only kisses and caresses were allowed, but in 1819 Platen wrote rapturously of

---

* Leibig has to take some responsibility for today's problems of soil infertility and nitrate pollution of rivers, lakes and seas.

Schmidtlein that 'Eduard at last gave himself up to me with a tenderness without reserve, a tenderness equal to mine. We were simply one soul, and our bodies were like two trees whose branches interlace closely forever.' His poetry chronicled their affair.

> Mid flowery perfumes, Oh here let us lie,
> Cheek against cheek, at dusk beneath the trees,
> Breast pressing close to breast and thigh to thigh.

But rapture declines and in the third sonnet it is disclosed that 'thou hast a heart as black as thy black eyes'. These amorous affairs with his student colleagues ended once Platen began to travel.

Once he had discovered Italy, Platen seems also to have discovered a more relaxed sexuality, but sadly his diaries remain reticent about the details. In Rome he 'made the acquaintance of a big, beautiful blond Roman who is a captain in the local regiment'. In Naples he sees, 'handsome, cheerful and adorable' men and he is happy to report that 'love between men is so common that one cannot choose to refuse the most daring demands'. He loved Venice and wrote seventeen sonnets to celebrate it; one describes a gondolier, the first but by no means the last romantic attachment writers were to have for Venetian boatmen.* Thomas Mann was fascinated by the relationship between Platen's poetry and his sexuality. Though a fervent admirer of his verse, Mann was critical of Platen's life. He speaks of love filling Platen's whole work: 'melancholy adoring love, ever and again rising to higher flights of ardour; endless, unquenchable love, which issues in death.' Platen's death inspired Mann to create Ashenbach in his novel *Death in Venice*. When a cholera epidemic hit Italy, Platen fled Naples, but he had already contracted the disease and he died a few days later in Sicily.

A few years earlier, Ralph Waldo Emerson (1803–82) had

---

*John Addington Symonds, Baron Corvo and L.P. Hartley all had romantic attachments to gondoliers.

suffered all the ardour and anguish of suppressed romantic love for a fellow student, Martin Gay. His journal begins in 1820, when Emerson was seventeen and a student at Harvard, and records his growing fascination for Gay. Emerson begins: 'there is a strange face in the Freshman class whom I should like to know very much.' Two months later, in the new term, the two students were eyeing each other, and Emerson talks of the Indian doctrine of eye fascination. But some time after writing these entries Emerson returned to the pages and censored the name and some of the thoughts, so there are gaps in the record. However, pen-and-ink sketches known to be of Gay by Emerson have been left.

Emerson listened anxiously to gossip about Gay, and was disappointed to hear that he was lazy, but others spoke of Gay as a superior man. Later, in the spring of 1821, Emerson was sorry to learn that Gay was dissolute: 'I wished my friend to be different from any individual I had seen. I invested him with a solemn cast of mind, full of poetic feeling, and an idolater of friendship, and possessing a vein of rich sober thought.' But Emerson was still entirely unacquainted with him and for a year he had entertained the same feelings and would be 'sorry to lose him altogether before we have ever exchanged above a dozen words'.[23]

A month later Emerson was dawdling in the morning, putting himself in the path of Gay, then noticing with alarm that Gay was taking pains to avoid him. The diary is confused and puzzled: 'All this baby play persists without any apparent design, and as soberly as both were intent on some tremendous affair.' He was worried that the diary would fall into the wrong hands and decided to burn it. But it was another whole year after graduation from Harvard before Emerson could write: 'the ardour of my college friendship is nearly extinct.' In all this time it would seem that they exchanged only a few words, and those were awkward, ill-at-ease, desultory comments.

Martin Gay graduated from Harvard in 1826 and in time became a well-known doctor, chemist, member of the Boston Society of Natural History and Fellow of the American Academy of Arts and Sciences. Without doubt Gay would have read the poetry and essays of Emerson. Did it ever cross his mind that the famous and distinguished philosopher had once been tormentedly in love with him? Such intriguing information was another victim of the self-censorship imposed by a society afraid to allow its citizens the freedom of natural feelings. The agony and depths of stoic frustration in Emerson's diary are so strong that our reactions now are likely to veer towards anger at the indoctrination which Emerson and countless others suffered, which so successfully killed the roots of friendship and love.

There was at this time one exception to the repressed agony of unspoken love, one throwback to the glorious days of overt expression which men like Rochester celebrated, and he was another poet – Lord Byron (1788–1824). There is no doubt that Byron was bisexual, some might say omnisexual for his sensuality extended in all directions without anxiety, although he had the sense not to pursue young men and boys until he was across the English Channel. As a youth at Harrow and then at Cambridge, Byron fell in love with fellow students. One, John Edlestone, he immortalised (though changing the pronouns to the feminine) in the 'Thyrza' section of *Childe Harold*.[24] Elsewhere in the same poem, the Apollo Belvedere statue which had so excited Winckelmann was praised, though such praises were seen through the eyes of a woman. John Edlestone was fifteen and Byron seventeen when they first met, and as the boy's background was humble Byron assumed the role of aristocratic patron to a talented youth. Byron was generous and when Edlestone wished to give him a gift he could only afford an inexpensive stone, a cornelian. Afraid that Byron would dismiss the ring, the boy burst into tears of humiliation which moved Byron into writing 'The Cornelian'. There is some doubt as to whether this relationship was carnal, but it was certainly intensely romantic on both sides. They planned to live together, but also thought it best to separate for a year and a half. Edlestone left Cambridge and took a post in London as a clerk at the Admiralty. Byron wrote:

Edlestone and I have separated for the present and my mind is a chaos of hope and sorrow. We shall probably not meet till the extirpation of my minority, when I shall leave to his decision, either entering as a Partner through my Interest, or residing with me altogether. Of course he would in his present frame of mind prefer the latter, but he may alter his opinion previous to that period, however he shall have his chance, I certainly love him more than any human being and neither time or Distance have had the least effect on my changeable Disposition ... He is certainly perhaps more attached to me, than even I am in return. During the whole of my residence in Cambridge, we met every summer and winter, without passing one tiresome moment and separated each time with increasing reluctance. I hope you will one day see us together. He is the only being I esteem, though I like many.[25]

But Byron always tended to grow tired of his affairs with both men and women, and a year or two later, when Byron was travelling, Edlestone died. Byron carried around a lock of Edlestones hair for the rest of his life.

In Albania, a chieftain and his son were both much taken by the handsome aristocrat. Byron wrote: 'In England the vices in fashion are whoring and drinking, in Turkey, Sodomy and smoking. We prefer a girl and a bottle, they a pipe and a pathic.'* Later, in 1809, he speaks of his young Greek companion, one Eustathius, who has 'ambrosial curls hanging down his amiable back ... we travelled very much enamoured ... our parting was vastly pathetic, as many kisses as would have sufficed for a boarding school, and embraces enough to have ruined the character of a county in England'.

When staying in a monastery in Athens, Byron started a passionate sexual relationship with a fifteen-year-old youth, Nicolo Giraud, a French citizen of Italian and Greek background. They

---

* The word 'pathic' comes via Latin from the Greek 'pathikos' meaning passive.

travelled around Greece together, Giraud taught Byron Italian, and they visited Malta.

On his return to England, Byron had affairs with women. The first decade of the nineteenth century was stained by a series of trials and hangings for sodomy, so it is hardly surprising that Byron contained any longings for a 'pathic' that he might have. But there are signs in his comments on the *Satyricon* that he had so much sexual expression with Giraud that he was almost tired of it. It was not until he returned to Greece in 1823 to fight for Greek independence that he began a new relationship with a youth, one Lukas. In his last poems, suppressed after his death and not published until 1887, the power of this passion is revealed.

> I am the fool of passion – and a frown
> Of thine to me is as an Adder's eye
> To the poor bird whose pinion fluttering down
> Wafts unto death the breast I bore so high –
> Such is this maddening fascination grown,
> So strong thy Magic – or so weak am I.

WEST AND EAST

There was one other factor – besides the rise of capitalism, consumerism and the Calvinist work ethic – that was responsible for the homophobic societies of the West: the breakdown and dissipation of a rigid class structure.

In the East, both China and Japan retained a rigid class structure until they were finally invaded by the West in the late nineteenth century. In both societies one finds an acceptance of pederasty and same-gender loving, for it is largely based upon the privileged exploiting the less fortunate, so one finds sexual relationships marked by a difference in class as well as by a difference in age. Western observers were horrified to find boy-brothels in Shanghai. While in Japan, 'we find a society in which male homosexuality was integrated into normal sexual life by means of social conventions governing relations between men and youths in much the same way that male–female relations were regulated.'[26] In neither country was there a powerful middle class, setting up new ethical role-models for the socially ambitious.

In the West, the burgeoning rise and power of the bourgeoisie was a continuing threat to the rule of the elite; social change had quickened its pace and it was possible for the sons of bankrupt cobblers to be the centre of attention in the salons of Venice. A sugar plantation owner could become the richest man in England. There was a feeling of insecurity; nothing was quite what it seemed.

To add a blurring of gender to this shifting world must have seemed like the last outrage. For there was a powerful need to feel that gender definition was secure, and in the eighteenth century we find a redefinition, in a much more precise way, of both male and female, which is linked to class. The middle classes had to create their own customs and manners; in this creation they imposed limits and restrictions, criteria by which they might be judged worthy of the social position they occupied.

Those qualities that were becoming associated with the truly feminine were celebrated in the romantic and sentimental fiction of the period. Women had to be gentle, kind, obedient, dutiful, passive and acquiescent, they must involve themselves with domestic duties. Hannah More in 1783 wrote of the 'almost sacred joys of home'.[27] These joys, though not specified, included sexual ones, for by this time the notion of the husband as romantic lover was one of the expectations that a bride had. Sex was seen not just as a marital duty, but in its modern role of expressing, sustaining and strengthening love.[28] In this context, the idea of a man masquerading as a woman became obscene and repugnant to the ethical concepts that the market economy had created. Female values resided in childcare, welfare work and to a lesser degree the fine arts and crafts. The middle-class woman's role was defined in terms of emotional sensitivity, in the way she cared for children and animals. She was idealistic and romantic, credited with aesthetic responsibility for furnishings and dress.[29]

Women's clothes became more frivolous in this age, but the men, instead of wearing a dress and being covered in powder, paint and perfume, had to be in the midst of the marketplace, competing. The logic of the market demands egoism and individualism, it is a matter of fighting your corner for what you believe are your rights. A man needed new skills, more subtle and devious forms of aggression and antagonism, flexibility and ingenuity, for the male was alone, not acting as part of a group. He also responded to the puritan ethic, becoming zealous and bureaucratic, yet rational and pragmatic. In England, too, at this time there was a sense of national pride in the spirit of free trade and in the growing influence of Britain in the world at large.

The aristocracy kept itself as a small elite. Middle-class wealth did not admit you into the top rank who were defensive about their rituals and privileges, constantly creating new rules so that outsiders would be both recognised and alienated. Admittance to the burgeoning and influential bourgeoisie, however, required a clear distinction between genders; the more profound the difference between men and women, the more the middle classes were impressed. This rigidity of class and the significance it placed on distinct gender difference grew throughout the next century until it became a shibboleth characteristic of Empire and Colonialism.

X

EMPIRE
AND INDUSTRY

England at the beginning of the nineteenth century was on the brink of an era of prosperity and world influence unrivalled in its whole history. Yet society had been wounded by two revolutions – that of the Americans and the French – which influenced public awareness by spreading ideas of individual freedom and responsibility, of humane ethics free from a patriarchal deity. These ideas were feared as something bound to disrupt and destroy orthodox society. Sodomy had been thought to come from France and Italy and the new revolutionary ideas were tainted by the same sexual anarchy.

The burgeoning empire and the spread of colonialism brought about the need to project a particular image. You can see it in portraits of the military and the statesmen – there is nothing relaxed or genial about these male figures, they are authoritative and arrogant, proud and inflexible; they wear a carapace of superiority; they are rulers and, to some, including themselves, almost gods. What marks the age of empire so distinctly is the conviction that the image is the reality, the male as superior being, as all-conquering and masterful, the ultimate judge and arbiter of morals. It was an age when the puritan ethic reached a zenith, for powerful men used it as a weapon to oppress and exploit.

Fuelling this superiority was a pride in the industrial riches that Britain had created. The Great Exhibition of 1851 not only symbolised this wealth of invention and talent but also exhibited it, while the building itself, nicknamed the Crystal Palace, in Asa Briggs's phrase showed 'the visibility of human progress'. The man of technology was the architect of the great leap forward, and the partner of the man of business. 'Commerce is the grand panacea, which like a beneficent medical discovery, will serve to inoculate with the healthy and saving taste of civilisation all the nations of the world,' wrote Richard Cobden (1804–65), the leading apostle of free trade. He went on:

> Not a bale of merchandise leaves our shores, but it bears the seeds of intelligence and fruitful thought to the members of some less enlightened community . . . while our steamboats, that now visit every port of Europe, and our miraculous railroads, that are the talk of all nations, are the advertisements and vouchers for the value of our enlightened institutions.[1]

Such high-falutin' imagery was commonplace, for there was a gulf, a great chasm, between the ideology and the reality, and the age was littered with examples of self-censorship, and a deliberate deadening of awareness which allowed inhumanity and barbarism to flourish. It was an age which celebrated a continuing narrowing of blinkered vision; an age which honoured the blindness bequeathed by intolerance and bigotry.

THE PERSECUTION CONTINUES

In a great many ways the new century took on many of the prejudices, fears, beliefs and sexual canons of the old, allowing them to sink deeper into national consciousness.

In the first few years of the century a spate of hangings for sodomy took place. In 1806 at the Lancaster assizes five men were convicted of sodomy. They had assembled regularly at the home of Isaac Hitchen (aged sixty-two), had called one another brother, and had engaged in sexual pleasure with one another.[2] The judge, sentencing all five of them to hang, 'lamented that such a subject should come before the public as it must do, and above all, that the untaught and unsuspecting minds of youth should be liable to be tainted by such horrid facts'.[3]

Mathusalah Spalding in 1804 was hanged at the Old Bailey for 'a venereal affair' with James Hankinson. In 1808 Richard Neighbour was convicted for buggery with Joshua Archer and sentenced to be hanged.[4] In the same year, the Home Secretary – later, the Prime Minister, Lord Liverpool – wrote to the rangers of Hyde Park and St James's Park, urging that the parks should be locked at night to stop men picking each other up: 'We must prevent these scandalous practices in such a way that the public is kept ignorant of the disgrace of them.'[5]

Then we have the Vere Street scandal involving the discovery of a molly house which catered for mock marriages. The house contained a chapel and rooms with four beds in them, so that nuptials were frequently consummated by 'two, three or four couples in the same room and in the sight of each other'.[6] It is interesting to note that, again, the customers in this male brothel were all working-class people: a chimney sweep, a coal merchant, a runner at the police office, a drummer in the Guards, a butcher, a waiter, a blacksmith and a grocer. Robert Holloway, who wrote a contemporary account of the case,* thought that most of these men were married. He cites one case where a 'Miss Read' lived with his lover, the chimney sweep, and his wife. Cook, the owner of the brothel, was married, and his wife ran a tavern in Long Acre. Many of the men arrested were set free because of lack of evidence, but six were pilloried and the scenes of mob fury were unprecedented. Holloway refers to a 'ruffianly scene of human degradation'. Another journalist commented: 'it is impossible for

---

* Robert Holloway, *The Phoenix of Sodom, or The Vere Street Coterie* (1813).

language to convey an adequate idea of the universal expressions of execration which accompanied these monsters on their journey.'

It is clear that sodomites and their sin were loathed with greater revulsion than ever before. Some sense of this profound disgust comes across in the words of a sailor court-martialled for buggery on HMS *Africaine* in 1815. Attempting to clear his name he spoke of 'a crime which would to God t'were never more seen on earth from those shades of hellish darkness whence to the misery of Man its propensity has been vomited forth'.[7] Four members of the crew were hanged for buggery the following year.

The idea that the act of sodomy was almost to consort with the devil was stressed even more in the United States. In 1810, one Davis was indicted in a court in Maryland 'for assaulting and attempting to commit sodomy on the body of WC . . . not having the fear of God before his eyes, but being moved and seduced by the instigation of the Devil . . . with force and arms . . . in and upon one WC, a youth of the age of 19 . . . intending the most horrible and detestable crime.' Davis was found guilty and was sentenced to be fined, gaoled and to stand in the pillory.[8]

Nor did condemned sodomites receive any understanding from their fellow convicts. A clergyman attached to one London prison reported in 1819: 'for unnatural offences the other prisoners themselves feel detestation, and I have continually heard them say, that the sufferers (those executed) richly deserved it.'[9] The irony was that the other convicts turned to fellow inmates for sexual relief, but because they despised themselves for it, they took their fury out on the condemned sodomites.

Louis Dwight was a prison visitor in Massachusetts and Georgia. In April 1826 he sent his findings to a government official: 'Boys are prostituted to the lust of old convicts . . . I am aware that the mere suggestion of this subject is so revolting, that we should gladly omit the further consideration of it; but if we would meet the evil and remove it, we must give our attention to the facts.' Dwight quotes another witness who was now a respectable man living in society, but who had served four years in a penitentiary: 'I have known boys . . . who, in consequence of a criminal association with the profligate and vile, have, in less than three months, become so perfectly brutalised as publicly to glory in every species of abomination.' Dwight then quotes a second witness, also an ex-prisoner: 'when a boy was sent to prison, who was of a fair countenance, there many times seemed to be quite a strife between old grey-headed villains, to secure his attention. Numerous presents were given for this purpose; and if it could be obtained, no art was left untried, to get the boy into the same room and the same bed.' Dwight ends his letter with a plea to separate juvenile delinquents from hardened offenders: 'Nature and humanity cry aloud for redemption from this dreadful degradation.'[10]

ROMANTIC LOVE...

Among young men of the middle and upper classes, an intense romantic fervour surrounded the idea of 'special friendship':

> At school friendship is a passion . . . All loves of after-life can never bring its rapture, or its wretchedness; no bliss so absorbing, no pangs of jealousy . . . so keen! . . . what bitter estrangements and what melting reconciliations; what scenes of wild recrimination, agitating explanations, passionate correspondence . . . what earthquakes of the heart . . . are confirmed in that simple phrase, a schoolboy's friendship!'

Nothing could be more romantic, more emotional, than this fervent statement from Disraeli's novel *Coningsby* (1844).

Charles Metcalfe (later, Governor-General of India) wrote to his sister in 1824: 'joys . . . in the pure love which exists between man and man, which cannot I think, be surpassed in that more alloyed attachment between the opposite sexes, to which the name of love is in general exclusively applied.'[11] Young men of this class and age walked about arm in arm, talked of loving friendships and wrote emotional letters to each other. The romance and ideology of friendship grew throughout the century; intimate, emotional relationships spawned poems and letters all of which seemed

257

curiously unaware of any possible sexual content. It was as if the whole ethos of romantic love had spilt over into male bonding, seemingly without a sexual component, yet we know that such a lack of carnality would have been both unreasonable and unlikely. There are vague references to 'base feelings' or to being 'a damned beast' in the stories of the time, but all we can do is speculate that if some genital pleasure had occurred in one of these friendships, then it would somehow have been transmuted into pure love by the alchemy of self-deception. In the lovers' minds it would have had no connection with the sodomy trials and punishments going on elsewhere in society.

Alfred, Lord Tennyson, Arthur Hallam and their coterie are examples of the dilemma of passionate love among students. Tennyson's poem *In Memoriam* expresses 'manly love' constantly in its devotion to Hallam's memory (Hallam had died tragically young in 1833). Scholars and biographers consider that there was no sexual expression in this relationship, yet Tennyson was not unaware that such a relationship had sexual implications. His intimate circle at Cambridge included the Apostles,* many of whom would never marry, but there were also two friends, both Apostles, William Butler and Richard Monckton Milnes, who certainly seem to have had sexual relations with both men and women. Milnes, according to his biographer James Pope-Hennessey, recorded a number of intimate friendships, including one with Arthur Hallam that lasted for a few months in 1829. Milnes travelled through Greece, Egypt and the Orient, gathering stories about pederasty, including an anecdote which referred to a young English officer named d'Arcy who had been assaulted by a Turkish soldier and was, in Milnes's view, a 'male Lucretia'.[12]

Tennyson's most devoted friend, second only to Hallam, was James Spedding, who appears always to have been sexually attracted to men. Another Apostle, Henry Lushington, remained

---

* The Apostles, an undergraduate society at Cambridge, was an elitist group, liberal conformist in politics, but with a sympathy for feminism and aware of the need to alter conventional gender roles.

unmarried and shared a house with yet another Apostle, George Venables. The latter's unpublished journals exhibit a one-sided devotion to Lushington, but also a commitment to a conservative moral code.[13]

As to Hallam, he wrote to Milnes in 1829: 'Though I have been the creature of impulse, though the basest passions have roused themselves in the deep caverns of my nature and swept like storm winds over me, . . . I will struggle yet, and have faith in God, that when I ask for bread, I shall not receive a stone.'[14] Is this a confession of powerful sexual desire for men? The Victorians were masters of not saying what they meant. In Hallam's prize-winning essay 'On Cicero' in 1831, he speaks of 'Greek love'. Though he refers to it as 'the noblest kind of love' with the effect of regenerating the soul, 'this highest and purest manly love' also devalued Athenian women. In his essay he appears to have entirely overlooked the dilemma of sexual fulfilment in these manly love relationships. Yet people were falling over themselves to fall in love with Hallam – not only Tennyson and his sister Emily, and Milnes, but the young William Gladstone as well. His intelligence, good looks and charm attracted men to him who were then halted by his reserve and air of superiority. Certainly the surviving letters which he wrote to these friends portray a priggish, over–idealistic soul obsessed with defining and redefining friendship so that it could not contain anything remotely base in it. Milnes wrote back at one point, a rather practical, down-to-earth note which one warms to, saying that he never thought 'we ever were or ever could be friends' in that exalted sense. Hallam died suddenly in 1833 while holidaying with his father in Vienna. He was suffering from the ague and though his father had sat with him all morning, in the afternoon he went for a walk and when he returned his son was dead. The doctor was called and opened up a vein in the wrist and another in the hand to determine that Hallam was dead – an odd procedure which gave rise to later rumours that Hallam had slashed his wrist. An autopsy was performed which declared he had had a stroke. Tennyson was heartbroken.

In later life Tennyson was worried that *In Memoriam* (published in 1850) was too overt in its expression of the love he held for Hallam and in the late 1870s he began to change personal pronouns. 'His living soul was flashed on mine' became 'The living soul . . .' 'And Mine in his was wound' became 'And mine in this . . .' Yet it is not difficult to see why the poem was such a huge success: it contrives to fulfil Victorian expectations of manly love and beauty. Hallam was too good and beautiful to live. He dies and this is his memorial. It has passion, ideals, death and no sex. The Victorians could hardly ask for more.

There is an interesting observation of Tennyson by the ever acute Jane Carlyle: 'Alfred is dreadfully embarrassed with women alone – for he entertains at one and the same moment a feeling of almost adoration for them and an ineffable contempt! adoration, I suppose for what they might be – contempt for what they are.'[15] The Victorian male tended to see women either as angels or demons, hardly ever as flawed human beings like themselves. This fantasy about women being either lofty and unapproachable or else luring the male into torrid sex is the inverse of the passionate male friendship – both divorce the Victorian male from a commonplace and pragmatic reality.

In American literature the same ideology of friendship existed, but where Europe contained the lure of the Mediterranean, with sun-burnished youths and the Byronic image of Greece, America contained unexplored wild territories and erotic natives as popularised by Fenimore Cooper. *John Brent*, a novel by Theodore Winthrop published in 1862, went through twenty-eight editions. It tells of the adventures of Richard Wade. On his first meeting with Brent, Wade takes him for an Indian and is struck by his beauty: 'Adonis of the copperskins . . . A beautiful youth! . . . There are a dozen romances in one look of that young brave . . . What a poem the fellow is! I wish I was an Indian myself for such a companion; or, better, a squaw, to be made love to by him.'[16] Is it likely that Winthrop's readers were unaware of the sub-text? Apparently so, for Richard Wade's remark was seen as a decent, manly appreciation of beauty. The handsome brave turns out to be an old school chum, once 'a delicate, beautiful dreamy boy' whom time has brought into harmony with the natural world. The two men search for Wade's sweetheart Ellen who has been captured by hostile Indians. For most of the novel Ellen is conveniently off-stage, either kidnapped or with her father in England. Wade learns about the natural world and also learns 'to love the man John Brent, as I had loved the boy; but as mature man loves man. I have known no more perfect union than that one friendship, nothing so tender in any of my transitory loves for women.' It is as if Winthrop is trying to communicate a rationale of sexless romantic love, but can do so only by debasing women. Later he says of the two men that in 'brotherhood they had trained each other to high thoughts of courtesy and love'. It is a form of 'knight errantry' (the Victorians, of course, had a fantasy that medieval chivalry was sexless too).

In another novel by Winthrop, *Cecil Dreeme*, the hero has to choose between two male loves; one is sinister and the other is gentle. Though attracted to the sinister man, he ultimately chooses the gentle one because it is discovered that he is a woman in disguise. The plot is a paradigm of the nineteenth-century male trauma and is summed up by what one scholar has called 'homosexual panic'.[17]

> [R]omantic love and the romantic novel grew together after 1780, and the problem of cause and effect is one that it is impossible to solve. All that can be said is that for the first time in history, romantic love became a respectable motive for marriage among the propertied classes, and that at the same time there was a rising flood of novels . . . devoted to the same theme.[18]

Love and love alone became the sovereign consideration in the choice of marriage partners, and the concept of romantic love that we are familiar with today originated then: that there is only one person in the whole world suitable for you, that love at first sight is like a thunderbolt out of the blue, that romantic love is the most important thing in the world to which everything should be sacrificed, and that we are entitled to give full rein to our emotions however absurd our conduct may seem to others.

The idea of a personal morality which is instinctive and which, if need be, ignores the dictates of church and state, grew in strength throughout the nineteenth century. It was a necessary ethic for the solitary lover of his or her own gender. But the ideas of romantic love were taken on board too, and as the century progressed, men like Walt Whitman, John Addington Symonds, Oscar Wilde and Edward Carpenter, extolled their youthful male lovers in the passionate language of sentimental novels where the hero woos the heroine. But there was another strong concept which stimulated the male psyche in homosocial relations.

... AND SELFLESS HEROISM

It was an age in which novels about single-sex boarding schools and special friendships were hugely popular. Inevitably they concerned worship by a pupil of an admired teacher or older student. Such schools and colleges were a response to the industrial wealth and rise of the affluent bourgeoisie; they taught a new structure of morality, stressing selflessness, public duty, responsibility for one's actions and a recognition of their consequences for others. The schools reflected the ethos of imperial Britain – pride and chauvinism in both the nation and religion. Sports and games were considered healthy and morally uplifting; beautiful bodies in boys and young men were fused with the idea of beautiful souls.

Edward Lefroy, a Victorian clergyman who devoted most of his output to the celebration of boys, was open in his dislike of heterosexuality yet stubbornly maintained that what he felt for beautiful youths was nobler and purer than any lustful desire for women:

I have an inborn admiration for beauty, of form and figure. It amounts almost to a passion, and in most football teams I can

find one Antinous . . . some folk would say it was . . . senti-
mentalism to admire any but feminine flesh. But that only
proves how base is the carnality, which is now reckoned the
only legitimate form. The other is far nobler . . . Platonic passion in any relationship is better than animalism.[19]

In all the stories there is a sacrifice – a little innocent dies to save another; a worthless scoundrel redeems himself at the last moment
by an act of heroism – and plots revolve round dark secrets which
are never quite explained. Innocent boys have no curiosity and are
confused when masters lecture them on 'those crimes far worse
than stealing'. And if they get involved with some older reprobate,
the little innocent redeems the sinner at the last moment.

Stories of boyish chivalry were complemented by tales and
paintings for adults which celebrated self-sacrifice. In Walter
Pater's *Studies in the History of the Renaissance* (1873), the first essay
concerns a medieval French romance. This is a story of the love between two men, one of whom replaces the other in battle; in return
the friend willingly sacrifices his own children so that his friend
can be healed of a disease which afflicts him, whereupon the gods
restore the children to life. In such stories, imbued with a homophile sub-text, there is no mention of what the wife and mother
thought when the father returned to sacrifice their children. It is in
the ancient Greek tradition in which the power of masculine love
somehow erases the mother.

CENSORSHIP

The very idea of sex between men in love was not only demonic,
the most hideous of all taboo subjects, but the act itself was never
talked about directly. Sir Robert Peel referred in Parliament to 'the
crime *inter Christianos non nominandum*', the crime Christians could
not name, largely because such behaviour was thought to be contagious. Lord Liverpool wanted the parks shut without the public
knowing why. Edward Gibbon thought sodomy was spread by

luxury, so simple poor people were 'exempt from this moral pestilence'.[20] It is the extent and intensity of the alarm and fear expressed which marks this age so distinctly.

There were other taboos which provoked explosive fury. This is the anonymous 'Walter' remembering his childhood:

> Just after I had one night exhausted myself by masturbating, my godfather came to see me. He stared hard at me. 'You look ill.' 'No, I'm not.' 'Yes you are, look me full in the face, you've been frigging yourself . . .' I denied it. He raved out. 'No denial, sir, no lies, you have sir; don't add lying to your bestiality, you've been at that filthy trick, I can see it in your face, you'll die in a mad house, or of consumption, you shall never have a farthing more pocket money from me, and I won't buy your commission, nor leave you any money at my death.' I kept denying it, brazening it out. 'Hold your tongue, you young beast, or I'll write to your mother.'[21]

A little later Walter tells us:

> My two intimate school-friends left off frigging, the elder brother who had a very long red nose, having come to the conclusion with me that frigging made people mad and, worse, prevented them afterwards from fucking and having a family. Fred, my favourite cousin, arrived at the same conclusion – by what mental process we all arrived at it, I don't know.

Walter was a sexual hedonist for the rest of his life, so it is all the more extraordinary for him to have exerted control in this matter, but his book serves to prove clearly the universality of the belief in the destructive effects of masturbation. It is also interesting that he genuinely seems not to realise how they all came to the same conclusion. Walter, always the realist, ever pragmatic, is at a loss to understand their group decision. Nor throughout his long pro-miscuous life did Walter stop believing in the evils of masturbation, though intermittently he still performed the 'sol-itary vice'. Unaware of the social indoctrination, he complains of depression, guilt, fatigue and general feelings of debilitation after a nocturnal emission or masturbation. None of this he feels, of course, after he has had sexual intercourse.

Considering that the marital age still remained high all over Europe – around thirty for men – it is not surprising that the num-ber of prostitutes on the streets continued to rise. In the mid-century, Norwich had 888 prostitutes – one for every twenty-three adult men. There were around 2,000 prostitutes in 360 houses in the City of London, parishes with a population of 59,000.[22] Walter is a mine of information about why working-class girls and those in domestic service became street women. A girl of fifteen who had to look after her younger sisters and brother while her mother went out all day charring did it for the food. All the mother could afford for her children was bread and scraps, but the girl with the pennies she earnt from whoring would buy herself pork pies and sausages. Another younger girl spent the money on sweets and bus rides. Two hundred child prostitutes under twelve were recorded in Liverpool in 1857. In these glimpses one sees how casual this promiscuous sex was and how socially acceptable. Alas, Walter was strongly heterosexual, so he tells us almost nothing about male prostitution. He did reach a time in his life when he felt that he should experiment and explore all forms of sexuality, but these incidents took place in a brothel and involved a prostitute with another man. Walter found that a powerful stimulus to fuck-ing a tart was imagining the sperm in her cunt as being from 'handsome, very young men'.

Brothels containing boys and youths certainly existed in England, but on nothing like the scale they did in Paris and Berlin. In 1837 David Romaine and William Sheen of Spitalfields were arrested for running well-established brothels specialising in young boys at the onset of puberty.[23] When these houses were closed the boys took to Piccadilly, the parks and railway stations.

'Don Leon'

Perhaps it was one of these young lads who led to the downfall of Richard Heber, the MP for Oxford and a well-known bibliophile. (At his death he left a magnificent collection of early English books, the volumes contained in eight different houses.) Heber suddenly fled to Brussels in 1826 and Walter Scott, a friend and admirer who had nicknamed him 'Heber the Magnificent', wrote in his journal: 'God, God, whom shall we trust!! Here is leaving wit, gaiety of temperament, high station in society and compleat reception everywhere, all at once debased and lost by such degrading bestiality. Our passions are wild beasts. God grant us power to muzzle them.'[24] Scott had heard only the vaguest rumours of 'unnatural practices' and once Heber had fled the details of the case remained unknown.

They are recalled, however, in a poem, 'Don Leon', which was published in 1866 but which was written in the 1830s. The poem bore Lord Byron's name as author, but as it refers to events which occurred after Byron's death it could not possibly have been a serious attempt at a literary forgery.

By 1833 Russia, Austria, Prussia and Tuscany had all dropped the death penalty for sodomy. Late in the eighteenth century, France had decriminalised all adult male sexual relationships, while in Britain the persecution had grown harsher. Lord Castlereagh in 1819 had judged an assault to commit unnatural offences – meaning soliciting – to be of the same seriousness as the crimes of murder and rape. From 1800 to 1834, eighty men were hanged for sodomy. In 1828 Peel sponsored a Bill making conviction in sodomy cases easier. Up to then the prosecution had had to prove penetration and emission, now proof of penetration would be sufficient. The passage of the Reform Bill in 1832 and the election of a more liberal government gave hope to society's oppressed minorities, but though capital laws against housebreaking and robbery without violence had been repealed, when the Criminal Law Committee issued its report in 1836 all it had to say upon the subject was: 'A nameless crime of great enormity we, at present, exclude from consideration.' In the following twenty years, 200 men were executed.

'Don Leon' begins with a strong protest against the barbarism of the hangings. Whoever wrote the poem had a talent for creating forceful couplets, a sharp wit and an intimate knowledge of Byron's pederastic passions; he also knew much about parliamentary debates and personalities between the years 1824 and 1833. He writes of Byron at school and then at Cambridge. Of Byron's love for his page, Robert Rushton, he wrote:

> Full well I knew, though decency forbade
> The same caresses to a rustic lad;
> Love, love it was, that made my eyes delight
> To have his person ever in my sight.

At Cambridge he hears a fellow student, John Edlestone, singing in the Trinity College choir and friendship ripens into love: 'Friendship's the chrysalis which seems to die, / But throws its coils to give love wings to fly.' The whole early section of 'Don Leon' shows the poet awakening to the sensuality of homoeroticism.

But the author also delivers a polemic to the effect that male loving is less of a social evil than adultery and extra-marital pregnancies. As well as referring to the case of Robert Heber, he also mentions MPs Baring Wall and William Bankes, and James Stanhope, the younger brother of Leicester Stanhope who fought with Byron in Greece. This young man, a year before Heber's disgrace, hung himself in an outhouse in Caen Wood.

Baring Wall, MP for Guildford, was accused by a policeman of making sexual advances to him in Harley Street. Wall was tried on the charge of attempting to commit unnatural offences, but the government, greatly embarrassed, trotted out prestigious character witnesses and the jury refused to believe the policeman's story. A similar incident occurred with Bankes, another friend of Byron's, who was arrested in a public convenience near the House of Commons and charged with sexual misconduct with a guardsman. The two were kept at the police station all night and an angry crowd of 2,000 people collected, calling for justice and punishment. In the end they were disappointed: the government used the same ploy as they had with Baring Wall, and a stream of prominent parliamentarians insisted on Bankes's virtue and probity, and the jury, duly impressed, found them both not guilty. When, eight years later, a similar offence was alleged, Bankes fled to Venice where he retired, dying there in 1855.

The poem ends with verses in praise of the act of sodomy. Scholars think that these were added later, but they are the main reason why the whole poem was published by a pornographer. 'Don Leon' remains a curiosity of its time, one of the first documents to argue passionately for humanity and justice for those expressing the taboo of 'the love that dare not speak its name'.

THE VICTORIAN ART OF DUPLICITY

The Yokel's Preceptor or *More Sprees in London*[25] recorded the increase of 'monsters in the shape of men, commonly designated Margeries, Poofs', and then went on to state that such bestial crime must be stamped out by the death penalty. It was in fact a guide to the brothels of London, naming the streets where such 'Margeries' could be found. Around Charing Cross, visitors to London would find posted bills in the windows of respectable pubs warning the public to 'beware of sods'. This convenient guide was of course used by the 'sods' themselves, as the guide well knew, even assisting a 'fledgling sod' by telling him how to recognise a 'fellow sod': 'They generally congregate around the picture shops, and are to be known by their effeminate air, their fashionable dress etc. When they see what they imagine to be a chance, they place their fingers in a peculiar manner underneath the tails of their coat, and wag them about – their method of giving the office.' The guide, of course, relied on such 'peculiar manners' for the success of its information, and must have added to the popularity of the meeting places then used, which was the only way most men had of finding a partner.

Horatio Alger (1832–99) was the son of a poor Unitarian minister who tutored him in reading from the age of six. By the time he graduated from preparatory school he was able to read French, German, Spanish and Italian. He became one of the most popular American authors in the last part of the nineteenth century, and certainly the most socially influential American writer of his generation. However, before he became famous, at the age of thirty-four he was expelled from the Unitarian Church at Brewster, Massachusetts. In 1866 a special investigating committee of the church reported that two boys, John Clark and Thomas Crocker had admitted that Horatio Alger had been practising deeds upon them too horrible to relate. Alger, who had officiated as minister to the church for fifteen months, was charged with gross immorality; 'he neither denied or attempted to extenuate' but received the evidence of his guilt with the 'apparent calmness of an old offender and hastily left town on the very next train for parts unknown'.[26]

Alger moved to New York where he wrote *Ragged Dick; or, Street Life in New York*, first serialised and then published in book form, which became a huge success. He had found a theme to which he would stick closely all his life. He began to visit charitable institutions, in particular the Newsboy's Lodging House, a home for foundlings and runaway boys. His concern was for homeless and abandoned boys struggling to survive on the streets of New York City. Later in life he informally adopted three street boys: Charles Davis, John Downie and the latter's brother Tommy. Alger continued to write stories about poverty-stricken boys who rose to middle–class respectability. His numerous books stuck to a formula that changed little apart from the characters' names. He preached that with honesty and industry, hard work and sticking to a code of honour, a poor boy could leave poverty and hardship behind and gain the fruits of affluent respectability. It was just the message the middle classes loved to hear, and his work gave the term the 'Alger hero' to the American language. It is a typical irony of the age that Alger's welfare work and his fiction obviously stemmed from his pederasty, yet so successful was he that society adored him, at the same time refusing to give name to his behaviour.

Duplicitous behaviour was characteristic of the age. Up to around 1850 boys at boarding school shared beds. Thackeray found the first order he received from a schoolfriend was 'come and frig me'. Three times as many single-sex public schools were founded between 1841 and 1870, a sign of the growing affluence of the middle classes. J.A. Symonds remembered Harrow in 1854, where every handsome boy had a female name and was recognised either as a 'public prostitute or as some bigger fellow's "bitch".' This word was used to indicate a boy who yielded to his lover.[27]

Masturbation was rife. Its perils were further stressed by William Acton in *The Functions and Disorders of the Reproductive Organs*, a huge success when it was published in 1857. This is Acton's description of a boy who habitually masturbates:

> The frame is stunted and weak, the muscles underdeveloped, the eye is sunken and heavy, the complexion is sallow, pasty, or covered with spots of acne, the hands are damp and cold and the skin moist. The boy shuns the society of others, creeps about alone, joins with repugnance in the amusements of his schoolfellows.[28]

Acton goes on: the boy will be unclean and untidy, sluggish, enfeebled and in the end a drivelling idiot. There is nothing unique about Acton's prognosis, it is the official view, repeated by medical opinion all over Europe and America. Masturbation was considered to be the cause of disease, impotence, consumption, curvature of the spine and insanity. The Reverend Edward Lyttelton, writing in 1887, thought masturbation so deplorable because it was learnt and was not instinctual; innocent boys were inspired to foul practices by other boys who spread corruption throughout a school.[29]

'Masturbators and What Shall Be Done With Them', an essay by Dr N. Emmons Paine, a physician at the New York State Homeopathic Insane Asylum, published in 1878, advises readers that as masturbators will inevitably end up insane or suicidal, the vice must be checked. He recommends a garment made of canvas, very close fitting from knee to waist: 'at the proper place a hole three-and-one-half inches in diameter, is cut in the canvas to allow the penis and scrotum to pass through into a tin receiver. This apparatus allows the use of the hands, but prevents their reaching the dangerous parts.'[30] If mechanical restraints do not stimulate a mental change, then Dr Emmons Paine recommends castration, but if the patient is far advanced in dementia even castration would be useless to bring about an improvement. The doctor hoped that a change of law could occur whereby operations for castration would not require permission from relatives or patients. The results, he thought, could only be beneficial. Dr Emmons Paine believed that masturbators married, had families and taught their children to masturbate.

People like Acton and Emmons exhibit a curious lack of logic. Acton agrees that masturbation is almost universal among boys, yet never questions why boys do not fit the description he gives of being stunted, grey, spotty, sluggish and enfeebled. While Emmons Paine believes that all masturbators become insane, he also tells us they marry and have families. There is a total lack of any common sense founded upon observation and experience; it is as if medical gurus have given themselves over to mass hysteria upon this issue which is so closely entwined with that of masculine loving. It is as if a deep and guilty disturbance within the male sexual psyche is expressed in fantasies held with a zealot's conviction. In this phenomenon we see the first step towards the medicalisation of homosexuality.

To doctors, the link is clear. George Beard, a neurologist, wrote in 1884 that: 'long-standing masturbators of either sex care little for the opposite sex; are more likely to fear than to enjoy their presence, and are especially terrified by the thought of a sexual connection.'[31]

BOULTON AND PARK

Ernest Boulton and Frederick William Park were arrested outside the Strand Theatre in April 1870.[32] They were both dressed as women. Boulton was wearing a scarlet dress with a white muslin shawl and Park a white dress; both wore false hair and jewellery. They had been closely followed and watched by William Chamberlain of the detective police force.

Boulton was the son of a respectable middle-class family from Peckham; he worked for his uncle, a stockbroker. He was thought handsome but had a soprano voice. His mother had dressed him as a girl from the age of six. Later, when he was older, she dressed him as a maidservant and had him wait at table. Park was articled to a solicitor. In May 1871 they were charged with 'conspiring and inciting persons to commit an unnatural offence'. The police had had a year to collect evidence and during that year another person arrested, Lord Arthur Clinton, third son of the fifth Duke of Newcastle, had committed suicide.

The Attorney General and the Solicitor General both appeared for the prosecution – the establishment, it would seem, was intent upon getting a conviction. The Attorney General began by pointing out that Boulton and Park were in the habit of dressing up for private theatricals; this in itself was not a crime but they had allowed it to carry through into their public outings. They had been seen in the Alhambra, in Leicester Square, in the Surrey Theatre, south of the river, and in Burlington Arcade, where the higher-priced prostitutes plied their trade. They were seen to pick up men, though some were friends, like Lord Arthur Clinton, who had lived with Boulton for a few months in 1868. It was alleged that Boulton had flirted with a Mr Cox in a public house in the City. Mr Cox's deposition read: 'I kissed him, she or it, believing at the time it was a woman.' Cox could not be at the trial for he, too, had died in the intervening year. Boulton had played the piano and had given Cox his photograph, but Cox had admitted that at no time had Boulton ever said he was a woman.

The prosecution read extracts from the correspondence between Boulton and Lord Arthur. Boulton wrote: 'I am consoling myself in your absence by getting screwed.' When the couple quarrelled, Boulton signed himself, 'Yours, Ernest Boulton'. At other times he was 'Stella'. Other letters were read out from various men, supposedly lovers, including ones from a Mr Fiske who lived in Edinburgh. From these amorous notes ('I have a heart full of love and longing') we know that they were fond of taking photographs ('but I cannot find those filthy photos'), and that they used glycerine as a lubricant. Fiske writes that another friend, Hurt, told him that Ernest was living in London in drag. He writes: 'What a wonderful child it is! I have three minds to come to London and see your magnificence with my own eyes. Would you welcome me? Probably it is better I should stay at home and dream of you – Lais and Antinous in one – is ravishing.'

When the pair were arrested the police committed several errors. In the year between the arrest and trial the London police had overstepped their jurisdiction by going to Edinburgh without the warrant of any Scottish judge or magistrate and taking possession of papers, including these love letters from Fiske. Equally as serious was that on the night of Boulton's and Park's arrest they were taken to Bow Street and examined by a magistrate and a surgeon to the Metropolitan Police, Dr James Paul, who ordered Boulton to take off his clothes behind a screen. Dr Paul then examined Boulton's anus for signs of penetration. He noted 'extreme dilation of the posterior . . . The relaxation was such as I had never seen before.' But Dr Paul was floundering in a sea of ignorance, he had never examined any male before in this way and his only knowledge came from a half-remembered case history in Dr Alfred Swaine Taylor's *Medical Jurisprudence*, where the unclaimed body of Eliza Edwards in 1833 had turned out to be on inspection the body of a twenty-four-year-old male: 'The state of the rectum left no doubt of the abominable practices to which this individual had been addicted.'[33] Dr Taylor himself gave evidence, but none of the doctors could agree on what were the signs of sodomitical activity. The Attorney General opined that it was fortunate that there was 'very little learning or knowledge upon this subject in this country', while the defence attacked Dr Paul for relying on 'the newfound treasures of French literature upon the subject – which thank God is still foreign to the libraries of British surgeons'.

The authorities had buried the subject so deep, had censored all the information so thoroughly, that both the medical and legal 'experts' were entirely ignorant. They suspected, of course, that Boulton and Park were male prostitutes – some of the letters read out in court mentioned money – but as there were no witnesses to any carnal act with an exchange of money, it was all conjecture. The Attorney General in his opening remarks hinted that it was their transvestism and their soliciting men as women that was their real crime.

Dr Paul was not let off lightly in the witness stand. The judge was perturbed by the examination at Bow Street. Dr Paul replied: 'I imagined I had to examine them for everything.' The judge asked: 'But didn't you think you had to have an order from the magistrate?' Dr Paul replied that he never waited for a magistrate's order, and in the eyes of the jury this did little good for the prosecution's case. But others had performed an anal examination as well. The surgeon to Newgate Gaol was cross-examined at length, while in May, Boulton and Park had had their own expert, the examiner at the Royal College of Surgeons, who claimed there was no evidence at all of penetration. Dr Paul had to agree that what he had noticed could have resulted from natural events.

In Lord Chief Justice Cockburn's summing-up, he said that the police surgeon had behaved in a most improper way and that the London police had overstepped their jurisdiction. Nevertheless, he found transvestism deeply offensive, speaking of an 'outrage to decency', and it was his opinion that whenever it occurred, even in the spirit of frolic, it deserved severe punishment. He went on to suggest two or three months' imprisonment, with the treadmill attached. If the offence was repeated, 'a little wholesome corporal discipline, would, I think, be effective'.

The jury was not impressed, and after only fifty-three minutes they brought in a verdict of not guilty. Not only had the police and doctors shown complete incompetence, they had been unable to decide what they were searching for and how to go about a prosecution. There was also no account taken of the powerful factors of environment and parental influences. Though Mrs Boulton gave evidence in court of how she brought up her son as a girl, the authorities seem to have considered this as irrelevant.

Though Boulton and Park had had a London audience for a short time before they passed back into obscurity, their case had repercussions, for it revealed how confused and helpless the law had become in this area.

THE LAW

The death penalty for sodomy was tacitly abandoned after 1836 and finally abolished in England and Wales in 1861, replaced by penal servitude of between ten years to life. This was the Offences Against the Person Act which replaced Henry VIII's legislation. But this Act had seldom been invoked and successful prosecutions were rare.

The change in the law came about because of a campaign against prostitution or the 'white slave trade'. There was a growing number of influential groups and citizens led by Mrs Josephine Butler who formed the London Committee for the Exposure and Suppression of the Traffic in English Girls for the Purposes of Continental Prostitution. In the Criminal Law Amendment Bill they attempted to raise the age of consent for girls to sixteen. But though the Bill passed the House of Lords in 1883, in 1884 and in a modified form in 1885, on each occasion the House of Commons refused to pass it.

In the early 1880s, a campaigning journalist, W. T. Stead, editor of the *Pall Mall Gazette*, started to investigate the sale of young girls into prostitution. He wrote a series of articles on prostitution that shocked Victorian England. Entitled 'The Maiden Tribute to Modern Babylon', Stead told how girl virgins were for sale at £5 a time, bought by elderly libertines. The mother was given £1 for the child, an intermediary was given £2 and a further £2 was given after the child's virginity had been certified by a competent authority. The five-day series of articles caused a storm of shock and horror throughout the land; for a moment, the great bourgeoisie, smug and self-righteous in their urban Utopia, saw and smelled the seamy underclass beneath them. Yet it merely served to reassure them in all their prejudices against working-class values and sexual depravity. The nation's prurient horror delighted Mrs Butler and her agitators for social reform who welcomed the exposure. The Criminal Law Amendment Bill, thought to be doomed, was finally carried through the House of Commons without a division.

However, there were opponents. George Cavendish-Bentinck, a typical high Tory, believed that everything in Britain was going to the devil. Henry Labouchère (1831–1912) was equally cynical. Labouchère was the grandson of a financier whose fortune he inherited. Like Bentinck, he had a taste for the stage door and flirtations with actresses. He had sprung to prominence in the siege of Paris where he wrote dispatches for the *Daily News*. His periodical, *Truth*, founded in 1877, was devoted to the exposure of frauds. He sat in the House of Commons as a Liberal and then as a Radical. He urged the abolition of the House of Lords. Some feared him, seeing that he could be an unscrupulous mischief-maker. Labouchère and Bentinck introduced an amendment to fix the female age of consent at twenty-one. When this was defeated they presented another amendment fixing the age at eighteen. Labouchère attacked the Bill for being badly drawn up and for its muddled amendments: 'The greatest care ought to be taken not to confound immorality with crime, not to over-run in well-meaning enthusiasm . . . and not to play in the hands of the blackmailers.'[34]

Labouchère's amendment, the eleventh clause of the Bill read:

any male person who, in public or private, commits, or is a party to the commission of, or procures or attempts to procure the commission by any male person of any act of gross indecency with another male person, shall be guilty of a misdemeanour, and being convicted thereof shall be liable at the discretion of the court to be imprisoned for any term not exceeding two years, with or without hard labour.

Did anyone who passed this legislation realise the devastating effect such a vague clause would have? Admittedly, it was less brutal than the death sentence or life imprisonment for buggery, but Britain was the only country in Europe which penalised mutual masturbation and all other sexual acts between males in private. The clause played right into the hands of blackmailers with its reference to 'public or private', and it equated all homosexuals with prostitutes – a fact that could not have much pleased some of the noble lords in Parliament, though it is doubtful that they realised it. Jeffrey Weeks comments: 'It is striking that all the major enactments concerning male homosexuality were drawn from Acts designed to control prostitution (1885, 1898, 1912).' Yet female prostitution, as we have seen, was tolerated as fulfilling a social need. Whores may have been pariahs, but homosexuals were cast out, unnameable and unrecognisable. The clause sent homosexuality further underground. Because male prostitution had to be far less public, it also became far less defined; places for meeting and making contact had to be both secret and temporary. The clause also increased guilt, doubt and confusion in the male adolescent, while it emphasised homophobia in the rest of society.

There is some reason to believe that the whole clause dreamt up by Labouchère was there simply to make the law ridiculous, an extravagant whimsy. This view was held by Frank Harris. Certainly when it was put to the House of Commons, a lawyer MP queried the clause as to its pertinacity within the Bill, as it dealt with an entirely different class of person. At that point it could have been ruled out of order, but MPs were keen to clear the backlog of legislation, so that the caretaker government could call a general election. It was late at night, few members were present, and in the end only one MP spoke against the amendment and he did so without conviction. Once passed, the clause succeeded in increasing hostility to homosexuals for there were suddenly more prosecutions under the 1861 law.

At around the same time, in the decades after 1879, most American states amended their sodomy statutes, or passed new legislation to make both fellatio and mutual masturbation a crime.[35] As a result, the rate of prosecution and imprisonment rose steadily. The reasons for these changes in law were complex, but one major factor was the growing influence that medical opinion now had within society.

THE CLEVELAND STREET SCANDAL[36]

In 1889 the editor of the *North London Press*, Ernest Parke, noticed that at a trial for homosexual prostitution, in which Veck, a minister aged forty, and Newlove, a clerk aged eighteen, were sentenced to four and nine months' imprisonment, the evidence was rushed and the sentences were both light and hurriedly given. Parke told his journalists to probe – after all, twelve months earlier a Hackney minister had been sent to prison for life for gross indecency. The newspaper found that in the summer a sum of money had gone missing from the Central Post Office and a telegraph boy with more money to spend than he had earned was suspected. Under questioning he told the story that a Charles Hammond had given the money to him, that many telegraph boys were involved as well as members of the Household Cavalry and that it all occurred at 19 Cleveland Street. This was a homosexual brothel where men could also meet and make assignations, run by Charles Hammond. But Hammond had not been arrested or tried. After the telegraph boy had confessed, a constable watching the house saw a great deal of activity, men coming and going, and furniture being removed. Hammond fled to France but two men from Scotland Yard were following him. He wrote to his sister-in-law: 'If we only go across the road from the Hotel they follow us. If I ask any questions they go and ask the people what I said to them. It makes me feel so ill I can scarcely eat my meals. I wish to god I knew what they are going to do.'

Parke continued to ask questions in his newspaper about Veck and Newlove's mild sentences. Who had told Hammond to flee to the continent? Who was protecting the secrets of Cleveland Street?

But Parke already knew the aristocratic customers that Hammond had fostered. There was the Earl of Euston, the eldest son of the Duke of Grafton, and Lord H. Arthur G. Somerset, the younger son of the Duke of Beaufort and assistant equerry to the Prince of Wales. Eight days after the telegraph boy had been questioned, a warrant was issued against Lord Arthur Somerset who fled to Boulogne. Parke hinted at all this in his newspaper with a satirical poem on Lord Arthur, called 'Lord Gomorrah', safe in France while those 'raw, cash-corrupted boys' lay in prison.

Other newspapers ignored the whole case or else dismissed it as a 'hideous and foetid gangrene'. The *Birmingham Daily Post* said loftily: 'The less that has to be said in these columns of the terrible scandal in London the better we shall be pleased.' The scandal delighted the working classes who congratulated themselves that, unlike the aristocracy, they were free of taint.

Lord Euston eventually heard of the rumours circulating and he promptly sued Parke for libel. Euston gave an explanation: he had been in Piccadilly and he had been offered a card stating that *poses plastiques* were being staged at Cleveland Street. Several days later, being in the neighbourhood, he called at the address. The door was opened by a man who asked for a sovereign. Lord Euston paid and entered the house, whereupon the man made an indecent suggestion. Lord Euston called the man an 'infernal scoundrel' and threatened to knock him down, promptly leaving the house for ever.

The police were keen to convict Euston. Witnesses who knew the Cleveland Street clientele were taken all over London in cabs so that they could pick out Lord Euston at various places. A head-and-shoulders photograph of Euston was shown to all the witnesses and they agreed basically that he was a man of medium height, stout, with a dark moustache and thin on top. But the authorities were equally as keen to convict Parkes. None of the campaigning papers and periodicals mentioned the case, and the *New York Herald* accepted Lord Euston's story.

The trial began and the witnesses were shocked when Lord Euston appeared in the witness stand, for he was all of six feet four inches tall. But Parke produced a witness who swore he had introduced Euston to Cleveland Street. This was John Saul, a man in his mid-twenties with a 'stagey manner and a peculiar effeminate voice'. The prosecution could barely hide its disgust for this man, and attempted without success to prove he was a prostitute. Even so, Saul had to confess that the police had promised to let him alone if he would take the witness stand.

In his summing up, Lord Justice Hawkins said that Lord Euston had been accused of 'heinous crimes revolting to one's common notions of all that was decent in human nature'. The jury was out for half an hour and found Parke guilty of libel. He was sentenced to one year's imprisonment. It was the end of the *North London Press*. Other newspapers were far from sympathetic, taking the line that Parke had ministered to a foul taste with fouler lies and that society was grateful to Lord Euston for stamping upon a miscreant.

As in the Boulton and Park case, there seems to have been an extraordinary ignorance about the underclass, for the middle classes had cut themselves off from knowing, hearing or seeing what actually went on in the streets around them. The Englishman's home was his castle, indeed, for each suburban villa was a small empire insulated (except for the tradespeople knocking at the back door) from the vulgarity of labour and street life. The labouring classes were always looked down on as weird in looks, manner and diction, as if verging upon the alien, and so were presented as either comic (as in *Punch*) or depraved (as in the trials).

OSCAR WILDE (1854–1900)[37]

Though these trials caused scandal, they did not imprint themselves upon the conscience of the nation, nor did they fuse a sexual activity with a name which conjured up a particular set of unappealing characteristics, as did the trials of Oscar Wilde. The tragedy is that this great writer, with an enormous range within his work from glittering wit, incisive social percipience to the most profound anguish, was tried and punished under the Labouchère amendment only nine years after the Act was passed. There has never been a more towering victim of such an inhuman clause.

Wilde at Oxford was part of the aesthetic movement, sporting velvet suits, long hair and lilies. There is little doubt that he was an extravagant poseur, an exhibitionist with a strong sense of mockery and a superb self-publicist. But he was also an intellectual and an accomplished classicist, a friend of both John Ruskin and Walter Pater. He married Constance Lloyd in 1884 and they had two sons. He published a book of fairy tales, *The Happy Prince* (1888) and a novel *The Picture of Dorian Gray* (1890) but by then he was also having relationships with men. His first affair was with the seventeen-year-old Robert Ross. Though the sexual nature of their relationship waned, they remained devoted friends until the end.

Wilde's next major love affair was with the poet John Gray. They probably met in 1889 and Wilde named the hero of his novel after him. Gray would sign his letters to Wilde 'Dorian'. A friend wrote: 'I have made great friends with the original of Dorian: one John Gray, a youth in the Temple, aged thirty (actually twenty-five), with the face of fifteen.' Bernard Shaw observed that Gray was one of the more abject of Wilde's disciples.

Then in 1892 Wilde fell in love with Lord Alfred Douglas, the youngest son of the Marquess of Queensberry. Douglas discovered his sexual persuasion at public school. He liked young, working-class lads and he introduced Wilde into the London underworld. They met because Douglas had begged Wilde's help: Douglas was being blackmailed because of an indiscreet letter he had written. Wilde got his solicitor to buy off the blackmailer for £100. Wilde compared Douglas, he now called him Bosie, to a narcissus – 'so white and gold'. But Bosie was a spendthrift, vain, egocentric, selfish and extravagant youth, given to terrible rages when his will was thwarted or when his work was criticised. Wilde wanted a great passion, and he was no doubt flattered by Bosie's youth, beauty and aristocracy.

Bosie wanted to flaunt their friendship to the world, no doubt flattered to have caught the attention of the most successful play-wright of the time. Bosie also had a powerful compulsion to shock his father, so he implied that he was Wilde's catamite. Bosie was insensible to the dangers of his lifestyle, dragging Wilde further and further into grubby intrigues. There was the time when Bosie stole a sixteen-year-old boy from where he was staying in London with Robert Ross and took him to stay with Wilde and himself in Goring. The boy, Paul Danney, son of an army colonel, had been at school in Bruges when Ross (who had known him for a couple of years) took him away for the London holiday. Danney slept with Bosie first and then with Oscar. He arrived in Bruges three days late. His master inquired into the facts and Ross and Bosie had to go to Bruges to attempt an explanation. Colonel Danney wanted to prosecute the offenders but his lawyer told him that his son would be liable for six months in prison. Ross's relations heard of the affair and called him 'the disgrace of the family, a social out-cast, a son and brother unfit for society of any kind'.

In spring 1894, Queensberry wrote to his son begging him to stop seeing Wilde: 'It must either cease or I will disown you and stop all money supplies. I am not going to try and analyse this in-timacy and I make no charge; but to my mind to pose as a thing is as bad as to be it. With my own eyes I saw you both in the most loathsome and disgusting relationship as expressed by your man-ner and expression.' Bosie telegraphed back: 'What a funny little man you are.' Wilde was horrified at the vulgarity of this, saying: 'it was a telegram of which the commonest street-boy would have been ashamed.' Queensberry reacted with another furious letter which included the prophetic threat: 'If I catch you again with that man I will make a public scandal in a way you little dream of.' Wilde refused to be a cat's paw in this battle between father and son, but though they had the sense to go abroad for a while (to Florence where they met André Gide), Wilde allowed himself to be manipulated by Bosie.

Wilde returned alone to London where, in June, there was a scene in his Tite Street house involving Queensberry: 'In my library waving his small hands in the air in epileptic fury, your father, with his bully, or his friend, between us, had stood uttering every foul word his foul mind could think of, and screaming the loathsome threats he afterwards with such cunning carried out.' Bosie was delighted. He wrote to his father: 'If O.W. was to prosecute you in the Central Criminal Court for libel, you would get seven years penal servitude for your outrageous libels.' It did not seem to occur to Bosie that if the libel was proved true, and with their open lifestyle that would hardly be difficult, his father would win and they would be prosecuted. But Bosie seemed to demand misfortune as the price of Wilde's love.

From August to October, Wilde was with his family in Worthing, working on *The Importance of Being Earnest*. In October he decided that he would never under any circumstances see Douglas again, and had decided to tell his lawyer to inform Queensberry of this. Yet fate was against him. Leaving by train, he opened his morning paper to discover that Queensberry's eldest son had committed suicide.

Drumlanrig, heir to the title, had been killed in a shooting incident, the papers reported, but it was thought that he had killed himself because of his love affair with Lord Rosebery, the Minister for Foreign Affairs. Queensberry, convinced that his favourite son had died in a homosexual scandal, was determined that a second should not die the same way. Wilde reading the report felt all his hatred for Bosie melt away to be replaced by infinite pity. He telegraphed him at once. They were back together again.

Wilde felt it was intolerable for his conduct to be dictated by a boor and a bully, but he entirely overlooked his own vulnerability. He never regarded his behaviour with the working-class tarts to whom Bosie introduced him as being of any consequence. As he had long since stopped having any sexual relations with Bosie, he could afford to think of their love as Platonic and ideal. But in the summer of 1894 some passionate letters from Wilde to Bosie came into Queensberry's hands. His solicitor told him that the letters in themselves would not sustain a charge of sodomy, so in February 1895 he left his card for Wilde at the Albemarle Club to which both belonged. On it was written: 'To Oscar Wilde, Posing as a Somdomite!' Instead of dismissing this silly, misspelt note, Wilde sued

Queensberry for criminal libel. Wilde was pedantic, he wrote exquisite prose, did the misspelling irritate him more than the accusation? Then again, was Wilde a sodomite? Bisexual men who are happily married – and Wilde was before Bosie appeared in his life – generally do not commit sodomy on youths (for they prefer to penetrate their wives), but have a strong desire to fellate them. There is evidence to incline one to this view, alluded to in Bosie's autobiography. Douglas poured fuel upon the flames, for he had always encouraged a public fight between Wilde and his father. But *hubris* played its part too: Wilde was arrogant, he had two plays running in London at the time and he felt that the fiendish little Queensberry could not touch him.★ He meant to teach the wretch a lesson.

There were three trials in all. In the first Wilde understood he was in trouble, for the defendants had gathered enough evidence against him for Queensberry to be proved right, and Wilde withdrew his suit. Private detectives had visited a shop in the West End and when they asked a prostitute how business was, she said it was bad because of the competition for men from boys under the influence of Oscar Wilde. The detectives, wanting further information, were told to go to a top flat in Little College Street. There they found the lodgings of one Alfred Taylor and a box containing the names and addresses of boys that Wilde had consorted with. The defendant in a libel action had to enter a Plea of Justification with particulars before the trial began. So Wilde understood that in fifteen separate counts (names and dates were given) he was accused of soliciting more than twelve boys, ten of whom were named, to commit sodomy.

On the strength of that evidence Wilde was arrested with Alfred Taylor who had been arrested before, but not charged as no one would give evidence against him. Taylor, who had inherited and spent a fortune, liked dressing up in women's clothes and shared his room and bed with a bevy of young men. At the second trial

---

★ Lord Euston's successful prosecution for libel must also have encouraged Wilde.

the jury could not agree on the guilt or innocence of either Wilde or Taylor. In the Plea of Justification Wilde denied all the charges which had to do with sodomy. He was tried separately a third time and found guilty of several acts of indecency. In the third trial, when Wilde heard the closing speech of the prosecution, he said later that it was like 'a thing out of Tacitus, like a passage in Dante, like one of Savonarola's indictments of the Popes at Rome.' He was sentenced to two years' hard labour.

Wilde was asked by the prosecutor to explain what the title of a poem meant. He answered:

> The love that dare not speak its name in this century is such a great affection of an elder for a younger man as there was between David and Jonathan, such as Plato made the very basis of his philosophy, and such as you find in the sonnets of Michelangelo and Shakespeare . . . on account of it I am placed where I am now. It is beautiful, it is fine, it is the noblest form of affection. There is nothing unnatural about it. It is intellectual and it repeatedly exists between an elder and a younger man, when the elder man has intellect, and the younger man has all the joy, hope and glamour of life before him.

Max Beerbohm wrote to Reggie Turner:

> Oscar has been quite superb. His speech about the Love that dares not tell its name was simply wonderful and carried the whole court right away, quite a tremendous burst of applause. Here was this man, who had been for a month in prison and loaded with insults and crushed and buffeted, perfectly self-possessed, dominating the Old Bailey with his fine presence and musical voice. He has never had so great a triumph.[38]

But Beerbohm was horribly wrong. When the judge sentenced Wilde he said: 'It is the worst case I have ever tried.' He further admitted that the crime was so bad that he had to restrain himself as to the language he used. The conviction sent a wave of horror to homosexual men of means across England. Henry Harland wrote to Edward Gosse that 600 gentlemen had crossed from Dover to Calais on a night when normally only sixty would have done so. Wilde's name was removed from the hoardings of the theatres where *An Ideal Husband* and *The Importance of Being Earnest* were playing to large audiences. It would not be long before both plays were taken off. Outside the court, when the verdict was heard, Yeats said that the harlots danced in the street.

The French newspapers were bewildered, commenting that in England sodomy ranked only a little below murder. The English press almost universally praised the verdict, fulminating with horror and shock. The London *Evening News* in an editorial on the day of Wilde's conviction, wrote: 'He was one of the high priests of a school which attacks all the wholesome, manly, simple ideals of English life, and sets up false gods of decadent culture and intellectual debauchery.' Wilde was 'a gross sensualist' to whom 'we owe the spread of moral degeneration amongst young men'. The editorial thought that such people as Wilde find their 'fitting environment in the artificial light and the incense-laden air of secret chambers' and that 'these abominable vices' were the 'natural outcome of his diseased intellectual condition'. The editorial is particularly interesting for it manages to embrace many of the shibboleths of the day which will be explored in the next chapter. The word homosexuality had only just passed into the language and Wilde was its first victim. In his conviction, institutionalised homophobia reached its highest peak, though unfortunately this peak flattened out into a high plateau that was to continue for the next seventy years.

Douglas wrote a series of letters to the press and gave interviews. He told a French journalist that he knew of forty or fifty men in the best society, hundreds of undergraduates at Oxford, not to mention a light sprinkling of dons, who were homosexual. Then he wrote to W. T. Stead who refused to publish his letter, but used most of his comments and comparisons in a piece he wrote himself. He was one of the very few public figures who had the moral courage to defend Wilde. He wrote:

If Oscar Wilde, instead of indulging in dirty tricks of indecent familiarity with boys and men, had ruined the lives of half a dozen innocent simpletons of girls, or had broken up the home of his friend by corrupting his friend's wife, no one could have laid a finger upon him . . . Another contrast . . . is that between the universal execration heaped upon Oscar Wilde and the tacit universal acquiescence of the very same public in the same kind of vice in our public schools. If all persons guilty of Oscar Wilde's offences were to be clapped into gaol, there would be a surprising exodus from Eton and Harrow, Rugby and Winchester.[39]

The exodus from England to France continued, if we are to believe Frank Harris, not always a reliable observer:

Never was Paris so crowded with members of the English governing classes; here was to be seen a famous ex-Minister; there the fine face of a president of a Royal Society; at one table on the Café de la Paix, a millionaire recently ennobled and celebrated for his exquisite taste in art; opposite to him a famous general. It was even said that a celebrated English actor took a return ticket to Paris for three and four days just to be in fashion. The mummer returned quickly; but the majority of the migrants stayed abroad for some time. The wind of terror which had swept them across the Channel opposed their return, and they scattered over the Continent from Naples to Monte Carlo and from Palermo to Seville under all sorts of pretexts.

In prison Wilde, after first being denied writing materials, wrote *De Profundis*, a passionate diatribe which explores his relationship with Douglas and the events that led up to his conviction. It was entrusted to his loyal friend Robert Ross, who published it in 1905 in an expurgated form. After Wilde was released from Reading Gaol he lived in France under an assumed name where he wrote *The Ballad of Reading Gaol*. His wife Constance gave him an allowance and wanted to attempt a reconciliation, but the old fascination for Douglas never faded and instead of going to Constance he visited Bosie in Naples. His health declined, money was desperately short and he died in Paris on 30 November 1900. The prison governor had remarked to Ross at the end of Wilde's sentence: 'He looks well. But like all men unused to manual labour who receive a sentence of this kind, he will be dead within two years.'

Wilde has extra significance for this history because he stamped an indelible character upon homosexuality itself. His conviction and imprisonment criminalised it; after this date no homosexual could be free of the fear of being arrested, charged and thrown into prison. In the public's mind the homosexual was something unthinkable. (My mother who was born in the year that Wilde died told me that throughout her growing up, in a fairly bohemian household, Wilde's name was never mentioned.) This self-censorship within society grew more impregnable, if society was forced to think about the crime, as they were as scandals continued, then the imagery which had become attached to Wilde was exhumed.

But Wilde also gave us a stereotype which prevailed throughout the twentieth century:

> The trials helped to produce a major-shift in perceptions of the scope of same-sex passion. At that point, the entire, vaguely disconcerting nexus of effeminacy, leisure, idleness, immorality, luxury, insouciance, decadence and aestheticism, which Wilde was perceived, variously, as instantiating, was transformed into a brilliantly precise image.[40]

Not just the homosexual, but the opulent parasite – the queer.

XI

COLONISATION
BY
MEDICINE

Throughout the nineteenth century, succeeding generations of physicians in Europe and America were intent on searching for a cause for what they considered to be a sexual dysfunction. As we have seen, up to 1700 it was thought a sin against God, hence a moral and theological flaw. Then it became a social crime which the state legislated against. Now it was to become a medical and psychological inadequacy which very quickly could become a mental illness. This move from sin to crime to insanity was brought about by social changes.

A COMPETITIVE PROFESSION

In the nineteenth century the bourgeoisie produced doctors and medical professionals in far greater numbers than before, and they began to have more and more power within society. The world of medicine was highly competitive and very poorly paid, unless one made one's mark and it was difficult, if not impossible, to maintain a standard of living expected of an educated gentleman. The character of Lydgate in George Eliot's *Middlemarch* is an example of the difficulties experienced by a young doctor. One way of making your mark was to do research into a social problem, though hard-working young doctors rarely had the time or energy to write a thesis. So, many of the medical professionals who pronounced upon homosexuality had struggled to reach eminence and were in the upper ranks of their profession. Not surprisingly, they represented orthodox views on sexuality, very much reflecting their own struggles for respectability and their own bourgeois roots.

Louis-René Villermé, in an 1824 report on the state of French prisons, thought that active pederasts were born with that condition and had inherited it. Adolf Henke's textbook (1832) named the condition an 'abominable vice' and described its medical consequences so that guilty parties could be identified in court.[1]

The Hungarian physician, Karoly Maria Benkert, who changed his name to Kertbeny in 1848, first coined the term 'homosexual', in 1869. He wrote:

> In addition to the normal sexual urge in men and women, Nature in her sovereign mood had endowed at birth certain male and female individuals with the homosexual urge, thus placing them in a sexual bondage which renders them physically and psychically incapable ... even with the best intention – of normal erection. This urge creates in advance a direct horror of the opposite sex.[2]

The term gradually came to be used by academics, though Benkert's pamphlet was forgotten until the German physician Magnus Hirschfeld republished it in 1905. In English the word was used first in a letter by J.A. Symonds in 1892, and it first appeared in Charles Gilbert Chaddock's translation of Krafft-Ebing's *Psychopathia Sexualis* at around the same time. But it was Hirschfeld and Havelock Ellis who brought it to a wider public.

Other words had been coined, but they did not catch on. Karl Heinrich Ulrichs (1825–95) was one of the first pioneers to plead for justice and humanity for same-sex lovers. In the years between

1865 and 1875 he published many pamphlets, safe from the law because he lived in Hanover. He coined the term *urning*, derived from an allusion to Uranus in Plato's *Symposium*. He argued that so-called 'abnormal' instincts were inborn and therefore natural; that in early foetal development all embryos were the same, after which they divided into three, male, female and *urning*, the last group having the physical characteristics of one gender but with sexual instincts which did not correspond to their sexual organs. Ulrichs had been much impressed by the discovery that each gender had the rudimentary organs of the other. His belief that *urnings* were born that way permeated slowly into orthodox medical opinion, but his pleading for humane understanding of the third sex fell upon deaf ears.

One can see in the pronouncements of many of these physicians how the tone was set, even down to the use of stock phrases, for the judicial and medical world to use this information throughout the next century. Take, for example, a paper first published in a French medical journal in 1893, and translated and published in the *American Journal of Comparative Neurology* in the same year, by Marc-André Raffalovich. He begins by saying that we cannot cure inverts, then goes on: 'If he were the superior being that he imagines himself and if he had any religion, he would shake off the bonds of flesh and make himself useful to humanity . . . The day when the invert ceases to call for the indulgence of society he will begin to justify himself in the eyes of truly superior men.'[3] It is a terrible indictment of our homophobic societies that these words might have been said (and something very like them no doubt has been) by someone in every year since Raffalovich wrote his paper.

André Raffalovich is something of a quisling. When Oscar Wilde was at Oxford, Raffalovich disliked him, saying that Wilde boasted of having as much pleasure in talking of homosexuality as others had in practising it. Later, he fell hopelessly in love with the poet John Gray, giving sumptuous dinner parties and courting Gray until, with the arrival of Bosie in Oscar Wilde's life, Gray allowed himself to be seduced. Wilde was amused, commenting: 'André came to London to start a salon, and has only succeeded in opening a saloon.' In the midst of the Oscar Wilde trial Gray fled to Berlin where he was soon joined by Raffalovich. He and Gray remained together for some years. His equivocal attitude is explained by his fervent Catholicism. Tortured by guilt, he lectured others on restraint.

DEGENERACY AND CASTRATION

In 1899 a Dr John D. Quackenbos treated with hypnotism the sexual perversion called 'unnatural passion' for persons of the same sex. He also treated and 'cured' nymphomania, masturbation and gross impurity. He agreed that his success depended upon the patient's desire to be cured. He claimed that hypnosis could remove criminal impulses and 'substitute conscience-sensitiveness for moral anaesthesia'. Quackenbos was only one of a huge number of doctors who all devised different treatments under the influence of one book: R. von Krafft-Ebing's *Psychopathia Sexualis*. First published in 1886, it reached a wide audience and was hugely influential. Krafft-Ebing had been provoked by Ulrichs into compiling hundreds of case histories. He was a Roman Catholic so held the simple view that sex was perverse if it was non-procreative. His case histories included sadism, masochism and various fetishisms, while the vocabulary used to discuss all these subjects expanded to include 'transvestism' and 'necrophilia'. Krafft-Ebing thought that homosexuality more often than not went with transvestism, and that both were a sign of degeneracy. He also cast a distinctly morbid light upon lesbianism, which he associated with insanity due to cerebral anomalies, a sign of 'an inherited diseased condition of the central nervous system', and a 'functional sign of degeneration'.[4]

Nor was anything very positive said by Havelock Ellis in the book that he wrote with J.A. Symonds on the subject of lesbianism. In *Sexual Inversion*, Ellis begins with the story of Alice Mitchell, referred to as a 'typical invert', who cut her lover's throat. He follows this with two other cases of lesbian murder and attempted murder. He makes it clear that he believes homosexuality in women is also the main cause of suicide. Perhaps in this area Ellis was not as objective as he might have been, for his wife was a lesbian. As to Symonds, he was not interested in lesbian love, and it was only at Ellis's instigation that female homosexuality was included in their book.

The great problem with the theory that homosexuality was genetic and inherited was that parents of homosexuals were very rarely bisexual. Krafft-Ebing got around this by saying: 'In almost all cases where an examination of the physical and mental peculiarities of the ancestors and blood relations has been possible, neuroses, psychoses, degenerative signs etc have been found in the families.'[5]

His views did not take long to reach America. In 1893 a Dr Daniel presented a paper on eugenic castration at a congress in New York, originally entitled 'Should Insane Criminals or Sexual Perverts Be Allowed to Procreate?' In it Daniel asserts that all perversions are transmitted by heredity and that they appear with alarming frequency in the lower classes, especially among negroes. Daniel lumps together as perversions, alcoholism, insanity, criminal tendencies, rape, sodomy, masturbation and pederasty. These, he says, 'are shocking to every sense of decency, disgusting and revolting.' He complains that there is no attempt to cure sexual perversion, or to suppress its gratification, and that the law is defective. He bases his belief in castration as a cure by quoting research which indicates that hysteria in women can be cured by the removal of the ovaries. He asks: 'Is it not a remarkable civilisation that will break a criminal's neck, but will respect his testicles?' He ends by saying: 'Rape, sodomy, bestiality, pederasty and habitual masturbation should be made crimes or misdemeanors, punishable by forfeiture of all rights, including that of procreation; in short, by castration, or castration plus other penalties, according to the gravity of the offence.'[6] This is the science of improving the human race by selective breeding, which was to have a great vogue in the following century, notably in Nazi Germany.

The total worthlessness of castration as a cure for sexual desire is illustrated in the most poignant fashion in the case history of Guy T. Olmstead sent to Havelock Ellis by a Dr E. S. Talbot of Chicago. In 1896 Ellis published a report of it in the *British Journal of Mental Science*. Olmstead, at the age of thirty, fired three shots into the back of William L. Clifford and then tried to shoot himself but was arrested. He had had a short affair with Clifford which the latter had halted, worried as to the propriety of their relationship. He urged Olmstead to get medical treatment, even offering to pay his expenses. But Olmstead was in anguish, writing passionate love letters to Clifford and following him about, for they both worked at the Post Office. In 1893 Clifford placed the letters in the City Postmaster's hands and Olmstead was asked to resign. Olmstead complained of unfair dismissal, and applied for reinstatement without success. Then, on the advice of friends and in despair, Olmstead went into hospital and had his testicles removed. No report of this operation was kept at the hospital.

The result was far from beneficial. Olmstead began to suffer from hysterical melancholia, writing to Dr Talbot from the Mercy Hospital, Chicago:

> my vileness is uncontrollable and I might as well give up and die. I wonder if the doctors know that after emasculation it was possible for a man to have erections, commit masturbation and have the same passion as before. I am ashamed of myself; I hate myself; but I can't help it. I am without medicine, a big, fat stupid creature without health or strength and I am disgusted with myself. I have no right to live and I guess people have done right in abusing and condemning me.

This poor wretch, reduced to a helpless state of humiliation and mortification by society's terror and loathing of homosexuality, at first thought he had killed his lover, but Clifford survived. He asked Dr Talbot: 'I should like very much to know if you really consider sexual perversion an insanity?' Olmstead then demanded his testicles back from the City Postmaster whom he accused of being in a conspiracy against him. By now he was paranoid and was sent to the Cook Insane Hospital.

Dr H. C. Sharp, a physician at the Indiana Reformatory, first instituted a treatment programme in 1899 which sought to end the procreation of the lower working class and social deviant groups of many kinds. Sharp lumped together the insane, the epileptic, the imbecile, the idiotic, sexual perverts, as well as confirmed inebriates, prostitutes, tramps and criminals, even paupers and children in orphanages. Sharp tells us that in 1898 the superintendent of the Kansas Feeble-Minded Institution castrated forty-eight boys in that institution.★

Tragically, castration is still performed. In 1993 a pederast in prison begged for the operation to cure him of his dangerous desires, his plea was publicised and a private surgeon performed the operation. A year later the pederast had fallen obsessively in love with a twelve-year-old boy and social services were asking for the boy's protection. One would have imagined that the uselessness of castration might have occurred to the medical profession by now.

As we can see, the 'degenerate' theory of homosexuality led to punitive action and visions of new forms of social control. It also allowed physicians to exert power, claiming they could treat and cure a range of mental disturbances. The decline in the French birth-rate, the rise in crime and alcohol consumption gave ammunition to prophecies of national decline. The Calvinists took to the degeneracy theory, as it fitted in with their concept of their own perfection as chosen by God; they reasoned that the rest of the human race, having turned its face away from God, was rapidly becoming degenerate. In England the theory had widespread middle-class support due to the rural exodus and agricultural depression and the increase of working-class discontent.[7] Riots by unemployed workers frightened the middle classes (with distant

---

★ Sharp also believed in vasectomy as a cure and performed the operation on 236 men, claiming proudly that the patients exhibited a sunny disposition and ceased excessive masturbation.

memories of the French Revolution) and the degenerate theory was used to explain away the workers' 'unreasonable' anger. The theory was necessary to confine social pathology to a restricted class of degenerates.

In America the high demand for scarce labour had driven wages up and attracted streams of immigrants from Europe and the Orient. This caused violent labour disputes and the new immigrants threatened the dominance of the Protestant middle and upper classes. When the security of an established order is threatened, then theories which typify the enemy as inferior and morally degenerate are thought necessary in the struggle to dominate the newcomer.

The medical theories of homosexuality were rapidly absorbed by the educated classes. Both the Catholic and the Protestant churches agreed on the medical explanation, declaring that sexual inversion was an anomaly of nature, a sickness.

THE REBELS

Thankfully, some highly singular people refused the medical labelling and fought the stigma: Walt Whitman, J. A. Symonds, Edward Carpenter and Havelock Ellis were all pioneers in their own way. The last three professed a fervent admiration for the American poet Walt Whitman (1819–92), who seemed to reject guilt and all notions of depravity and in their place advocated a vision of health and holism, of a unity which sprang from nature. All four men were eager to humanise approaches to homosexuality, radically to change society's concept of it. They consciously played down the role of sodomy, insisted that effeminacy was a caricature of male homosexuality and rejected pederasty. They wanted to present a homosexual relationship as manly and healthy, equal and non–exploitative, as stable and long-lasting as heterosexual relationships. To be all this the homosexual relationship had to be presented as a harmless congenital anomaly.

Symonds, Carpenter and Ellis advocated a political approach

which emphasised dissemination of information and the education of the authorities. This was to be a prelude to reform of the law.[8]

What did the intelligent, educated homosexual feel at this time, when he was being traduced by science and threatened by the state? Edmund Gosse explained: 'the position of a young person so tormented is really that of a man buried alive and conscious, but deprived of sleep. He is doomed by his own timidity and ignorance to a repression which amounts to death.'[9] Much of the work which might have enlightened his ignorance, and given him courage was, alas, privately printed or suppressed altogether. Symonds spoke of a vast subterranean literature, and his own books were all privately printed in limited editions.

John Addington Symonds was born in 1840 into a middle-class family in Bristol. His father was a senior physician. Even as a small boy Symonds was aware of his attraction towards his own sex. At Harrow he was appalled at the gross carnality of the boys and the hypocrisy of the headmaster, Dr Vaughan, who preached purity and moral cleanliness, but had sexual relations with his pupils. Symonds told his father who threatened to expose Vaughan if he did not resign. (Vaughan resigned.)

At the age of eighteen Symonds read Plato and thus became fully aware of his own sexual nature. From then on, he identified closely with the Greeks. In 1876 he wrote *Studies of Greek Poets*, the final chapter of which shows homosexuality as an integral part of Greek social life. Then in 1883 he wrote *A Problem in Greek Ethics* which Weeks considers has a claim to be the first serious work on homosexuality published in Britain. In it Symonds claims that the Dorians, migrating into the Greek peninsula in the eleventh century BC, brought the cult of homosexuality with them. These were fighting men: 'To be loved was honourable, for it implied being worthy to die for. To love was glorious, since it pledged the lover to self-sacrifice in case of need. In these conditions the pederastic passion may well have combined manly virtue with carnal appetite.'

For some years Symonds suppressed his sexual appetites and then married on medical advice. He fathered four children. This appeared also to have released his inhibitions about making assignations with young men. Symonds was an advocate of the 'adhesive' theory which originated with Franz Joseph Gall (1758–1828) who suggested that one of the brain functions was 'adhesiveness', the faculty responsible for friendship. This was all part of the phrenological school of psychology, as several of the leading figures in this movement lived in stable and passionate relationships with other men. They claimed that excess adhesiveness gave rise to overly strong feelings of friendship, and were constantly giving examples of adhesive behaviour in the past, such as David and Jonathan or Achilles and Patroclus. Walt Whitman, too, was much encouraged by these theories.[10] Because Symonds believed in this concept of masculine comradeship, he found Wilde's behaviour and work particularly nauseous, thinking *Dorian Gray* was morbid and perfumed.

The poet Swinburne had coined the word 'Calamites' for Symonds and his followers, after the *Calamus* section in Whitman's *Leaves of Grass* (see below). Symonds had first encountered Whitman's work in 1865 and was much struck by the lines:

> I proceed for all who are or have been young men,
> To tell the secret of my nights and days,
> To celebrate the need of my comrades.

Symonds admitted later that Whitman gave him the courage to express opinions previously held only timidly; he loved to quote the Whitmanesque thought that if anything is sacred it is the body. He wrote adulatory letters to Whitman over a span of twenty years, feeling that no one before had ever expressed 'the manly attachment, the athletic love and high towering love of comrades' as Whitman had.[11] Symonds longed to hear the poet confess in his own words that sexual expression was at the heart of his love for men, but he could never quite come out and ask the question, while Whitman, aware of what Symonds was after, refused to divulge anything. By this time Symonds was working on a study of the poet and in 1890 he at last posed the question, did adhesiveness include sexual relations with men? Whitman wrote back an indignant reply denying that such a connotation should ever be put upon his work: 'such morbid inferences are disavowed by me and seem damnable.' (Symonds, however, was unaware that all the evidence tells a very different story.) In his study, Symonds writes with great tact: 'Whitman never suggests that comradeship may occasion the development of physical desires. On the other hand, he does not in set terms condemn, deny, or warn his disciples against their perils.'[12]

In his books, Symonds denies that masturbation leads to homosexuality, or that it could be hereditary. Together with Havelock Ellis he wrote the first volume of *Sexual Inversion* which was to explore the subject in depth. It was to be published in Germany to avoid English censorship, but by the time it came out, Symonds had died and his outraged family demanded that his name be removed from it. They bought and destroyed the whole edition, extracting an agreement from Ellis that any further publication would be in his name only.

Leaves of Grass was published in 1860, a group of forty-five poems which focus on the spiritual love that exists between men, and symbolised by the calamus flower which has fascicles that cling together for support, representing the adhesive love of friendship. Symonds wrote that 'Calamus' had a passionate glow, a warmth of emotional tone beyond anything we are used to. There is nothing reticent about the verse, it is astonishingly overt in its emotional feelings for men.

> I will make divine magnetic lands,
> With the love of comrades,
> With the life-long love of comrades
> . . .
> We two boys together clinging,
> . . . Arm'd and fearless, eating, drinking, sleeping, loving.

As a young man Whitman went daily to the public baths. As

these were for men only and nakedness was customary, perhaps Whitman merely used such a venue for aesthetic satisfaction. He served as a male nurse in the Civil War, and formed deep attachments to the young Union and rebel soldiers he tended. 'I believe no men ever loved each other as I and some of these poor wounded, sick and dying men love each other,' he wrote.[13] Before he left at night he kissed the 'poor boys'. Of a nineteen-year-old Southern captain he declared: 'our affection is quite an affair, quite romantic – sometimes when I lean over to say I am going, he puts his arm round my neck, draws me face down etc.' After the war it was clear that Whitman liked uneducated workmen, ex-soldiers, men who toiled. To Tom Sawyer, a former soldier, he wrote: 'My soul could never be entirely happy, even in the world to come, without you, dear comrade.' He worked as a clerk in the Indian Bureau of the Department for the Interior until he was fired, supposedly for the pornographic quality of the poems 'Children of Adam' in *Leaves of Grass*.

Two unpublished notebooks of Whitman covering the year 1862–3 list the names of men he met while travelling around New York. Many of them he took home for the night. One is described as 'somewhat feminine', another was in 'dry goods'. Salesmen were looked down on as effeminate (so much for manly comradeship). The notes are short, almost terse descriptions, ending often with the two words 'slept with'.

One young man, Peter Doyle, was in the army and later became a streetcar conductor. They met in 1866. Whitman wrote: 'Dear Comrade, I think of you very often. My love for you is indestructible, and ever since that night and morning has returned more than before.' Doyle recalled the night they met: 'He was the only passenger, it was a lonely night, so I thought I would go in and talk to him. Anyway, I went into the car. We were familiar at once – I put my hand on to his knee – we understood. He did not get out at the end of the trip – in fact went all the way back with me.' Though they spent long hours exploring the city together, when they were apart they exchanged loving letters. In 1869, when Doyle was depressed because he feared he had caught syphilis, Whitman wrote kindly: 'It seemed indeed to me (for I will talk out plain to you, dearest comrade,) that the one I loved, and who had always been so manly and sensible, was gone . . . My darling, if you are not well when I come back I will get a good room or two in some quiet place . . . and we will live together, and devote ourselves to the job of curing you.' A correspondence between them was published posthumously under the title *Calamus*. Some misunderstanding must have occurred which estranged them, for there is a curious and painful message in Whitman's notebook in 1870: 'I never dreamed that you made so much of having me with you, nor that you could feel so downcast at losing me. I foolishly thought it was all on the other side.' He went on to write a coded message of grief: 'This feverish, fluctuating, useless undignified pursuit of 164 . . . much too long persevered in so humiliating.' (164 is thought to be code for letters of the alphabet with 16 standing for P and 4 for D, the initials of Peter Doyle.)[14]

We know that the Victorian man was extravagant in his emotions and in the expression of them to other men. Behaviour in the Civil War hospital which would now merit a court martial was entirely acceptable then. The whole ideology of the age exalted passionate friendship, and self-sacrifice, masculine heroism and strength were all part of the colonial spirit. But it seems not unlikely that beneath the social façade of comradely friendship a great deal of carnal fulfilment took place. Yet, the carnality was hidden by society, so that a male nurse kissing a wounded soldier goodnight did not suggest anything homoerotic but only the bonding of comrades.

There is one last piece of evidence that Whitman in old age was drawing a thick veil over the truth. Allen Ginsberg prodded Gavin Arthur in 1977 to recall his meeting with Edward Carpenter in the twenties. Mutual friends took the youthful Arthur to meet Carpenter, some sixty years his senior. Arthur asked whether he and Walt Whitman had ever had sex together. Carpenter told him that they had, for Whitman thought it the best way to get to know somebody. Arthur then asked how Walt made love and inevitably the aging Carpenter said he would show him. They went to bed together, naked beneath an eiderdown, first holding hands and lying on their backs, then Carpenter kissed his ear and began to fondle his body very lightly, ignoring the lad's genitalia, but licking, 'flickering all over me like summer lightning'. This went on for some time and Arthur became excited, having an orgasm just at the moment that Carpenter fellated him. 'The emphasis was on the caressing and loving. I fell asleep like a child safe in father-mother arms, the arms of God.'[15] Admittedly this could have been a complete fiction of Carpenter's, a neat ploy to bed a young man, we shall never know. He was not beyond making a pass at young men who visited him in the 1920s. Michael Davidson had his bottom pinched and was much amused.[16]

Edward Carpenter (1844–1929) was born in Brunswick Square in Brighton. He went to Cambridge and took orders, becoming a curate to the early Christian Socialist F. D. Maurice. He had a great loathing for his background and the way in which women were brought up to expect nothing from life but a respectable marriage. Later in life he was to say that the homosexual man has a clearer, more sympathetic understanding of women. But like Symonds, Walt Whitman's poetry came as a revelation to him: 'It was not until I was twenty-five that I read Whitman – and then with a great leap of joy – that I met with the treatment of sex which accorded with my own sentiments.'[17]

Carpenter was a polymath. He wrote books on 'science, industry, art, religion, economics, sex, marriage, women, the Empire, war, police, prisons, nature, vivisection, nudism, anthropology, Whitman, Beethoven, Wagner, anarchism, socialism, market gardening, pollution, the East, mysticism, transcendentalism.'[18] His most famous book, *Towards Democracy*, exhibits a fervent pantheism. It begins:

> The sun, the moon, the stars, the grass, the water
> that flows around the earth, and the light air of heaven:
> To You greeting. I too stand behind these and send
> you word across them.

Carpenter attacked the industrial bourgeois society which had destroyed the sacredness of life and sex; he loathed its conventions, manners and beliefs. He was of course right to do so, for we have seen how in the rise of the middle classes and the power that they wielded through their daily rituals, one strand of the homophobic society was forged. He thought science served this social structure rather than the aspirations of man. He challenged the legal codes which expressed class power: 'Law represents from age to age the code of the dominant or ruling class . . . Today the code of the dominant class may perhaps best be denoted by the word respectability.'[19]

He began market gardening in 1883 in a house, Millthorpe, outside Sheffield, where he could escape from what he called 'the domination of Civilisation in its most fatal and detested forms, respectability and cheap intellectualism'. In 1891 he met George Merrill – aged twenty – in a railway carriage. They exchanged a few words and a look of recognition – it was love at first sight. Carpenter gave Merrill his address and their friendship began. Merrill stayed with him for the rest of his life. He died one year before Carpenter in 1926, leaving him heartbroken.

The two men were devoted to each other. George wrote: 'Dear Ted . . . I shall be glad to see thy dear face again as I have such longings to kiss those sweet lips of thine. I will wait till I hear from you, first. So I must close dear heart as I am feeling a little low and lonesome. I'm always with thee every night in spirit, fondest love from your dear Boy. G XXX'[20]

Carpenter's decision to live with Merrill openly as a couple was for its time an astonishingly brave act. They lived through the Oscar Wilde trials, Carpenter complaining, anonymously, when Wilde's name was removed from billboards. Many of Carpenter's friends disliked the menage and thought Merrill would be a bad influence. They also considered that the house would be filthy without a woman living there, but Merrill proved to be domesticated and efficient.

This relationship marks another change in the life of the homosexual. Before, if two men who were lovers wished to share a house together, it could only be done as master and servant, like

Bacon and his various minions. These relationships, which must date back to the ancient world, were always exploitative in some way, not always to the master's credit. However rich and powerful the servants became – as in Castlehaven's household – they were still servants at the end of the day. Though Merrill was from the working class and uneducated, when he arrived at Millthorpe his relationship with Carpenter was as near equal as the older man could contrive. Carpenter proved that a homosexual union could be as loving, kind and considerate, and as stable and intimate, as any heterosexual union. In choosing this mode of loving and living, Carpenter had adopted the very bourgeois structure he so detested. But at least Millthorpe was not Brunswick Square.

One person who thoroughly approved of Merrill being at Millthorpe was Edith, the wife of Havelock Ellis. When Ellis first read *Towards Democracy* he thought it was 'Whitman and water', but later he grew more appreciative. Carpenter and Ellis wrote to each other throughout their lives.

Ellis (1859–1939) was born into a lower-middle-class home in Croydon. As a teacher in Austria he had a revelation that he must dedicate his life to the study and exploration of sexuality. When he returned to London he began to move in radical and socialist circles making life-long friendships with Eleanor Marx, the early Fabians and women like Olive Schreiner, the South African feminist and writer. He began to write himself, on philosophy, travel, religion, politics and art. Though he was not homosexual himself, he was fascinated by variations on what was considered orthodox sex (Ellis himself found the sight of women urinating highly erotic). He published two books in 1890: *The New Spirit*, which showed a passionate declaration of the 'new age', and *The Criminal*, based on Lombroso's theories of the biological basis of criminality. Ellis believed that criminal behaviour was determined by congenital factors. This theory would be extended to cover a congenital view of homosexuality. His next book, published in 1894, *Man and Woman*, convinced him that major differences came about because of biological predisposition. His views, however, were very similar to those of both Symonds and Carpenter, in that he considered it was society which inhibited the real potential of human nature.

Symonds collaborated on the book that was to become *Sexual Inversion* by writing an analysis of ancient Greece, as well as providing most of the case histories. Symonds died in 1893, and Ellis continued to write the book the way they had planned it. Ellis was an observer of human nature, collecting case histories without giving judgement. The book is a plea for tolerance, asking society to accept that deviations from the 'normal' were harmless and could perhaps even be valuable. One section of the book lists homosexuals of note throughout history. Ellis argues that homosexuality is not a product of periods of social decay or a particular national vice. He rejected all theories of 'degeneration', arguing that anything so natural and spontaneous could not be a manifestation of a morbid disease.

Soon after the book was published in England it was banned, called 'a certain lewd, wicked, bawdy, scandalous libel'.[21] Future editions were printed in the United States. However, the publicity caused by banning the book prompted hundreds of homosexuals to write to Ellis with their problems and life histories. Many of these he passed on to homosexual friends like Carpenter and much in their stories became case histories for future editions. Ellis argued, first, that homosexuality is characteristic of a fixed minority and incurable; second, that the law must be changed to leave this minority in peace; and third that reform could occur only after a long period of public education.

The book, though never publicly available in a British edition, became a landmark in the understanding of homosexuality. It is possible that when the homophobia of a society becomes as hysterical as it did in the 1890s, a voluble opposition automatically springs into action which, however small, makes a subtle impact that eventually will bear fruit. In this case it took eighty years.

THE URANIANS[22]

In this negative climate it is odd to discover that the love of boys was quietly celebrated without much social awareness. The society that had countenanced passionate friendship and comradely love took little notice of the attachment between a man and a boy. The Uranian movement* began as early as the 1870s. Symonds wrote of Horatio Forbes Brown to a friend: 'I am sorry that he has chosen to tread this wearifully barren and solitary and heart saddening path of paiderastic poetry.' The Uranians were all minor poets, sometimes teachers, clergymen and painters, who churned out verses of almost unspeakable sentimentality and coyness. The poems share some common themes. First, the fleeting days of boyhood: the bud blossoms, the fruit ripens and then it falls. Of all romances, the pederastic love is quickly done. All mourn its shortness. Second, guilt: a boy might be damned for his beauty, so mesmeric is its power upon the beholder. Then there is the frustration of nurturing a forbidden love in oneself, knowing the immorality of the urge to love and fondle. Third, peeping: the lover watches the boys at games, sees them strip for swimming, can only look and yearn. Fourth, lost youth: the Uranians recalled their own youth, when they were equal in beauty and strength with the boys they now long for. There is in this a strong element of narcissism, perhaps even nostalgia for lost physical embraces and carnal play. Fifth, the angelic vision: the Victorians were inordinately fond of the angelic cherub asleep and rosy-cheeked. In this case the boy is never grubby, ink-stained or uncouth, but is the essence of beauty. Sixth, the supremacy of Uranian love: they argued that it belonged to a higher order than mere heterosexual love, quoting the friendship of Jesus and John, echoing Marlowe, James I and Diderot. True male comradeship created far stronger bonds than the marriage tie. The Uranians also liked the beloved to be a working-class boy, desiring the Socratic relationship between teacher and pupil. Besides, it was far more likely that such boys would be more sexually frank and uninhibited than boys from the middle or upper classes, and they would also be more

---

* A term given to them by Timothy d'Arch Smith in his book on the subject, *Love in Earnest*.

vulnerable to a bribe or willing to enjoy a steady flow of cash and presents.

These poets wrote as a form of sublimation, not daring to expose their private longings in print. On the rare occasions when a poem was published, the author would change the sex of the beloved. They wrote for themselves and for each other, to share their poetry and their obsession with like-minded men. They were blameless in their lives and did no harm to their young friends; it is very likely that they gave genuine help and guidance to many deprived boys who were hungry for affection and knowledge.

As we know from the ancient world, adult men loving boys was a uniform and common practice. Examples of such relationships appear throughout history, even at times when it was socially unacceptable. But when that unacceptability is intensified into horror and hatred, it is reasonable to suppose that most men who might have enjoyed pedophilia in a more homophile society, now turn their libido into sexual areas which are socially approved of. Nevertheless, there are always men throughout history who choose not to change; generally they would say they cannot and they, after all, should know. We should not forget that brothels containing young boys existed throughout the nineteenth century, but brothels were not what the Uranists desired; they wanted a sentimental attachment, to look after and guide their young protégés. It is curious that throughout their short history, from the 1880s to the outbreak of the Second World War, the Uranians were ignored by society and left to their own devices. This is something that would not happen today.

STRUGGLING WOMEN

The nineteenth century was an era during which alternative forms of loving multiplied, when orthodox sexuality was opposed, when freedom for the individual was trumpeted. It was the age when the term 'free love' was coined, meaning that love, rather than marriage, should be the precondition for sexual relations. The movement started with Frances White, a Scottish orphan with independent wealth and a close friend of the Utopian Socialist Robert Owen. White emigrated to America in the 1820s, where she opposed religion, slavery and marriage. She started an interracial community and encouraged miscegenation. She attacked 'ignorant laws, ignorant prejudices, ignorant codes of morals', and condemned society for allowing 'one portion of the female sex to vicious excess, another to vicious restraint . . . and generally the whole of the male sex to debasing licentiousness, if not to loathsome brutality'.[23] The press loathed her and caricatured her as a demon threatening the stability of holy marriage. She died in 1852, worn out with the battle.

None of the factions and groups in nineteenth-century America, including anarchists, though they trumpeted individual freedom, ever seemed to have considered that same-sex loving needed social recognition and acceptance. The term 'Boston marriage' was used in New England to describe a long-term monogamous relationship between two unmarried women. The women needed to be financially independent of men in order to remain unmarried, but Boston society in the late nineteenth century was an affluent one. Henry James in *The Bostonians* (1885) celebrates such a friendship. Olive Chancellor is a wealthy young feminist who meets Verena Tarrant, a charismatic personality whose talent for speaking could advance the cause. Olive tutors her and forms a passionate attachment to her. Such passionate friendships among women were common at the time, especially among writers and champions of the women's movement, yet we do not know whether or not they contained a physical element. It seems reasonable to suppose they did, but lesbianism was not one of the causes advocated by feminism. There was of course no need to campaign for reform of the law, and there was no punitive threat held over lesbian relationships – they were merely something best left unspoken.

Yet times were changing rapidly and if 'Boston marriages' were not explicit, others were. In 1896, in an article published in the *American Journal of Insanity*, a Dr Hamilton discussed the problem of soundness of mind when male or female homosexuals bequeathed large sums of money or property.[24] The doctor described two cases where families questioned the sanity of homosexual relatives in disposing of their property. He begins: 'Until within a comparatively recent period the mere insinuation that there could be anything improper in the intimate relations of two women could have drawn upon the head of the maker of such a suggestion a degree of censure of the most pronounced and enduring character.'

The secret is out. Women living together in close harmony can no longer rely on public naivety or ignorance as to the nature of their relationship. Dr Hamilton continues by commenting that a great many attachments entail sexual feelings, 'which leads to moral degradation, as well as impairment of rights, when a stronger will dominates a weaker'. The doctor envisaged lesbian couples as being one frail and feminine and the other large-framed and masculine. Hence, to his mind, this was sexual exploitation. He went on to quote the first case. A quiet, religious young woman had inherited a million dollars. Her brothers invested the money over which she retained complete control. A friend wanted her to consult a doctor in New York over certain trivial uterine disorders. The doctor was a masculine-looking woman of about forty with a deep raucous voice who swore, in marked contrast to the quiet and refined patient. The girl stayed on in New York for some months, until her worried family went there to try and get her back. The girl refused angrily. At last she did return while the woman doctor went off to Europe for the summer, but the girl was depressed and constantly spoke of her friend, the doctor. After a while letters arrived and she became elated. She returned to New York where she began living with her medical adviser. Large sums of money were spent by the girl to build a large and expensive house for her friend.

Dr Hamilton was asked to intervene and interviewed the girl, but he found her angry and obstinate and was unable to influence her in any way. So a private detective was enlisted who discovered that the girl was totally infatuated and went everywhere with the doctor, even sharing her bed. Letters were also found written by the doctor which 'burn with love for her'. More inquiries revealed that the doctor had debauched several young women, driving one to commit suicide. Hamilton was in a dilemma. The circumstances did not warrant an assumption of insanity. There was nothing about the girl that could have convinced a jury that she was of unsound mind, for at that time her mental perversion did not show. Hence, it would have been futile, Hamilton says, to have declared her a lunatic. The family could have taken criminal proceedings against the woman doctor, but they were loath to do so, for it would have meant unwelcome publicity.

At this point we are still within a phallocentric society, though feminism has made a dent in it. Society has absorbed the fact that a sexual relationship can exist between women even without a penis. But it can only envisage such a couple as male/female; the 'male' partner has to be coarse and unrefined, has to have a past of debauchery, has to be evil in her intention, while the 'female' partner is the innocent party and has to be saved.

As society's awareness grew, so did the awareness of those girls who were slowly finding their sexual identity. Ellis in *Sexual Inversion* quotes the story of a twenty-one-year-old woman being nursed by a married friend and neighbour, fourteen years her senior. Each felt a great warmth for the other and an ardent friendship built up. But the mother of the younger woman and the husband of the older woman took steps to end the friendship, sending the younger woman away to a distant city. The young woman had always been a great favourite in her circle of friends; she was athletic, religious, a singer and active in clubs and societies. The older woman belonged to an aristocratic family and was loved and respected by all. Soon after being sent away, the young woman shot herself in the head in front of her mother.

A report dated 1913, in the US *Journal of Abnormal Psychology*, by Margaret Otis paints a picture of lesbian love between white and black girls at a reform school. It was a tradition of the school that, on arrival, a white girl would receive a lock of hair and a note from a coloured girl asking her to be her love. 'The notes when captured show the expression of a passionate love of a low order, many coarse expressions are used and the animal instinct is seen to be paramount. The idea of loyalty is present. A girl is called fickle if she changes her love too often.' Otis points out that it was often asked if only the 'defective' girls indulged in such practices, but this was not the case, for some of the girls indulging in this love had the most highly developed intellectual ability in the school.

The reform school wisely seems to have just accepted this tradition without attempting to suppress it. Other institutions were far more sensitive. Ellen Coit Brown tells of a story at Cornell University in 1880 when a handsome girl student turned up at a concert escorted by a young gentleman who was not immediately identifiable. It was then seen that the 'gentleman' was another woman student dressed in a man's suit. The story was all over town the following day. The university expelled the handsome girl but not the girl in drag. For days afterwards the women of Cornell were in a 'mood of chastened gloom', feeling the injustice keenly. Then the handsome girl beat upon the closed doors of the university so persistently that they let her in again. She graduated successfully and Coit Brown tells us 'lived a long and exemplary life'. Cornell obviously took the view that if a student dressed up in male attire and accompanied another, they must be having a lesbian relationship. Yet if they were, the public flaunting of their relationship is most unlikely. Coit Brown is most discreet in the telling of the tale, never disclosing the names of the students for fear such scandal might harm them. No doubt she knew that transvestism was still an issue which provoked the authorities into a state of appalled horror.

In 1894 a man, Frank Blunt, was sentenced to one year in prison for stealing. It was then discovered that he was a woman who had worn masculine attire her whole life. Gertrude Field claimed to have married the prisoner and furnished all the money for Blunt's defence.

But the scandal that rocked New York was the discovery that an influential politician in the Tammany Hall Democratic machine, Murray Hall, was a woman. Murray Hall had a reputation as a *bon vivant* and man-about-town. He had been an influential politician throughout the 1880s and 90s, a friend of a state senator. He registered and voted at primaries and general elections for many years. He drank whisky, smoked big black cigars and had been married twice. The discovery of the true gender of Murray Hall happened only after his death, ironically from breast cancer.

Joseph Young, one of the senator's aides, was quoted in the obituaries as saying: 'A woman? why, he'd line up at the bar and take his whisky like any veteran, and didn't make faces over it, either. If he was a woman he ought to have been born a man, for he lived and looked like one.'

In this continuing horror at the successful cross-dresser we see a need not only to have gender defined absolutely, but to be able to recognise it. Joseph Young was duped and it is as if he is claiming that society cannot be stable unless the genders are kept within defined boundaries. He also believes that Murray Hall should have been born a man (no doubt a belief shared by Hall) if he lived and looked like one – a notion which is still fervently believed in by transsexuals and those psychotherapists who treat them and now encourage surgery. (See Chapter 14.) There is no doubt that the exposure of a successful life-long transvestite caused social anxiety, for a crack had appeared in the façade of the nation's morals, reflecting a different light which made people feel uneasy, even to the point of panic. Generally, anger and vilification were the result.

THE EULENBURG AFFAIR

Within the first decade of the twentieth century, Germany was outraged by a series of trials for homosexual offences which affected the military and the circle that surrounded the Kaiser. In one very real sense, their effect was similar to that of the Wilde trials in England a decade earlier, giving the nation a new and highly unpleasant view of itself to which it was difficult to adjust.

Scapegoats were then sought and easily found. A spirit of self-disgust began to germinate which had to be rooted out.

In 1908 the German Kaiser had given a bombastic interview to the *Daily Telegraph* offering unwanted advice and suggesting a future where the seas would be ruled in peace by the two nations. Members of the Reichstag were furious, not unreasonably expecting a degree of tact and discretion from their Kaiser. Distressed by his error, the Kaiser fled to the Black Forest estate of a friend. One evening, after much food and drink, the Military Secretariat, Dietrich Count von Hülsen-Häseler, dressed in a ballerina's tutu danced a solo. In the midst of this he had a heart attack and dropped dead. The whole thing was quickly hushed up, but shortly afterwards the Kaiser, still in the midst of what was to become the 'Eulenburg affair', suffered a nervous breakdown.

Ever since Wilhelm II had ascended to the throne in 1888, observers in his inner circle were alarmed by his mental balance. He struck older politicians as brash and incompetent. In fact, one of his first political acts was to dismiss Bismarck and the network of treaties which had guaranteed the European balance of power.

The Kaiser's favourite adviser during the 1890s was Philipp Prince zu Eulenburg-Hertefeld. This bosom friend was swiftly promoted to an ambassadorship, for it was rumoured in court circles that 'His Majesty loves Philipp Eulenburg more than any other living being.'* Bismarck refused to name his suspicions, but in a letter to his son he did remark that he supposed there were some good generals among the ancient Greeks but he had yet to find 'any good diplomats of the sort'. This was repeated to Maximilian Harden, who was told more detailed suspicions which he would keep to himself for fourteen years.

Harden was a Jew and a journalist, editing and largely writing by himself *Die Zukunft*, a campaigning weekly calling for progressive domestic reforms and a coherent foreign policy. He began attacking Eulenburg's influence from 1893, but refrained from

---

* Attributed to Wilhelm von Liebenau by Herbert von Bismarck in a letter dated 5 October 1888.[25]

personal innuendo. As government policies continued, Harden's patience waned, and in 1902 he issued an ultimatum: if Eulenburg did not resign from public life, his private life would be exposed. Now ambassador to Vienna, aged fifty-five, Eulenburg capitulated. Excusing his departure on the grounds of ill-health, he retired to his estate and remained a recluse for the next few years.

Then Harden discovered that from late 1905 and into 1906 Eulenburg had been contacting foreign diplomats; what was more, he coveted the post of Chancellor. Harden published two articles which linked Eulenburg with his friend, General Kuno Count von Moltke, the military commandant of Berlin, revealing that the latter's nickname was 'Tutu'. The pair were identified as 'the Harpist' (Eulenburg was a composer) and as 'Sweetie' (a slang word for homosexual). Eulenburg fled to Switzerland. Harden was convinced that homosexuality was rampant, and thought a blow against Eulenburg would halt its spread. In the preceding three years court martials had convicted twenty officers of homosexuality and in 1906-7 six officers committed suicide after being blackmailed.

Eulenburg returned to Germany to accept the honour of being initiated into the High Order of the Black Eagle, a particularly silly move on his part for, soon after, Friedrich Heinrich, Prince of Prussia, refused investiture as Grand Master of the Order of the Knights of St John because his homosexual proclivities made him 'unsuitable'. It was a gift to Harden who denounced Eulenburg as a pervert on 27 April 1907, commenting that since his *vita sexualis* was no healthier than Friedrich Heinrich's, he should have the decency to follow the prince into exile.

The Kaiser was brought all the papers by the Crown Prince and appeared to be horrified by them. The Kaiser, after all, was well known for his liking for all-male company on his annual holiday cruise on the royal yacht and his frequent hunting trips. The Crown Prince thought that his father was feeling unwell because of the disgusting revelations. The Kaiser then conferred with his minister of police affairs, who presented him with a carefully edited list of fifteen prominent aristocrats who were thought by the Berlin vice squad to be homosexual. They had to resign their commissions and Eulenburg was forced to go into exile again. Harden was hailed as the hero of the day.

There was now a flurry of legal activity. Moltke filed a suit against Harden for civil libel. But Eulenburg avoided Harden altogether and accused himself of violating the penal code, presenting this to his local district attorney who started an investigation. In three months he had declared Eulenburg innocent. In the meantime the imperial Chancellor, Bernhard Prince von Bülow, was linked romantically with his secretary, one Privy Councillor Schaefer, by Adolf Brand, who had founded the first homosexual magazine, *Der Eigene*, in 1896. So Bülow pressed criminal libel charges against Brand.

At the Moltke *v.* Harden trial, Lili von Elbe, Moltke's former wife who had divorced him nine years earlier, testified that in two years of marriage sex had occurred only twice. Eulenburg had opposed their marriage and her husband always spent more time with him than with her. Moltke called him, 'my soulmate, my old boy, my one and only cuddly bear'. It had never crossed her mind that her husband might be homosexual because she did not know of its existence. Then a soldier, Bollhardt, testified that in Potsdam regiments, sexual relations between officers and enlisted men were common knowledge. He described at length his own participation in champagne orgies and stated that he had seen Moltke there. He went on to describe the powerful eroticism of the white pants and knee-high boots of the cuirassiers' uniform, saying that any guardsman who wore it in public was bound to be solicited.

The court agreed that Moltke's homosexuality had been confirmed and Harden was acquitted of libel. The nation was outraged, both by revelations of perversion in the upper echelons of the military, and by the fact that these bad tidings had been brought to their notice by a Jew. The authorities felt impelled to act, the trial was declared void because of faulty procedure and the state prosecutor called for a re-trial against Harden on the grounds of criminal libel. But the second trial had already started of Bülow *v.* Brand. This was rushed and over within a day. In 1902 Brand had founded an organisation dedicated to repealing Paragraph 175 which punished 'unnatural vice'. He was charged with distributing a libellous leaflet which stated that Bülow had been blackmailed because of his homosexuality. It further alleged that Bülow at all-male gatherings hosted by Eulenburg had embraced and kissed Schaefer. Brand argued that Bülow, as a homosexual, should use his considerable influence to repeal Paragraph 175. This was to be Brand's defence. Bülow took the stand and denied all the allegations; then Eulenburg swore that he had never hosted parties of that description and that, like Bülow, he had never violated Paragraph 175. (His local district attorney had cleared him of that charge, though he had accused himself of it in the spring.) The judge withdrew for a short time, then returned with a verdict of guilty and an eighteen-month prison sentence for Brand. The nation heaved a sigh of relief, perhaps nothing was terribly wrong with the established order of things after all. The filth came from the Jews and homosexuals and now they were being punished.

The retrial of Moltke *v.* Harden opened in December. Lili von Elbe returned to the witness stand and the prosecution destroyed her earlier testimony by using expert medical witnesses, painting her as a classic hysteric. Moltke and Eulenburg spoke in defence of male friendship and declared it had nothing to do with a homosexual orientation. Moltke's reputation was cleared and Harden was convicted of libel and given a four-month prison sentence. The Kaiser began to relax and to feel that the scandals had perhaps come to an end. But Harden had a persistent nature, he knew that Eulenburg had committed perjury by claiming he had not violated Paragraph 175. So Harden set out to trap him. He colluded with a Bavarian ally, editor Anton Staedele, to publish an article alleging that Eulenburg had given Harden a million marks to stop his attacks. Harden then sued Staedele for libel and used the court room to present his evidence on Eulenburg. A trial was arranged in Munich where people would be more likely to be sympathetic.

Harden had subpoenaed Georg Riedel, a Munich milkman, and Jakob Ernst, a Starnberg farmer and fisherman in the Bavarian lakes. Riedel admitted that while serving in the military in 1881 he had engaged in sexual relations with Eulenburg who had introduced him to Moltke. Ernst admitted that he had been seduced by Eulenburg when he was nineteen and that they had had a long relationship which always included sex. He was married and had children but he always thought what he had done with Eulenburg was just good fun: 'Fooling around. I don't know of no real name for it. When we went rowing we just did it in the boat.' He was proud of his friendship with the prince, all his friends and neighbours knew of it and they were rather in awe of him because of it. He even went on holiday with the prince, to Rome, the Riviera and Egypt. Staedele was convicted of libel and sentenced to a hundred-mark fine, which was reimbursed by Harden.

Germany was stunned by these further revelations. Some thought Eulenburg should commit suicide, others believed that Ernst and Riedel were paid to give such testimony by enemies of the state. Eulenburg was arraigned on perjury charges in May 1908. The state prosecutor had confiscated books and letters found at Eulenburg's Liebenberg Castle, including one letter to Ernst written before the Munich trial begging him to be silent. Eulenburg was so weak he had to be brought into the court room on a litter. The prosecution planned to call thirty witnesses, but Eulenburg collapsed and medical attendants declared him dangerously ill. The judge resumed the trial in the hospital where Eulenburg lay ill, but it was repeatedly postponed. Eulenburg would faint one hour into the proceedings and be granted a conditional postponement. He was to be examined every six months to see whether he was fit or not. This continued for a decade until he died in 1921.

In the 1920s Harden was to admit to Magnus Hirschfeld that getting rid of Eulenburg had been the worst mistake of his life, for he later realised that Eulenburg had had a moderating influence upon the Kaiser. Without him, Germany was set upon war. But the series of trials had an immediate effect upon the nation, and fears were generated which appeared to threaten its very survival. An editor asserted that the continuing spread of homosexuality threatened the German race with extinction. The court chaplain in

the Reichstag argued that homosexuality, the spread of porno-
graphy and the rise of the women's movement for emancipation
were all part of the corruption of society. The exposure of sexual
liaisons between officers and men, between a prince and a farmer,
suggested that the pillars of society were riddled with moral decay.
This was, for one speaker at the Reichstag, a portent of barbarism;
homosexuality was a contagion which could become an epidemic,
and such an epidemic would destroy culture and civilisation. A
campaign for moral rearmament began. Dr William Hentschel
commented that the Eulenburg affair had been beneficial if it had
driven homosexuals to poverty and suicide. Perhaps, he suggested,
the extermination of all homosexuals should become necessary to
the nation. A prophecy indeed, for such a policy would be put into
practice within thirty years. The campaign to repeal Paragraph 175
was dead and buried, for the scandals led to far harsher enforcement of the law and to efforts to strengthen and extend it.
Another widespread fear was expressed in the Reichstag, that
thousands of people previously ignorant about homosexuality
would now be tempted to explore it. Because of Harden's star part
in the proceedings there was an intensification of anti-Semitic feelings. Military discipline was heightened, middle-class morality
was praised and the German nation was preparing itself for a leader
such as Hitler. Thirty years later the fascists would identify both
Harden and Hirschfeld as responsible for the Eulenburg affair, insisting that it was a Jewish conspiracy which lay behind the
scandal.

KILL OR CURE

The degeneracy theory rode high. In the 1880s a St Louis physician, Charles H. Hughes, reported: 'Male negroes masquerading in
women's garb and dancing with white men is the latest St Louis
record of neurotic and psychopathic sexual perversion.'[26] The
blacks were arrested and their names and addresses taken, while
the white men who danced with them were allowed to go.

It was established by medical practitioners that a male homosexual was effeminate: they feel 'the need for passive submission,
they become easily enraptured over novels and dress.' When it
could be proved that some male homosexuals were not effeminate,
then it was thought they must belong to that variety which had a
female brain inside a male body. These were the same physicians
who opposed greater freedom for women, claiming that sharp sex
distinctions were biologically based, even threatening that if these
were violated, women's capacity for reproduction could be lost.

When population growth was on the decline, as it was at times,
then politicians, physicians and the church together inveighed
against both homosexuals and the rise of the women's movement.
But even the liberals had their say on this matter. Edward Carpenter, Havelock Ellis and Marie Stopes all criticised lesbianism and
feminism for encouraging women to abandon motherhood and
marriage. It was also widely thought that the downfall of Greece
and Rome was due to rapacious homosexuality. (Indeed, this particular canard refuses to be shot down.) The Bishop of Ripon, at a
public meeting in Leeds in 1904, worried about the birth-rate
decreasing because the wealthy and the well-to-do were not doing
their duty, instead leaving it to 'the tramp, to the hooligan and the
lounger to maintain the population. This was not the way to rear a
great Imperial race.'[27]

Freud's hugely influential contribution to the homosexual debate
was highly equivocal. It filtered through society slowly, though
much of his real message was too obscure to be absorbed. His attitude towards homosexuality was confused, and because of social
bias he stressed its pathological aspects. Freud was beneficial in
some ways, for, on the one hand, he dismissed such notions as
masturbation being harmful or leading to later homosexuality. He
attempted to destroy the Victorian portrait of childhood innocence
by returning to the child its sexuality, nor could he ever agree that
homosexuality was a sign of hereditary degeneration. (He was
aware that the degeneracy theory was being used in anti-Semitic
campaigns.) Instead he concluded that homosexuality was a de-
velopmental disorder – this meant that it was in everyone's

psychological history, never fully eradicated from the heterosexual adult. His theories made heterosexuality a product of family interaction as much as homosexuality.

His Letter to an American Mother displays a positive attitude to homosexuality: 'I gather from your letter that your son is a homosexual. I am most impressed by the fact that you do not mention this term yourself in your information about him. May I question why you avoid it? Homosexuality is assuredly no advantage, but it is nothing to be classified as an illness; we consider it to be a variation of the sexual development.' Freud goes on to list famous homosexuals and states that it is a great injustice to persecute homosexuality as a crime. He also tells her to read Havelock Ellis.[28] But this letter was written in 1935, at the end of Freud's life and career, and though he states homosexuality is not classified as an illness, his early work, which dealt in terms like the 'Oedipal complex', 'anal fixation', and 'penis envy', made it seem as if he regarded it as an illness, and many psychotherapists, influenced by Freud's work and theories, have attempted to 'cure' it.

Indeed, there is something highly confused within Freud himself on the matter, for in 1905 he told a newspaper reporter that 'homosexuals must not be treated as sick people, for a perverse orientation is far from being a sickness'.[29] 'Perverse' strikes a distinctly discordant note, why not 'different'? Though Freud refused to treat homosexuals unless they were also neurotic, he did not seem to understand that it was society's attitude to their homosexuality which made them neurotic. In 1930 he signed a statement saying that to punish homosexuality was an 'extreme violation of human rights'. The confusion lies in the fact that Freud never quite adjusted to his own homosexuality. In the 1890s he had felt an ardent intimacy with Wilhelm Fleiss, an ear, nose and throat specialist from Berlin. Fleiss had written to Freud with admiration and from then on Freud used Fleiss as a confidant, discussing all the problems which beset him. Later, Freud agreed that his attachment to Fleiss had contained a homosexual element. Then there was Sandor Ferenczi, a psychoanalyst from Budapest, who made exorbitant demands on Freud for intimacy and love. Freud complained about him: 'a very dear fellow, but a little awkwardly dreamy and infantile towards me . . . he has let everything be done for him like a woman and my homosexuality, after all, does not go far enough to accept him as one.'[30]

However, the judgement of psychoanalysis, which included both Freud's followers and his critics, was still that homosexuality was pathological. This judgement clouded the whole of the twentieth century until very recently: 'Many post-Freudian analysts have been less tolerant, and in the 1940s and 1950s American psychoanalysts such as Bieber, Bergler and Socarides mobilised an almost McCarthyite zeal in labelling homosexuals as sick, inadequate personalities, and "grievance collectors".'[31] Psychoanalysts believed that homosexuality was incompatible with happiness, yet psychoanalysis generally held out the hope of an eventual heterosexual adjustment. Homosexuality, it was stated, was a sign of a disturbed personality.

There was a general consensus in the medical world that the homosexual should change his orientation if he could; if not, it must be repressed and strictly controlled; if this could not happen and the man was constantly getting into trouble with the police, then the inference was that suicide was always an option. It is not too harsh, I believe, to typify the approach of kill or cure as being the over-riding one for the first two-thirds of the twentieth century.

XII

WARS
AND
PERSECUTION

The world of the nineteenth-century autocrats, secure in their insularity and self-deceit, continued until the outbreak of war in 1914. Feelings against the abhorrent crime whose name no Christian lips should utter had intensified, so that the homosexual act now became treachery against the state in the minds of many people. For men to consort carnally together was thought to be a political act of insubordination, a flagrant act of betrayal to the moral *zeitgeist* which all must honour, yet it took another sixty years before homosexual men began to be aware of the political nature of their acts.

IGNORANCE AND IGNOMINY[1]

Throughout the post-Wilde period, suppression and censorship were so successful that a large majority of people were totally ignorant that anything like same-gender sex even existed. The laws against soliciting had been strengthened in 1898, and the Vagrancy Law Amendment Act had been changed specifically to 'lay hold of a certain kind of blackguard who is unmentionable in society'. The state's continual persecution of homosexual men must have had some deterrent effect, but in Edwardian London homosexual haunts, clubs and pick-up places still existed. There were enough victims of police arrests for a deputy chairman of the London Sessions in 1911 to bring back the birch. There were twenty-three sentences of fifteen strokes in London during the twelve months to October 1912. Not surprisingly, the men who were punished were all from the lower middle classes. The rich, if caught, could generally avoid the situation by bribery or influential connections; besides, they had their own clubs and a network of discreet pimps to furnish them with lads from the working classes. The rich took enormous pains to hide their proclivities, and had the wealth to make such concealment easy. They also had connections: the Canon of Westminster, Robert Eyton, escaped prosecution and was allowed to leave quietly for Australia, while the Governor of New South Wales, the seventh Earl Beauchamp, was allowed to remain and get married, though he was deprived of office for ten years.

How did the working man, aware of his homosexuality, feel about his life? Indifferent, is the impression one gets, if you look at the army. The Guards were as infiltrated with homosexual practices as their future enemies in Germany: 'When a young fellow joins, someone of us breaks him in and teaches him the trick; but there is little need of that, for it seems to come naturally to almost every young man, so few have escaped the demoralization of schools or crowded homes. We then have no difficulty in passing him on to some gentleman.' Another Guardsman said that most of the soldiers were married, but they didn't let on to their gentleman customers because they didn't like married men.

A Norfolk man, Gerald, born in 1892, had had fun as a farm boy with his mates in the loft of the stables, but was only seduced by a sergeant in 1914 when he joined up. At that time there was no talk of homosexuality, they just did it. (One is reminded of the attitude of the Bavarian farmer, Ernst.) At Le Havre in 1917 Gerald met another soldier and they just knew they were meant for each other. They remained together, sharing a house in Ilford for the next

324

eight years. Gerald seemed throughout his life to be unconcerned that he was living outside the law; nevertheless, he was acutely aware of the situation, always taking care to be discreet.

The picture one gets from reading interviews with other men from this time is of their ignorance and naivety. (The word 'homosexual' was not in general parlance until fifty years later.) Generally, their sexual awakening was delayed until their twenties, and was followed by very little actual sexual contact because of shyness, inhibition and confusion. There was a great deal of loneliness, for there was no one to discuss their feelings with, nor were they aware of any places where they could meet others like themselves. On the whole they had very low self-esteem, for they knew they were different, marked down by society as sinister misfits and social outcasts, reviled if they dared to speak out and say how they wished to be loved. Happiness rested on a chance encounter, a lucky meeting in the street or pub. A bachelor could go for a lifetime without this ever occurring and very often did. No doubt these men would have been heartened, if sceptical, had they been told that groups existed who were working hard for reform.

PIONEERS

Magnus Hirschfeld (1868–1935), who happened to be both a homosexual and a transvestite (he coined the latter term), compiled a vast amount of information on homosexuality, including 20,000 volumes and 35,000 pictures to assist his research. He was a Jew who had given evidence in the Eulenburg trials and was accordingly hated in Germany for such treachery. In 1897 he founded the Scientific-humanitarian Committee in Berlin, with the aim of abolishing Paragraph 175, as well as to educate the public and to interest homosexuals themselves in fighting for their rights.

Hirschfeld devised a psychological questionnaire containing 130 questions which was sent out to 10,000 men and women. He established a marriage counselling service, gave advice on contraception, as well as writing books and monographs upon the subject. He was also concerned with social welfare, alcoholism and prostitution. He claimed that homosexuals had special virtues, being more democratic and altruistic – a claim that particularly annoyed his opponents. He considered homosexuality to be innate, influenced by internal secretions of the glands, a theory which has found few admirers until very recently. Unfortunately, all of his research material was destroyed when Hitler came to power. Nazi hoodlums broke into his Berlin Institute for Sexual Science (which he founded in 1919), burned the records and destroyed the building. Hirschfeld was luckily abroad at the time.

In 1907 Dr George Merzbach, a member of Hirschfeld's committee, gave a lecture in New York and then wrote to Hirschfeld to tell him how it went. From the questions asked in the discussion afterwards, we can gauge the ignorance of this audience of 'distinguished doctors and legal scholars'. 'Can homosexuality be eradicated by castration?' 'Doesn't homosexuality lead to paranoia?' 'Can homosexuals have children?' 'What are the names of historic or famous homosexuals and the evidence thereof?'[2] Merzbach considered this lecture to have been a huge success, simply because of the amount of interest engendered in such an audience.

In the same year, the periodical that Hirschfeld published printed an anonymous letter from Boston. Part of it reads:

> Here, as in Germany, homosexuality extends throughout all classes, from the slums of the North End to the highly fashionable Back Bay. Reliable homosexuals have told me names that reach into the highest circles of Boston, New York and Washington D.C., names which have left me speechless with astonishment. I have also noticed that bisexuality must be rather widespread.

Hirschfeld was known and admired in select groups in England, and one of his most famous maxims, *Per Scientiam ad Justitiam* (Through knowledge to justice), was taken to heart by the sexual reformers. 'I have no doubt we shall win,' Oscar Wilde wrote to the criminologist, George Cecil Ives in 1897, 'but the road is long, and red with monstrous martyrdoms. Nothing but the repeal of the Criminal Law Amendment Act would do any good. That is essential.'[3]

Ives was born in Germany, illegitimate offspring of two aristocratic families (but he was brought up by his grandmother the Hon. Emma Ives in France and England). He was aware of his homosexuality from as far back as he could remember: 'I could not understand why such a wonderful thing should not be sanctioned.' From the mid-1890s Ives began a secret homosexual society called the Order of Chaeronea, named after the battle in 338 BC when the sacred band of Theban lovers had all been killed. The cause of homosexual liberation dominated Ives's life. Only those prepared to work for a reform of the law were admitted into the secret society, members were exhorted to be secretive about their comrades, and there were seals and insignia, rules and purposes: 'We demand justice for all manner of people who are wronged and oppressed by individuals or multitudes or the laws.' Laurence Housman (1865–1959) was chairman of the society but because of its secrecy it is difficult to discover who actually belonged. Some of the Uranists certainly, and C. Kains Jackson, editor and publisher of Uranian material, Laurence's brother, A. E. Housman, and Leonard Green, a writer of Uranian prose and friend of T. E. Lawrence. It is thought that there were members in America, France, Italy and Germany, and meetings were held in Vienna and Paris. Most of the known members seemed to have had an interest in working-class youths.

This is another aspect of homosexuality that marked the era, the romance of 'rough trade', the desire among educated and cultured older men who were reasonably wealthy for labouring men or youths. Money came into this sexual exchange, of course, benefiting the youths, but in many cases it was a mutually beneficial exchange because the older man wished to teach and the younger had a genuine desire to learn. Many of the younger men would later marry and have families but still keep in touch with their old lover. The older men then had the added bonus of a vicarious family where they were in the position of being an uncle or godfather to young children. E. M. Forster's policeman lover, Bob Buckingham, christened his son Morgan, and he in turn christened his first son Morgan.

It is impossible to say how effective the Order was in advocating the necessity of reform. One of its activities was to encourage distinguished and prominent but secretly homosexual men to use their influence. Members of Parliament, writers and artists, men in the legal profession were all canvassed and encouraged. But in an era where the word could barely be uttered, when if any hint of the subject was mooted a person ran the risk of being suspected of the crime, it must have seemed foolhardy to do anything. So a public defence of homosexuality did not exist. Possibly the Order's most significant function was in being a support group for its members at a time of antipathy and persecution.

In July 1914 the British Society for the Study of Sex Psychology (BSSP) was established, making Edward Carpenter a life member and first president. It was inspired by Hirschfeld's Scientific-humanitarian Committee, so its aim was to adopt a humane and rational approach to the problems of sex. They planned lectures and pamphlets to 'organise understanding in the lay mind on a larger scale, to make people more receptive to scientific proof, and more conscious of their social responsibility'. There was a clear assumption that the women's cause and sex reform were all part of the same struggle. Many of the pamphlets were relevant to feminist politics (such as Havelock Ellis's *The Erotic Rights of Women*), but the discussion of homosexuality was at the core of the society's work. Its second pamphlet was an English digest of a German pamphlet published in 1903, *The Social Problem of Sexual Inversion*, which said in its introduction: 'that any courage should be needed in a demand for facts to be recognised and scientifically investigated, is in itself a sufficient condemnation of the obscurantist attitude which prevails so largely among us in regard to this question.'

The BSSP continued to publish pamphlets on a wide range of homosexual topics: Carpenter wrote on Whitman's homosexuality; Laurence Housman wrote on fellow feeling in sex; Stella

Browne wrote on sexual variety for women; a leading anthropologist wrote on the origins of sexual modesty. But in the 1920s it had around only 240 members, forty to fifty of whom would attend a meeting. Yet its membership of progressive intellectuals now seems impressive: G. B. Shaw and E. M. Forster, Vyvyan Holland, Harley Granville Barker, Harriet Weaver Shaw, Radclyffe Hall and Una Troubridge, Bertrand and Dora Russell and Norman Douglas. Until the early 1930s it remained the only British organisation concerned with the issue.

In 1928 the World League for Sexual Reform was founded. Hirschfeld, August Forel and Havelock Ellis were its first honorary presidents. It comprised (according to Wilhelm Reich) the most progressive sexologists and sex reformers in the world; it had representatives from the USSR as well as from capitalist countries, but its stance was decidedly apolitical. The 1928 Congress appealed 'to the legislatures, the Press and the Peoples of all countries, to help to create a new legal and social attitude (based on the knowledge which has been acquired from scientific research in sexual biology, psychology and sociology) towards the sexual life of men and women.'

The League worked for the political, economic and sexual equality of women and men, the reform of marriage and the divorce laws, improved sex education, control of conception, reform of the abortion laws, prevention of venereal disease and prostitution and the protection of unmarried mothers and illegitimate children. 'Sexual equality' covered homosexual injustices, but when society was in such a panic over the subject, little progress could be made outside the insular world of medicine, and there was no consensus there either.

A more modest society, though with equally humane and ambitious aims, met with a savage and quick end. In 1924 the state of Illinois issued a charter to a non-profit organisation named the Society for Human Rights, located in Chicago. This was the brainchild of Henry Gerber who had fought in the First World War. He had spent some time in Germany and had subscribed to homosexual magazines there, impressed that homosexuals had organised themselves and were pressing for reforms. He wanted to do the same for homosexuals in the United States, for 'being thoroughly cowed, they seldom get together'.[4] Gerber borrowed the German name for his own society and once home began to spend his savings to get the society working. With a small circle of new but enthusiastic friends (John, a preacher who earned his room and board by preaching brotherly love to small groups of blacks; Al, a laundry worker; and Ralph who worked on the railways), he planned a series of lectures, a membership drive, and a publication called *Friendship and Freedom*. Gerber soon found out that his new friends were both illiterate and penniless, and it was he who had to write and pay for the magazine. Two issues were sent out. What Gerber also did not know was that Al, the vice-president of the society, was married and had two children. One Sunday morning at 2 a.m. Gerber returned to his single room. Soon after there was a knock on the door and two men insisted on entering. One was a city detective and the other a reporter from the *Examiner*. The detective asked where the boy was. 'What boy?' Gerber asked. The detective told him that he had orders to take him down to the police station. They searched his room and took his typewriter, papers and a diary.

At the police station Gerber found John and Al, and the young man that Al had in his room at the time. He was shown a copy of the *Examiner* with the front-page headline 'Strange Sex Cult Exposed' and told how Al had brought his male friends home and had sex with them in front of his wife. When the police searched Al's rooms they found a pamphlet which 'urged men to leave their wives and children'. The police had no arrest warrants.

The day after the arrest, a detective in the police court triumphantly produced a powder puff and said he had found it in Gerber's room. This was solemnly admitted as evidence of Gerber's effeminacy. The judge adjourned the court, saying that he thought they had violated federal law by sending obscene matter through the mail. However, nothing in *Friendship and Freedom* could be considered obscene.

Gerber got himself a lawyer but it was not until the third trial that a new judge reprimanded the prosecution for arresting persons without a warrant and ordered the case to be dismissed. When Gerber left, a detective said: 'What was the idea of the Society? Was it to give you birds the legal right to rape every boy on the street?' Gerber said of the experience that it convinced him 'they were up against a solid wall of ignorance, hypocrisy, meanness and corruption. The wall had won.'

There was an unexpected spin-off from this short-lived experiment: the Mattachine Society founded by Henry Hay. In 1930 when Hay was seventeen he picked up his first man who then brought him out into Los Angeles's homosexual society. This man had in turn been picked up by a man who was a member of the Chicago group, so Hay first heard about such an organisation then. It stayed in his mind but it was not until 1948 that the Mattachine Society was conceived (see p. 357).

FRONTIERSMEN

Little is known of the sexual life of cowboys, except that though they occasionally married Indian women and used brothels when they were available, their work made it well nigh impossible for them to be family men. For many thousands of cowboys, where they worked was a day's journey or more from frontier towns and hamlets. Often they lived on the range or in camps where there were likely to be no women at all. Often two men would pair off and become 'partners' or 'sidekicks'. There are a few poems and limericks still in existence which give a picture of a boisterous sexuality among these rough-necks who had opted out of orthodox society and would remain outside for the rest of their lives.

> There was a cowboy named Hooter,
> Who packed a big six-shooter,
> When he grabbed the stock,
> It became hard as a rock.
> As a peace-maker it couldn't be cuter.[5]

An Oklahoma cowboy early in the century recalled how his trail boss urged them always to pair off with another man. In a letter he wrote: 'At first pairing they'd solace each other gingerly and, as bashfulness waned, manually. As trust in mutual good will matured, they'd graduate to the ecstatically comforting 69 . . . Folk know not how cock-hungry men get.' At first, he goes on, attraction for another cowboy is rooted in admiration, a need for an ally which ripens into love.

A poem published in 1915 by a ranch-hand who lived in South Dakota and Arizona tells of how he felt when his partner died. The last verse reads:

> The range is empty and the trail is blind,
> And I don't seem but half myself today.
> I wait to hear him riding up behind
> And feel his knee rub mine the good old way.[6]

Another man recalls his work in the early 1900s in an isolated logging camp, where nine men were snowed in for months during the winter. He stresses the fact that none of them was effeminate, abnormal or psychotic, but all but two engaged in homosexual activities, sodomy being the most favoured act. Then he spent two years in a gold-mining camp where fifty-five men were employed. Here there were raids on the vaseline in the first-aid cabinet and easily half of them were having sex with each other. Two of the most 'masculine', a tram operator and a jackhammer man, paired off exclusively with each other. The rest envied them.

Kinsey in his famous report talks about sexual contact among older males in rural Western areas, and believed it was common among the pioneers and cowboys:

> Today, it is found among ranchmen, cattle men, prospectors, lumbermen, and farming groups in general – among groups that are virile, physically active. These are men who have faced the rigors of the wild. They live on realities and on a minimum of theory. Such a background breeds the attitude

that sex is sex, irrespective of the nature of the partner with whom the relation is had.[7]

These words are true of any all-male, enclosed society. An elderly woman in Interior, South Dakota, remembered the pioneer bachelors of the 1890s. When asked if she thought they ever had a sexual relationship, she replied that people then didn't talk about sex, so it would never have crossed their minds, but they probably did. No one was that worried about it.[8] At least these bachelors, far away from prying eyes, could get on with their lives in the way they wanted, without the persecution that others suffered.

VICTIMS

What is the connection between the military mind and the love of boys? One certainly exists, for there are many examples of high-ranking military commanders having sentimental attachments to boys before they have reached puberty. Montgomery is a fairly recent example: one young friend, aged nine, had to perform naked drill after his bath and was puzzled afterwards as to why Montgomery seemed so extremely affectionate.[9] Lord Kitchener was a mysogynist who liked to surround himself with a circle of handsome young officers whom he described as his 'happy family of boys.' His aide-de-camp, Oswald FitzGerald, also a bachelor, remained with Kitchener until they met death together in 1916. Their devotion to one another was well-known.[10]

The case which shocked the nation was that of Sir Hector MacDonald, hero of Omdurman, who committed suicide in 1903 after the European edition of the *New York Herald* had reported that he was travelling back to Ceylon, where he was Commander-in-Chief, to be court-martialled for the crime of misbehaviour with several schoolboys. When he shot himself in the Hotel Regina in Paris, he was taking the advice of the king with whom he had had an audience a few days before. It was thought that Edward VII had said that the best thing he could do in the circumstances was to shoot himself. Why did the establishment not protect him as it had so many others in similar cases?

MacDonald, however, was not one of them. Born in 1853, he was a crofter's son who became a draper's assistant, and then enlisted in the ranks in 1870. Seventeen years later he became a captain in the Egyptian Army, making his name as the hero of Omdurman, and then went on to fight in South Africa – a Scottish national hero. In 1902 he was appointed to his position in Ceylon and within the year he had been discovered by a planter in a railway carriage, with the blinds drawn, with four Sinhalese boys in a communal masturbation circle. Once the word got around, several schoolmasters and clergymen came forward to lay more charges of MacDonald being friendly with other young boys.

When Kitchener heard the news (he was Commander-in-Chief of the Indian Army), he demanded that the brute be court-martialled, then shot. The Governor, Sir Joseph West Ridgeway, claimed that MacDonald was involved with scores of boys aged twelve and upwards: 'Some, indeed most of his victims . . . are the sons of the best known men in the colony, English and Native.' It was rumoured that Ridgeway's son himself was involved, and the Governor was desperate to ensure that 'no more mud would be stirred up'. Later, when he was accused of hounding MacDonald to his death, he defended himself by asking what else he could have done, for the clergy and planters had formed a Vigilance Committee and were about to take out a warrant for MacDonald's arrest. The Governor congratulated himself that the revolting details of the case had so far not been made public. They never were, because after MacDonald's suicide, his case file was destroyed.

Sir Roger Casement (1864–1916) wrote a note in his diary about MacDonald: 'The reasons given are pitiably sad. The most distressing case this surely of its kind, and one that may awake the national mind to saner methods of curing a terrible disease.' This is an amazing entry, considering that Casement was avid in picking up tall, well-hung young men and being the passive partner. His diaries, which began in this same year, detail the size and appearance of their genitalia ('it was huge and curved and he awfully keen') and the payment (from four and sixpence to ten shillings) given to the men whom he picked up. The only explanation for a diary entry such as the one about MacDonald, is that Casement felt that a pederast was as alien to him as a heterosexual, but why should it be 'pitiably sad' and a 'terrible disease'? Surely this shows in Casement a degree of self-deception and disorientation, those same feelings which were to bring about his exposure and downfall, working for an independent Ireland in the midst of the First World War. The British government unashamedly used the diaries to blacken Casement's name and reputation, and, helped by a popular tide of feeling against the Irish patriot, Casement was convicted and hung. There was a general hysteria among the authorities that such vice was continuing to spread. Reading about Casement's easy conquests and the availability of them must only have served to intensify the establishment's alarms and fears.

QUEER OR STRAIGHT?

The military elite were always particularly concerned with the 'nameless crime' in the armed services, believing that such perversions, if not ruthlessly stamped on, would decimate the aggressive fighting spirit within the forces. Stories of the sacred Theban band pulled no weight here. Decoys had long since been used to trap men suspected of such acts, so there was nothing new in the ploy when, in the spring of 1919, officers at Newport (Rhode Island) Naval Training Station sent men into the community to associate with suspected 'sexual perverts'.[11] What was new was the scale of this mission. A squad of young enlisted men, who were expected to have sex with other men, were ordered to bring back evidence with which the 'perverts' could be charged, leaving the decoys who had committed the same acts to go free. The whole enterprise was magnificently impractical, besides being, in the light of the sexual mores of that time, grossly immoral, and if anyone but a bunch of authoritarian zealots had ordered it, they would have foreseen that it would undoubtedly end in farce and humiliation for themselves.

The scheme began with a Dr E. M. Hudson, the welfare officer at the naval hospital, who was concerned about the flagrantly displayed effeminacy of his male nursing staff. What the decoys discovered must have been a revelation to the naval authorities, as their naval base was the busy hub of the perversions they were hunting. There were designated pick-up places called 'cruising grounds', the beach in the summer, the cliff walk, a cemetery and a bridge, where sailors and civilians could meet. But the most significant discovery was the part that the YMCA played; it was a rendezvous for homosexual parties where drag acts were performed, where sailors new to the area were given the once-over by more experienced men and where private rooms could be engaged for sex. The YMCA was the place where the 'queens' hung out. They referred to themselves as the 'gang'.

From the evidence of the first trial, 406 pages of testimony over twenty-three days, a whole new sub-culture springs to life with all its slang and beliefs. The civilians were largely men from outside the area, who would spend weekends in Newport so as to visit their sailor friends, and servants, residents of New York, who worked in the grand houses of Newport. Only two civilians were local residents. The YMCA at Newport was famous, it seemed, for offering a good time. The sailors who dominated the social life of the YMCA were the drag queens, notorious, when not in uniform, for wearing women's clothes. A local paper praised Billy Hughes whom everyone fell in love with in *Pinafore*, for he danced 'like a Ziegfeld girl'. The paper went on to quote an admiral who thought Billy was a 'corker' and 'she is the daintiest little thing I ever laid eyes on'.

The homosexual sailors called themselves 'queers', but within that group they distinguished among themselves three categories: 'fairies or cocksuckers', 'pogues' – men who liked to be anally penetrated – and 'two-way artists', men who enjoyed both. A second group of sailors participated but always took the male role. Some of them were married, indeed, some of them, according to the 'queers', were also married to them. To be accepted by the 'gang', you had to be either fairy, pogue or two-way or a husband, and present yourself unashamedly at their public social

336

events in that role. Some of them blurred their roles a little, a drag queen and fairy, for example, attempted on the quiet to 'brown' another member of the gang. This was an infringement of the tacit code.

Before the trial the Navy's attitude had been to ignore the occasional sexual liaisons between straight men and the queers, for they had not thought them important. But the investigation brought out the fact that many more men than they had ever imagined were regularly consorting with queers. When they found themselves prosecuting men who were not normally labelled as queer, the authorities were forced to redefine how they categorised people who participated in such acts. The gang defined the male population beyond their circle as 'straight', but then they sub-divided that group into men who rejected their advances and men who accepted them. The last group were 'trade'; some would participate, the gang agreed, rather more enthusiastically than others. The gang pretended to prefer all their men straight and not to reciprocate in any way. But one of the decoys recorded that the fairy he was with 'wanted to kiss me and love me . . . and insisted and begged for it'. The fairies might take their straight companion out to dinner, give him presents, and provide him with a place to stay where they would have sex. Or a fairy might pick up a straight sailor one evening at the YMCA, have sex the same night and never see him again.

A decoy testified that in order to get admitted into the gang, all he had to do was sit with them in the YMCA lobby one evening. One of the gang members expressed his surprise at seeing him with them all. The decoy told him that he belonged with the gang. The answer was: 'So we can consider you trade?' The decoys observed how the gang would pick up young recruits and go to bed with them, but it is clear that they never thought such recruits were queer because of it. 'Normal' men, the decoys thought, could take advantage of the fairies, for they were men who offered themselves to you like women did. The decoys believed that normal men could participate in such sexual acts without questioning their own sexual nature. The decoys were happy to become trade for this mission because it was no threat to their self-image. Trade was socially acceptable. There were always straight men who engaged in certain ritual behaviour after sex with a queer, designed to reinforce their difference and their 'masculinity'. These were men who ridiculed the queers and after sex generally beat them up.

The court of inquiry was told of a great number of straight sailors who regularly had sex with the queers. One had fellated 'something like fifteen or twenty young recruits from the Naval Training Station in a single night'. But as the investigation proceeded, they began to be so appalled at the extent of homosexual activity that the chairman of the first court told the chief investigator to curtail the investigation, saying of the decoys, 'that if your men do not knock off they will hang the whole state of Rhode Island'. The Navy was trying to prosecute only those men in whom homosexual desire was a persistent, constituent element of their personality, whether it manifested itself in effeminate behaviour or not. They chose not to prosecute the straight men who were the queers' customers, but as the trial proceeded it became increasingly difficult to keep the two categories separate.

The decoys testified that they had submitted to the queers' advances only to rid the Navy of their presence, but the defendants pointed out that the decoys had taken pleasure in their work. The lawyers asked one decoy after another, gently pressurising them, about the work that they had volunteered for; they knew, didn't they, that this work involved sucking and sodomy, and yet they still volunteered? The decoys began to get nervous, especially when some of the gang claimed that the decoys took the sexual initiative. At the second court of inquiry, the decoys were asked how much sexual pleasure they had experienced. One protested, saying he was a man and if someone touched his cock, then it got erect and he could not do anything about it. In 1920 the Dunn Inquiry condemned the original investigation and the Navy offered clemency to some of the men who had been imprisoned. It knew it had been defeated.

But the church had become involved too. The decoys had testified that five of them had sex with an Episcopal clergyman,

Samuel Kent, and a YMCA volunteer and churchman, Arthur Leslie Green. Kent fled Newport but the Navy found him and brought him to trial on sodomy charges. Two courts acquitted him because he denied the charges and he was a widely respected figure, well-liked and admired by his colleagues, and because he had worked tirelessly in the hospital throughout the influenza epidemic. After Kent's second acquittal, the Bishop of Rhode Island and the Newport Ministerial Union charged that the Navy had used immoral methods in its investigation, by instructing young enlisted men in details of a nameless vice. The Bishop wrote letters to the President and to the Secretary of the Navy, condemned the exposure in the press, and forced the Navy to convene a second court of inquiry.

The anger of the Episcopal church was not just that two of their men were seriously implicated, it was that the naval inquiry had associated the church in perversions because of their perceived effeminacy. Kent and Greene had been continually described in the court as 'peculiar' or 'sissified' or 'effeminate'. During the daily visit to the hospital, a witness had declared that Greene held the patients' hands and did not 'talk like a man', for he spoke quietly and with concern. Hospital visiting was impugned, it was not a man's work, nor was it suitable for a man to loan the sailors money, take them for drives or out to dinner or to the theatre.

Kent and his supporters argued that this was part of the ministry, that they had acted in the spirit of Christian brotherhood, that in the war thousands of sailors had come through the Naval Training Station and needed support and sympathy. Besides, the Episcopal War Commission provided Kent with funds every week to take servicemen to the theatre and to maintain his automobile in order to give them drives. The church managed to defend Kent by denying that he had ever had any sexual contact with the men, but at the same time they celebrated his profound emotional devotion to them.

What is perhaps surprising is that throughout the trials no medical evidence was ever given. Though the trials occurred only thirty years after the medical model of homosexuality had been created, in 1919 no such concept of homosexuality as a sickness seems to have permeated through to the authorities. No medical expert was ever invited to give an opinion on the issues. Dr Hudson took the view that homosexuals were wilful criminals who should be rounded up and punished.

There was no uniform policy within the Navy to combat homosexuality. The Newport sailors were fortunate compared with James Ray Harwell, who had enlisted in 1917. He was a carpenter's son from Miami, Florida, and he eventually achieved the rank of chief quartermaster. Then in 1921 his commanding officer, on the basis of a love letter, charged Harwell with sodomy and 'scandalous conduct tending to the destruction of good morals.'[12] He was convicted and sentenced to fifteen years' hard labour with a dishonourable discharge and forfeiture of pay. His parents appealed, adding that they had depended upon Harwell's meagre pay in order to survive. The Navy was adamant, refused clemency and defended their need to exact a heavy penalty so as to bring about this 'eradication of evil'.

THE POLITICS OF THE JAZZ AGE

The old autocratic order had become enfeebled by the time the twentieth century 'began' in 1914. Intellectually bankrupt, it clung to moribund values and in a panic could do little but send millions of young men to their deaths. (My father, aged sixteen, had enlisted at the beginning of the war, lying about his age as thousands did, and I grew up through the Second World War hearing vivid stories of the First; stories which were so horrific and vile for the men in the trenches, that my father's traumatic experiences touched me as well.)

Wars on the scale of the two this century have huge revolutionary power, they have a dynamic which reverberates throughout all levels of society, starting at the lowest depths. It is as if a series of explosions rips through all the walls and partitions that have been carefully built up to segment society's rituals and pretensions. War exposes the false and the faithless, the synthetic and spurious, the cosmetic dreams in which society clothes its baser desires.

When blunt working-class men are grouped together in their thousands, a hitherto buried loyalty and trust are discovered which bond the group, making a new dynamic with the potential for change. In Russia, led by Lenin, it created the revolution of 1917. But in the West, though changes were fermenting, there was no leader charged with fervour to fuse all the elements into a new social structure. So in the 1920s we find chaos, old and new in constant friction, if not battling in public.

This has its comical side, for though homosexuality insisted on being flagrant and public in its customs, clothes and slang, the old order never recognised it. Memoirs and autobiographies of the time constantly refer to friends visiting their upper-middle-class homes perfumed and delicately made-up, with flowers in their buttonholes, while the parents coolly agreed how pleasant the young men were.* The word in homosexual circles was 'so', as in 'Is he so?' Quite often this was accompanied with the downward flick of a languid hand, showing the limp wrist. Parents could be astonishingly obtuse, as in Beverley Nicols's case where Egerton Edwards, who painted his face and wore an orchid in his buttonhole, was thought a dark horse because he proclaimed his aversion to women – the parents were sure he kept a mistress on the sly. His made-up face was amusing and bohemian and, as his grandfather was a baronet, his taking Beverley out to dinner and to concerts was simply 'kindness'.

These were the homosexuals in the upper echelons of society, often bolstered by private incomes. Like characters by Firbank, they turned the whole of life into a rather trivial aesthetic. Why did they ape the effeminate so outrageously? Partly, these were the signs that marked the group, gender-blurring was a way of making a statement. In an age which still delineated gender in

---

* For example, J. R. Ackerley, *My Father and Myself*; Beverley Nicols, *Father Figure*; T. Cuthbert Worsley, *Flannelled Fool*.

absolute stereotyped terms, it was an effective way of showing disagreement and rebellion. Yet others, who committed homosexual acts throughout their lives, opted out of labelling themselves and merged with social convention and the idea of the masculine heterosexual: 'Sailors, explorers, Australian station-hands, cowboys, athletes, head prefects of schools, policemen who importuned other men in urinals . . . soldiers who went to homosexual pubs for repeated bouts of sex . . . all of these . . . engaged in the activity, but were excluded from the identity.'[13]

At the same time, the 'new woman' had appeared, obscuring the image of the restricted Victorian matron. The new woman rejected both patriarchy and her mother's domesticity. Society felt she was dangerous, for her behaviour constantly threatened its most cherished values. At the same time people were mesmerised by her exhibitionism, drawn in to her world of short hair and flashy automobiles, riveted by the suspicion that there were simply the exterior icons of something far more sinister. The new woman was felt to be promiscuous and it was whispered that she was almost certainly bisexual. She wore trousers – that was highly suspicious in itself. Bosoms were flattened and the crotch was stressed. Skirts, of course, veil the genitals. Trousers, on the other hand, accentuate the loins, hips, bottom, thighs and, depending upon how tight they are, the crotch itself. Tight trousers say, I am sexually available – do you want me? No wonder they were thought so shocking in themselves. Krafft-Ebing linked lesbianism with crossdressing. 'Uranism may nearly always be suspected in females wearing their hair short, or who dress in the fashion of men, or pursue the sports and pastimes of their male acquaintances'[14]

The jazz age of the 1920s sounds to those born later to have been a great age of rebellion against the prison walls of the nineteenth century. Yet lesbian women who wished to write about their experiences openly found it impossible to get published; books were either privately printed* or suppressed by the author herself.†

---

* *Ladies Almanack* by Djuna Barnes.
† The autobiographical fiction of Hilda Doolittle (H.D.).

Novels could take flight in another way, but they were still a disguise, as in Virginia Woolf's *Orlando* – a surreal *Bildungsroman* – or Djuna Barnes's *Nightwood* – a Jacobean tragedy in prose poetry – or the deliberate camouflage of gender and events in the novels of Gertrude Stein. But when you have deliberately burnt a historic past, broken the cast of the social image of woman, where do you find a new political role?

Gertrude Stein was in fact content to use the old structure. She and Alice B. Toklas lived together in Victorian domesticity, the only roles they changed were those within the family. Stein was at first 'husband', then she also became 'baby', while Alice was 'Mama': 'Despite her sexual preferences, Stein never ceased to believe in bourgeois heterosexuality: its decencies, norms and families.'[15] Stein was in fact a patriarch, she treated Alice at times with great cruelty, she represented the law and so was allowed to transgress it, and though she was husband and father, she had the freedom to be baby too. Alice was as exploited a female as any Victorian spinster looking after the needs of a wilful father. This need in Stein to be a dominating force made her blind to the realities of Nazism and the German occupation; self-hatred of her own Jewishness made her brush aside the fate of the Jews in occupied Europe. It was only because she was protected by her wealth and connections in occupied France that she was left alone, managing to acquire eggs and butter every day when millions in the same country were near starvation.

As a German sympathiser she was not alone among the great lesbian artistic salons of the Paris inter-war years. Natalie Barney, who was one-quarter Jewish, was also, like Stein, attracted to fascist theories of economics. She fell under the sway of Ezra Pound's theory of usury with its anti-Semitic base, convinced that both wars were caused by Jewish efforts to secure greater profits on their investments. She fled Paris in 1940 and went to Italy with her lover, Romaine Brooks, a painter. They lived in a large villa near Florence where they ordered trenches to be dug in the garden so that they could lie in them on sun-loungers and sun-bathe, safe from enemy bombs and guns. From there Barney wrote: 'Why all this mystery about financing the second act of this continuous war? Are not its bankers secured against loss either by the victory of the Allies or assured of their revenge by getting their money's worth of Aryan flesh?'[16]

In glaring contrast, other lesbians of the time living in Paris – Djuna Barnes, Sylvia Beach, Colette, Nancy Cunard, Hilda Doolittle – were all resisting the patriarchal power of such totalitarian regimes as had been created in Italy. While Bryher secretly smuggled Resistance workers, Jews and intellectuals (including Walter Benjamin and Arthur Koestler) out of Nazi-occupied territories, Sylvia Beach and Adrienne Monnier helped Gisele Freund, the literary photographer, to escape from Germany and later from occupied France. Both Bryher and Cunard had already shown their left-wing sympathies when they had been involved in the Harlem Renaissance and in movements for black equality.

The Harlem Renaissance was an explosion of equality for black and white lesbian and homosexual men which occurred in the 1920s in New York's Harlem. It spawned a homosexual subculture that was uniquely Afro-American, where black and white, straight and queer were meeting together on street corners, in cafés, night clubs and in private salons; where blues music and its lyrics mirrored this new world.

Madame Walker, a tall coloured woman who carried a riding crop and wore a jewelled turban, gave opulent parties at her lavishly furnished house in Sugar Hill, parties crammed with artists and writers, and celebrities of stage and screen. These parties would attract luminaries such as Cole Porter, Cary Grant and Bessie Smith. There were also 'buffet flats', an after-hours entertainment in someone's apartment where gin was poured out of milk pitchers, and where gambling and prostitution were sometimes also on tap: 'They had a faggot there that was so great that people used to come there just to watch him make love to another man. He was that great. He'd give a tongue bath and everything. By the time he got to the front of the guy he was shaking like a leaf.'[17]

344

There was a similar sex circus on 140th Street, the 'Daisy Chain' or the '101 Ranch' – a place so notorious that both Fats Waller and Count Basie composed tunes commemorating it. At another 'buffet flat' a young black entertainer called Joey played the piano and sang, then did a striptease and extinguished a lighted candle by sitting on it until it completely disappeared. At Harry Hansberry's Clam House, Gladys Bentley, a 250-pound dark-skinned lesbian, performed all night long in a white tuxedo and top hat. She was celebrated for her obscene lyrics to popular contemporary melodies. Novels of the time often included scenes based on these parties in Harlem.★ Forty years later, the lesbian socialite and lover of both Garbo and Dietrich, Mercedes de Acosta recalled: 'Everyone rushed up to Harlem at night to sit around places thick with smoke and the smell of bad gin, where Negroes danced about with each other until the small hours of the morning.'[18]

The stock market crash of 1929 and the following Depression brought the Harlem Renaissance to an end. Several of its leading lights died in the early 1930s. What is significant is that equality between black and white, and male and female, appears to have been generated by homosexuality itself. Ignored by the rest of society, such equality never spread. In one of the novels of the period (*Strange Brother*), the hero frequents the homosexual underworld of Harlem because he finds social acceptance there, and because he identifies with others who are also outcasts from American life. Outcasts ferment revolt and this was a true revolt against the established mores of the last century, though there had been signs of something similar occurring in Louisiana in the 1840s. It is one aspect of homosexuality that the rest of society unconsciously fears, that if it had the power it would enact legislation, not just to remove all stigma and injustice from itself, but from all other oppressed minorities as well.

When the rest of society did notice what was going on, all the old pejorative terms were trotted out, as in this 1936 article in *Current Psychology and Psychoanalysis* which describes the degenerates

---

★ *Strange Brother* by Blair Niles (1931); *The Young and Evil* by Charles Henry Ford and Parker Tyler (1933); *Nigger Heaven* by Carl Van Vechten (1926).

of Greenwich Village. This was once a happy, carefree abode, the writer said, for struggling writers and artists. Now it has become a place of 'Freak Exhibits'. These are the sexual inverts, members of the third sex who flaunt their traits in the Village, 'Lady Lovers', teenage girls with their 'wives' roving in dark streets and alleys, clothed in mannish togs, flat-chested, hair slicked back, faces thin and hard with voices as low as a man's.

Boys, known as 'pansies', wore heavy mascara, rouge and lipstick, smirking indecent suggestions to each other. They all used drugs, consuming large quantities of marijuana. At Village parties, sexual exhibitionism with physical degradation was quite 'the thing'. The article sums up by saying that all they care about is to be noticed: 'They have never grown up.'[19]

Such stereotyping was to continue; it was one method by which society distanced itself from what it saw as a social problem. By coarsening and simplifying homosexual behaviour, reducing it to a few physical characteristics of gender exchange, while proclaiming it an abomination and a type of blasphemy to make the flesh creep, society tried to ensure that homosexuals were alienated from everyday life.

The most famous homosexual novel of the era was Radclyffe Hall's *The Well of Loneliness*, but politically it served only to emphasise gender stereotyping. Hall had studied Kraff-Ebing and compiled a set of notes which were from 'the latest and revised editions of the works of the highest authorities on sexual inversion.'[20] The novel thus pretended to medical accuracy and for decades was the only literary image which lesbians had. The pity of it is that Hall intended writing a polemic which would convince society that homosexuals needed mercy and understanding, so she contrived to make heterosexual readers feel sorry for her lesbian characters. Her heroine is therefore trapped by an accident of birth – Stephen has a superior moral disposition which is constantly being overthrown by self-pity and self-loathing.

Hall's own costume and manner – monocle, breeches and brusqueness – fitted society's stereotype like a glove, while her lover, Una Lady Troubridge, frail and feminine, was the perfect foil. But the real harm that Hall did to homosexual self-respect was by believing in the congenital inversion theory, thus giving a morbid aura to natural impulses and healthy views. Hall believed that lesbians were women who were born into the wrong body and so made them sound freakish, instead of merely communicating that women love women because it is as natural to them as breathing air.

THE SECOND WORLD WAR[21]

This war and the years of Nazi rule before it, are marked by the savage persecution of homosexuals in Germany. There are no official figures for how many homosexuals died in concentration camps (for many camp records were destroyed by the SS), but it is thought nearly 50,000 were convicted for homosexuality and died in the camps. It was the Jews, homosexuals and gypsies, who wore yellow, pink and brown triangles respectively,★ who suffered most from the tortures and violence of the SS and the Capos. They were described as the scum of humanity who had no right to live on German soil and should be exterminated.[22] The rest of the world knew nothing of this savagery and at the end of the war, when discovering the holocaust of Jewish people, few had compassion left also to consider the fate of the homosexuals and gypsies.

Throughout the war, the US Army and Navy both described homosexuality as a 'constitutional psychopathic state' and homosexuals as 'sexual psychopaths'. Screening tests were set up so that the services should not admit such people. It listed three possible signs for identifying male homosexuals: feminine bodily characteristics, effeminacy in dress and manner and a patulous or expanded

---

★ The distinguishing triangles in different colours were red for politicals, green for criminals, black for anti-socials, blue for emigrants and purple for Jehovah's Witnesses.

rectum. Again, we see the need to isolate the phenomenon by identifying flagrant physical signs; for the armed services, homosexuality could not exist in men or women who appeared to be similar to themselves. The screening process, then, was doomed to failure.

The majority of homosexuals, hearing that they were being rejected for military service, took pains to hide any give-away characteristics they thought they might have. It was not difficult. The nineteen-year-old Richard Fleischer was astonished that the psychiatrist had not noticed his curly blond hair was partly bleached, or had not picked up on the sissy S in his voice. All the psychiatrist had asked was whether he liked girls and as he genuinely did, he had answered 'yes' and was passed.

Once in the Army and at military base, where sometimes 100,000 military personnel might be stationed, they quickly found like-minded kin and groups would begin to form. Bob Ruffing, a chief petty officer in the Navy, told of the eye contact that very soon alerted him to the presence of other homosexual men: 'Very quickly you had a vast network of friends.'[23] Both men's and women's cliques soon developed a basic rule to protect themselves; such was the fear of discovery that they would never talk about homosexuality, even among themselves, and never reveal another's homosexuality, especially to the military authorities. So even among lovers, the habit was never to name or attempt to describe their relationship. Cliques, nevertheless, found it useful to identify themselves with a secret code, slang, signal or nickname. Women in one lesbian clique wore a particular ring, while women in another whistled the tune of the Hawaiian War Chant. Male GIs gave each other nicknames based on *Gone with the Wind*, and another clique called themselves the Legion of the Damned.

At the beginning of the war, GIs discovered in the homosexual act were sent to prison, for there was no other way of getting rid of these undesirables except by convicting them of sodomy. Throughout the 1920s and '30s homosexuals in Army and Navy prisons had been a continuing problem. The authorities were anxious that the vice should not spread, so homosexuals were segregated. At Fort Leavenworth, Kansas, in an effort to punish the sodomists further, they had to wear a large yellow D on their backs to signify 'degenerate'; but as this seemed to have no effect, the practice was abandoned. Naval authorities then decided to make Portsmouth Naval Prison in New Hampshire a 'place of confinement for moral perverts regardless of length of sentence'. In the 1930s, more than 40 per cent of all new admissions to Portsmouth were men convicted of sodomy or fellatio.

As this procedure was putting great strain on the military prisons, an alliance of military officials and psychiatrists proposed that as homosexuality was a mental illness, people suspected of it should be dishonourably discharged without trial. The new policy began in the spring of 1941 and Lt Colonel Burt toured the States to discover how Army officers were handling their 'sodomist' problems during mobilisation.

Before their discharge, homosexual GIs had to face lengthy interrogations, physical abuse and systematic humiliation, for the authorities had to be certain that they were not malingering heterosexuals. A psychiatrist interviewed them to discover whether they were a habitual homosexual, a pathic, sexual pervert, a true sodomist, confirmed pervert or moral pervert – the new categories which had been set down. Then hospital staff observed their behaviour where they were confined in the sick bay, Red Cross workers compiled their life histories and contacted their families. Intelligence officers would interrogate them to obtain names of other personnel and sexual partners. A medical report which reflected all this was then sent to an administrative board, which decided whether the patient would be discharged, remain in hospital or return to duty. If they did not accept the dishonourable discharge, they could be court-martialled and sent to prison.

In 1944 Woodie Wilson and his buddy 'Kate' were court-martialled in South Carolina for publishing the gay servicemen's newsletter, the *Myrtle Beach Bitch*. They were sentenced to a year in prison. They found a whole wing of a huge prison filled with homosexuals. Wilson was a typist and messenger inside the prison and often visited other inmates. He was shocked by the age of some of the prisoners: 'There were old, old men with white hair.' They had a separate part of the dining-room to eat in and if they went to the cinema they had to sit always in a separate section.

By 1945 military officials had broken down the sodomist into yet more categories: latent, self-confessed, well-adjusted, habitual, undetected or known, true, confirmed and male or female. Not content with that, their categories continued into almost twenty other variations and it must have struck them that it was well-nigh impossible to classify the 'variants of deviant sexuality', in the way they were doing. Whether anyone reflected that they could have done the same with heterosexuality, that in fact there are as many variants as there are human beings, is doubtful. Such a lack of relative values shows the extreme rigidity of the military mind, even when labouring under the illusion that they were being liberal and humane.

Tragically, their work produced only an expansion of the military's homophobic structure, adding to its complexity and inevitably ended by creating new forms of surveillance and punishment. If a homosexual or lesbian was hauled up in front of the authorities because they were under suspicion, it was now no good claiming innocence of all carnal acts, for they had to prove that they were not homosexual in mind or nature. Nor did a suspected person have any right to cross-examine witnesses or have the benefit of counsel. Instead of being locked up behind prison bars, they now might be forcibly committed to a hospital psychiatric ward and eventually be discharged as a psychopathic undesirable. What is particularly offensive is the opinion of even the most sympathetic army psychiatric consultant, William Menninger. Homosexuals, he wrote: 'have immature personalities which make them and their lives and some of the personal relations grossly pathological. Like any sick person, they deserve understanding instead of condemnation.'

However, from the war there was a huge positive bonus. For many Americans the war years were an unforgettable experience; pulled away from families, from small sleepy towns and ethnic ghettoes in large cities, and suddenly deposited into a sex-segregated and non-familial context, each individual was thrown into a new world crammed full of information which had the valuable potential of radical change. For the first time in their lives, many homosexuals realised they were not alone, and they could begin to articulate a homosexual identity which was shared with others. For the first time in history since the ancient world, homo-sexuals had a network which they could use, a new life offering them a dramatic alternative to years of isolation. Homosocial groups grew up quickly which were never to fade away. Support groups rallied when injustice was done, even though there was at first little that could be done publicly. The battles of gays against the military had begun. They continue today.

THE TREATMENT CONTINUES

The war years appear to have been a boom time for physicians attempting experimental treatment upon homosexuals. In 1937 a Dr Owensby of Atlanta, Georgia, began treating homosexuals with convulsive shock therapy inducted with a chemical stimulant, Metrazol. He was concerned that the prevalence of homosexuality was increasing with 'an unparalleled rapidity'. He regarded it as an 'atavistic form of degeneracy'[24] and went on to detail six different cases where homosexuals had been given up to ten convulsive shocks and afterwards appeared to be healthy in every way, many of them marrying and beginning a 'normal' life. But no one else after him had any success in the use of this therapy. In 1949, Dr George S. Thompson reported that Metrazol-induced shock had no effect on sexual orientation.

However, much trust was placed in electric-shock treatment without the Metrazol which continued to be practised. A Dr Samuel Liebman treated a young black man in 1941 who showed marked effeminacy (he was termed overtly homosexual). In the hospital he made advances to many of the male patients. He was also considered to be a transvestite and psychotic. Over three months he had electric-shock therapy and Dr Liebman saw great advances. But a year later he was back in hospital for more treatment. 'Effeminate' blacks seem to have been a target for the medical profession. Another case, dating from 1941, deals with a short, stocky negro who, except for his large masculine genitals, was 'in every respect a woman'. Over thirty-five years of showing marked homosexuality he had been given hormone medication, a variety of oestrogenic, androgenic and gonadotropic preparations. They had no influence whatsoever upon his behaviour and personality. One is stunned at the immorality of the medical profession which uses a person as a guinea-pig for substances known to be carcinogenic.

Performing a lobotomy was considered a suitable form of treatment. One of the first patients to undergo the operation was a fifty-four-year-old white male in 1941 who liked to be spanked. When he was twelve his mother had discovered him in mutual sexual play with another boy and had immediately spanked him hard. Thereafter he seemed to have enjoyed being found out, so her spanks became part of the sexual experience. After the lobotomy the patient was highly confused and frightened, he was also incontinent. Though he left hospital and was found work as a secretary, he was too confused to keep his job. He insisted that all homosexual longings had left him, that the operation had been a success, but he could no longer look after himself, his memory was poor and he got lost easily. When taken back into hospital, various scraps of paper with notes written on them were found in his luggage. They detailed meetings in local parks with boys and sailors, but he still denied that any homosexual encounters had occurred since the operation. By 1945 the doctors had decided that though the patient had showed rapid improvement in the post-operative period which had stabilised him for a year, he had then showed progressive decline. He was then recognised as psychotic and later as demented and they concluded that the lobotomy had produced the dementia.

Lobotomies continued to be done. In 1959 a report was written on 100 lobotomised males selected at random from the patients at

Pilgrim State Hospital, New York. Patients often showed an increase in their sexual desire for men after the operation; they often became aggressive and posed problems for other patients whom they were trying to seduce. The report concluded that lobotomies, in the majority of cases, do not change the pattern of sexual behaviour which existed prior to the operation.

Aversion therapy was continued in Czechoslovakia by doctors J. Srnec and Kurt Freund. A Dr Louis Max had tried electric aversion therapy in 1935. Srnec and Freund used emetics (nausea-inducing drugs) and slides. The patient was first given coffee or tea with emetine, ten minutes later a subcutaneous injection of emetine, apomorphine, pilocarpine and ephidrine was given, and he was shown slides and film of men in the nude and told to visualise the men as sexual partners. About five minutes later the man would begin to feel ill and vomit. This would happen about six times. The patient was then shown films of women which would arouse the sexual appetite in 'normal' men. These films were shown in the evening before bedtime when the patient was given an injection of testosterone. Out of twenty-five patients, ten were 'cured' completely and three adapted so that their homosexual inclinations faded. Out of the ten, several lapsed after a few months. Nevertheless, the doctors hoped to continue with more effective methods than the ones described.

In 1953, in the *Journal of Social Hygiene*, Dr Bowman and Ms Engle advised therapeutic castration in an article called 'The Problem of Homosexuality'. They asked for a really serious investigation of the actual results of castration, for they believed it to be a valid subject for research.

WITCH-HUNTS

Enlisted men and women were not the only ones to gain a new sense of freedom in the war; it was true of homosexual civilians too. When I was a teenager, immediately after the war, speaking to older 'queer' men and women, I gained the impression that the war years had been a sexual golden era which they looked back on with a lingering sense of nostalgia. Cruising the streets at designated areas always brought an opportunity for picking up a serviceman and the blackout made it fairly easy to have sex in doorways, bomb-sites or shelters. Tom Driberg, the MP, was caught *in flagrante delicto* just inside an air-raid shelter by a policeman in Edinburgh. He was with a Norwegian sailor who had 'a long, uncircumcised, and tapering, but rock-hard erection'. When the policeman discovered he wrote the William Hickey column for the *Daily Express*, he was allowed to go free.[25]

Something of the thrill of the new freedom is caught in the following extract which tells of the added erotic stimulus of the uniform. Stephen, a civil servant, remarked: 'one's gay friends suddenly appeared in the most gorgeous uniforms and all joined rather exotic regiments. You've probably heard there was some anti-aircraft defence unit . . . in Kent which was wholly gay. I think it was some MP who organised it, one of the gay MPs'. Later Stephen reflects: 'I think the war led to a sort of breaking down of old inhibitions and customs and family ties. A lot of people had affairs with service people, though not necessarily within the services where it was much too dangerous. One now met people and arranged to see them on leave . . . the blackout helped undoubtedly.'

Stephen quotes Forster on working-class people, that they did not have the same sort of hang-ups as middle-class people. Stephen found this in the war, that working-class men in the services were very obliging, they didn't make a fuss about sex, they seemed to enjoy it and made a bit of money from it.

Another man, Roy, born in Brixton in 1908, enlisted in the Royal Army Medical Corps. He spoke of a lesbian friend who said: 'I hate to say this, Roy, but I must tell you it was such a lovely war. What went on was no one's business . . . it was a riot.' Roy picked up a Canadian in London and found a bed for them at the Union Jack Club: 'He was willing, he was TBH [to be had]. I know a lot of married men. I used to have married men.'

Donald Vining, who had lived in southern New Jersey when the war began, moved to New York and lived and worked in the YMCA. He found it to be a sexual paradise. At the end of the war he had a huge circle of homosexual friends and an encyclopaedic knowledge of homosexual meeting places.

Lisa Ben, raised on a ranch in northern California, sought work in Los Angeles and lived in a rooming house filled with unmarried women. She got talking and was immediately asked whether she liked girls or boys. On confessing that she liked girls she was introduced to other lesbians and to lesbian bars.[27]

The war for all these people on either side of the Atlantic was a revolutionary process within their lives, a process which, once begun, had no foreseeable end, for it could not be halted after 1945 when peace came. Homosexuals worldwide then gained encouragement and support after the publication of Kinsey's report *Sexual Behaviour in the Human Male*, in 1948. Orthodox sexual values were scandalised by the incidence figures for homosexual behaviour. Fifty per cent of males acknowledged erotic responses to their own sex, one-third had had a post-adolescent experience; 4 per cent were exclusively homosexual as adults; one out of eight males was predominantly homosexual for at least a three-year period. 'Persons with homosexual histories are to be found in every age group, in every social level, in every conceivable occupation, in cities, on farms, and in the most remote areas of the country.'

This was heresy, both in Britain and America. The enemy within the heart of society was felt to be a 'red poofter', one who could strike within society's most valued institutions, undermining their moral integrity. As if to emphasise such fears, in 1951 two British diplomats, Guy Burgess and Donald Maclean, were revealed as Soviet spies when they fled to Russia. What was more, Burgess was an unrepentant homosexual and Maclean was bisexual. Homosexuals became a dark threat to national security for, it was explained, they were so vulnerable to blackmail and thus became the target of widespread witch-hunts.

In Britain, Sir Theobald Mathew, who was appointed Director of Public Prosecutions in 1944, believed that homosexuality was spreading. He blamed National Service which created an un-precedented atmosphere in which 'homosexuality can be easily acquired and become ingrained'.[28] The men who came before the courts, Mathew thought, were not genuine homosexuals, they were men who had allowed themselves to be initiated and had per-sisted in the behaviour. They had to be taught that these habits were dirty, and society had to ensure that those in charge of young men were free of the taint.

There was a strong feeling within society that as the British Empire disintegrated, such loss of power was linked with potency. The decline and destruction of the Roman Empire, after all, was due to unnatural vice. As the whole of the sub-continent of India was lost, and territories in Africa and Malaysia also became in-dependent, it seemed to many that it was no coincidence that homosexuality was spreading like a contagion. US Senator McCarthy now placed pressure upon the British government to hunt out the perverts and bring them to justice.

In 1950 McCarthy had claimed that the Department of State was riddled with communists. A State Department official, John E. Peurifoy, in charge of security, then testified in Congress that ninety-one employees had resigned while under investigation since 1947, most being homosexuals. McCarthy had already declared in the Senate that a 'flagrantly homosexual' employee discharged in 1946 had been reinstated because of pressure from a high official. Later, he admitted he did not know the name of the official but it was on the files and could be found by a sub-committee. News-papers had a field-day. A Republican, Guy George Gabrielson, asserted that, 'sexual perverts who have influenced our Govern-ment in recent years' were perhaps 'as dangerous as the actual communists'.[29] Governor Dewey of New York State accused the Democratic national administration of tolerating spies, traitors and sex offenders. A sub-committee was ordered to investigate police reports that about 3,500 sex perverts held federal jobs. Senator Kenneth Wherry talked to Max Lerner, a columnist on the *New York Post*, about his crusade to harry every last pervert from the federal government. In the interview Wherry made no distinction between a homosexual and a communist. He said: 'a man of low morality is a menace to the government.' Later he was asked to define homosexual, and replied: 'he is a diseased man, an abnormal man.'

The FBI chief, J. Edgar Hoover, not to be outdone, agreed that his agency had identified 406 'sexual deviates in government service'. One supposes that he did not include himself and the friend with whom he lived and worked throughout his life. A lie detector was employed to test men and women involved in sensitive jobs related to national security. Then there was the theory of Congressman Miller, who claimed with authority that 'homosexual desires follow the cycle closely patterned to the menstrual period of women. There may be three or four days in each month that the homosexual's instincts break down and drive the individual into abnormal fields of sexual practice. Under large doses of sedatives during this sensitive cycle, he may escape such acts.'

At this time the Newport Naval Base was again in the news. An accused officer and twenty-four enlisted men were dishonourably discharged. In 1954, McCarthy complained that the Army had attempted to stop his exposure of communists in its ranks and had suggested that he turn his attention to subversion and homosexuality in the Navy, Air Force and the Defense Department. Roy Cohn, McCarthy's counsel, went on television to claim that the Army counsel, John G. Adams, had reported to his office specific information on Air Force bases where there were a large number of homosexuals and had even provided a map.

It was in this heated climate of harassment and hysteria that Henry Hay founded the Mattachine Society.[30] The society was conceived in 1948, a prospectus written the next year and a third version produced in 1950. The group was described as 'a service and welfare organisation devoted to the protection and improvement of Society's Androgynous Minority'. The main reason given for its birth was encroaching American fascism and the guilt of androgynity by association with communism. The name derived from *Société Mattachine*, a secret medieval French society of unmarried townsmen who conducted dances during the Feast of

Fools, often rituals which were peasant protests against oppression, but never performed in public unmasked. Hay took the name because he felt homosexuals in America in the 1950s were also masked people, unknown and anonymous, who, once organised, could be engaged in social and legal reform to redress injustices.

Hay was married with children, his mother was on the Mattachine council and their address was her home. In the spring of 1952, one of the original Mattachine members, Dale Jennings, was arrested by the Los Angeles vice squad on the charge of soliciting an officer. He denied the charge but publicly admitted his homosexuality. The Mattachine Society organised his defence and he was acquitted. In 1953, they organised a convention attended by 500 people. Hay felt that this was the first time in the history of the United States that 500 men, all vilified and hounded by the rest of society, had shown up in a public place to declare their willingness to fight for their human rights.

All along the Mattachine Society had insisted that it was non-political in its objectives, wishing only to stir up the debate on the place of homosexuals in American society. But the continuing purges within government agencies of hundreds of homosexuals had thrust Hay into the political arena. In a speech to the convention he pointed out: 'not one single political or pressure group among the liberals, let alone the left wing, lifted either voice or finger to protest the monstrous social and civil injustice.' In the same speech he defended the refusal of the Mattachine lawyer to testify before the House Un-American Activities Committee (HUAAC), based on the Fifth Amendment. But the Society was split between the founders and the conservatives who were keen always to appear respectable and who wanted to limit the activities of the society to pressure for legal change.

In 1954 a scandal-mongering periodical named *Confidential* carried an article warning America against the Mattachine Society, saying that the organisation was recruiting across the country and had funds of $600,000. It added that Henry Hay had already been mentioned in testimonies before the HUAAC and had been quoted as a prominent Marxist teacher. Hay was then subpoenaed to appear before the HUAAC. He saw five lawyers before he found one who would brief him – a Portuguese who represented Chicanos, Mexicans and Puerto Ricans in Los Angeles. They rehearsed possible questions and answers. The strategy worked. Hay had recently resigned from the Communist Party (after eighteen years), and when he denied membership the attorney for the committee lost his temper, pushed over his desk and forgot to use the phrase 'or have you ever been a member of . . .?' Further, Hay learnt that they were entirely ignorant about his creation of the Mattachine Society. The committee's information was more than five years old. Hay was prepared to take a Fifth Amendment position but there was no need for him to do so.

What is so deeply shocking that it veers almost upon the unbelievable, is that the architects of this oppression, McCarthy, Cohn and Hoover were all homosexual themselves, contriving to hide their natures from the general public until after they were dead. Here again, society colluded with them, for among their inner circle it was public knowledge. As ever, the great and the powerful were indulged while the nameless suffered.

On occasion, the rich and powerful are made to suffer as an example to others. This was true of Britain's witch-hunt in 1954 when Lord Montagu of Beaulieu was tried. The year before he had been accused with another man of committing an unnatural offence and an indecent assault on two boy scouts. But the judge found that the police had tampered with an important piece of evidence, so it was decided that Montagu should be re-tried at the next sessions. Soon after, Peter Wildeblood (diplomatic correspondent to the *Daily Mail*) and Michael Pitt-Rivers were arrested on several charges of indecency with two RAF men two years before. All three men were also accused of conspiring to commit these offences.

The principal witnesses for the prosecution were the two airmen, Edward McNally and John Reynolds (they were promised immunity from prosecution), who had happily allowed themselves to commit these 'unnatural acts' in return for lavish hospitality. The prosecution exhibited horror and distaste for the class difference between the two airmen and the accused. Sir Theo-bald Mathew (see p. 355) was determined to ruin Montagu, for he believed that men in authority had a special moral responsibility in their care for the lower orders. Pitt-Rivers and Wildeblood were both given eighteen-month sentences and Montagu twelve months. McNally and Reynolds incriminated other men who were never pursued by the police.

Like the Wilde trials, these too sent tremors of terror and panic through British homosexuals. Michael Davidson, then foreign correspondent for the *Observer*, destroyed two suitcases of letters, diaries and photographs of friends. He was far from alone. Late-night burning of incriminating material occurred far and wide; many personal mementoes kept for years as sentimental tokens of a barely recalled romance went up in flames. The richer homo-sexuals decided to spend more time abroad. Robin Maugham sailed his yacht around the Mediterranean, others moved to more sympathetic cities such as Tangiers and Rome. Less affluent 'queers' just tried to keep a low profile, but fear was in the air they breathed and stories of police harassment were swopped among them daily. Police *agents provocateurs* were in common use. 'Cot-taging' (picking up men for sex in urinals) was a dangerous business, the blond beauty beside you who smiled sweetly when you glanced at him could easily be a plain-clothes policeman. Junior policemen rose in the ranks on the number of convictions they secured, so homosexuals were easy prey for an ambitious policeman. Convictions for male soliciting rose to an average of about forty a month in the West End of London in the early 1950s. There were also increasing numbers of prosecutions promising im-munity if the man testified against others, the legal precedent established in the Castlehaven case in the early seventeenth century. Between 1945 and 1955, the number of annual prosecu-tions for homosexual behaviour rose from under 800 to just over 2,500 of whom over 1,000 were given custodial sentences.[31]

In this country-wide trawl of intrigue and persecution, old cases were dredged up again, married men committed suicide, some had their reputations ruined and their businesses failed, others endured years of being blackmailed and reduced to misery and penury because of it. After a scandal, men had to move away from their families, never allowed to show their faces at home again. Stoking the fires of the witch-hunts were the cheaper Sunday papers like the *News of the World*, *The People* and the *Sunday Pictorial* which gave lurid accounts stressing the depravity and degradation of such people and the imminent decline of a nation which was so riddled with such contagion.

There was another hazard which homosexuals faced. The strenuous effort needed to conceal the very fact of their homosexuality over a period of years or even a lifetime often led to the death of the heart, a phenomenon which Lady Ayer detected in Somerset Maugham.[32] There were many who suffered that fate, isolated and alone. Afraid to take a second glance at an attractive man in public, they became reclusive, content to stay within their private world, always alert and suffering tremors of fear when there was an unexpected ring at the door. For homosexuals of this era, Britain had become a police state.

XIII

REFORM, LIBERATION AND INEQUALITY

The intensity of the witch-hunts and their obvious injustice had the effect of provoking the opposition into some kind of action. In the House of Commons there were calls by members of the Labour Party, including Desmond Donnelly, to correct the gross injustices. The only Conservative to protest was Sir Robert Boothby who had been bisexual all his life. The *Sunday Times* also published a leader (on 28 March 1954) backing a review of the existing laws.

MOVES TOWARDS REFORM

In August 1954 the government appointed a Home Office departmental committee under the chairmanship of John Wolfenden, who was vice-chancellor of Reading University. The committee's brief was to study and then report on the state of the law relating to homosexuality and prostitution. The appointment of the committee did not modify continuing police persecution. In March 1956, after being interviewed by police at Evesham, a forty-year-old barman gassed himself, and a forty-six-year-old carpenter, married with three children, threw himself under a train.[1] The authorities seemed to be utterly oblivious to the private hell into which they plunged individuals. If they did notice, they expressed satisfaction that society had been cleansed of another deviant.

The committee was made up of parliamentarians, clergy, lawyers and doctors. The first person they interviewed was Lord Chief Justice Goddard who had once confessed that he felt physically sick when trying 'buggers'. It was not surprising, then, that he thought buggery should be punished far more severely than it was, that penalties for male soliciting should be drastically increased, and that male prostitutes should be whipped.

Other witnesses from the legal profession and the police all believed that if the young were seduced they would inevitably become part of the homosexual world, which was an exclusive and insidious freemasonry. This idea, held with the zealousness of a fundamental faith, was broadcast in the media by many parliamentarians and clergy, and it greatly alarmed parents. (It still does.) The medical witnesses who gave evidence to the committee dismissed the idea that seduction was powerful enough to change a youth's sexual orientation.

The Law Society opposed any change. They thought that both buggery and gross indecency, when committed in private, should remain criminal offences. The British Medical Association's evidence was given by a committee which suggested that a cure for homosexuality could be sought through Christianity mixed with forestry, farmwork and market gardening.[2] The BMA further thought that homosexuals would be always loyal to each other rather than to their government or country, hence they would always pose a problem in the civil service, the armed forces, Parliament and the church. A report by Anglican doctors and clergy thought that a sodomite should face his sin without self-excuse and that all homosexuality was a rebellion against God.

It is astonishing, then, that when the Wolfenden Report[3] was published in 1957, its main recommendation was that 'homosexual behaviour between consenting adults in private be no longer a criminal offence'. The report received shock–horror headlines in the tabloid press. The *Daily Telegraph* thought that, once legalised, homosexuality would spread like an infection, while *The Times*, the Manchester *Guardian*, *Observer* and *News Chronicle* welcomed it with some reservations.

Within this climate the Homosexual Law Reform Society was formed in spring 1958. It began with a letter to *The Times* in support of the Wolfenden Report from a list of distinguished figures.★ They immediately began to put pressure on MPs to urge Lord Kilmuir to adopt some of the Wolfenden recommendations. A pamphlet, 'Homosexuals and the Law' (drafted by Peter Wildeblood), was circulated with a draft Bill. But the debate in the House of Commons brought no immediate hope that the law might be changed. The consensus seemed to be that though reform might be desirable, it was premature to accept it now.

Six years later the government made it clear that they would not implement reform until a shift in public opinion had occurred, but when shown such a shift by the Reform Society they regarded it as unreliable information as it constituted special pleading. Reform had to wait for a change of government. In 1966 the Labour Party won the general election and Leo Abse introduced a Bill to amend the law of England and Wales relating to homosexual acts. It became law the following year.

The change of law did not apply to the merchant navy or the armed forces. The 1967 Act strengthened the law against offences with minors and soliciting. The term 'in public', which was where all homosexual acts were against the law, meant not only in a public place but also in private if more than two people were present. Both hotels and prisons were considered to be public places, though a homosexual act might well be committed in a locked room with no one else present. Certainly most homosexuals would have considered a hotel room to be a private place.

If this was a victory, it was conceded grudgingly and it was severely limited. It soon became clear that the change in the law

---

★ Noel Annan, A. J. Ayer, Isaiah Berlin, David Cecil, J. B. Priestley, Trevor Huddleston, Stephen Spender and Angus Wilson were but a few.

was unpopular with the police; arrests for indecency and importuning offences increased. Clubs where men danced together were raided and fined for gross indecency. Plain-clothes policemen were still used as decoys in public lavatories, public parks and open spaces.

There was a need for a more militant reforming group to come into being. At the end of the 1960s, revolution was in the air. The student revolts in May 1968 in Paris, the rise in student militancy across the world, mass open-air concerts and the smoking of marijuana, anger in the USA over the Vietnam War, the 'Prague Spring' in Czechoslovakia, the rise of the hippie movement with its maxim 'make love, not war', all these elements inspired a new generation to believe that the old order was crumbling away and a new dawn had begun.

THE GAY LIBERATION FRONT

Dawn, when it arrived, seemed more like a volcanic eruption. At the time, straight America viewed the Stonewall riots as no more than drag queen hysteria. But the riots abruptly changed the mood of many of the gay populace from low-key compliance to militant fury. Secrecy was abandoned and closet doors were smashed.

The Stonewall Inn, a gay bar on Christopher Street, Greenwich Village, had been raided by the police on an alleged infringement of its liquor licence. The customers, joined by gays from the bars, backrooms and bedrooms of the street, fought back for two days and nights. The riot was an explosion of anger and frustration from a small group of young homosexuals. The poet Allen Ginsberg said: 'the guys there were so beautiful, they've lost that wounded look that fags all had ten years ago.'[4]

By a strange irony, the Friday the riots began saw the funeral of Judy Garland, the adored icon of gays around the world. Not only was she dead, but what she stood for had died too. Two years later, Tom Burke commented in *Esquire* that the new 'clone' gay of the 1970s thought 'Over the Rainbow' was merely a place to fly to on LSD. A few weeks after Stonewall, a new movement began to demand respect and equal rights from straight society, including the right to go anywhere 'where straights go and do anything with each other they do'.[5] The new spokesmen were young and left-wing, impatient with the old diplomatic methods that had insisted on always making a favourable impression upon the straight elite. Now you had to be proud to be what you were and a new phrase was born: 'Coming Out'. The word 'homosexual' was to be ditched and 'gay' was to be proudly acknowledged.

A year later, at the National Gay Liberation Front student conference in San Francisco, Charles P. Thorp told the conference that 'the word "homosexual" is the sick-psychiatrist's definition of us, it is the straight concept of us as sexual. While "gay" is a lifestyle. It is how we live. It is our oppression. It is our Tiffany lamps and our guns. Gay is our history and the history we are just beginning to become."[6]

On 28 June 1970, to mark the first anniversary of Stonewall, between 5,000 and 20,000 people marched from Greenwich Village to Central Park. The *Village Voice* reported: 'They stretched in a line, from Gimbels to Times Square, thousands and thousands and thousands, chanting, waving, screaming – the outrageous and the outraged, splendid in their flaming colors.'* On the same day 1,200 people marched down Hollywood Boulevard in Los Angeles. The Los Angeles *Advocate* remarked: 'Probably the world had never seen anything like it since the gay days of Ancient Greece.' The gay pride march had begun and over the years it would spread around the world.

At last, what Carpenter and Symonds had worked and hoped for, a time when homosexuals would organise themselves and campaign for justice, had arrived. The transition from 'homosexual-equals-secrecy' to 'gay-equals-publicity' was as radical a change as that which we saw occur around 1700.

---

* Twenty thousand people stood in line to view Garland's body at an uptown funeral parlour.

The British were inspired by Stonewall and the formation of militant groups in the USA. GLF (Gay Liberation Front) described itself as a revolutionary organisation, its members were aged roughly between twenty-five and thirty-five, and they included a high proportion of artists, drop-outs and social security claimants as well as students, teachers and sociologists. What united them was the unique inebriation that resulted from being open about their gayness.[7] Kissing, embracing and holding hands on the street marches were accompanied by demands that discrimination and oppression must end. This 'coming out' was the first step towards anyone involving themselves in GLF, a necessary process with family, friends and colleagues. But it was essential first for gays to come out to themselves (friends and lovers who had already done so were an invaluable help), to be able to face their nature and to find no fault in it, not to see themselves through society's eyes. Once they had found pride in themselves, then it was possible to speak to family and colleagues without feeling the shame and humiliation into which young gays had so often been forced.

GLF had a deeply personal role to play in their members' lives, for the coming-out phase was essential to the group's strength. It also challenged all the old homosexual stereotypes, the values of the ghetto, gay bars and pubs, the cruising areas called the 'meat market', the touring of cottages, the piss-elegant fairy and the limp-wristed queen. The 'camp' aesthetic of appearance and the manner of speech had always lent itself to subversive attack; men had deliberately turned themselves into female caricatures so as to deflect aggression and invite laughter. GLF would present society with a different and more aggressive range of semiotics.

GLF demonstrated publicly outside pubs that had turned away men and women whom they considered gay. They began their own gay discos where homosexual men and women could meet and spend an evening together in a relaxed atmosphere without the tension and grubbiness of the traditional cruising area. The Women's Liberation Movement joined forces with GLF in all of these activities.

Gradually a new awareness of what society had done to homosexuals began to permeate the movement. The GLF *Manifesto*, written by a mixed collection of men and women in early 1971, tried to pin it down. Oppression, they believed, starts in the gender role playing within the model family, consisting of the dominant male, the wife as a slave and their children who are asked to model themselves upon them. Homosexuality is excluded and appears as inferior or a sickening perversion. Gay people themselves tended to fall into the same role models where one partner would ape the husband and the other the wife. Up to the 1960s gay men had no other choice but to follow the heterosexual social structure, their only way of opting out was to forgo a partnership and to become a secret pursuer of brief sexual connections with strangers. All gay men were acutely conscious that society viewed them as failed men, that they were isolated, and liable at any time to be treated by psychiatry as sick or deviant, or to be punished by public trial and prison sentences. They also were often ostracised and taunted by colleagues and not infrequently physically attacked by gangs of drunken hoodlums. Gay men formulated techniques to defend themselves, the first being secrecy – various complex signals and language came into being. The second, in direct contrast, was the cultivation of an extrovert camp manner or the parading of drag queens, to invite laughter and obtain a social niche in straight society. Last, some felt a tacit agreement with society's view of themselves, which led directly to self-hatred, shame and guilt.

This portrait is true of gays in both Britain and the USA. Homosexual oppression was then defined as cultural indoctrination, related historically to the oppression of women. This should have drawn the two groups closer together, but women felt that GLF meetings were overwhelmingly male-orientated, and that sexist attitudes were as prevalent inside the gay movement as outside. In 1972 the women in GLF broke away and set up their own organisation. Beneath the split was the idea that what was crucially wrong with society was the 'inherent maleness' of men, and that male homosexuals were merely another aspect of this. Logically they should now relinquish all power to the women and give up their male privileges. Gay liberation would be the first step to the cultural de-manning of man. A few men put this tenet into practice and would march wearing thick make-up over stubble and a medley of women's clothes. It is doubtful if any observers of this travesty ever got the political point that was being made; most merely saw a freak show, which is exactly the image the whole movement had been struggling away from. Much the same battle was being waged in the USA where feminist pioneers moved away from mixed gay liberation to form feminist lesbian groups.

Under these pressures it was inevitable that GLF would fragment. Though the spirit of gay liberation was to continue, it was no longer under the aegis of GLF. The organisation had appalled many thousands of homosexuals who felt, rather as Leo Abse had wanted them to feel when he introduced his Bill in 1966, that they were no longer illegal and could now quietly continue with their lives. All this marching in drag and make-up and shrieking slogans seemed to them to be in very bad taste. Many thousands more, who saw beneath the veneer, were perhaps if anything more alarmed, for they disliked GLF's extreme Marxist analysis and militancy. The secretary of the Committee (later Campaign) for Homosexual Equality (CHE) claimed that if people wanted something more 'reasonable' they should write to CHE. Small gay organisations began to spring up across the country, campaigning against books, TV programmes and films which showed homophobic attitudes. They arranged social nights for members and some even attempted a counselling service.

The newspaper *Gay News* was founded in 1972. Essentially populist, it reviewed books, films and TV, contained articles on relevant people and subjects and its front page highlighted a current news topic. It was quick to report incidents of homophobia and injustice. It was good gay entertainment and none of the big newsagents, such as W.H. Smith, would stock it. Distribution at first was a problem and it was not helped by the attitude of the police who kept an eye on the paper's contents. One of its undoubted successes was its contact advertisements – 'Love knoweth no Laws' – which allowed isolated gays across Britain to join their local gay groups and so make vital contact with others. Within four years it had a circulation of 20,000.

In America gay liberation actively campaigned and sometimes succeeded in forcing localities to repeal sodomy laws or to cease police harassment. They also pressurised medical faculties to remove homosexuality from the official list of psychological disorders. They encouraged the acceptance of gay men in the family, the media and the workplace. The reduction of social and legal sanctions against gay existence allowed gay recreational services and a variety of professionals – doctors, lawyers, dentists – slowly to move from their self-imposed secrecy.

The gay movement, perhaps inevitably, also had its martyrs. Early in the 1970s Harvey Milk settled in the Castro neighbourhood of San Francisco and decided to run for the board of supervisors as an openly gay candidate. It took him a few years of hard canvassing and of changing the gay image held by straight voters (one commented that he had always thought 'gays are little leprechauns tip-toeing to florist shops')[8] who became impressed by Milk's charisma. By this time the 'new' homosexual, the Castro Street clone with gym membership, had colonised parts of San Francisco and swelled the gay vote. When Milk ran for city supervisor a third time in 1977 he was elected, as was Dan White, a police officer and fireman.

Milk introduced a Bill banning discrimination against homosexuals in housing and employment; White was the only supervisor to oppose it. In the autumn of 1978 White abruptly resigned, then ten days later he asked the Mayor to reinstate him. When the Mayor refused, White shot him dead. He then went to Milk's office and shot him four times, twice in the head.

The trial was a farce. White received a sentence of seven years, eight months on two counts of voluntary manslaughter. He was released in early 1985 and returned to San Francisco, but before the end of the year he had committed suicide.

In 1977 forty US cities agreed to repeal their sodomy statutes. Anita Bryant, pop singer, born-again Christian and publicist for Florida orange juice, pledged herself to lead a campaign to repeal the ordinance in Dade County. She rallied support from a wide range of people who quickly repealed the gay rights law by a landslide in June 1977.

Such serious setbacks rang alarm bells in the gay rights movement. The heady euphoria of post-Stonewall had faded and they could now see the fierce struggle that lay ahead.

SEX AS BIG BUSINESS

Throughout the 1960s, sex had been becoming increasingly visible; what you could see on film and read between the covers of a book was far more explicit than it had ever been before. The authorities had attempted to stifle this process, bringing works like D. H. Lawrence's *Lady Chatterley's Lover* and Hubert Selby Jr's *Last Exit to Brooklyn* to trial (the latter was homosexually explicit), but their success was minor and they only served to make themselves appear foolish. Besides, the end result for the books they wished to ban was a vast amount of publicity and huge sales. In 1968 the Lord Chamberlain's office was abolished, allowing playwrights uncensored freedom upon the stage. Kenneth Tynan staged his erotic revue *Oh! Calcutta* in 1970. It offered a series of sketches, often with complete nudity, on masturbation, flagellation, simulated intercourse, sado-masochism and transvestism. Over the years it grossed $360 million.[9]

Though witnesses at the *Last Exit* trial said that the book was nauseating and Sir Basil Blackwell, the Oxford bookseller aged eighty-seven, claimed that it had corrupted him, through a loophole in the law the book continued to be on sale. Public taste was for greater access to sexual exposure, and pornographic films were beginning to be shown across Britain and America at the same time as homosexual soft porn was considered to be obscene and counted as a criminal offence. The cult favourite, *Deep Throat*, for example, is the story of a girl who has the ability in fellating to take a complete penis in her mouth; if she had been a man, the film would have been banned in hysterical outrage.

Sex began to be seen by society as pleasure and entertainment, not just something that happened in the privacy of a darkened bedroom. Sex manuals were written in an easy style and often became bestsellers. In the 1970s and 80s the over-riding social ethic was self-fulfilment, the gratification of inner needs and desires, the encouragement of consumerism and erotic exploration. Sex was no longer linked to procreation – very few people were virgins when they got married – ideas like wife-swapping had their vogue, the divorce rate was climbing, and people began to have partnerships instead of going through a ceremony that seemed an anachronism. Indeed, that was not the only alternative to marriage, for the homosexual debate had allowed men and women to discuss, albeit with great caution, the possibility that homosexuality and bisexuality were options for themselves. The new popular literature about sex allowed people to acquire a greater repertoire of sexual techniques. All these changes should have made heterosexual society closer to the homosexual world, but though the link between procreation and the sexual act was weakened for heterosexuals, it was still there. I believe that because the act is procreative, it carries with it a distinctive difference, which allows heterosexuals to feel a superiority, which in turn induces them to treat gays as inferior, even though much heterosexual activity involves contraceptive devices.

There is, then, in these twenty-five years from the law reform of 1967, a tension within straight society which was forced to show greater compassion and understanding for gays only because they demanded it; it also allowed a hardening and strengthening of homophobia. (Why this should be so is explored in the next chapter.) But in those twenty-five years the pace of change was hectic. Ever since the onset of GLF, Britain had followed the lead that was given in the US.

CLONES

As we have seen, the gay liberation movement radically altered how gay men saw themselves. One of the greatest changes which liberation wrought was to encourage the belief that same-sex love was natural and healthy. The new definition of gay love destroyed all concept of gender deviance and thus removed the need for the artifice of camp or cross-dressing, provoking a new pride and a sense of integrity in the wholeness of the gay man.

Now that recreational facilities were open for gays, social networks formed in public – in bars, restaurants, bookshops and baths – surrogate families were created by circles of men, and every crowd in a gay place was composed of several circles and cruising strangers. Furthermore, these meeting places formed a circuit; men dined in a certain restaurant, worked out in one particular gym, used the same three or four bars and had sex in a particular bath-house. The gays in the circuit fashioned themselves on the male icon of a Marlboro cowboy/body-builder; they strove for a hard, muscular 'butch' image and wore flannel check shirts, button-up Levis, work boots, short haircuts and moustaches. The jeans stressed the buttocks and genitalia – they wore no underclothes to increase the exposure – and their pockets displayed keys and a handkerchief which signalled a preference for sexual acts and positions.[10]

Bars set aside places for cruising and 'tricking', meaning sexual contact. Using Western imagery – wagon wheels, corral posts and leather upholstery – their staff dressed up in cowboy hats and boots. Some bars showed pornographic films in back rooms and gave themselves erotic names – the Cockring or the International Stud. The erotic ideal for clones was men of the same type, butch, muscular, good-looking and 'well hung'; these would be signals and eye-contact, and 'tricking' was often quickly arranged.

Sex was rough, uninhibited and phallocentric. Tricking involved 'deep-throating', 'hard fucking' and 'heavy tit work'. Drugs were usually used to alleviate the pain of these sexual experiences: pot, poppers and Quaaludes were the most popular.★ Deep-throating involved the penis being rammed down the other's throat in such a way that there was a chance of choking. Fucking meant slapping the buttocks while ramming the whole penis into

---

★ That is, marijuana, amyl nitrites and barbiturates.

the other's anus, and the tit work involved heavy biting, sucking and pinching of the nipples.

This strenuous giving and receiving of sado-masochistic sex was surely only another form of self-punishment. It was the gay aping the worst excesses of the chauvinistic sexist male, treating his sexual partner with insensitivity and cruelty. What is more, the receiver fully colluded with the act. Both the gays in the partnership were as fully locked in to the heterosexual structure as they had been when they played at domesticity and keeping house together. Further, the butch imagery and the semblance of masculine normality was as artificial a pose as the frock that had been worn before. But trying to create a social niche in a society which still negates you forces caricatures of that society upon you.

AIDS

These sexual encounters were hardly ever repeated, but by the early 1980s the clone culture was in decline. Income had fallen and a yearning for stable relationships made promiscuous sex, consumerism and drug-use seem unwise. Yet the event which provoked the greatest change was the insidious appearance of AIDS. It was this that made many men embrace ideas of constraint and commitment; they gave up alcohol, cigarettes and drugs, they went into rigid regimens of exercise, altered their diet and worked out in the gym.

For many men it was too late. Their previous erotic patterns meant that many were infected with HIV. Some of the earliest fatalities in New York were among the clones: more than half of three intensely studied cliques or circles died.[11] One survivor, a corporate executive in his forties, said in 1991: 'Almost all the guys from my group have died. The lovers Tom and Jim went first in '82. Then Bob, Chad, and Ted in '83 and '84. Frank died a year later. Only Steve and I are left, but Steve has KS [Karposi's Sarcoma] and my lymph glands are swollen.' The disintegration of the cliques destroyed the crowds which had frequented the bars and they slowly closed down or changed their clientele. Health officials closed bath-houses and sex clubs as being public health risks.

The relation between drug-use, lack of sleep and promiscuous sex with damage to the immune system which AIDS highlighted made cruising, all-night partying and tricking seem unhealthy and dangerous, while the fear of AIDS removed the need for erotic butch imagery leading to rough sex. Clones still wore obvious masculine gear, but the clothes no longer had to enhance the musculature of the body. Health maintenance, hoping to boost the immune system, and community service, caring for men sick with AIDS, became the chief spare-time occupations among clones.

The government's slow and inadequate response to AIDS (both in the US and Britain) repoliticised gay men. They came to realise that they had been ignored because they were still oppressed. What was more, within straight society there was a powerful feeling that AIDS was divine retribution; a part of straight society even exulted in the fact that thousands of gay men were dying a laboriously slow and tortuous death. Gay men began to ask themselves, had anything really changed? Was society still as deeply homophobic as it had been for the last three hundred years?

AIDS hit Los Angeles as early as it did New York; the first five cases of pneumocystis were diagnosed in 1981. By 1990 the county had recorded the second highest cumulative incidence of AIDS in the US after New York. Over 95 per cent of the cases were among gay and bisexual men.[12] The first AIDS response agency had been formed in late 1982. The county government refused to acknowledge the threat posed by the disease as they were basically unsympathetic to the problems of minorities like gays and intravenous drug-users. This laxity from government forced gays to organise themselves. In New York Larry Kramer became renowned for his fight to incite gays into action and to wake the government from their self-induced torpor.

Painfully the gay community had to confront the terrible crisis. They had to learn that sex could no longer be spontaneous and carefree; it had to be cautious and planned. By the end of the 1980s it was clear that sexually-transmitted diseases and hepatitis B had begun to decline among gays and bisexual men. Safer-sex practices emerged such as 'phone-sex' – one Gay Pride issue of a gay newspaper in the 1980s contained seventeen pages of phone-sex ads out of ninety-four pages of text.

The HIV epidemic forced the gay community to confront the anguish of losing friends and lovers long before their time; they had to cope with the long and painful process of dying and with death itself. A 1989 random-digital-dial telephone survey of 300 gay and bisexual men in gay neighbourhoods of Los Angeles found that these men knew an average of eighteen persons diagnosed with HIV, and one in twelve knew fifty or more. A woman said: 'We have more friends dying than our parents. We can tell our parents where to get the best deals on funerals.' The epidemic also had a positive side: it brought out a sense of solidarity, it inspired heroism and selflessness, it emphasised the need to survive and triumph over an indifferent heterosexual authority.

In Britain there were about twenty known cases by mid-1983. These fuelled a moral panic which was to colour the next few years. The tabloid press printed headlines on the theme of the 'gay plague', hospital staff became hysterical, ambulance drivers disinfected their vehicles, policemen refused to give the kiss of life to known gays who were badly hurt in accidents and wore gloves and protective clothing when they raided gay bars, children with the virus were banned from school and theatre personnel refused to work with gay actors. In 1986 the Chief Constable of Manchester, James Anderton, saw the spread of AIDS as a result of 'degenerate conduct', and went on: 'People at risk are swirling around in a human cesspit of their own making.' Draconian measures were suggested by various pressure groups. They called for testing of all known groups at risk, and for the complete segregation of the sick and dying. They also wanted to test people coming into the country. To combat this, the first gay self-help groups came into being. The Terrence Higgins Trust, founded in late 1982 in memory of the first Briton to die from AIDS, organised the first national conference on the subject in 1984. A year later they obtained some public funding.[13]

By the end of the 1980s there were over 100,000 cases of AIDS in the US, half of whom had died. By this time it was no longer just a gay disease; increasingly it was affecting the very poor and black populations. It was estimated that one million people had been in contact with the virus in East Africa.[14] Society is still struggling to adjust to the fact that, unless a cure is found, AIDS is a pandemic whose repercussions will last well into the next century. Unfortunately, the fact that everyone is potentially at risk has not tempered the homophobic reaction. Gays are still being blamed for bringing devastation upon the rest of society. But then they have been the scapegoat for great disasters ever since Justinian made the connection just under two thousand years ago.

One famous victim of AIDS was Leonard Matlovich who had been relieved of his duties in the US Air Force after coming out publicly as a homosexual in 1975. Up to then Matlovich's career had been considered exemplary: he had volunteered for three tours of duty in Vietnam because 'that's where my nation needs me'.[15] He voted for Goldwater and had erected an 18-foot flagpole in his front yard. He had been brought up in a conservative Catholic family where sex was not discussed, but at the age of thirty he lost his virginity to a man. The experience wrought a huge change in him. He became ashamed at the stand that he had taken against the integration of blacks, and was aware of the irony that at the base the blacks were the ones supporting his case against unfair dismissal. At his trial Sergeant Matlovich was asked whether he would sign a contract never to practise homosexuality again. He blanched in disbelief then declined. A huge amount of evidence was given at the trial by experts, two of whom suggested that homosexuality was congenital and due to a hormonal difference in pregnancy. What bearing this had on a serviceman who genuinely wanted to stay serving his country is difficult to see. When Matlovich finally lost the trial he held up a Bicentennial 50-cent piece with the inscription '200 years of freedom'. He said, 'Not yet, maybe some day, but not yet.'

Matlovich died of AIDS in 1991. The headstone he chose for his grave reads: 'A Gay Vietnam Veteran. When I was in the military, they gave me a medal for killing two men, and a discharge for loving one.'

IN THE PROVINCES

Gay resources tend to be located in large cities, but in the 1980s, certainly in the US, there was a move away from large centres of population. Over half of all Americans live in the suburbs. Cities are increasingly seen as beset with problems of social dis-organisation, crime, poverty and racial tension. Furthermore, the recession had bitten deep into funds which might allow a more adventurous life-style for young gays, severely limiting travel into city centres.

How do the young in the provinces find their sexual identity when there are no social organisations to help them? Various studies in America have looked at the lifestyles of suburban homo-sexuals,[16] and have concluded that they are more circumspect about coming out, worrying about exposure and anticipating more intolerance. They try to pass as heterosexuals for as long as possible and so join in a great deal more social involvement with straight society. Among young students 'gay' means 'stupid and silly' while 'faggot' is the most humiliating insult a male teenager can give another. These attitudes, it was observed, were also com-mon among parents of students and male teaching colleagues.[17]

Their initial awareness of sexual identity was in reinterpreting childhood experiences (same-sex physical contacts) in the light of later desires, though these were inevitably suppressed. This might happen at any age from twelve to thirty. The next step was being taken on a visit to a gay bar; it was noticed that women friends were often perceptive in noticing a young male colleague looking lost and divining what his problem was. Some males confessed that until they entered a gay bar they had no idea what their prob-lem was. One man was taken to the bar by his wife, another by a lesbian colleague.

The next stage was some form of commitment. Ninety-one per

cent of the subjects interviewed valued their own sexual orientation over any 'conversion' to heterosexuality, though a few agreed that being straight would make life easier. Very few of them had come out with their families and work colleagues. Most of them thought that their parents suspected, but such things were not mentioned.

Most of the men were weekend excitement seekers, going to the gay bar to find sex and, perhaps, 'Mr Right', for they also wanted to settle down with the one perfect partner and build a home together. A strong middle-class background, which most of them had, was influential in their identification with middle-class values, relegating sexual experience to a lower priority than creating a home together. A wide range of sexual activity was reported, from three or four contacts within a year, to three or four contacts per month.[18]

Taking a long-term lover was the final stage of commitment. At first there was an emphasis on surrounding themselves with gay friends, partly due to pride in their own new domesticity. But then the threat of the gay circuit would create problems and the lovers would return to a mixed milieu. Problems also arose with family and colleagues and lovers could often be alienated by the attitude of one set of parents.

The middle-class suburban context reinforced devotion to work, home maintenance and ownership and a continuing relationship with the heterosexual world. Most men were content to pursue routine and daily social activities, ignoring the possibility of creating a viable gay social network. A gay partnership has no legal or religious supports and no cultural guidelines. There are rarely any children to impose a structure on daily life and plans for the future. Without children, people have fewer ties with the community, for there are no relationships with schools, parent associations or the parents of the children's friends.

Lack of marriage and conventional families induce gay couples to place great emphasis on gay friendships; these in a sense form a vicarious family. Edmund White speaks of the durability and

breadth of homosexual friendships, that a common sexual orientation can bind people from different and highly diverse
backgrounds, crossing the boundaries of race, class and creed.[19]

The advent of AIDS was slow to percolate into suburbia. It was
not until the mid-1980s that its significance struck home. As it continued its devastating course, AIDS changed people's lives,
increasing their caution, and emphasising the close-knit circles that
they had already created. Gay bars lost their attraction, and many
gays became increasingly isolated. According to the barmen, the
first men to disappear from the circuit were the married ones.
AIDS made bisexuals question where their sexual orientation
really lay, and provided a powerful motive for examining the
strength of their commitment to their sexual preference.[20]

SECTION 28[21]

Throughout the 1980s British society grew more homophobic. In a
poll in 1983, when asked if they approved of homosexual relationships, 62 per cent of respondents had censured them; in 1985
the figure was 69 per cent, and in 1987 it was 74 per cent. When
asked in 1987 if homosexuals should be allowed to adopt children,
86 per cent said they would forbid lesbians to adopt, while 93 per
cent wanted to forbid gay men. Such growing hostility can partly
be explained by public reaction to AIDS but other factors had also
played their part.

The 1967 Act which had legalised homosexual acts in private did
not give homosexuals equal citizenship. It did not by any stretch of
the imagination protect them or their jobs from discrimination. It
did not protect them from abuse, intolerance and violence. People
suffered constantly from the inequity of one law for straight
society and another for gay. One glaring example of this was the
age of consent: for homosexuals it was twenty-one, while for
heterosexuals it was sixteen. Another injustice (though Lady
Wootton had twice tabled amendments to change the clause) was
to allow conspiracy charges to be brought against people committing, seeking to commit or to facilitate homosexual acts. This

allowed the police to charge magazines and gay newspapers with conspiracy to corrupt public morals if they carried homosexual contact advertisements. Homosexuality was (and still is) a crime in the armed services and many gays and lesbians are discharged if they are discovered in possession of gay love letters or are seen to enter a gay bar.

But in the 1970s and early 1980s, understandably enough, homosexuals behaved as if they were equal, and some sections of liberal society colluded with this ideal or fantasy. What is more, Labour-controlled local authorities, inspired by the radical Greater London Council (GLC), were adopting equal opportunity policies for lesbians and gays, setting up and subsidising gay centres and encouraging a positive image of homosexuality. The GLC's charter on homosexuality had been deeply concerned about gay and lesbian pupils and students who would see in the curriculum only 'negative images'.

Appalled at what they felt was the spread of a pernicious evil, the authorities showed their concern in 1984 by the raid and seizure of books by HM Customs and Excise from Gay's the Word bookshop. In 1983, the gay-rights activist Peter Tatchell had been smeared in the tabloid press when fighting a by-election campaign at Bermondsey. Labour supporters canvassing on housing estates knew that the subject of lesbian and gay rights would almost certainly bring forth hostility. The Labour candidate at another by-election in Greenwich in 1987 was virulently attacked for her sympathy with gay rights.

The Conservative Party and most of the media fuelled the flames of this growing resentment and alarm felt by large sections of the public. These feelings increased in the run-up to the 1987 general election, prompting the comment from *Capital Gay* that 'a gay who votes Conservative is like a turkey voting for Christmas'.[22] There was a strong feeling that authoritative rule should act, and in the 1980s an authoritarian *par excellence* was in charge – Mrs Thatcher. At the Party Conference in 1987, following her third election victory, she said: 'Children who need to be taught to respect traditional moral values are being taught that they have an inalienable right to be gay.' It was the green light.

It took only two months to introduce a new clause, Section 28 of the Local Government Act, which was passed into law in 1988. All the lesbian and gay rights organisations were horrified; 20,000 lesbians, gays and sympathisers took to the streets on marches against Section 28 in 1987 and 1988, while intensive lobbying continued. An advertisement in the *Independent* was signed by 280 distinguished people alarmed at the unthinking intolerance that was expressed in the clause. All to no avail, the Thatcher government was riding the crest of the wave.

The clause was designed to prevent the 'promotion' of homosexuality by local authorities, to promote greater inequality and also deeply embarrass the Labour Party. It decreed that a local authority should not: '(a) intentionally promote homosexuality or publish material with the intention of promoting homosexuality; (b) promote the teaching in any maintained school of the acceptability of homosexuality as a pretended family relationship. It was exactly what the public had been baying for. David Wilshire, the Tory MP who introduced the clause, remarked: 'Homosexuality is being promoted at the ratepayers' expense, and the traditional family as we know it is under attack.'

'Family values', the public felt, were being threatened and Mrs Thatcher and her party were the great defenders of them. A Gallup Poll (*Sunday Telegraph*, 5 June 1988) reflected this view: 60 per cent thought that homosexuality should not be considered an accepted lifestyle, compared with 34 per cent who approved. On the same day the same paper asked 'Is there a Homosexual Conspiracy?' and concluded that there was. Gays were beginning to feel like Jews in Nazi Germany. This flagrant injustice did provoke a new gay rights organisation to come into being, the Stonewall lobbying group, which had the objective of putting gay rights and homosexual equality back into the political arena.

A national survey on homophobic violence which Stonewall released in 1994 claimed that 155 gay men had been murdered since 1986. A Gallup survey undertaken in 1991 found that 44 per cent of lesbians had been physically threatened and 72 per cent verbally abused. In 1992 a study of gay men in Lewisham found that 81 per cent had suffered verbal abuse and 45 per cent endured physical abuse because of their sexuality.★

In the four years from 1991 to May 1994 the UK armed services had discharged 260 people from all ranks. (In the Army that included four majors and four captains and other non-commissioned officers as well as 113 privates). The cost to the taxpayer in abortive training, according to the *Guardian* (5 August 1994), ran into many millions of pounds. The attitude of the authorities might be summed up by Air Chief Marshal Armitage who spoke on television of 'fairies in the armed services' by whom he was repelled; he claimed to 'feel queasy in their physical presence' and that 'all normal people should be repelled.'

To dismiss gays from the armed services, claimed a *Guardian* leader (5 August 1994), is a breach of their civil rights: 'A military establishment that sets itself apart from the social and moral values of the society it seeks to defend is eroding its own foundations.' But have the armed services set themselves apart? Do they not more accurately reflect the feelings and views of the majority in society than does the *Guardian*?

WORLD VIEW[23]

Out of 202 countries in the world, homosexual behaviour is illegal in seventy-four of them. Generally, only males are specified. The situation is, on the whole, worst in Africa and best in Europe.

One hundred and forty-four countries show no support for gay and lesbian rights, and in fifty-three countries where homosexual behaviour is illegal, the culture is predominantly Islamic, or formerly communist or they were once part of the British Empire. In fifty-six countries a gay and lesbian movement exists, and in eleven of these countries a majority of the population is in favour of equal rights for lesbians and gay men. In ninety-eight countries homosexual behaviour is not illegal, although different ages of

★ Stonewall National Survey from, 2, Greycoat Place, London, SW1P 1YX

consent operate and there is no law against discrimination. In only six countries does the law protect gay men and lesbians against discrimination. Such protection also exists in some parts of the US, Canada and Australia.

The British heritage of sexual prejudice and bigotry has often left punitive legislation in its former colonies which has continued unrepealed, while the effects of French, Dutch, Spanish and Portuguese colonisation were far less severe. However, there is no doubt that Christian-based homophobia has percolated into many cultures which were amiably positive before. Very recently, a new heady potion of Christian puritanism fused with Islamic fundamentalism has generated hysteria and hatred.

Throughout the world countries exhibit a great range of differences in their legislature and in their social attitudes. In Argentina, for example, homosexuality is not mentioned as a criminal offence, but many provinces have rules which are used against gays; they can be detained for thirty days for offences against morality. In both Bahrain and Bangladesh, homosexuality is illegal and the official view is that it does not exist. Islamic law applies. 'Homosexuality in Iran, treated according to the islamic law, is a sin in the eyes of God and a crime for society. In Islam generally, homosexuality is among the worst possible sins you can imagine.* Punishment is whipping, chopping off of hands and feet and stoning. In Iraq there is no mention of homosexuality in the law, but it is taboo and is punished with fifteen years' imprisonment. In Cuba homosexuality is illegal – men found guilty are liable to three months to one year in prison – society is extremely hostile towards it and homosexuals try to emigrate. In Cyprus homosexuals are punished with a maximum penalty of five years in prison. The Greek Orthodox Archbishop of Cyprus in his Christmas message in 1990 said he would excommunicate known homosexuals. This is in direct contrast to Greece where there is no mention of homosexual behaviour between consenting adults in

---

* Answer from the Iran Embassy in The Hague when sent a questionnaire for *The Third Pink Book* (see note 23).

the law, and where, since 1987, the age of consent for homosexual and heterosexual is fifteen years. Iceland lowered its age of consent to fourteen for all its citizens in 1992, but only a minority of the population is in favour of gay and lesbian rights. The age of consent in The Netherlands is sixteen for all citizens, nor has homosexuality been mentioned in the penal code since 1971. Nor is it mentioned in New Zealand where the age of consent was lowered to sixteen in 1986. In Poland, the general age of consent had been fixed at fifteen since 1932, but because of the strong influence that the Catholic church has over society, homophobia is widespread.

In Pakistan homosexual behaviour is illegal: 'carnal intercourse against the order of nature with any man' is punished with two years' to life imprisonment. 'The homosexual individual is not accepted as a decent individual and homosexual acts constitute an offence punishable with imprisonment for life.'* In Saudi Arabia homosexual acts are punished with the death penalty. In China, homosexuality is not mentioned in the law as being a criminal offence, but it is considered to be 'a foreigners' disease'. (These officials had perhaps not read the accounts of their travels through China made by the Jesuits from the fifteenth century onwards who complained of the Chinese addiction to the abominable sin.) Chinese gays have fled their country and been accepted by Australia as political refugees on the grounds of their persecution in their home country. All visitors to China from Hong Kong, Taiwan and Macau have to present certificates of HIV negativity before they can enter the country. Reports exist of homosexuals being subjected to electric-shock therapy.

Australia passed anti-discrimination laws in 1986 which affect employment, but homosexual relationships are still discriminated against in the areas of residence permits, adoption and fostering. In 1991 new immigration laws gave legal recognition to homosexual

---

* Answer from the Embassy of Pakistan in The Hague when sent a questionnaire for *The Third Pink Book*

relationships, and the ban on homosexuals in the armed services was lifted in 1992. Homosexuality was legalised in Tasmania in 1994. In Austria, male and female homosexual acts were decriminalised in 1971. Homosexual prostitution was legalised on the same basis as heterosexual prostitution in 1989. Gays from repressive countries have been given asylum. In Denmark, legal protection against discrimination exists, the age of consent was lowered to fifteen in 1976, and since 1979 homosexuals have been able to enlist in the armed services. Since 1989 homosexuals have been able to engage in a registered partnership, a status similar to marriage, which has been recognised by the state.

In France, homosexuality has not been included in the Penal Code since 1986, but there is no legal protection against discrimination. However, in 1987 the major gay magazine, *Gai Pied*, was banned, using a 1949 law to protect minors. There was a public outcry and the ban was reversed. Only 24 per cent of French people object to having gays as neighbours. In Germany there is no mention of homosexuality as a criminal offence, but the age of consent in what was East Germany is fourteen while in West Germany for homosexual acts between men it is eighteen. This anomaly still exists, but the government of the united Germany have plans to alter the law to fourteen throughout the country. In August 1992, in over fifty German cities, more than 250 gay and lesbian couples submitted marriage applications in an attempted mass wedding – they were all rejected.

In the United States legal protection against discrimination now exists in the states of California, Connecticut, New Jersey, New York, Massachusetts, Vermont and Wisconsin. Though up to 1961 anal and oral sex were crimes between people of the same sex in every state, the American Law Institute developed a Model Penal Code during the 1950s which suggested that all non-violent consensual sexual activities between adults in private should be decriminalised. Twenty-four states have adopted this code, but six states still keep anal/oral sex between persons of the same gender as a crime. (They are Arkansas, Kansas, Oklahoma, Texas,

Montana and Nevada.) In 1992 the third court of appeals in Austin decided that the sodomy law in Texas infringed the laws of the United States and declared it illegal. The ban on gays in the armed services has been estimated to have cost $500 million during the last decade. President Clinton promised in 1993 to lift the ban on homosexuals in the military, causing an outcry of protest. Nothing has been done up to the time of writing.

In Britain a homosexual partner cannot be allowed to stay or enter the country on the basis of his or her relationship with a UK citizen. Thirty-one per cent of the British (48 per cent in Northern Ireland) object to homosexuals as neighbours. In 1992, the court of appeals in London upheld the conviction against five men guilty of sado-masochistic sex in private with consenting adults. They received sentences of up to four and a half years in prison.

Lesbian and gay men demand equality from the law and require safeguards against discrimination, but no international human rights treaty explicitly distinguishes the rights and freedoms of people with an alternative sexual orientation. Discrimination exists because the majority in society still consider gays and lesbians to be 'sick, sinful, perverse, unnatural, dangerous, contagious for children, shameful to the family . . . it is regarded as inferior to heterosexuality, particularly since lesbian and gay couples cannot procreate'.[24]

Human rights legislation is supposed to be concerned with the protection of individual and collective rights of minority groups. At the core of lesbian and gay rights is a demand for a broader, less heterosexually biased interpretation of the established basic rights that most people consider are naturally theirs. The right to have a private and personal life, a home, photographs, diaries and correspondence which are sacrosanct. The right to freedom of expression which Section (now Clause) 28 demolished. The right to freedom of assembly. The right to marry and found a family. (The European Court does not recognise same-sex cohabitants as a couple entitled to marry and have or foster children.) The right to non-discrimination.[25] Lesbian and gay rights do not enjoy sufficient protection under any recognised human rights code. It is thought that this is not so much the textual shortcomings of the major treaties, but rather the conservative interpretation of them given by people in authority.

XIV

ANALYSIS
AND
REFLECTIONS

Throughout history every society has exhibited forms of same-sex loving. We can therefore conclude that what we now call homosexuality is a constant aspect of the sexual nature of *homo sapiens*. Or to put it another way: 'the production of a population of human males who are (supposedly) incapable of being sexually excited by a person of their own sex *under any circumstances* is itself a cultural event without, so far as I know, either precedent or parallel, and cries out for an explanation.'[1]

This conclusion in no way detracts from, or invalidates, the main sexual drive of our species which, like all others, demands preservation and survival by procreation. There is, however, throughout the mammalian genus, an imbalance in the amount of eggs each sex produces, for there is always a huge surplus in the male. Because human society – up until very recently – strictly controlled the number and availability of women, while also selecting which males would procreate, there was also a surplus of males.

It would seem, then, that homosexuality rests, as it does in zoology, partly on a simple biological equation. Surplus males will cohabit with surplus males if there are no females readily available.

But it is not as simple as that, because there are always males and females who do not want to cohabit with members of the opposite gender even when they are available. But let us stay with the simple explanation for the moment and view how society has coped with the surplus, especially in the very young, curious and lustful.

YOUTHFUL LOVE

Ever since the decline of the ancient world, societies have failed to create an acknowledged method by which the biological extravagance of semen in the young male can be dissipated in an enjoyable and harmless way. The early church countenanced prostitution rather than pederasty and masturbation, as it seemed the lesser of the three evils. Yet sex was a subject the church was unwilling to confront in a humane and civilised manner; sex had to be severely restrained, for without discipline and caution, indulgence in the flesh was the certain way into the arms of Satan. The whole world of the adolescent boy, bursting with strange new feelings and essences, was ignored. Previously, magisters guided youths, often with desire and affection, but church and state combined to erase such roles, deeming them a wicked influence. The roles of socially acknowledged loving teacher and pupil, who might also be lover and beloved, took many hundreds of years to fade away; society was always equivocal about such relationships, seeing their worth but also terrified of their sexual content.

From then on, the youth, bursting with sexual potency, was left to his own devices, surrounded by threats and warnings of disease and madness; every sexual alternative before he was old enough to marry was beset with dangers. It is as if society feared the power of male children and so deliberately furnished the path to sexual knowledge with mythical dangers. Ancient societies had established a sexual rule over young males so that they could be taught and trained in citizenship – in all these societies pederasty was portrayed as an essential part of learning how to be a man. Male loving was closely entwined with valour, heroism, bravery and manliness. Christendom, terrified of these truths, attempted to suppress all knowledge of them and over the years reinterpreted biblical text when it spoke of same-sex loving, so that it placed a greater emphasis on sinfulness and degradation.

Adult males in modern society who feel fulfilled in giving concern and tuition to boys and youths are portrayed as being interested only in boys' bodies (though this may be a small part of the attraction) and are spurned and traduced as sexual monsters. I believe we reap the harvest of our hysterical fear and homophobia today in juvenile crime, drug use and delinquency. Consider the ethical training which boys and youths gained through *shudo* in Japan or in the system in classical Greece, the tuition in manners, customs and humanity, the degree of civilised values imparted to them, the ideas of loyalty, honour and truthfulness; this highly personalised education with love and sensuality at its centre must be far more effective than any other. We in the West are bigoted fools to dismiss it with such horror.

STUDS

How do men and women pick each other out as mates? What lies behind the experience of 'falling in love'? Male and female are searching for a mate who will produce healthy, successful children because that is the in-built need for the species. Males ensure their genetic survival, if they are already powerful enough, by choosing as many mates as possible; the chosen females will be the most attractive in physical beauty, health and strength, because those are the genes the male desires for his children. In this situation, where all the males are selecting the best females, the males will be in competition with each other. Only the best males get to breed, the constant extinction in reproduction of the less attractive males purges their genes from a species. We should not forget that same-sex coupling is non-procreative and that if it serves a function biologically, it could be either an effective form of birth control or the purging of unwanted genes. This, of course, ignores the likely possibility that the chosen male, the stud of the group, is penetrating both genders.*

Males compete with each other for the choice females, but it is the latter who finally choose which male they are going to mate with. Both peacocks and sage grouse in the mating season have male circles in which they strut and preen and are on view to the females who observe and then finally choose between them. What they choose is not a partner (for the males fly off immediately after mating) but the genes. The females are selecting on beauty, that is health, strength and power, and these will be passed on to the next generation.

In human society it is apparent that, depending on the cultural context, at different times both the male and the female have made the final choice. Enormous emphasis is placed on the beauty and accoutrements of the other, for wealth and social position will influence offspring. Yet throughout history there have been non-procreative partnerships, the choice of which cannot be based upon selection of genes. Some of these partnerships are alternative arrangements continuing while the procreation is committed elsewhere, but some are not. Because the evidence of a definite refusal to procreate is so overwhelming, because there are many who opt out of the stud competition, we have to conclude that in many men and women this amounts to a definite choice. The choice may exist on an unconscious level, but nevertheless it is still there. Why some people but not others are obsessed with the survival of their species is a fascinating question. I would suggest that it may well be that, in times like the present, this is an instinctive but nevertheless responsible reaction to an over-populated planet which needs, if it is to survive, either to stabilise its birth-rate or to engineer a decline.

---

* In Xenophon's *Symposium*, the beautiful Critobulus is the beloved of older men, lover of the younger Cleinias, and newly married.

THE TREATMENT OF WOMEN

How a society expresses its sexuality is a direct result of its political structure and ideology. How a society views its women also relates closely to the manner in which it expresses its maleness. As we have seen, where the women were severely limited and well-nigh oppressed, there was likely also to be a cult of pederasty as part of the social fabric. Consider the severely restricted role that women had in Celtic societies, where they were treated as if they were almost sub-human, and look at the cults of male warrior love, of male bonding and the ritual pederasty of adolescents that also existed. Classical Greece is, of course, a major example: women were confined in quarters and not welcomed in public (unless they were intelligent courtesans) and boys were idealised as being by far the greater love object. In these societies, to be passive in cohabitation was to be despised; it was approved of only in boys and women, but in the older man it was a source of vulgar jokes and satire, which it still remains today. For a male to allow himself to be used as women are used was to debase the idea of masculinity. What was socially approved of was a form of sexual fascism, for the superior partner took sexual precedence, he alone might initiate a sexual act, penetrate the body of his partner in a situation which lacked both social and sexual reciprocity.[2] In these phallocentric and despotic societies, the political system engendered the sexual form. The case for the theory that political structures shape sexuality grows stronger once we look at other societies.

In societies where women are more equal with men (as in the American Indian tribes), there is a greater relaxation in gender exchange. Males can opt to be women, or women to be men, if they wish, and dress accordingly. Such people are valued as being greatly talented. In such societies gender is seen as something fluid, not holding the great significance which the Western powers gave it, and still do.

Because of the rise of feminism, and a corresponding decrease in the suppression of women in Western societies, there is a little more overt transvestism, but it is accorded no respect; it often incites pity and embarrassment, if not downright abuse. Today we appear to be locked into gender absolutism, where the definition of male is fixed and limited by capitalism, which insists on the exploitation of anything else that does not conform to it.

When the political structure changed at the beginning of the eighteenth century, sexual expression was very quickly redefined. The change from public approval of bisexuality to its condemnation, and the new approval of heterosexuality, was astonishingly sudden, but it serves to show how the demands of the market needed a new concept of the masculine in its aggressive leadership in order to survive and grow.

There are now a few women in leadership roles, but alas they have had to adopt 'masculine' psychological attire, as Mrs Thatcher did, in order to stay as leaders of capitalism. Other women are working to redefine their identity, for it should be possible to become a powerful elite without adopting traits from the opposite gender.

We now live in an age where there are no restrictions on the availability of women, except those that women themselves adopt. To my knowledge this has not occurred before in any society. Usually, the male autocracy imposes a social structure which defines the age at which a woman can marry and emphasises the punishments that are meted out to her if she does not submit. This slowly vanished after the Second World War with the availability of contraception and the struggle for women to control their own destiny. Today, young girls, some even before puberty, allow sexual intercourse with boys of roughly the same age. Adolescent boys are aware of the availability of girls of their age and class, and the mating ritual of viewing and selecting starts early. Because of the general homophobia of society which is strongest in relation to this age group (parents possibly feel that their adolescent children are at their most vulnerable then), same-sex loving is not on the agenda, though there are some certainly who would wish to explore it.

Society seems to be in two minds over this cultural phenomenon, exulting in youthful heterosexuality, but deploring the inevitable consequences – pregnant thirteen-year-olds. It seems not to occur to them that what used to be thought of as a natural adolescent homosexual phase (we never hear this sentiment expressed now), has a valuable social function. Such a relationship between two girls or two boys is useful experience for the adult; it releases the suppression of intense emotions, teaches the individual something about kindness, consideration and sharing without the threatening responsibility of a baby. What is more, it is enlightening sexually while, contrary to popular myth, it does not create an indelible sexual identity for the rest of one's life.

REBELS

Given that political structures dictate the sexual form, every new orthodoxy that is accepted acquires its heresy, each defining the nature of the other. Being a real rebel, that is striving to create a viable alternative, takes time and hard work. Being a sexual rebel, refusing to accept the sexual orthodoxy of one's time, is one of the most powerful and significant of all rebellious acts; to opt for the pursuit of non-procreative sex is a form of blasphemy, for it strikes at the heart of society's belief in its own immortality. A hatred of the hypocrisy and ideals of one's age could well lead individuals to make a statement of this kind, a statement which can germinate at a very young age.

Another vivid form of political rebellion is to don the clothes of the opposite gender. Women do not now have this political weapon as they once did, for women in suits, whether boiler- or pin-stripe, cause no outrage but society still finds it offensive to see men in frocks. A man wearing a frock is somehow threatening and has to be dismissed with laughter or vituperation.

Transvestites always talk in very personal terms about their desire; they feel somehow wrong dressed as a man, but in a frock they tell the interviewer, they feel relaxed and at home. Transsexuals, on the other hand, always talk about being inside the body of the wrong gender and how they long to change the body to suit their feelings. One transsexual expressed very definite views on child-rearing: 'I would definitely teach my kids that boys should be boys and girls should be girls.' Other male transsexuals viewed themselves as 'passive, nurturing, emotional, intuitive'.[3] Transsexuals are highly conservative in how they view social roles. They see themselves in what they feel are the feminine roles, dress-making, sewing, housework, secretarial work. They see their future in terms of finding 'the right man' to take care of them, with whom they will adopt kids and rear them. They all tend to view their present existence as somehow deeply and profoundly wrong, out of kilter with everything they are familiar with inside.

I would suggest that the only thing that is wrong is society itself which has a vested interest in gender stereotypes: a society which is appalled at the thought of men sewing or a woman stevedore; a society which cannot accept gender fluidity, where women have a clitoris they might use as a penis and men have large breasts as well as a penis they can penetrate with. There are medical histories of a few lesbian women with a clitoris that, when erect, was the size and thickness of a finger. Brazilian male transvestite prostitutes swear they earn a fortune in Italy when going with Italian men who desire the illusion of having sex with large-breasted women who then sodomise them. But these examples are extravagant ones and the gender fluidity I am citing needs only slight physical attributes or maybe none at all. For significant sexual desire exists within the mind.

What concerns me about transsexuals is that cutting off a penis does not make a woman. Psychotherapists and the colluding surgeons are trading in myths, and they know it. Men who wish to have such an operation often state stridently that they are not gay or even bisexual, indeed, many of them are married and have fathered children, but once they have the operation they tend to search for a man to love, as if they have been suppressing their gayness before. Yet another example, I would suggest, of the indoctrination of a homophobic society, the message being that only a woman (or a simulated woman with a contrived vagina and a daily shot of oestrogen) can have sexual intercourse with a man.

What we are seeing in transsexual cases is society's gender system being maintained and therefore vanquishing concepts of same-sex loving. These are rebels who hate their rebellion and long to conform. They realise after the operation that they have failed in both genders. Society has duped them, it has pretended to wave the magic wand and to change Cinders into Cinderella, but they were Buttons at the time and both sides knew it.★

OVER-POPULATION

At the United Nations Conference on population, in Cairo in 1994, one would have thought that the issue of homosexuality might have been discussed positively, instead of neglected entirely. No nation went as far as suggesting that sex should be finally separated from reproduction, that we should teach our young that not only is contraception necessary, but that abortion is available and that sexual desire is pleasurable. No nation would have dared to suggest that our young should be taught that homosexuality is a viable lifestyle. Yet, in the next century, over-population will place so great a strain on our planet's resources, that governments might have to turn to encouraging homosexuals by subsidising their lifestyles at the expense of heterosexual couples.

Yes, it strikes us as most unlikely. But why should it? The ancient world where homosexuality was entwined into the social fabric was barely two thousand years ago, a mere second in the age of *homo sapiens*, and we have seen how quickly a political structure

---

★ This point of view is explored brilliantly and in great detail by a transsexual, Sandy Stone, in an essay, 'The Empire Strikes Back: A Posttranssexual Manifesto', included in Epstein and Straub (eds.), *Body Guards*. The essay includes many quotations from the accounts of transsexuals of that moment when they woke up from the anaesthetic and felt themselves to be 'real' women for the first time. Nothing, I would suggest, could be more persuasive in inclining the reader to the view above.

will change sexual mores. Ecological disasters might make such radical changes a necessity, ushering in a time when the homophobic societies of the past, the Nazi extermination of homosexuals, the castrations and electric-shock therapies, will strike people with horror that such barbarian practices could have existed in a society that counted itself 'civilised'.

WHY HOMOPHOBIA?

Would homophobia have existed without the constant nourishment it gains from biblical exegesis? Why should a great section of the world accept with seriousness, believing devoutly in, folk tales often violent and barbaric, from a tiny group of nomadic tribesmen on the edge of the eastern Mediterranean? Why should those biblical sections which appear to deplore same-sex loving be believed in so fanatically, when other sections that praise it, for example, the love of Jonathan and David, are ignored?

We have seen that within the Roman Empire itself there was a move towards stoicism and restraint before Christian belief took hold. We do not know whether that movement would have continued, but as philosophy and pagan religions countenanced same-sex loving, it is unlikely. The sources of homophobia have to be the Old Testament and St Paul; both have fuelled it over the centuries.

Yet homophobia has deeper roots. It seems possible that homosexuality is psychologically offensive to some people because it appears to strike at the survival of our species. Onan spilt his seed on the ground and that is what offended the Lord God. In so many early societies we get the worship of semen itself as being the precious life-giver. In same-sex acts the semen is not wasted, it is swallowed as nourishment or it is absorbed by the rectum. Prehistoric tribes had rituals where semen was either ingested or sprinkled over the ground as fertility magic. The idea that semen has magical qualities is still held by rational men today.★ I would suggest that such reverence for semen and the worship of the phallus are both atavistic and linger on in our consciousness. There is indeed, in all homosexual love, an element of adoration of the male as icon of beauty, as sexual paragon, as golden Greek god; there are undeniably powerful themes of pagan love and desire that lie within the act.

Fear of the homosexual act therefore includes fear of paganism, fear that the barbarians are at the gates – indeed, this kind of language is often used by preachers and writers who fulminate against it. It is a fear, then, that has its roots within the dawn of history, a fear that pagan worship can destroy today's civilisation. Homosexuals and masturbators are seen as pagan wastrels in the most profound sense, dissipating the life-force of humanity for the sake of a passing sensual thrill. However, at times of population explosion, one would think even fundamentalists might become rational upon the subject. But sexual pleasure is the most intense experience in our lives, it is the essence of being alive, it is the final opposition to death, therefore it carries within it the possibility of continual resurrection, the immortality of the selfish gene which must never be extinguished.

Society clearly spelt out this fear of the pagan very early on when it fused the crime of sodomy with heresy and struck terror into Christendom. No wonder then, that this fear culminated in such harsh legislation. But such fears can be fanned by the authorities to become a means of manipulating the masses into submitting to laws of restraint and control. There can be no doubt that, within Christian states, laws against sexuality were part of the corporate fiction used to influence and subjugate rebellious beliefs and peoples. Thus, I believe, homophobia was and is useful to all forms of government that pay lip-service to the Christian faith. It is a method of disciplining unorthodox codes, controlling

---

★ Tom Driberg thought a daily consumption was essential to health and long life (see Francis Wheen's biography), while Michael Davidson, with only a little self-mockery, believed the same (in a letter owned by the author).

'anarchy' and suppressing rebellion. It was no mere accident, after all, which saw the McCarthy era in America linking homosexuality with communism – both were as one, the enemy of the state. Again, after the American and French Revolutions, it was no coincidence that it was thought in England that revolutionaries bred sodomites. This package of populist myths lies within reach of any government in times of economic decline, or when threatened with alien forces, to be picked up, unwrapped and detonated as a device to achieve solidarity and unison.

Nor is there any sign that homophobia has lessened over the last few decades. At times of recession it often seems paramount. Homophobia wrapped in the guise of wisdom and compassion is perhaps the most pernicious and repulsive of its manifestations. Professor Charles Socarides, a New York psychiatrist, has been writing books and journalism devoted to a rabid anti-homosexual view, believing it to be nothing less than a threat to mankind. His arguments are banal, which is why they have a following. He speaks of homosexuality as being 'a revision of the basic code and concept of life and biology, that men and women normally mate with those of the opposite sex and not with each other . . . homosexuality cannot make a society or keep one going for very long. It operates against the cohesive elements in society.'[4] These views are pernicious, and because they are so commonplace and obvious anyone can grasp them. They exhibit a paranoid fear that homosexuality will take over the world. (It is perhaps not irrelevant to Socarides' views that his son, Richard Socarides, is a highly successful civil rights lawyer and gay.)

However, psychiatric practices in the US and the UK are imbued with these views. A consultant psychotherapist at Addenbrookes Hospital in Cambridgeshire is quoted as saying: 'if you go to the NHS for psychotherapy and you're a gay man the chance of meeting a therapist who will view your homosexuality as pathological is very high'.

That Socarides' views are being listened to with some attention now when we are still within a recession is, of course, no accident.★ For if you are suffering a degree of economic hardship, you relieve your feelings by kicking and spitting at the underdog.

GENDER

It is clear that the defining of gender in a highly limited manner is not only necessary but is of great significance to society, its importance fluctuating according to its usefulness at any given period.

Since 1700 there has been a growing need to redefine 'male' and 'female' as having qualities which oppose each other. Our current expectations of male and female stem from this period: the male as aggressor, and the female as a docile receptor. These stereotypes are used to judge people and as the basis for punitive laws. We live now in a time when the stereotype's mould has been cracked, and although it has not broken apart, at least we can see through the cracks that gender is actually blurred. Because of this, the male and female stereotypes are clung to with rising hysteria. Society is in a state of ferment in its exploration of a new gender awareness, and does not seem to know which way to turn.

By 1800 society had acknowledged that from the two bodies, male and female, there were four genders: men, women, sodomites and sapphists, the last two being social pariahs. Today, the last two under different names, gays and lesbians, have been grudgingly admitted to the fringes of society, and a fifth gender, the transsexual, is also acknowledged, though hardly welcomed, and survives on the social perimeters. What confuses society about this arrangement is that these three last categories refuse to know their place. Gays and lesbians 'come out' and they look like 'normal' people while some transsexuals can carry off their transformation with a spirited *elan* and convince everyone (as in

---

★ Socarides was to give the prestigious annual lecture to the Association for Psychoanalytic Psychotherapy at Middlesex Medical School, London, on 28 April 1995, but earlier that week the organisers received letters from gay activists threatening barracking if the lecture took place. They called it off.

the case of Ms Caroline Cossey). No wonder society feels insecure about identifying precisely what is male or female.

Why should this excite so much concern? Alas, we return to the powerful cultural indoctrination imposed by the Old Testament. The story of Adam and Eve still carries enormous significance, and these distinct ideas of male and female lie behind our legal and social structures to such an extent that to question the truth of the definition becomes an anarchic act. Hebraic and Talmudic texts further defined male and female roles and much of this, considered as divine law and therefore sacrosanct, in great detail permeated Christendom.

A great deal of our anxiety over gender is made manifest in our intense obsession with sex and children. The last decade has seen an enormous amount of pain and suffering wrought upon parents and children when medical specialists have diagnosed 'child abuse' where no such thing has occurred. (Evidence on anal dilation in children is reminiscent of the Boulton and Parks case; at least that jury had the sense to disbelieve it.) I am not saying that child sexual abuse does not exist, it always has, but whether more of it exists than before is not known. But our obsession with it sheds light upon our own problems with sex and gender.

Our children are sacrosanct. We do not think of them as sexual beings, yet we do think of them very distinctly as boys and girls. Their gender is important to us. We believe strongly that all children are innocent and must be kept that way for as long as possible. (Children, of course, are no more innocent than anyone else, they are simply inexperienced and we tend to confuse the two.) If any child exhibits characteristics associated with the opposite gender we ignore it, telling ourselves it is only a phase, or we encourage them in some other activity which we think is more suitable. We are very keen to thrust gender indoctrination on to our children, whatever their own wishes on the matter.

It is our fear of a natural growth into sexual maturity of one gender or another being abruptly halted or thrust into an alternative direction which drives us into a panic, seeing the potential for sexual abuse everywhere. All rape is loathsome because it uses

404

power, dominance, sadism and cruelty to achieve its ends, and the terror and pain inflicted on small children is one of the most unspeakable aspects of child abuse. But in my view, the gender indoctrination we give to children, from the moment they are born, often gives them a false pattern which they strive to fulfil to their cost.

We need, of course, to broaden the stereotypes; we need to say that both male and female can mean a whole range of sexual identities. We need to break the link between male and aggression, female and docility, gay as camp, and lesbian as butch. Thankfully, gay liberation has worked on the last two categories and succeeded in breaking that link, though not in everyone's eyes. Last, and most important, we need to allow the bisexual out of society's closet.

What this historical survey has shown me is that all previous histories (except for very recent ones) have deliberately changed bisexual men and women into homosexuals. It is as if society cannot endure the thought that human beings can find eroticism in either gender. If an individual is known to like his or her own gender, then he or she is immediately labelled homosexual. This need to remove bisexuality from society by attempting to erase it altogether continues unchanged today. Bentham thought an exclusive taste for only one gender was very rare. I would agree.

This is anathema to the media, who have not even begun to grasp a definition of 'homosexual'. Is it, as a letter to the *Guardian* asked: '(1) A person who earlier was heterosexual but now has gay relationships; (2) a person who had gay relationships before but now has only heterosexual relationships; (3) a person who has bisexual relationships? Is a person who had just one brief homosexual relationship in his life a homosexual?' The writer, Gordon Wilson (author of *The Third Sex*), goes on to comment: 'The problem was highlighted after the recent report from America that homosexuals' brains differ from those of heterosexuals: a letter to a newspaper asked whether, if a homosexual had heterosexual relationships, his brain would then alter?' Wilson highlights the absurdity of so much that is written about the subject. But why is

405

it so often so absurd? It would seem that the sheer mention of homosexuality induces panic, a rush to explain it all away by any means, however, bizarre, instead of merely accepting it as but one aspect of our sexual nature.

We need a new theory of human sexuality which avoids dominance in one gender and compliance in the other. People can work, live and love together in greater harmony if they honour and respect both male and female within themselves. Society appears to be edging towards this concept, albeit with great nervousness, but for the majority it is still an area of condemnation.

THE FUTURE

There is now an active cell of gay solidarity which is quick to stamp on all signs of homophobia. This cell is likely to grow in numbers and strength. There is also some evidence that the same-sex marriage ceremony which took place within the Christian church from the earliest beginnings has returned: 'A network of vicars is conducting clandestine wedding ceremonies for gay couples in churches.'[5] Gay vicars have admitted that they have hosted homosexual blessings in their parish churches in the last ten years. The Church of England is deeply divided over the issue of gay relationships which include physical expression. Hampered by the condemnation implicit in biblical texts, many churchmen cannot embrace the humanity of Christian love without a harsh judgemental view. The ordination of women (unpopular with many of the same churchmen) has possibly quickened the pace with which the orthodox church will embrace a gentler, forgiving and more accepting view of human nature. Yet against that hopeful prognosis one must place the vigorous rise of fundamentalism throughout the world. So the future is one of polarisation, a humane acceptance of the bisexual nature of people, against a zealous structure, both repressive and domineering, which involves the concept of distinct differences in gender which are always in opposition.

Capitalism seems to need this fierce and limited gender stereo-typing. So as long as capitalism is in control we are stuck with it, unless the feminist and gay liberation movements can change these caricatures of sexual identity. But as crises in the world's ecology and population loom, capitalism must change within the next fifty years or wither away.

As capitalism also creates and maintains a homophobic society, and as societies in crisis deepen homophobia, there is little hope that that too will wither away in the next few decades. In fact, I see it getting worse.

What homosexuals have endured through the centuries is of such monstrous inhumanity and injustice that it is difficult to accept that a mere sexual and emotional preference can rouse such cruel opposition. How many times must homosexuals have thought, But what harm did we do to anyone? How could such an act of impetuous pleasure be this terrifying, demonic thing which endangers the love of God and a civilised society? What a tragedy it is, then, to see how Western views on this subject have poisoned much of the rest of the world and driven former colonies into homophobic legislation. How deeply tragic, too, that Islamic fundamentalism has reneged on its own cultural roots and declared itself so bitterly against homosexual acts. The world picture is grim, and, because of it, one is more and more grateful for those recent laws across the world in more enlightened countries which have been against social discrimination.

SELECT BIBLIOGRAPHY

Aldrich, Robert, *The Seduction of the Mediterranean* (London: Routledge, 1993).

Allen, Peter, *Cambridge Apostles: The Early Years* (Cambridge: Cambridge University Press, 1979).

Anderson, Michael, *Approaches to the History of the Western Family, 1500–1914* (London: Macmillan, 1980).

Ariès, Philippe and Béjin (eds), *Western Sexuality: Practice and Precept in Past and Present Times*. Trans. A. Forster (Oxford: Blackwell, 1985).

Ariosto, Ludovico, *Orlando Furioso*. Trans. W. S. Rose (London: Bell, 1907).

Barber, Malcolm, *The Trial of the Templars* (Cambridge: Cambridge University Press, 1978).

Bentham, Jeremy, 'Essay on Pederasty', introduced and ed. L. Crompton, *Journal of Homosexuality*, vols 3–4 (1978).

Bérubé, Allan, *Coming Out Under Fire: The History of Gay Men and Women in World War Two* (London: Penguin, 1991).

Beurdeley, Cecile, *L'Amour bleu*. Trans. M. Taylor (New York: Rizzoli, 1978).

Boswell, John, *Christianity, Social Tolerance and Homosexuality: Gay People in Western Europe from the Beginning of the Christian Era to the Fourteenth Century* (Chicago: University of Chicago Press, 1980).

——, *The Marriage of Likeness: Same-Sex Unions in Pre-Modern Europe* (London: HarperCollins, 1995).

Boucé, Paul G., *Sexuality in Eighteenth-century Britain* (Manchester: Manchester University Press, 1982).

Bray, Alan, *Homosexuality in Renaissance England* (London: Gay Men's Press, 1982).

Brown, Peter, *The Body and Society* (New York: Columbia University Press, 1988).

Brundage, James A., *Law, Sex and Christian Society in Medieval Europe* (Chicago: University of Chicago Press, 1988).

Bullough, Vern L., *Sexual Variance in Society and History* (Chicago: University of Chicago Press, 1976).

Burford, E. J., *Wits, Wenchers and Wantons* (London: Robert Hale, 1990).

Burg, B. R., *Sodomy and the Perception of Evil: English Sea Rovers in the Seventeenth-century Caribbean* (New York: New York University Press, 1983).

Burton, Sir Richard, *The Book of the Thousand Nights and a Night* (10 vols) (Benares, 1885).

Cadden, Joan, *Meanings of Sex Difference in the Middle Ages* (Cambridge: Cambridge University Press, 1993).

Cameron, Averil and Kuhrt, Amelie (eds), *Images of Women in Antiquity* (London: Routledge, 1993).

Campbell, Colin, *The Romantic Ethic and the Spirit of Modern Consumerism* (Oxford: Blackwell, 1989).

Cantarella, Eva, *Bisexuality in the Ancient World*. Trans. C. O'Cuilleanain (New Haven: Yale University Press, 1992).

Carpenter, Edward, *My Days and Dreams* (1916), in *Selected Writings*, vol. 1 *Sex* (London: Gay Men's Press, 1984).

Cavendish, Richard (ed.), *Mythology* (London: Macdonald, 1987).

Chamberlin, E. R., *The Bad Popes* (London: Hamish Hamilton, 1970).

Chaney, E. and Ritchie, N. (eds.), *Oxford, China, Italy: Writings in Honour of Sir Harold Acton on His Eightieth Birthday* (London: Thames and Hudson, 1984).

Cohn, Norman, *The Pursuit of the Millennium* (London: Paladin, 1970).

Coote, Stephen (ed.), *The Penguin Book of Homosexual Verse* (London: Penguin, 1983).

Crompton, Louis, *Byron and Greek Love: Homophobia in 19th-Century England* (Berkeley and Los Angeles: University of California Press, 1985).

——, 'Homosexuality in Imperial China', paper presented at the Conference on 'Homosexuality, Which Homosexuality?' (Amsterdam, 1987).

Cuttino, G. P. and Lyman, T. W., 'Where is Edward II?', *Speculum*, vol. 53 (1978), pp. 522–44.

Davenport-Hines, Richard, *Sex, Death and Punishment: Attitudes to Sex in Britain since the Renaissance* (London: Fontana, 1990).

Davidson, Michael, *The World, the Flesh and Myself* (London: Gay Men's Press, 1986).

Deacon, Bernard, *Malekula: A Vanishing People in the New Hebrides* (London: Routledge, 1934).

SELECT BIBLIOGRAPHY

Dekker, Rudolf M. and van de Pol, Lotte C., *The Tradition of Female Transvestism in Early Modern Europe* (London: Macmillan, 1989).

Dellamora, Richard, *Masculine Desire: The Sexual Politics of Victorian Aestheticism* (Chapel Hill: University of North Carolina Press, 1990).

D'Emilio, John and Freedman, Estelle B., *Intimate Matters: A History of Sexuality in America* (New York: Harper and Row, 1988).

Diogenes Laertius, *Lives and Opinions of the Eminent Philosophers.* Trans. C. D. Yonge (London: Bell, 1891).

Driberg, Tom, *Ruling Passions: The Autobiography of Tom Driberg* (London: Cape, 1977).

Duberman, Martin, *About Time: Exploring the Gay Past* (New York: Gay Presses of New York, 1986).

Duberman, M. B., Vicinus, M. and Chauncey, G. (eds), *Hidden from History: Reclaiming the Gay and Lesbian Past* (London: Penguin, 1991).

Earle, Peter, *The World of Defoe* (London: Weidenfeld and Nicolson, 1976).

Ellis, Peter Beresford, *The Celtic Empire* (London: Constable, 1990).

Ellmann, Richard, *Oscar Wilde* (London: Hamish Hamilton, 1987).

Epstein, Julia and Straub, Kristina (eds), *Body Guards* (London: Routledge, 1991).

Faderman, Lillian, *Surpassing the Love of Men: Romantic Friendships between Women from the Renaissance to the Present* (New York: Morrow, 1981).

Fernandez, Dominique, *Signor Giovanni* (Paris, 1981).

Ferris, Paul, *Sex and the British* (London: Michael Joseph, 1993).

Foord, Edward, *The Byzantine Empire* (London: A. and C. Black, 1911).

Foucault, Michel, *The History of Sexuality* (3 vols), Trans. R. Hurley (London: Allen Lane, 1979–88).

Fout, John C. (ed.), *Forbidden History* (Chicago: University of Chicago Press, 1992).

Gay, Peter, *Freud: A Life for Our Time* (London: Dent, 1988).

Gerard, Kent and Hekma, Gert (eds), *The Pursuit of Sodomy: Male Homosexuality in Renaissance and Enlightenment Europe* (New York: Harrington Park, 1989).

Gibbon, Edward, *The History of the Decline and Fall of the Roman Empire* (1776–88; Everyman edn, 1910, 1993).

Gibson, William, *Church, State and Society, 1760–1850* (New York: St Martin's Press, 1994).

Greenberg, David F., *The Construction of Homosexuality* (Chicago: University of Chicago Press, 1988).

Grey, Antony, *Quest for Justice: Towards Homosexual Emancipation* (London: Sinclair Stevenson, 1992).

Grosskurth, Phyllis, *John Addington Symonds: A Biography* (London: Longmans, 1964).

Guiart, J., 'Native Society in the New Hebrides: The Big Nambas of Northern Malekula', *Mankind*, vol. 4 (1953), pp. 439–46.

Halperin, David M., *One Hundred Years of Homosexuality and Other Essays in Greek Love* (London and New York: Routledge, 1990).

Hampson, Norman, *The Enlightenment* (London: Penguin, 1968).

Harry, Joseph and DeVall, William B., *The Social Organization of Gay Males* (New York: Praeger, 1978).

Heger, Heinz, *The Men with the Pink Triangle* (London: Gay Men's Press, 1980).

SELECT BIBLIOGRAPHY

Hendriks, A., Tielman, R. and van der Veen, E. (eds), *The Third Pink Book: A Global View of Lesbian and Gay Liberation and Oppression* (Prometheus, 1993).

Herdt, Gilbert H. (ed.), *Ritualized Homosexuality in Melanesia* (Berkeley: University of California Press, 1984).

——— (ed.), *Gay Culture in America: Essays from the Field* (Boston: Beacon Press, 1992).

Higgins, Patrick (ed.), *A Queer Reader* (London: Fourth Estate, 1993).

Hill, Christopher, *The World Turned Upside Down* (London: Penguin, 1975).

Hinsch, Bret, *Passions of the Cut Sleeve* (Berkeley: University of California Press, 1990).

Hyam, Ronald, *Empire and Sexuality: The British Experience* (Manchester: Manchester University Press, 1991).

Irwin, Robert, *The Arabian Nights: A Companion* (London: Allen Lane, 1994).

Junod, Henry A., *The Life of a South African Tribe* (London: Macmillan, 1927).

Katz, Jonathan N., *Gay American History: Lesbians and Gay Men in the U.S.A.* (New York: Crowell, 1976).

Kellogg, Stuart (ed.), *Literary Vision of Homosexuality* (New York, London, Norwood, Australia: Haworth Press, 1983).

Keuls, Eva C., *The Reign of the Phallus: Sexual Politics in Ancient Athens* (New York: Harper and Row, 1985).

Kimmel, S. M. (ed.), *Love Letters between a certain Late Nobleman and the Famous Mr Wilson* (New York: Harrington Park, 1990).

Kinsey, A. C., Pomeroy, W. B. and Martin, C., *Sexual Behaviour in the Human Male* (Philadelphia: Saunders, 1948).

Kosofsky Sedgwick, Eve, *Between Men: English Literature and Male Homosocial Desire* (New York: Columbia University Press, 1985).

La Barre, Webster, *Muelos: A Stone Age Superstition about Sexuality* (New York: Columbia University Press, 1984).

Levin, Eve, *Sex and Society in the World of the Orthodox Slavs, 900–1700* (Ithaca, NY: Cornell University Press, 1989).

Licht, Hans, *Sexual Life in Ancient Greece.* Trans. J. H. Freese (London: Routledge, 1932).

Maccubbin, Robert P. (ed.), *'Tis Nature's Fault: Unauthorised Sexuality During the Enlightenment* (Cambridge: Cambridge University Press, 1987).

Marcus, Steven, *The Other Victorians* (London: Weidenfeld and Nicolson, 1966).

Memoirs of the American Museum of Natural History (2 vols) (New York, 1904).

Miller, John C., *Alexander Hamilton: A Portrait in Paradox* (New York: Harper and Row, 1959).

Miller, Nancy K. (ed.), *The Poetics of Gender* (New York: Columbia University Press, 1986).

Miller, Neil, *Out of the Past* (New York: Vintage, 1995).

Moore, R. I., *The Birth of Popular Heresy* (London: Edward Arnold, 1975).

Morgan, Ted, *Somerset Maugham* (New York: Simon and Schuster, 1980).

Moss, Cynthia, *Portraits in the Wild: Animal Behaviour in East Africa* (London: Hamish Hamilton, 1972).

Munroe, R., Whiting, J. M. and Hally, D., 'Institutionalized Male Transvestism and Sex Distinction', *American Anthropologist*, vol. 71 (1969), pp. 87–91.

Norton, Rictor, *Mother Clap's Molly House* (London: Gay Men's Press, 1992).

Ogden, C. K., *The Theory of Legislation* (London: Kegan Paul, 1931).

Parkin, Tim G., *Demography and Roman Society* (Baltimore: Johns Hopkins University Press, 1992).

Parrinder, Geoffrey, *Sex in the World's Religions* (London: Sheldon, 1980).

Pearsall, Ronald, *The Worm in the Bud* (London: Weidenfeld and Nicolson, 1969).

Pequigney, Joseph, *Such is My Love: A Study of Shakespeare's Sonnets* (Chicago: University of Chicago Press, 1985).

Pope-Hennessey, James, *Monkton Milnes: The Years of Promise, 1800–1851* (London: Constable, 1949).

Porter, Kevin and Weeks, Jeffrey (eds), *Between the Acts: Lives of Homosexual Men, 1885–1967* (London: Routledge, 1990).

Reischauer, Edwin O., *The Japanese Today: Change and Continuity* (Cambridge: Cambridge University Press, 1988).

Roberts, Nickie, *Whores in History* (London: HarperCollins, 1992).

Rousseau, G. S. and Porter, Roy (eds), *Sexual Underworlds of the Enlightenment* (Manchester: Manchester University Press, 1987).

Rousselle, Aline, *Porneia: On Desire and the Body in Antiquity* (Oxford: Blackwell, 1988).

Rowse, A. L. *Homosexuals in History: A Study of Ambivalence in Society* (London: Weidenfeld and Nicolson, 1977).

Ruggiero, Guido, *The Boundaries of Eros: Sex Crime and Sexuality in Renaissance Venice* (Oxford: Oxford University Press, 1985).

Sergent, Bernard, *Homosexuality in Greek Myth*. Trans. Arthur Goldhammer (Boston: Beacon Press, 1986).

Sinfield, Alan, *The Wilde Century* (London: Cassell, 1994).

Smith, Timothy d'Arch, *Love in Earnest: Some Notes on the Lives and Writings of English Uranian Poets from 1889 to 1930* (London: Routledge and Kegan Paul, 1970).

Spier, Leslie, *Klamath Ethnology* (Berkeley: University of California Press, 1930).

Stanton, Donna C. (ed), *Discourses of Sexuality from Aristotle to Aids* (Michigan: University of Michigan Press, 1992).

Stone, Lawrence, *The Family, Sex and Marriage in England, 1500–1800* (London: Weidenfeld and Nicolson, 1977).

Strachey, C. (ed.), *The Letters of the Earl of Chesterfield to His Son* (2 vols) (London: 1932).

Summers, Claude (ed.), *Homosexuality in Renaissance and Enlightenment England* (New York: Harrington Park, 1992).

Swidler, Arlene (ed.) *Homosexuality and World Religions* (Valley Forge, PA: Trinity Press, 1993).

Teal, Donn, *The Gay Militants* (New York: Stein and Day, 1971).

Thomson, David, *England in the Nineteenth Century* (London: Penguin, 1950).

Thorn, Michael, *Tennyson* (Boston: Little, Brown, 1992).

Tuchman, Barbara W., *A Distant Mirror* (London: Macmillan, 1979).

Turner, James Grantham (ed.), *Sexuality and Gender in Early Modern Europe* (Cambridge: Cambridge University Press, 1993).

Waal, Frans de, *Chimpanzee Politics: Power and Sex Among the Apes* (London: Cape, 1982).

——, *Peacemaking Among Primates* (Cambridge, MA: Harvard University Press, 1989).

'Walter', *My Secret Life* (London: Panther, 1972).

Watanabe, Tsuneo and Iwata, Junichi, *The Love of the Samurai*. Trans. D. R. Roberts (London: Gay Men's Press, 1989).

Weeks, Jeffrey, *Coming Out: Homosexual Politics in Britain from the Nineteenth Century to the Present* (London: Quartet, 1977).

Weinberg, T. S. and Williams, Colin, *Male Homosexuals: Their Problems and Adaptations* (New York: Oxford University Press, 1974).

Wheatcroft, Andrew, *The Ottomans* (London: Viking, 1993).

White, Edmund, 'Paradise Found', *Mother Jones* (June 1983).

Williams, Walter L., *The Spirit and the Flesh: Sexual Diversity in American Indian Culture* (Boston: Beacon Press, 1986).

Yerkes, Robert M. and Yerkes, Ada W., *The Great Apes* (New Haven: Yale University Press, 1945).

REFERENCES

Foreword

1. R. Trumbach, 'The Birth of the Queen: Sodomy and the Emergence of Gender Equality in Modern Culture, 1660–1750', in Duberman et al. (eds), *Hidden from History*.

1. Prehistory and Early Civilisations

1. R. Fox, 'The Conditions of Sexual Evolution', in Ariès and Béjin (eds), *Western Sexuality*.
2. Moss, *Portraits in the Wild*.
3. Yerkes, *The Great Apes*.
4. Waal, *Peacemaking Among Primates*.
5. Waal, *Chimpanzee Politics*.
6. Herdt (ed.), *Ritualized Homosexuality in Melanesia*.
7. Guiart, 'Native Society in the New Hebrides'.
8. Deacon, *Malekula*.
9. G. M. Herdt, 'Semen Transactions in Sambian Culture', in Herdt (ed.), op. cit.
10. La Barre, *Muelos*.

REFERENCES

11. Munroe et al., 'Institutionalised Male Transvestism and Sex Distinctions'.
12. A. Sorum, 'Growth and Decay: Bedami Notions of Sexuality', in Herdt (ed.), op. cit.
13. E. Schwimmer, 'Males Couples in New Guinea', in Herdt (ed.), op. cit.
14. Spier, *Klamath Ethnology*.
15. W. Bogores, 'The Chukchee', in *Memoirs of the American Museum of Natural History*, XI, pp. 449–51.
16. Junod, *The Life of a South African Tribe*.
17. Sergent, *Homosexuality in Greek Myth*.
18. Quoted in Roberts, *Whores in History*.
19. Greenberg, *The Construction of Homosexuality*.
20. Roberts, op. cit.
21. Bullough, *Sexual Variance*.
22. Greenberg, op. cit.
23. Quotations about the myth of Seth and Horus come from Greenberg, op. cit.
24. Some material in this section (China) is based on Hinsch, *Passions of the Cut Sleeve*.

2. The Conflict: Greeks and Jews

1. Sergent, *Homosexuality in Greek Myth*.
2. Translated by M. Barnard, in Coote (ed.), *The Penguin Book of Homosexual Verse*.
3. Translated by J. A. Symonds, in Coote (ed.), op. cit.
4. Quoted from Cantarella, *Bisexuality in the Ancient World*, which also contains extracts from other poets mentioned in this section.
5. Lycurgus, quoted in Licht, *Sexual Life in Ancient Greece*. Other material in this section (Women in Classical Greece) is also taken from Licht.
6. Xenophon, *Memorabilia* II, quoted in Bullough, *Sexual Variance*.
7. Licht, op. cit., p. 358.

8. Diogenes Laertius, *Lives and Opinions of the Eminent Philosophers*.
9. Greenberg, *The Construction of Homosexuality*.
10. Quotations in this section (Ethics) are taken from Cantarella, op. cit.
11. For the lexical proof and for other quotations referred to in this section (Passive Love), see Cantarella, op. cit.
12. Ibid.
13. Quoted in Parrinder, *Sex in the World's Religions*.
14. Greenberg, op. cit.
15. Boswell, *Christianity, Social Tolerance, and Homosexuality*.
16. Boswell, op. cit., but Greenberg argues against this.
17. St Ambrose, quoted in Boswell, op. cit.

3. Rome, the East and Early Christianity

1. Greenberg, *The Construction of Homosexuality*.
2. P. Veyne, 'Homosexuality in Ancient Rome', in Ariès and Béjin (eds), *Western Sexuality*.
3. Cicero, quoted in Cantarella, *Bisexuality in the Ancient World*.
4. Boswell, *Christianity, Social Tolerance, and Homosexuality*.
5. Veyne, op. cit.
6. This and the following quotations from Martial and Catullus come from Cantarella, op. cit.
7. Veyne, op. cit.
8. Catullus, quoted in Cantarella, op. cit.
9. Ovid, *Amores* 1, 9, 1, quoted in Cantarella, op. cit. Cf. *Ars Amatoria* 11, 233f and 674.
10. Quoted in Greenberg, op. cit.
11. John Chrysostom, quoted in Brown, *The Body and Society*.
12. Foord, *The Byzantine Empire*.
13. Parrinder, *Sex in the World's Religions*.
14. Bullough, *Sexual Variance*.
15. Greenberg, op. cit.
16. Unless otherwise noted, material in this section (China in the Han Dynasty) is taken from Hinsch, *Passions of the Cut Sleeve*.
17. Crompton, 'Homosexuality in Imperial China'.

18. Watanabe and Iwata, *The Love of the Samurai*.
19. Reischauer, *The Japanese Today*.
20. Brown, op. cit. The following quotations from Tertullian and Quintillian can also be found in Brown.
21. Gibbon, *The History of the Decline and Fall of the Roman Empire*, vol. 4.
22. John Chrysostom, quoted in Boswell, op. cit.
23. Rouselle, *Porneia*.
24. Ibid., for a full account. See also Brown, op. cit.
25. Boswell, op. cit.
26. Minucius Felix, *Octavius*, quoted in ibid.
27. St Augustine, 'Concerning Heresies', quoted in Moore, *The Birth of Popular Heresy*.
28. St Basil of Nyssa, quoted in Bullough, op. cit.
29. Foucault, *The History of Sexuality*, vol. 3.
30. Boswell, *The Marriage of Likeness*.
31. St Augustine, quoted in Boswell, *Christianity, Social Tolerance, and Homosexuality*.

4. The Celts, Feudalism and Islam

1. E. Evans, 'The Celts', in Cavendish (ed.), *Mythology*.
2. Diodorus Siculus, quoted in Greenberg, *The Construction of Homosexuality*.
3. Polybius, quoted in Ellis, *The Celtic Empire*.
4. For example, the Irish saga *Tain Bo Cuailnge*, quoted in Greenberg, op. cit.
5. W. Davies, 'Celtic Women in the Early Middle Ages', in Cameron and Kuhrt (eds), *Images of Women in Antiquity*. St Columbanus' poem is also taken from Davies.
6. Ammianus Marcellinus, quoted in Sergent, *Homosexuality in Greek Myth*.
7. Material in this section (Germanic Tribes) is taken from Greenberg, op. cit.
8. Quotations in this section (Early Feudal Society) from Gregory of Tours, Alcuin, Hincmar of Reims and St Boniface are taken from Boswell, *Christianity, Social Tolerance, and Homosexuality*.

9. Quoted in Greenberg, op. cit.
10. Quoted in Bullough, *Sexual Variance*.
11. Quoted in Greenberg, op. cit. The following quotations from Samau'al ibn Yahya and William of Adam can also be found here.
12. Sir Richard Burton, 'Terminal Essay' (1886), in *The Book of the Thousand Nights and One Night*, vol. 10. Also quoted in Bullough, op. cit. and Greenberg, op. cit.
13. Pierre de Bourdeille, Seigneur de Brantôme, *Lives of Fair and Gallant Ladies*, quoted in Faderman, *Surpassing the Love of Men*.
14. See Irwin, *The Arabian Nights*.
15. Unless otherwise noted, quotations in this section (Later Feudalism) are taken from Boswell, op. cit.
16. Brundage, *Law, Sex and Christian Society in Medieval Europe*.
17. Quoted in Greenberg, op. cit.
18. Cadden, *Meanings of Sex Difference in the Middle Ages*. The following quotations from Peter of Abano and Albertus Magnus are also taken from here.
19. Quoted in Brundage, op. cit.
20. Ibid.
21. Greenberg, op. cit.
22. Boswell, op. cit.
23. Brundage, op. cit.
24. Boswell, op. cit.
25. Material in this section (The Trial of the Templars) is taken from Barber, *The Trial of the Templars* and Chamberlin, *The Bad Popes*.
26. Cuttino and Lyman, 'Where is Edward II?'
27. Cohn, *The Pursuit of the Millennium*.
28. Brundage, op. cit.
29. P. de La Palude, *Lucubratonium*, quoted in ibid.
30. Boswell, *The Marriage of Likeness*.

5. Medieval Europe and New Worlds

1. Foucault, *The History of Sexuality*, vol. 1.

REFERENCES

2. J. Cady, '"Masculine Love": Renaissance Writing and the "New Invention" of Homosexuality', in Summers (ed.), *Homosexuality in Renaissance and Enlightenment England*.
3. G. Ruggiero, 'Marriage, Love, Sex and Civic Morality', in Turner (ed.), *Sex and Gender in Early Modern Europe*.
4. Tuchman, *A Distant Mirror*.
5. Brundage, *Law, Sex and Christian Society in Medieval Europe*.
6. Ibid.
7. Ibid.
8. Greenberg, *The Construction of Homosexuality*.
9. Quoted in Bullough, *Sexual Variance*; Bullough also gives an account of Giles de Rais.
10. Unless otherwise noted, material in this section (Slav Sexuality) is taken from Levin, *Sex and Society in the World of the Orthodox Slavs 900–1700*.
11. Quoted in Bray, *Homosexuality in Renaissance England*.
12. Ibid.
13. Quoted in Greenberg, op. cit.
14. Quoted in Chamberlin, *The Bad Popes*.
15. Greenberg, op. cit.
16. Material about Venice is taken from Ruggiero, *The Boundaries of Eros*.
17. Ariosto, *Orlando Furioso*.
18. J. M. Saslow, 'Homosexuality in the Renaissance: Behavior, Identity, and Artistic Expression', in Duberman et al. (eds), *Hidden from History*.
19. Quoted in Greenberg, op. cit.
20. Quoted in Saslow, op. cit.
21. Rowse, *Homosexuals in History*.
22. Michelangelo, Sonnets XXX and XXXI, trans. J. A. Symonds.
23. Rowse, op. cit. has a similar list, but see Bray's Introduction to his *Homosexuality in Renaissance England* for a perceptive essay upon the subject.
24. Quoted in Saslow, op. cit.
25. Quoted in Bullough, op. cit.

26. See Boswell, *The Marriage of Likeness*, for a detailed history of this practice.
27. Material about South American civilisations is taken from Greenberg, op. cit.
28. Material about Japan is taken from Watanabe and Iwata, *The Love of the Samurai*.
29. Unless otherwise noted, material in this section (The Yuan and Ming Dynasties of China) is taken from Hinsch, *Passions of the Cut Sleeve*.
30. Quoted in Greenberg, op. cit.

6. Renaissance England

1. Bray, *Homosexuality in Renaissance England*.
2. Ibid.
3. Rowse, *Homosexuals in History*.
4. Norton, *Mother Clap's Molly House*.
5. Rowse, op. cit.
6. Norton, op. cit.
7. J. Cady, '"Masculine Love": Renaissance Writing and the "New Invention" of Homosexuality', in Summers (ed.), *Homosexuality in Renaissance and Enlightenment England*.
8. Material in this section (Effeminacy and Apparel) comes from D. Kuchta, 'Semiotics of Masculinity in Renaissance England', in Turner (ed.), *Sexuality and Gender in Early Modern Europe*; and G. Woods, 'Body, Costume, and Desire in Christopher Marlowe', in Summers (ed.), op. cit.
9. G.W. Bredbeck, 'Tradition and the Individual Sodomite: Barnfield, Shakespeare and Subjective Desire', in Summers (ed.), op. cit.
10. Quoted in Norton, op. cit.
11. Ibid.
12. Quoted in Bray, op. cit.
13. In this section (Shakespeare and the Sonnets) I am indebted to Joseph Pequiney's exhaustive study, *Such is My Love*.
14. Bredbeck, op. cit.
15. Quoted in Bullough, *Sexual Variance*.

REFERENCES

16. Quoted in Norton, op. cit.
17. Unless otherwise noted, material for this section (Who was the Sodomite?) is taken from Bray, op. cit.
18. Quoted in Norton, op. cit.
19. Hill, *The World Turned Upside Down*.

7. Puritanism and the Rise of the Work Ethic

1. Brundage, *Law, Sex and Christian Society in Medieval Europe*.
2. S. Saxey, 'Straunge and Wonderfull Examples of the Judgement of Almighty God upon two adulterous persons in London in 1583', quoted in Brundage, op. cit.
3. Bullough, *Sexual Variance*.
4. Greenberg, *The Construction of Homosexuality*.
5. Brundage, op. cit.
6. Norton, *Mother Clap's Molly House*.
7. Bullough, op. cit.
8. Greenberg, op. cit.
9. Katz, *Gay American History*. The following quotation from the New Haven colony's book of laws is also taken from Katz.
10. R. Trumbach, 'The Birth of the Queen: Sodomy and the Emergence of Gender Equality in Modern Culture, 1660–1750', in Duberman et al. (eds), *Hidden from History*.
11. Ibid.
12. D. Rubini, 'Sexuality and Augustan England: Sodomy, Politics, Elite Circles and Society'.
13. Quotations taken from G. S. Rousseau, 'An Introduction to the Love–Letters: Circumstances of Publication, Context, and Cultural Commentary', in Kimmel (ed.), *Love Letters*. Rousseau also suggests that the king was Wilson's lover. The quotation from Mrs Manley is taken from Rousseau.
14. Quoted in Norton, op. cit., who tells the whole fascinating story in some detail.
15. Ibid.
16. Trumbach, op. cit.
17. Quoted in Norton, op. cit.

18. Ibid. Originally from *Murders, Rapes, Sodomy, Coining, Frauds and Other Offences at the Session-House in the Old Bailey*, 3 vols, 1742.
19. Burford, *Wits, Wenchers and Wantons*.
20. Quoted in Bray, *Homosexuality in Renaissance England*.
21. Quoted in Burford, op. cit.
22. Norton, op. cit.
23. T. W. Laqueur, 'Sexual Desire and the Market Economy during the Industrial Revolution', in Stanton (ed.), *Discourses of Sexuality from Aristotle to Aids*.
24. Earle, *The World of Defoe*.
25. Laqueur, op. cit.
26. Ibid. Originally from William Petyt, *Britannia Languens, or a Discourse of Trade*, 1680.
27. Quoted in Norton, op. cit.

8. The Elite and Transvestism

1. Material about the Hervey family is taken from R. Trumbach, 'The Birth of the Queen: Sodomy and the Emergence of Gender Equality in Modern Culture, 1660–1750', in Duberman et al. (eds), *Hidden from History*.
2. Material about Robert Thistlethwayte is taken from Norton, *Mother Clap's Molly House*.
3. Quoted in Greenberg, op. cit.
4. Quoted in Norton, op. cit.
5. Quotations from Voltaire and Diderot are taken from M. Delon, 'The Priest, the Philosopher and Homosexuality in Enlightenment France', in Maccubbin (ed.), *'Tis Nature's Fault*.
6. Faderman, *Surpassing the Love of Men*. The quotation from Queen Christina of Sweden's letters above also comes from this book.
7. R. Oresko, 'Homosexuality and the Court Elites of Early Modern France', in Gerard and Hekma (eds), *The Pursuit of Sodomy*.

REFERENCES

8. G. Kates, 'D'Eon Returns to France: Gender and Power in 1777', in Epstein and Straub, *Body Guards*.
9. Material in this section (The Rise in Transvestism) is taken from Faderman, op. cit.; and Dekker and van de Pol, *The Tradition of Female Transvestism in Early Modern Europe*.
10. Quotations from Quinnin and Garrick are taken from K. Straub, 'The Guilty Pleasures of Female Cross-Dressing and the Autobiography of Charlotte Clarke', in Epstein and Straub, op. cit.
11. R. Trumbach, 'London's Sapphists: From Three Sexes to Four Genders in the Making of Modern Culture', in Epstein and Straub, op. cit. All Trumbach's papers on eighteenth-century sexuality are both arresting and profound.
12. Quotations in this paragraph are taken from Dekker and van de Pol, op. cit.
13. Quoted in Burford, *Wits, Wenchers and Wantons*.
14. R. Trumbach, 'Sex, Gender and Sexual Identity in Modern Culture: Male Sodomy and Female Prostitution in Enlightenment London', in Fout (ed.), *Forbidden History*.
15. Straub, op. cit.

9. Sex and the Enlightenment

1. Quoted in Hampson, *The Enlightenment*.
2. 'Introduction' in Rousseau and Porter (eds), *Sexual Underworlds of the Enlightenment*.
3. Quoted in R. Porter, 'Mixed Feelings in the Enlightenment and Sexuality in Eighteenth-Century Britain', in Boucé (ed.), *Sexuality in Eighteenth-century Britain*.
4. Strachey (ed.), *The Letters of the Earl of Chesterfield to His Son*.
5. Porter, op. cit.
6. P. Wagner, 'The Discourse on Sex – or Sex as Discourse: Eighteenth-century Medical and Paramedical Erotica', in Rousseau and Porter, op. cit. The following poem is also taken from Wagner.
7. Quoted in Wagner, op. cit.
8. Bentham, 'Essay on Pederasty', introduced and ed. L.

Crompton, *Journal of Homosexuality*, vols. 3–4 (1978); Ogden, *The Theory of Legislation*, includes an appendix 'Bentham on Sex'.

9. Quoted in Norton, *Mother Clap's Molly House*.
10. Quoted in Davenport-Hines, *Sex, Death and Punishment*.
11. R. Trumbach, 'Sodomy Transformed: Aristocratic Libertinage, Public Reputation, and the Gender Revolution of the Eighteenth Century', in Kimmel (ed.), *Love Letters*.
12. G. S. Rousseau, 'In the House of Madame Van der Tasse on the Long Bridge: A Homosexual Club in Early Modern Europe', in Gerard and Hekma, *The Pursuit of Sodomy*.
13. Quoted in Burford, *Wits, Wenchers and Wantons*.
14. Quotations from Winckelmann are taken from Aldrich, *The Seduction of the Mediterranean*.
15. Fernandez, *Signor Giovanni*.
16. Katz, *Gay American History*.
17. Miller, *Alexander Hamilton*. Quoted in Katz, op. cit., as are extracts from Hamilton's letter.
18. Quoted in Davenport-Hines, op. cit.
19. Katz, op. cit.
20. Material on William Hamilton, Huges/d'Hancarville and Richard Payne Night is taken from G. S. Rousseau, 'The Sorrows of Priapus: Anti-clericalism, Homosocial Desire and Richard Payne Knight', in Rousseau and Porter (eds), op. cit.; and F. Haskell, 'D'Hancarville: an Adventurer and Art Historian in Eighteenth-century Europe', in Chaney and Ritchie (eds), *Oxford, China, Italy*.
21. Keuls, *The Reign of the Phallus*.
22. Material on August von Platen is taken from Katz, op. cit.
23. Quoted in Katz, op. cit.
24. Aldrich, op. cit.
25. L. Crompton, *Byron and Greek Love*, quoted in Higgins (ed.), *A Queer Reader*.
26. P. G. Schalow, 'Male Love in Early Modern Japan: A Literary Depiction of the "Youth"', in Duberman et al. (eds), *Hidden from History*.

27. Gibson, *Church, State and Society, 1760–1850*.
28. Anderson, *Approaches to the History of the Western Family, 1500–1914*.
29. Campbell, *The Romantic Ethic and the Spirit of Modern Consumerism*.

10. Empire and Industry
1. Quoted in Thomson, *England in the Nineteenth Century*.
2. Norton, *Mother Clap's Molly House*.
3. Davenport-Hines, *Sex, Death and Punishment*.
4. Norton, op. cit.
5. Davenport-Hines, op. cit.
6. Quotations concerning the Vere Street scandal are taken from Norton, op. cit.
7. Weeks, *Coming Out*.
8. Katz, *Gay American History*.
9. Quoted in Davenport-Hines, op. cit.
10. Katz, op. cit.
11. Hyam, *Empire and Sexuality*.
12. Dellamora, *Masculine Desire*.
13. Allen, *Cambridge Apostles*.
14. Quoted in Dellamora, op. cit.
15. Thorn, *Tennyson*.
16. R. K. Martin, 'Knights-Errant and Gothic Seducers: The Representation of Male Friendship in Mid-Nineteenth-Century America', in Duberman et al. (eds), *Hidden from History*.
17. Kosofsky Sedgwick, *Between Men*.
18. Stone, *The Family, Sex and Marriage in England, 1500–1800*.
19. Quoted in Higgins (ed.), *The Queer Reader*.
20. Quoted in Davenport-Hines, op. cit.
21. 'Walter', *My Secret Life*.
22. Hyam, op. cit.
23. Ibid.
24. L. Crompton, quoted in 'Don Leon, Byron and Homosexual

Law Reform', in Kellogg (ed.), *Literary Visions of Homo-sexuality*.

25. See Davenport-Hines, op. cit.
26. Katz, op. cit.
27. Hyam, op. cit.
28. Marcus, *The Other Victorians*.
29. Davenport-Hines, op. cit.
30. Duberman, *About Time*.
31. Greenberg, *The Construction of Homosexuality*.
32. Details of the Boulton and Park case can be found in Pearsall, *The Worm in the Bud*.
33. J. Weeks, 'Inverts, Perverts and Mary-Annes: Male Prostitution and the Regulation of Homosexuality in England in the Nineteenth and Early Twentieth Centuries', in Duberman et al. (eds), op. cit.
34. Davenport-Hines, op. cit.
35. Greenberg, op. cit.
36. Details of the Cleveland Street scandal can be found in Pearsall, op. cit.
37. Unless otherwise noted, quotations in this section (Oscar Wilde) are taken from Ellmann, *Oscar Wilde*.
38. Quoted in Higgins (ed.), op. cit.
39. Quoted in Bullough, *Sexual Variance*, as is the following quotation from Frank Harris.
40. Quoted in Sinfield, *The Wilde Century*.

11. Colonisation by Medicine

1. Greenberg, *The Construction of Homosexuality*.
2. Quoted in Bullough, *Sexual Variance*.
3. Ibid.
4. Faderman, *Surpassing the Love of Men*.
5. Quoted in Greenberg, op. cit.
6. Quoted in Katz, *Gay American History*, as is Olmstead's letter to Dr Talbot and information about Dr H. C. Sharp.
7. Greenberg, op. cit.
8. Weeks, *Coming Out*.

9. Quoted in Grosskurth, *John Addington Symonds*.

10. Greenberg, op. cit.

11. Quoted in Bullough, op. cit.

12. Quoted in Weeks, op. cit.

13. Quotations from Walt Whitman and Peter Doyle's recollections are taken from D'Emilio and Freedman, *Intimate Matters*.

14. Bullough, op. cit.

15. Quoted in Duberman, *About Time*.

16. Davidson, *The World, the Flesh and Myself*.

17. Carpenter, *My Days and Dreams* (in *Selected Writings*, vol. 1).

18. N. Greig, Introduction to Carpenter, op. cit.

19. Quoted in Weeks, op. cit., as is the following extract.

20. Quoted in Greig, op. cit.

21. Quoted in Weeks, op. cit.

22. Detailed information about the Uranians can be found in Smith, *Love in Earnest*.

23. D'Emilio and Freedman, op. cit.

24. For material by and/or about Dr Hamilton, Havelock Ellis, Margaret Otis, Ellen Coit Brown and Murray Hall, see Katz, op. cit.

25. Quoted in J. D. Steakley, 'Iconography of a Scandal: Political Cartoons and the Eulenburg Affair in Wilhelmin German', in Duberman et al. (eds), *Hidden from History*. Other material in this section (The Eulenburg Affair) is also taken from Steakley.

26. Quoted in Greenberg, op. cit., as is the following quotation.

27. Ferris, *Sex and the British*.

28. Quoted in Bullough, op. cit. and elsewhere.

29. Quoted in Greenberg, op. cit., as is Freud's 1930 statement.

30. Gay, *Freud*.

31. Grey, *Quest for Justice*.

12. Wars and Persecution

1. Material in this section (Ignorance and Ignominy) is taken

from Davenport-Hines, *Sex, Death and Punishment*; and Porter and Weeks, *Between the Acts*.

2. Quoted in Katz, *Gay American History*, as is the following letter.

3. Quoted in Weeks, *Coming Out*, as are the quotations from the BSSP and *The Social Problem of Sexual Inversion* and the World League for Sexual Reform.

4. For information about Henry Gerber and the Society for Human Rights, see Katz, op. cit.

5. Quoted in Williams, *The Spirit and the Flesh*, as is the following letter.

6. Quoted in Katz, op. cit., Williams, op. cit., and others.

7. Kinsey et al., *Sexual Behaviour in the Human Male*.

8. Williams, op. cit.

9. Hyam, *Empire and Sexuality*.

10. Davenport-Hines, op. cit., which also tells the story of Sir Hector MacDonald, as does Hyam. The following quotation from Sir Roger Casement is also taken from this volume.

11. G. Chauncey, 'Christian Brotherhood or Sexual Perversion? Homosexual Identities and Construction of Sexual Boundaries in the World War I Era', in Duberman et al. (eds), *Hidden from History*.

12. Bérubé, *Coming Out Under Fire*.

13. Davenport-Hines, op. cit.

14. C. Smith-Rosenberg, 'Discourses of Sexuality and Subjectivity: The New Woman, 1870–1936', in Duberman et al. (eds), op. cit.

15. C. R. Stimpson, 'Gertrude Stein and the Transposition of Gender', in Miller (ed.), *The Poetics of Gender*.

16. S. Benstock, 'Paris Lesbianism and the Politics of Reaction, 1900–1940', in Duberman et al. (eds), op. cit.

17. E. Garber, 'A Spectacle in Color: The Lesbian and Gay Subculture of Jazz Age Harlem', in Duberman et al. (eds), op. cit.

18. Quoted in ibid.

19. Quoted in Duberman, *About Time*.

20. Faderman, *Surpassing the Love of Men*.

REFERENCES

21. Unless otherwise noted, material in this section (The Second World War) is taken from Bérubé, op. cit.
22. Heger, *The Men with the Pink Triangle*.
23. D'Emilio and Freedman, *Intimate Matters*.
24. See Katz, op. cit.
25. Driberg, *Ruling Passions*.
26. Quoted in Porter and Weeks, op. cit., as is the following quotation from Roy.
27. D'Emilio and Freedman, op. cit.
28. Davenport-Hines, op. cit.
29. Quoted in Katz, op. cit., as is Congressman Miller, below.
30. An account of the Mattachine Society is given in Katz, op. cit.
31. Grey, *Quest for Justice*.
32. Morgan, *Somerset Maugham*.

13. Reform, Liberation and Inequality

1. Grey, *Quest for Justice*.
2. Davenport-Hines, *Sex, Death and Punishment*.
3. Report of the Committee on Sexual Offences and Prostitution, CMND 247 (1957).
4. Quoted in Teal, *The Gay Militants*.
5. James Fouralt, speaking angrily at a public meeting called by the New York Mattachine Society.
6. Quoted in N. Miller, *Out of the Past*.
7. Weeks, *Coming Out*.
8. Quoted in N. Miller, op. cit.
9. Ferris, *Sex and the British*.
10. M. P. Levine, 'The Life and Death of Gay Clones', in Herdt (ed.), *Gay Culture in America*.
11. Ibid. The following quotation also comes from Levine.
12. M. E. Gorman, 'The Pursuit of the Wish', in Herdt (ed.), op. cit. Information about the LA telephone survey is also taken from this work.
13. See Weeks, op. cit.
14. Ibid.
15. Duberman, *About Time*.

16. Weinberg and Williams, *Male Homosexuals*; Harry and DeVall, *The Social Organization of Gay Males*.
17. F. R. Lynch, 'Nonghetto Gays: An Ethnography of Suburban Homosexuals', in Herdt (ed.), op. cit.
18. Ibid.
19. White, 'Paradise Found'.
20. K. Keishman, 'Heterosexuals and AIDS', *Atlantic Monthly* (February 1987), quoted in Lynch, op. cit.
21. Unless otherwise noted, material in this section (Section 28) is taken from Weeks, op. cit.
22. Quoted in Grey, op. cit.
23. R. Tielman and H. Hammelburg, 'World Survey of the Social and Legal Position of Gays and Lesbians', in Hendriks et al. (eds), *The Third Pink Book*.
24. E. van der Veen and A. Mattijssen, 'Lesbian and Gay Rights', in Hendriks et al. (eds), op. cit.
25. Ibid.

14. Analysis and Reflections

1. D. M. Halperin, '"Homosexuality": A Cultural Construct (An Exchange with Richard Schneider)', in *One Hundred Years of Homosexuality*.
2. Ibid.
3. Quotations from J. Shapiro, 'Transsexualism: Reflections on the Persistence of Gender and the Mutability of Sex', in Epstein and Straub (eds), *Body Guards*.
4. Taken from an article about Socarides by J. Rayner, *Guardian*, 25 April 1995.
5. L. Thomas, *Sunday Times*, 12 March 1995.

INDEX

INDEX

INDEX

INDEX

INDEX